# God as Form

*And out of what one sees and hears and out*
*Of what one feels, who could have thought to make*
*So many selves, so many sensuous worlds,*
*As if the air, the mid-day air, was swarming*
*With the metaphysical changes that occur,*
*Merely in living as and where we live.*

# GOD AS FORM

Essays in Greek Theology

with special reference to Christianity and
the contemporary theological predicament

by Curtis Bennett

State University of New York Press
Albany, 1976

God as Form

First Edition

**Published by State University of New York Press**
**99 Washington Avenue, Albany, New York 12210**

©1976 State University of New York

Printed in the United States of America

Library of Congress Cataloging in Publication Data

Bennett, Curtis, 1921-
God as form.
1. Gods, Greek.    1. God.    I. Title.
BL795.G6B46        292',2'11        75-43851
ISBN 0-87395-325-8
ISBN 0-87395-326-6 microfiche

Iesu Christi ministrorum

CHB et HCB

filius neposque memoriae

# Contents

# FOREWORD

There seems to be something incongruous about a *theology* of anthropomorphic Greek polytheism. The physicist C. F. von Weizsäcker, closing his book *The History of Nature* with a theological chapter on "Man: Inner History," states the difficulty with precision: "It is possible to reject religion, but it is not possible to accept religion and at the same time to strike out of it the transcendent godhead." The realm in which the Greek gods have reality is "not the material outer world, it is the human soul itself. And there, in the human soul, what are they? What now of their transcendence?" *God as Form,* being a tightly wrought set of "essays in the theology of poetry, with special reference to the contemporary theological predicament," answers: The Greek gods indeed have reality in the human soul, and it is perfectly possible to find out what they are, if one asks the Greeks, not the Christians. Their own understanding of the nature of godhead has too long been buried under the heavy assumption that godhead is by its very nature transcendent. One recalls Nietzsche crying out that Christianity has cheated us of the harvest of Greco-Roman culture — "All the labor of the ancient world *in vain:* I find no word to express my feelings at such an enormity." Still, how can a theology of Greek religion, let alone of poetry, extract an understanding of the nature of godhead from the religion of which Xenophanes said that horses, if they had hands and could paint, would portray their gods as horses, and oxen as oxen? What can such a religion do for the contemporary predicament? What has it to do with it, anyway?

*God as Form* attacks these questions with an intrepid logic that would have delighted Nietzsche, notwithstanding its implicit reduction of Superman to human measure. A classicist, a New Englander with a rebellious insistence on independence, systematically rectifies the first of Nietzsche's "Four Great Errors," i.e., mistaking effect for cause. Thus not the Olympian

Pantheon but Hebrew, Christian, Moslem monotheism must stand as "the most insistent anthropomorphism the world has ever known" as it hypostasizes human into divine will that tolerates no other. Thus, theology is not the study of scripture and revelation as sources of doctrine and dogma; theology in the Greek, the "vital" sense, is "*theos* as *logos,* the shape of mind in speech, form for perception and its rendering" or, briefly, god as form. Process and product of theological statement are poetic, and not in Greek religion only: the hall of the symposium in the poem of Xenophanes becomes "the room of our consciousness again" as

> . . . late
> Coffee and oranges in a sunny chair,
> And the green freedom of a cockatoo
> Upon a rug mingle to dissipate
> The holy hush of ancient sacrifice.

Wallace Stevens and Xenophanes, as Ahab and Agamemnon, bespeak the same understanding of godhead, in that Western tradition, now withering, "which reached its climax as direct statement in Nietzsche but was, perhaps, richest of all on this continent in the century that begins with Emerson and ends with Stevens." What, then, is the nature of godhead in the understanding of this theology of poetics as the shape of mind in speech?

As to the Greeks, the question is not simple but triple. There are the man-shaped gods of Homer: Zeus, Aphrodite, Athena speaking in person to Achilles. Then there is Xenophanes with his fatal question about these gods. Finally there is Plato, the greatest theologian of antiquity, walking among the statues of gods and goddesses, oblivious of them as his mind reaches towards the unreachable divine *nous.* How is the tri-unity of these forms of understanding achieved? And how does it relate to that other trinitarian conception grounded in transcendence, Incarnation and Resurrection? The structure of *God as Form* reflects these stages. "The Shape of Divinity" (chap. 1) is fundamental precisely because it investigates the nature of such godhead in the most difficult because most concrete case, that of Homer. "Xenophanes and Plasmata" (chap. 5) then corresponds to the second "modality," and the two closing chapters (7 and 8) on "Incarnation and Resurrection" bring into confrontation god as form and transcendent God. Let us briefly follow that articulation, starting off with Weizsäcker again.

"Nowhere in physical space are there such manlike beings as Zeus, or Athene, nor have they ever existed anywhere, barring lifeless statues," Weizsäcker says. But the "lifeless" statues were wrought by men; what reality do they express? In Bennett's exegesis, "The gods and goddesses are not men or women, or plants or beasts, or sunshine or shining water or laden olive tree. They are the appreciative forms for all these things, realized as *phenomena* by the human consciousness and stamped with the modality of that consciousness." Furthermore: "That the gods alone possess self-expressive power and man only expresses theirs is, without figure, the statement of the total dependence of natural form on the *process* creating, and expressed by, that form." This total dependence of natural form on the process creating it and expressing itself in it, explains why this theology of poetry is natural theology, why these gods are neither things in physical space nor fictions of the mind. Again the reversal: the gods alone possess *self-expressive* power, though the process of appreciation is in the human soul.

What, then, is the Xenophantic revolution? "What has history brought at this point? It has brought the maker of myths the recognition that he is making myths; it has brought to the imagination that conceives godhead the self-conscious awareness that it is doing just that." Xenophanes passes beyond anthropomorphism by isolating human awareness from what it perceives. He realizes the capacity to grasp the perceiving situation as itself phenomenal, as a given: he *understands.* "In the Greek view, the intellectual failure is a religious failure; the religious failure is always a failure to grasp *the structure of nature and man's perceiving position in it.*" Once the individual psyche recognizes itself as "a spectator of its own experienced process rather than its determinant, its willful master," the man-shaped gods and goddesses sink away before "god" to whose nature it is not proper to be in different places at different times, as Xenophanes says. Human will is not cause but phenomenon, "given not willed." What in monotheism appears as submission to divine will, is here acceptance of will as a given, neither supreme even in the soul, nor free.

With Thucydides and Plato we encounter a new, Athenian, modality of myth transformed into self-conscious discourse, sharply contrasted with the earlier Ionian stress on process. The reading of Thucydides is illuminating, but can "psyche-in-society, bound in by common values," can *eidos* or *idea* as "an as-if, just as a god or a god's act is an imaginative as-if," capture Plato's "wonder-watching yet analytical psyche" as it strains towards what is beyond imagining? A pale portrait compared to the coldly passionate second chapter on Freud who sees repression where the Greeks saw celebration, to whom the dream is a lie telling the truth, art a species of that lie, the consequence of a theology that divinizes human will in a struggle against the biological father.

If the Freud chapter pitted Aphrodite against Jehovah, the two great closing chapters attack the question how the mighty Greek understanding of god as form, of image, dream, art, symbol, speech as truth not fiction came to be perverted, how the harvest of Greco-Roman culture was destroyed before it could ripen. Again a confrontation: Pindar versus Paul, incarnation and its inseparable twin, resurrection—Castor and Pollux—versus Incarnation and Resurrection. Let the reader discover that drama for himself, since it is he who at the end of it will have to face the question of Pilate.

Seeing the modern predicament not in the revolt of human will against God but in its rebellion against its own givenness, in the reversal not of values but of effect and cause, *God as Form* pushes hard against the limits of the exploratory essay. What rises in the memory, though, with the force of the "realized" image as one lays down this book, are the readings of poetic texts from which the thesis springs: dawn breaking for immortals and mortals alike, the hall of the symposium, Sappho and Pindar in consonance across millennia with Whitman, Dickinson, Stevens. Demonstrating the claimed relation between poetry and theology in the critical act itself, these readings may one day do for literary criticism and the theory of poetry what Erich Auerbach's *Mimesis* has done in its time.

Whether, and to what extent, the reader accepts the book's thesis and its consequences will largely depend on where he stands in regard to the great issues that lie outside its pale. But it is safe to say that such a reader will never read his Greek and American authors nor view Greek religion and indeed the human condition with the same eyes again.

Gregor Sebba
Emeritus Professor
The Graduate Institute of Liberal Arts
Emory University

## Acknowledgments

Many books read over many years are somewhere buried in this one, but since it was largely written apart from them, let the debt be simply said. Instead obeisance to those who guided reading, or learning how to, at the university, John Finley and Werner Jaeger, E. K. Rand and C. N. Jackson, W. C. Greene and A. D. Nock, and before, John Roblin, Alfred Bacon, Augusta Osterloh, Thacher and Katherine Sears. Earlier still response to words and music, creed and ikon had been so interwoven, this writer can not, as these pages prove, separate them, anymore than he can distinguish genetic and formal awareness. No man can, but in this instance formulas found at home were rehearsed or analyzed at school, Handel and Milton, Emerson and James, and if unknown there coeval shades, Lawrence, Stevens, have now been confounded with it. And behind them, the ghost of Ariston's son, and an old philosopher in Rome.

Permissions:

"Esthetique du Mal," Copyright 1947 by Wallace Stevens. Reprinted from THE COLLECTED POEMS OF WALLACE STEVENS, by permission of Alfred A. Knopf, Inc.

"Sunday Morning," Copyright 1923 and renewed 1951 by Wallace Stevens. Reprinted from THE COLLECTED POEMS OF WALLACE STEVENS, by permission of Alfred A. Knopf, Inc.

"A Primitive Like an Orb," Copyright 1948 by Wallace Stevens. Reprinted from THE COLLECTED POEMS OF WALLACE STEVENS, by permission of Alfred A. Knopf, Inc.

All translations in the text are the writer's own.

# CHAPTER 1

## THE SHAPE OF DIVINITY

"And Dawn arose from her bed beside radiant Tithonus so that she might bring light to the immortals and to mortal men." *Odyssey* 5.1,2.

"One and the same is the clan of men and of gods. We both breathe from one mother. All determined power separates us, so that one is nothing, but the shining seat of heaven remains forever sure. Yet all the same we bear our likeness to the immortals or in our great consciousness or in our physical nature, even though we do not know by day or night toward what turning point fate has decreed for us to run." *Nemean* 6.1-7.

"Why should I want to see God better than this day?
I see something of God each hour of the twenty-four,
    and each moment then;
In the faces of men and women I see God, and in my
    own face in the glass." *Song of Myself* 1577-79.

Lifting idea and phrase from Eliot, Wystan Auden once condemned in verse "such as read the Bible for its prose." That, the detached aesthetic view, remains the fate of the theology of Greek poetry. Yet nothing but religious ethnocentricity prevents us from using Greek poetry, quite as much as the Old and New Testaments, to try to understand the process as well as the product of theological statement.

We can be easily deceived. The blithe anthropomorphism of divinity in Greek poetry, as in Greek painting and sculpture, has often enough been put down as 'primitive', naive; polytheism, the Greek many gods, has, from the traditional Christian point of view, been seen as intellectual failure or theological sin, either failure to conceive or blasphemy before one jealous God. Contemporaneously, anthropomorphism seems a radical obstacle to realizing divinity as the 'Other', 'not ourselves', as

1

polytheism seems a barrier to the unified consciousness or appreciation of divinity made manifest. These can not certainly be wished away, discarded, or even abruptly translated into other terms of discourse that, somehow, reassert the intent or result of Greek theology apart from its own formulation.

It will seem startling, then, to suggest that they are of great value in themselves, that we have much to learn from them both, from the forthright use of human shape and mind as the figure for divine power and from the separation of that power into discrete categories. The Greek gods are still relevant, not for poetic imaginative imitation, still less for ritual resuscitation, but to help to disclose anew in our own time the correct as opposed to the deeply imbedded erroneous view of the nature of godhead.

We might start with seeming paradox which is historical fact. The great tradition of the unknowability of deity, deity which hides its face, consciousness unlike our own, inscrutable in aim, all powerful of will, breaking into or denying the natural world, beyond it, outside it, coming into it from untouchable space and unthinkable time: that tradition has issued in the longest detailed discourses on the separate nature of deity, defining its unknowableness in intimate terminology, unraveling its differences in logical discourse, bespeaking its purpose as it heralds its mystery, declaring the unknowable in precise laws for our diet, rite, sex, social act. It is that unknowable deity which has expressed its full nature in specific, unique human form. It is the unknowable godhead which has lent itself to all the precise formulations and self-defining definitions of self-asserted mediators.

To the scandal of the Hebraic mind and its Christian descendant, the Greeks, as they crossed their agoras, walked among the statues of Zeus and Aphrodite, of Athena, Artemis, Apollo, Poseidon, and generations of artists vied with their predecessors to give those divine shapes clearer and lovelier articulation. Yet this theology, poetic or sculptural, did not issue in dogma or wearying discussions of the nature of deity. It issued in history, drama, philosophy and science. The great forms of Greek intellectual exploration are derived from its poetry, which, from Homer to Euripides, from the proem of the

*Iliad* to the epilogue of *The Bacchae,* is specifically the articulation of divinity in action. This contrast, this paradox we should ponder more than once.

Historically, the chiastic paradox of the end results of polytheistic anthropomorphism and mysterious godhead can be posited within the confines of theology itself. Plato, the greatest theologian of antiquity, was a man who walked among those statues of deity his life-long, as he must have sat for the enactment of their determinations in the Dionysiac theatre a thousand times. Yet his own theology is free of personality, of human form, of a sense that a man who has reached its apex is to be related to human mind or will. It is precisely what we are still told is impossible, theological intuition and discourse without a personal god.

By contrast, the putative theology of non-human deity issued in distinct but radically related Hebraic, Christian, and Moslem forms as the most insistent anthropomorphism the world has ever known, in willful Jehovah identified by one race or culture pattern, in crusading Allah, and in the Father of a given man in history. The radical distinction between the Greek and Christian views of incarnation will be a subject of our final chapters and does not concern us now. I point to it here to raise serious doubt in regard to clarity and honesty in the contemporary appreciation of the history of religion, as it applies to Greek anthropomorphism vs. the unknown Christian God, when the first sees god in man but never man as god, and the second can posit unknown and unknowable deity in the unique genetic relation of Father and Son.

Similarly, a later chapter is wholly devoted to Xenophanes' disclaimer of the Greek human forms for divinity, and my comment here is only meant to be oblique. It is this: from our viewpoint, which is to understand theology anywhere in process, including our own efforts, its significance is not what it was in its own time. Not much, after all, is now required of us to see whence the Greek forms for deity issued, from the human body, psyche, mind. The important disclosure of Xenophanes for us is that in the heyday of Greek theology in its mythological mode — with Pindar and the tragedians yet to compose — he should have been so simple and direct about those forms. His own insights, that is, proceed directly from the matrix of those forms' own use. By contrast Judaism had to wait until the 20th century for a comparably clear and compelling statement. However one may judge the historical distortions of *Moses and Monotheism,* theologically it is simply the very late Hebraic equivalent of the Xenophantic declaration, amid the efflorescence of Greek mythology, of the psychic source of the image of deity. And though those who are not professed Christians can apply the same attitude towards its imagery, the important point is that Christianity did not *of itself* come to terms with this awareness and *as* Christianity evolve from there. Xenophanes did not destroy Greek theology; he is the necessary point of transformation between Homer and Plato and sheds light on both their modes without invalidating either one. His real use to us is his definition of the transparency of the earlier modality *implicit in its own use.* Another way of saying that is that the greatest contribution of the Greeks to theology, from our present standpoint, is not what their own theology discloses (though that is of the greatest value, their imaginative efforts share most of their results with other peoples') but in their realization of the nature of theology itself, of theos as logos. Logos is the pattern of a man's mind, speech in action.

It is existence itself which is the great mystery, and all gods are the efforts of the human imagination to mediate that mystery. Godhead bespeaks the creation, not creation the godhead. The mystery of faith is a problem of human psychology, the form of god a problem of symbolism. To have made an imaginative effort the source of creation rather than an appreciation of it is the hubris of Judaic-Christian theology, from which not only Xenophanes, but Greek poetic theology on the one side and Platonic dialectic theology on the other are radically free. They are free because they are aware of form, its source and use. That that is as true of Homer and Pindar as of Xenophanes I trust will be made clear.

The historical progeny of the Greek exercise of theology in its poetic mode, history and philosophy, should have taught us that such a mode led, as Judaism and Christianity never could, to the awareness of the Other in its complexity and actuality,

4

and equally dramatically, within poetry, to the realization of the Other in the self. Unaware of form, its limitation but also its splendid use, the Judaic search for the Other remains, even through Buber, an attempt to establish the self in nature, primarily to establish human personality as the creator and spokesman for nature. Just as it is science, not our conventional religion, which confronts the Other as Other, while employing the human mind, as far as it can, for that exploration but not trying to coalesce the two, so, for the realm of human psychic performance, Greek poetic practice had to hand an instrumentality — anthropomorphic polytheism — not yet surpassed because its delineative function has not yet been adequately substituted for by terms or categories of analytic discourse, a means for realizing the Other in the working of that psyche in its natural situation. Polytheism is precious as a way to distinguish the modes of power in nature, the sort of distinction without which science could not exist; anthropomorphism as a means of relating those powers to the human mind and psyche for which psychology has yet to find an equivalent modality. Once the source of the older modality was made self-conscious, its exercise was increasingly inhibited, and a new means to the same end had to be found. But that problem which faced Plato still faces us.

But there is another historical reason why what Greek poetry, Greek theology in its poetic mode, led to is of contemporary importance: the death or distortion in our time of theology, particularly as it concerns those whose moral and intellectual life is bound up with poetry in its larger sense, imaginative literature, to whom the awareness of deity is of as great moment as to anyone else. We have now forsaken the heritage of the Enlightenment in poetry and religion, and the contemporary scene is divided between those who live oblivious of relation to all natural phenomena as given, determined — modern secularism — or those who attempt once again to define that relation in terms which the Enlightenment discredited, divided between those who are unaware of the psyche's forms for mediating the environment and those who misconceive the nature of those forms. And the price is the withering of that brief rich Western poetic production inspired by a new, a renascent natural theology, Goethe and Shelley, early Words-worth, Hoelderlin, Nerval, which reached its climax as direct statement in Nietzsche, but which was, perhaps, richest of all on this continent in the century that begins with Emerson and ends with Stevens, triumphant in Melville and Whitman, the last the religious and poetic progenitor of such disparate genius as Lawrence and Pound.

There were two radical errors in the conventional religious tradition which the long process of the Enlightenment exposed and rejected. One was the hypostasis of human will as source and governor of nature, the other the unselfconsciousness that made that possible, failure to realize religious symbol as a form of human imaginative seizure, not, as the secularists would have it, invalid because it was such — all science, after all, is such a grasp in a different mode — but wrong if conceived as autonomous.

The word Other as used in current theology can be deceivingly ambiguous. It can be that which is perceived by the percipient center but not itself, or it can be merely the form that center uses for its perception posited as having an independent existence. That confusion in the last analysis invalidates the thought of Martin Buber and Paul Tillich: the attempt of one to conceive a dialogue between the percipient center and an hypostasized source of creation and of the other to posit an unrealizable ground for mythic symbol outside the human mind are simply the last gasps of the religious tradition opposed to that of the Greeks, who never saw their gods outside nature and came to realize fully that their gods were their forms for appreciating nature.

Just such an attempt was made again in modern history, to recapitulate the predicament of the psyche in the natural world. The formulation for perceived power would not then attempt to escape the limitation of the psyche that had created the form in the first place, nor could such imaginative projection issue as omniscient, omnipotent, purposive deity, for that would be to claim that the form not only disclosed purpose and understood the predicament but had predicated it. On the contrary, the form or imaginative picture would be simply a means to come to terms with it, and that will mean realizing that the predicament is inescapable in a necessary world.

Ahab as much as Agamemnon is caught in the toils of pride and self-assertion, the lust for power, and is broken before the power of nature. Human defeat is a natural focus of the highest art. But there is nothing of defeat that is not from Zeus. But what is Zeus to Aeschylus? He is not the purposive god of Israel punishing Agamemnon to declare his own will. The only purpose he serves is to disclose the natural order. He is admittedly the means of the mind, the measure of the discerning mind, to come to terms with that predicament. Aeschylus is quite clear as to the use of the Zeus form in his poem as the mind's own measure. (*Ag.* 163-66.) The equivalent of Zeus for Melville is Ishmael's — or the writer's or the reader's, a distinction quite blurred — realization of the fate of Ahab. Zeus would be the realization of the white whale's power not, as some criticism would have it, the lashing tail itself. The imaginative grasp is not given a figure itself but it performs the function of Zeus in the *Agamemnon,* the only way to cast from the mind the revelation of Ahab's, as of Agamemnon's, predicament, to face it, meet, measure it, the mind's meditation on the terror of circumstance, the propriety of defeat and death.

> It may be that one life is punishment
> For another, as the son's life for the father's.
> But that concerns the secondary characters.
> It is a fragmentary tragedy
> Within the universal whole. The son
> And the father alike and equally are spent,
> Each one, by the necessity of being
> Himself, the unalterable necessity
> Of being this unalterable animal.
> This force of nature in action is the major
> Tragedy. This is destiny unperplexed,
> The happiest enemy.
>
> (Stevens, *Esthetique du Mal* XIII)

Zeus is that "universal whole," that "unalterable necessity," "this force of nature in action" which issues in tragedy, or rather, he is the earlier poem's form of all of these which, in the later poem, takes the "form" of direct statement of them.

7

The meeting of phenomena in the mind, that is the function of the Greek many gods in human shape before they gave way to later modes of disclosure. The price of the distortion of theology as autonomous form is the loss of the sense of relation of the created psyche, itself a phenomenon, to other phenomena, a relation which traditionally theology has expressed, the awareness of being and its conditions credited in the perpetual affirmation of process.

A stark example is provided by the presumed antithesis between the revelations of modern biology and the appreciation of ubiquitous natural teleology. Nor need one go back to the struggle over Darwinism. Recently this writer read a critical attack on a European biologist's attempt to see causes other than selection in the emergence and continuance of natural form. Whether he was right or wrong does not concern us, and one would be willing, in one's ignorance, to accept selection as the only agency in the stabilization or continuity of form. But the critic voiced his fear that that other biologist was once more raising the specter of teleology in biology. By that he meant, of course, purpose or intent outside the process itself leading to its results, an error derived directly from conventional theology. But that critic — and he is merely representative — was disclosing in his own argument a blinding ignorance or imaginative failure. Biological process is, of course, teleological from beginning to end: it is the evolvement and preservation of form, all selection a means to that 'end', all that does not help it discarded mercilessly, all that enhances it incarnated for reproduction in the form itself. The word 'survival' presumes teleology, as does the distinction 'species' or the generic phrase 'living being'. Yet — and this is the irony — a false conception of teleology is one of the dams to the flood of awareness of natural teleology and its implications, a teleology in the critic's reaction, in the attempt to reach a valid concept, as much as in the processes he assays to recapitulate. To a striking degree the scientific mind as secularist is unaware of the contingency of any process for which it seeks pattern or of the nature of the process involved in establishing that pattern, a mind-held form. Neither the status of the specific process under observation nor the modality of its formulation is expressed in the description or definition of the process itself. And the suggestion that the observed fact must be appreciated as phenomenon, that is, given transient imaginative form as determined entity, at once raises the specter of will anterior or exterior to its resolution. It should not, and it will not, if the Greek point of view from Homer to Plato is appreciated. For the latter, it should be stressed time and again, never stepped outside his awareness of human discourse as the only source of statement or figure, never used figure for process except as form, a means to see or realize enactment. There is still need to see process, the destiny of form, as phenomenon, whether as poetic figure or descriptive statement. Those who would deny this need disclose the limit ✓ of their own imaginations.

Yet secularist and Christian will be in extraordinary agreement, if to the fulfillment — the form and its trope — of process is given the ancient term of divinity in action. To one, divinity is something else, apart from, exterior or anterior to process, while such terminology suggests to the other a purely fictive fiat for what is grasped only as process. Paradoxically, the nature of deity seems pretty much the same to conventional Christian and secular scientist, however they may divide on subscription to it. That it is merely a necessary human shape for the appreciation of natural phenomena is inconceivable. To the Christian it should be sharply answered, by any Hellenist, that the Judaic-Christian hypostatization of human will is not history's only valid use of the term god or the gods. To patent a term as your own definition is to foreclose argument, though it is quite true that the bulk of Classical criticism of the term theos from Homer to Plato is an attempt to define its approximation to Christian intent, not to disclose its contradiction.

But the Greeks worshipped their gods as the shapes of very real pressures and powers, not only as the abiding energies but the reiterative forms of those energies, worshipped Aphrodite in copulation and caress, Poseidon in the timber-shattering sea or the phallus of the horse, Zeus in the thundercloud or the experienced force of the man-in-the-place-of-power, father of family or ruler of hosts. These gods are the discrete categories in shapes of the human imagination, drawn from awareness of self-process, for the intimately distinguished powers in process

9

and event of the natural, social, and inner psychological environment. That the supreme god, Zeus, is limited, defined by *moira,* the standard of natural event, that he bespeaks the established order of nature, is the mind's shape for that established order, which he is never intent on overturning or subverting to disclose his own power (nor for that matter is it a disclosure of himself or of his own 'will'; his 'will' rather defines its enactment): all this is a "problem" to criticism simply because that criticism is based on a belief in god as omnipotent will for man-congruent moral purpose. In Classical Greek theology the divinities arise from nature and are defined as far as possible by an appreciation of its events. In the beginning was *not* the Word; in the beginning was chaos. Word or logos is form; godhead itself is form for the appreciation of heretofore unrealizable and hence chaotic process. Theology is, in the vital sense, theos as logos, the shape of the mind in speech, form for perception and its rendering. And the gods' presence is in the literal sense poetic, made, attempts by the exercise of poetry to realize the natural powers through inherited verbal visual symbols. From Homer to Euripides the realization of divinity is itself at every moment an imaginative act.

The implications of that symbolism are quite as revealing in by-the-way statements as in ambitious constructs. They shine through the opening lines of the 5th book of the *Odyssey,* when Dawn brings light to the deathless ones and to men who must die. And she performs this daily brightening service for both *at one and the same time.* Somehow, then, the gods are living under the same conditions as men, receive the light of day as and when men do. That sun is our sun, shining on us, awakening us, making us rub our eyes and get to our feet. At this moment the immortals are here in this world, subject as ourselves to its natural processes, even if the crises which create their visibility for us, our acute consciousness of them gathered as shapes, have not arisen. They are not outside this world where there is neither light not shade, beyond the rim of dusk and dawn. They are as much within the horizon as the new-smoking village or the city whose altars take the morning light off marble surfaces, alive as the men who stretch and stalk, but for the moment invisible in contrast to the men who, walking to an early morning assembly, are clearly seen as single figures. The gods at this moment are unseen shapes but denotative of the same qualities, presumptive of the same appearance, open to the same fascinations and repulsions as men.

What, at this dawning hour, are they within this limited world, where all we see in the flesh are living men and their natural environment? They are forms in the mind *for* the powers and energies expressed in men and beasts and their entire terrestrial or celestial environment. They are also abstractions, though only in human shape, for the given natural forms in which these energies are expressed. They are not simply, that is, ascribed human shapes for immanent powers and energies. The poetic vocabulary makes no such analytic distinction, but they are also — if we are to make it — forms for natural forms, men, beasts, life-giving plants, the sea, the sky. They are always presented as identities in an inter-related vocabulary, but those imaginary identities are abstractions of reiterative natural identities expressive of energies and powers. Their immortality is not one whit supernatural; it is the immortality of those energies and their natural shapes, the immortality of living forms, their radiance the perpetual fresh renewal of those living, breathing shapes. The gods and goddesses are not men and women, or plants or beasts, or sunshine or shining water or laden olive tree. (Demeter is never the waving field of grain, nor Dionysus the vine, nor are those shapes ever 'in' the natural shapes; the natural shapes and their plangent power live in the mind *as* the god or goddess.) They are the appreciation of all these *as phenomena,* natural shapes or energies seen in the human consciousness, and stamped with the modality of that consciousness, as reiterative, determined forms.

As enduring elements in a traditional vocabulary the Greek gods do nourish an autonomous ideal existence, and Homer, though not the tragedians, dramatizes it. But we may lose our sense of the *function* of those shapes, if we yield to the blandishment of such entertainment. We must grasp the moment's interrelation between the *donnée* of this world, the men who rise and rub their eyes, and the forms in the mind for it, the gods who rise and rub theirs, the simultaneity of Dawn's mission for men and gods. We must grasp the mind forms and the actual scene at one and the same time to realize that the former are inherent in the latter, that they are the logos of life, that when a man arises, the form of that gesture is enacted, a recurrent shape springs into a recurrent position, that when a man looks kindly on new light in his own right, the everywhere summons of light and the eye's participation in it are once more blessed. This Platonic expression of the gods' formal function changes the mode but not its intent; the one is, after all, the other's successor. The world itself is not changed by the presence of deity recognized in it; its appreciation, however, is only so made possible, for its recurrent natural forms are grasped in separation from the passing instruments of their fulfillment. The nature of man and deity, as Pindar says, is precisely the same; the decreed limited capacity and temporary loveliness of the one is its expression of the immortal continuity and perpetual propulsion to clarified shape of the other.

The question can be posed in what way gods such as these may be said to exist, what is the nature of their existence. It is not only easy to see that the anthropomorphic figures are totally imaginary; it is also clear that a whole society as well as its creative poets endowed this functioning vocabulary with an independent as-if natural existence, and that vocabulary continued its "life" from one generation to the next in quite a different fashion from the energies and their natural shapes it recapitulated, and it died, of course, while they lived on. More strikingly, Plato's imaginary shapes have been endowed with an active quasi-natural autonomy that it is almost impossible to conceive that their creator, by the very act of creating them, could ever have been deluded into assuming. But, like his poetic predecessors, he did assume that the mind-made shapes dramatized or even fictionalized, if you will, not fictive but natural history, repetitive process established as the form of its enactment. And I do not think that our obstacle to an appreciation of Greek divinities, as supposed, is our historical detachment from their historical, and hence accidental contours, but a failure to grasp process, organic shape in its environmental destiny, as phenomenon. What is our term or appreciative formalization for the recurrence of man as opposed to identifying individual men, identifying societies, or defining the species biologically in relation to others? What is our term for his momentary fulfillment of form or deployment of recurrent energy? What is our term for the appreciation of will *in* process, not will *for* process, of natural form as expressive of — precisely what it expresses, not the fiat for that expression? Where will you find a figure or term as résumé of natural teleology or discrete terms for the varied modes of that teleology?

The causes are many. In science concentration on the disclosure of the effective elements and their interrelation in a pattern precludes, usually of necessity, any awareness of what is implied by the possibility of the pattern and its enactment, implications, I must always add, governing the establishment of the formal pattern quite as much as the natural process it seeks to resume. Similarly, even in the most deterministic analyses of history, the nature of what is so determined or that it can be so determined is usually clean forgot. The preoccupation of scientist and historian can be the more easily forgiven, in that all unconsciously they are taking for granted the phenomenal expression whose possibility they have no time and energy to concern themselves with, whose nature as enactment they fully accept without appreciation.

But not to be forgiven is either philosophy or religion which has failed of such appreciation, which has failed to define appreciation itself as phenomenon, or has confused the function of that man-made logos with what it is attempting to disclose, which even goes so far as to abolish the distinction between percipient center and what is perceived or assumed to be seen, has sometimes made the will of one the determination of the other. To understand the Greek gods, which means to accept them to be as valid as any gods promulgated by the human imagination, requires that we comprehend the processes of our natural existence, even the intellectual ones, as given. The momentary seizure of place in any one of the processes then becomes a form of relation between a mortal and immortal possibility for just such expression, including the possibility for that perception. But such a realization is a priori impossible, if the individual enactment is precluded from naturally disclosing

13

divine enactment, or if the situation and mode of that individual enactment, expressive or appreciative, are denied by the terms of its imaginative statement. The hypostatization of human will, which after all is itself totally given in nature, as autonomous omnipotent deity shuts the door on the awareness of divinity in action. The scandal of Emerson, that dogmatic Christianity is incompatible with revelation of divinity through nature, has not penetrated Classical criticism. Yet until we face it, we can not understand the function of the Greek gods as a vocabulary of natural theology.

As at other points in this work, we must insist on the radical difference in the nature of the projection illuminated by the Greek as opposed to the Judaic-Christian godhead. The "will" of God in the Judaic-Christian sense is absent from Greek religion. Divine will, which has many categories or aspects, is will *in* process, not fiat or intention. The will of Zeus which is proclaimed at the beginning of the *Iliad* is logos, pattern as theology, of psychic event propelling human action unrolled in the poem. It is not Zeus' will *for* the lives of Achilles and Agamemnon; it is the acts of Achilles and Agamemnon seen as necessary process. Similarly, the oracle or will of Apollo deployed in Oedipus' destiny is not moral purpose, illustrated in defiance or acceptance by his acts; it is the statement in theological terms of the inevitability of his existence, his essence, his unraveling of an insistent concatenation. To fight against that oracle's declaration is not the least impious — but the instinctive, if futile human effort to avoid a destructive life. The will of Zeus in the *Iliad* and the oracle of Apollo in the *Oedipus Rex* function for the human action of those poems precisely as Dawn bringing light to the immortals serves to restate simultaneously her bringing light to men. The actual process is both unified and transposed as its logos or form expressed as divine shape. By the symbol of the god the human event or process becomes phenomenon. Those two lines of the *Odyssey* can epitomize the function of the Olympic hierachy in Greek poetry as a mode of discourse. The will of Aphrodite, for Helen or Hippolytus, is simply the inherent force in her pressure, and if the goddess is glorified, it is not as beneficent or purposive but as permanent power. And if, in the *Agamemnon,* Paris and Agamemnon are punished, that is, in Emerson's term, "compensation," inevitable natural process working itself out in their destruction, as natural as the female, human or animal, giving birth after she has been impregnated — Aeschylus' own figure (*Ag.* 758-60). The Greek gods are not another world governing this one for their own moral or self-glorifying ends; they are the forms for the pressures, the energies, the processes revealed as event in this one. Nor is their source the source for that other world in Christian myth: the human desire for triumph, glory, success, yes, and for justice, too, projected as the controller of natural event, wish for omnipotence become Omnipotence, wish for security become omnipotent Beneficence. There is, of course, fructifying order, in nature as in society, and the better that order is established and sustained, the greater likelihood of individual prosperity. Zeus is the logos for such order, in nature as society, but even he is not the fiat for it. He is simply the symbol of it and its enactment in individual cases. You do not escape from the overwhelming presence of the actual with the Greek gods, turn the tables on event, disastrous event: a god's "will" will symbolize that too. But you are enabled to see pattern in event, and the gods' distinction from one another, polytheism as opposed to monotheism, is an aid to the elicitation of discrete patterns, is the means to distinguish the type of power or pressure signaled in specific case.

But the more fundamental issue is whether godhead is to be defined as transcendent will and purpose reforming or denying nature, or the mind's form for the relation of individual existence to the unwilled and ungovernable process of nature. The Christian does not argue that nature without supernatural intervention or direction works to moral purpose or in itself guarantees human security and happiness. These are all seen as dependent on the Divine Will for them. Certainly, then, natural process can not be said to reveal the true relation of individual will (for security) and divine will (the enactment of such natural process), unless the concept of Omnipotent Benevolent Deity is disclaimed as simple human wish fantasy. Nor is the symbolic rendition of natural relation to unwilled power as human subservience to godhead reconcilable with the hypostatization as independent being of human value. The Greek and Christian conceptions of godhead are incompatible, for all the effort from Gregory of Nyssa to Werner Jaeger to reconcile them.

But the premises of Greek theology have been open to Western thought, and for theology itself, since the time of the Enlightenment. It is remarkable how little Hellenists with direct access to a natural theology have contributed to the elucidation of those premises — though Nietzsche remains the most gifted exception — and it is doubly ironic in the case of American Classicists, since both poetically and religiously the post-Enlightenment possibility of religion based on these natural premises had a brief but most fecund flowering on these shores. It is conveniently overlooked, at least popularly, that the Nietzschean declaration, God is dead, is not a declaration of the death of divinity in the Greek sense at all but an invitation to its revival. It is a rejection of projection, of the projection of the human will as godhead. Nothing more. And it is also overlooked that the phrase did not begin with Nietzsche. Gerard de Nerval, in 1844, uses Jean Paul's proclamation at the end of the previous century, God is dead!, as the motto for his sonnets on Christ's immersion in death, almost a century before Stevens' parallel statement in *Sunday Morning.* Nor need we suppose idea or phrase an invention of Richter's. It is essential attar of the Aufklärung, spring of the "atheism" of such as Goethe and Shelley. And as early as the *Divinity School Address,* Emerson used the phrase conditionally, "as if God were dead," and he had already, unlike Nietzsche, transposed the premise for deity from its Christian to its Hellenic base. God as revealed contemporaneously through natural process would be dead, if the Christian view of revelation were accepted. The fertile line of American theology descends from Emerson, though it has now been lost to sight in debate on stakes he made irrelevant. But it has yielded a rich harvest in Melville, Whitman, and Stevens, and not least Santayana.

> Supple and turbulent, a ring of men
> Shall chant in orgy on a summer morn
> Their boisterous devotion to the sun,
> Not as a god, but as a god might be,
> Naked among them, like a savage source.

Their chant shall be a chant of paradise,
Out of their blood, returning to the sky;
And in their chant shall enter, voice by voice,
The windy lake wherein their lord delights,
The trees, like serafin, and echoing hills,
That choir among themselves long afterward.
They shall know well the heavenly fellowship
Of men that perish and of summer morn.
And whence they came and whither they shall go
The dew upon their feet shall manifest.

She hears, upon that water without sound,
A voice that cries, "The tomb in Palestine
Is not the porch of spirits lingering.
It is the grave of Jesus, where he lay."
We live in an old chaos of the sun,
Or old dependency of day and night,
Or island solitude, unsponsored, free,
Of that wide water, inescapable.
Deer walk upon our mountains, and the quail
Whistle about us their spontaneous cries;
Sweet berries ripen in the wilderness;
And, in the isolation of the sky,
At evening, casual flocks of pigeons make
Ambiguous undulations as they sink,
Downward to darkness, on extended wings.
                    (Stevens, *Sunday Morning* VII, VIII)

Melville wrote Hawthorne of *Moby Dick,* "I have written a wicked book and feel as spotless as a lamb." The sense of a violent assertion against traditional theology is mingled with the exultation of new innocence and freedom. That exultation is Emerson's as it was to become Nietzsche's. That line in Melville's letter rings again in the declaration of the German Hellenist turned wandering analyst and commentator, "That alone is the great liberation; with this alone is the innocence of becoming restored." What is the liberation, the new innocence? The sentences in Nietzsche which precede and explain them can serve as as good a commentary as has yet been written on

Melville's epic reassertion of ultimate determination by nature. Nietzsche wrote:

> No one is responsible for man's being there at all, for his being such-and-such, or for his being in these circumstances or in this environment. The fatality of his essence is not to be disentangled from the fatality of all that has been and will be. Man is not the effect of some special purpose, of a will, and end; nor is he the object of an attempt to attain an 'ideal of humanity' or an 'ideal of happiness' or an 'ideal of morality'. It is absurd to wish to devolve one's essence on some end or other. We have invented the concept of 'end': in reality there is no end.
>
> One is necessary, one is a piece of fatefulness, one belongs to the whole, one is in the whole; there is nothing which could judge, measure, compare, or sentence our being, for that would mean judging, measuring, comparing, or sentencing the whole. But there is nothing besides the whole. That nobody is held responsible any longer, that the mode of being may not be traced back to a *causa prima,* that the world does not form a unity either as a sensorium or as 'spirit' — that alone is the great liberation; with this alone is the innocence of becoming restored. The concept of 'God' was until now the greatest objection to existence. We deny God, we deny responsibility in God: only thereby do we redeem the world. *(Twilight of the Idols,* trans. W. Kaufmann, *Portable Nietzsche* 500, 1)

That antithesis between 'God' and existence, be it said, is not of Nietzsche's own making; it is the inheritance of traditional religion. This passage not only illustrates Melville's "wickedness" as judged from the pulpit which Hawthorne seems to have understood; it is the violent scream of what Emerson elicits so much more gently in his *Address.* And it is not only the assumption behind *Moby Dick;* it is the restatement of the theological premise implicit in *The Bacchae, Oedipus, Agamemnon.* Neither Oedipus nor Apollo is "responsible" for "these circumstances or this environment." The oracle is the announcement of what will be. There is no purpose, no illumination of divine will outside nature, no Job-like testing. There is simply the "fatality of Oedipus' essence," as there is the "fatality of Ahab's essence," or of Pentheus'. Dionysus' mocking laugh is the adumbration of the tragic humor of Melville's consciousness, his wickedness. Nietzsche, be it remembered, had been schooled in *The Bacchae* and *Oedipus Rex.*

It follows, too, that the individual human confrontation with deity in a natural theology is the confrontation of limited and donated will and perception with pressure or power not at all shaped by that will, congruous with its aspiration or expressive as its personality. Confrontation with deity cannot be dialogue with similar personality or parallel moral sense. Both the individual will and its moral sense are temporary creations in a field of forces and their pressure, and confrontation with those is likely to entail annihilation or the submergence of moral sense as self-affirmation or the affirmation of its sense of order. Hellenic tragedy is a series of paradigms of just such conflict, and by this tragic nomos or standard the Judaic-Christian dialogue with God becomes the imaginary discourse with the self and its aspirations projected as the Ruler of Nature, theology providing, as alcohol for the drinker, the means to a self-division and the satisfaction of illusory mutual conversation.

Yet the characters of Greek poetry are perpetually in conversation — not, be it said at once, "dialogue" — with their divinities, and those divinities are precisely shaped as human bodies, psyches, or minds, upbraid or bless, prod or discourage as one man or woman to another. Yet I claim that that Greek poetic anthropomorphic mode can express the relation of the individual to what is not the self or of the self's making or choosing, that that is its intent and function; that Greek anthropomorphism accomplishes what the contrasting religious sense which denies its own anthropomorphism never accomplishes: to picture self in a universe which is neither run by the self nor for it, to realize the predicament of self in that given universe not as end or purpose but as necessity.

Let me disclaim at the outset either perfection or transmissibility for this Greek poetic mode, for all its own revelatory history. The conditions for its seemingly contradictory use as a mode of natural theology perhaps never existed elsewhere and will surely not arise again, the historical realization in Homeric Ionia of transmitted figures as masks for felt pressures and powers. Conscious analysis of their function as masks finally inhibited the necessary illusion of their independent existence. We may in a later and different poetry attempt to render their function but never in this mode of man-derived shapes. This frankly man-centered mode of Greek natural revelation in its own time entailed imaginative *loss* as well as running a theological *risk,* though for that loss and at that risk it provided an as yet unparalleled *means* for the expression within the confines of psyche of the presence of realized natural power. These summary points, *loss, risk,* and rare *means* deserve separate, if brief comment.

The *loss* the Greek poets paid for the total anthropomorphism of their sense of divinity was the downgrading of the appreciation, felt sense and its symbolic expression, of the non-human centers of organic existence. This Hellenic exclusiveness lowers the symbolic value, the contribution to meaningful pattern, of the other recurrent forms as centers of will, focus of energy, display of creative might, most especially of the greater or perpetually visible animal and plant forms. For their full symbolic use we must go to more primitive religions, Sumerian, Egyptian, Mayan. Power blazes in the jaguar, the serpent, the eagle, the shark. They, too, ride the arc from non-existence to flourishing and back again to non-existence, as centered will focusing their own donation, expressive forms of evolved energy, as the jaguar leaps, the eagle swoops, or the tree burgeons. The Greeks, it is true, kept these forms in new subordinate roles for the great deities, in animal epithets, most especially of the great goddesses, as sexual symbols now made attributes or partial functions of man-form gods, or as areas of their mastery, as rulers of beasts, or made the god the form for the absorption into man-life of the benefits of plants or animals, as with Demeter and Dionysus. But they ceased to see or use godhead illustrated, made image by the animal forms in

20

independence of man-form deity. Man's relation to his environment and its other living members is recapitulated in the divine forms' ascendancy in human shape over all the others. (How natural these other forms are, however, when man goes back to the natural appreciation of biologic and psychic destiny and seeks images for his sense of recurrent vital power or action, can be seen in the wealth of animal symbolism unleashed for poetry by the Enlightenment's toppling of the symbolism of omnipotent and omni-centering deity in human shape, in Blake's Tyger and Devigny's wolf, Melville's White Whale, Whitman's she-bird and he-bird or eagles' dallying, in Shelley's plants. Significant animal form in Western poetry has had only this brief recent history and it is, I would claim, a direct result of theological revolution.)

The *risk* the Greeks ran with their human masks for natural powers or social orders was, of course, to fall into the Christian pitfall of seeing those powers or orders under the control of the psyche which lent its shape to the mask. But usually they did not — from the Zeus of the *Iliad* to the Apollo of the *Oedipus* and the Dionysus of *The Bacchae* — fall into this error, though it would take detailed exegesis to show how in each poet's instance that misstep was avoided. Summarily, I think they did not both because, in the use of the vocabulary, the intent of the symbolism in the great poets governed at every junction the deployment of the figures, natural process or power bespoken at every moment through the human mask, and also, more paradoxically, because the human mask was so transparent, because in its poetic exercise Xenophanes' self-consciousness of its source was always so close to hand. The clarity of the mode inhibited delusion, just as the Judaic-Christian denial of anthropomorphism opened the door to unconscious projection. Consciousness of form is always the key to the Greek power of revelation.

But they achieved a *rare means* at the price of imaginative restriction and the danger of delusion in the use of the human shape for divinity. The major use of the divine forms is to disclose man's own place in nature, the nature of his relation to the recurrent given elements in himself, or his relation to the forces or circumstances outside himself creating or defining his destiny. All these must be realized in the human mind or psyche and so must speak and appear as their host speaks or looks to be recognized and hold revealing communication with him. The ego-centricity of the Hellenic forms of divinity is in the last analysis determined by the imposed ego-centricity of human perception as statement.

It is certainly perfectly clear why, if man is to recognize himself not as fact but phenomenon, the divinity of his body and mind can be expressed as the immortal possibility or endurance of their forms. I turn now to the Pindar quotation at the beginning of this chapter, and for its appreciation we should apply to its blent antithesis-comparison the same temporal simultaneity we applied to the lines from the *Odyssey* which stand beside it.[1]

It is to be noted that Pindar does not make the gods or a god the creator or father of mankind. How easily, without arguing it, he has avoided the fiat or purpose or end which Nietzsche is at such pains to disclaim; and for one critic, at least, this avoidance means that his poetic statement is still valid theology — theos as logos — as the contrasting Christian myth of creation, man made in God's image by God himself, from this standpoint, can not be. Gods and men are born together, just as dawn brings light to men and the immortals simultaneously. The same "mother" is reiterated as the same "clan," the Greek term for the everywhere primitive categorization of blood relation. (From an anthropological rather than theological point of view, the identification of genos, clan, and mother is quite fascinating. Pindar's single theological clan is matrilinear.) "Mother" in our poem is strictly substitutable for "clan," the expression of natural blood relationship. I emphasize this to dispose of the scholiast note (Drachmann III 101) that by "mother" is meant the earth of the Hesiodic theogony. Not at all. The two figures, mother and clan-relation, taken together can best be summed, if not precisely, by the English Nature. Gods and men issue from the same Nature. I use capitals to suggest not only the oblique adumbration of Emerson and Whitman but the whole Enlightenment glorification of Nature, the rebirth in modern times of the Hellenic line in theology leading as theirs did to the exercise of science, of the mind truly at grips with environment and circumstance. That double *mias* — *single* mother, *single* clan — makes, in one sense, the existence of gods and men precisely coterminous, as does the *Odyssey's* act of light-bringing.

What is their essential distinction? One is immortal, the other transient. The "turning point of fate," the limit or definition, *stathmos,* which no man knows, is, as a scholiast well says this time (Drachmann III 103), death. (For the moral implications of the acceptance of death and the sacrilege of belief in triumph over it we must again await the discussion of the *1st Olympian.*) The shining seat of heaven is forever; that immortal continuity alone is power, alone possesses self-existence, self-will, and self-expression. Man alone only expresses that all determined capacity.

But he does express it; in his body's achievement, as in his mind's, the gods' life shines as his. We must be very careful in our interpretation of Pindar's description of man as "nothing," a description reiterated at the end of *Pythian 8,* and as quickly contradicted, in the logical sense, there as here, by its juxtaposition with the statement that in man's transient attainment of form immortal radiance shines. In the apogees of natural existence — and Pindar is concerned only with moments of perfect natural form — the god-given glory is announced. "Nothing" is not, as with the Christian, the dismissal of momentary achievements; they are, in fact, god-in-being. "Nothing" defines the potency of human *will* in relation to what it expresses. Divinity is, of course, the continuity of that expression defined by individuals and is instinctively figured in the form of its own expression, men's shape and mind. But the mortal-divine antithesis, from the point of view of man who makes it, is more than a distinction in time, of transiency vs. everlastingness. I call it relation, and so it appears dramatically when the divine propulsion and continuity are figured as human shape. But even when we dispense with anthropomorphism, the antithesis of process and its individual instrument is still in any language expressed quasi-anthropomorphically as a distinction in *will* quite as much as endurance. That the gods alone possess self-expressive power and man only expresses theirs is, without figure, the statement of the total dependence of natural form on the process creating and expressed by that form. It is the definition or disclosure to man's mind by word of himself as phenomenon, the dramatic grasp of himself as occurrence and occurrence as form. Theos is the logos of natural existence expressed as the form man, but the use of logos does not deny, distort, or even, as some have it, add something to nature. It is the animal's rare realization of his will-lessness in the enactment of his own history. For that rare animal, word, as mental form recapitulating natural form and its history, is a means to go outside himself and define his natural location. The effect of that exercise has always been stunning: the sense that the fullest power he employs or shape he enjoys is purely instrumental, never for a moment determined by that instrument. His awareness of his position in process is for Pindar his simultaneous expression of the potency for form in his own right and his spectator helplessness within the process of his own enactment. The greatest humility in regard to the individual as will — "nothing" — is combined with glorification of the individual as expression of the power for just such formal expression — "god-given radiance." This, I hold twenty-five hundred years later, is an accurate appreciation of man as natural phenomenon, a naturally expressive form of existence.

But the contemporary barrier to its acceptance is not alone the Christian denial of divinity revealed through nature, though I would be prepared to argue that the cultural rootedness of Christian insistence on deity outside and beyond nature has habitually inhibited theological intuitions and their terminology in the appreciation of nature. But the Pindaric insight is also pitted against the instinctive coalescence of given individual will and the natural expression defined by individual identity, so that the created individual will, both given and withdrawn, is made for its temporary passage determinant of its own history and the capacities utilized in it, the individual man's delusion of the ownership of his biological and intellectual endowments and the illusion of *self*-expression in his social use of them. Furthermore, the Pindaric vocabulary, his use of theos, runs up against a widespread contemporary failure to appreciate the function of symbolism, well exemplified (see below Chapter 5, pp. 161f) by the fatuous English analytic proposition, coming out of G. E. Moore, that divinity is something "added" to nature and contradictory of our instinctive appreciation of it. We lack both the psychological motivation for the use of, and an extant vocabulary, when correctly motivated, to denote the relation of individual expression to its continuing possibility or of the relation of the dramatic center of its enactment to that process, the terms by which to see the individual in nature as not self-determinant or self-expressive, to reveal in individual cases not just the individual but the form, its continuity, and the modality of its flourishing.

The word god, in all its manifold and often contradictory uses, underneath its varied imagistic contours or argued systematizations, Christian as well as Hellenic, Moslem quite as much as Hindu, alone historically has carried the dramatic intuition of the relation of the given individual to his own existence. To relinquish that term is to relinquish that intuition and to harden the delusion — a delusion as regards nature, I reiterate, not any specific theology — of the self-determinant individual. That delusion is hardened by the practice of psycho-analysis in its glorification of individual will, despite the fact that its own analyses are based on the elucidation of ineluctable generic form, of which individual case is only instance and by its illustration a fortiori not free agent. It is hardened by the practice of science contradicting its own possibility in a failure to realize its subject matter as phenomenal and the symbolic rendition of that subject in pattern itself a phenomenon, dependent on natural, given, not self-determined capacity. It is hardened by contemporary theologians, conventional or God-is-dead, who confuse divinity or a sense of it with a particular historical aberration glorifying human will. But above all it is hardened by insistent social practice which is not qualified by a religious appreciation of individual achievement and self-assertion as expressive of the given form for its enactment not of its given center of action.

I do not, in sum, as yet know any better way than Pindar's for expressing the relation of individual capacity and achievement to the continuing existence of its formal possibility, to the splendor of expression through that form, or of that form's existence, even in enactment, beyond the grasp of any of its participants. That is the gods. They exist in one sense only as formal appreciation, natural shape appreciated as phenomenal form. They are words as images by which the percipient defines dramatically his sense of relation to what is appreciated. Historically they are simply a symbolic vocabulary. But all our words have ancient histories which do not of themselves preclude their functioning, and that Hellenic vocabulary can still be revelatory of the position of that perceiving speaker in nature, man grasping the immortal formal expression beyond his own control of his own existence.

Why the symbol of man's own existence expressed as phenomenal, as beyond the will of any of its individual expressions, should itself be Human Shape and Mind as Divine is readily grasped. But the gods of the Greeks serve other analytic and revelatory functions, equally expressive of the relation of the individual not only to his capacities but to his instincts. Instinct and capacity for the individual are realized in as-if human forms of enduring existence, and the reason here is not only to recapitulate the generic as Everlasting Form, but to express the only way in which the pressure of that instinct or the employment of that capacity is realized in the human mind, as the voice, the will, the self-expression to the individual of his non-individual endowment. In dialogue with him the ever-living and self-expressive instinct or capacity must be momentarily focused to his own individuality. Though we do not give articulated anthropomorphic shape to just such locally realized pressures or capacities, we do the same thing embryonically when we use words like "instinct" or "will" or "need," "drive," "capacity." In natural fact there is neither "instinct" nor "will" nor "need"; there is simply process. The words for the varied processes are rendered as psychic entities, that is, from the point of view of the human mind which is under their influence. Its own history or its response to its own history *calls* the process a need or an instinct or a realized capacity. The Greek vocabulary of transparent anthropomorphic deities is not to be separated from the instinctive shaping of all speech which, in every jot of its promulgation, is anthropomorphic, too.

26

This can best be seen, perhaps, in Homer, in the confrontation and conversation by the heroes, as if with other human beings, with the immortal forms of their capacities or instincts. We left Homer with the awakening gods and goddesses of the *Odyssey* who were about to proceed to an assembly where Athena was to exorcise the woes of Odysseus. Let us instead follow the most radiant man (because most illustrative of eternal youth and vigor), Achilles, to a heroic assembly, not forgetting that the heroic like the divine assembly in poetry is formulative not representational, and be present at the confrontation of Radiant Man and Athena. I refer to the moment in the 1st Book of the *Iliad* (188-223) when Achilles in his anger is tempted to draw his sword and slay Agamemnon. He does, in fact, draw that great sword, at least part way, but he is restrained by the apparition of Athena who in poetically conceived conversation persuades him instead to chide and revile the leader of the host, with the promise of far greater gifts than that of which he is at the moment being deprived. The sword he is withdrawing at line 190 he replaces in its sheath at 220, without, however, drawing the attention of any man in the assembly immediately surrounding him. The confrontation with deity, then, takes place in less than the perception of an eye-glance, even though it requires thirty lines of poetry for its objectification. The poet's careful marking of the resumed action, without time enough for it to arouse reaction, is the sign that he is quite conscious of giving a purely poetic extension to a split second's inner experience. And if Achilles' fellow heroes never catch the moment of the sword's withdrawal, neither do they ever hear one word that passes between man and god. The poet also makes it sharp that Achilles alone (198) saw the goddess and her dread flashing eyes or felt her harsh restraining hand upon his head, holding him back from violence. We are abundantly prompted to understand this moment as isolated, inner reaction, as self-realization and consequent self-restraint. The goddess' intervention is pure poetic projection of grasp of reality, and inhibition which follows it, within Achilles, leading him to put the sword back in its place. This is simple enough: no one has or is likely to argue it. But it has not been stressed that the poet makes it clear that he knows what he describes is projection. That is what relates his self-conscious poetic consciousness displayed in imaginary act and speech to the poetic consciousness that elaborated the gold doubloon of the *Pequod,* as it is what relates Homeric practice to Xenophanes' examination of it.

But when I speak of the poetic objectification of an inner experience, we will be led astray if that phrase suggests to us the psychoanalytic view that a "subjective" experience has been given an illusory concretization as the picture of Athena, her acts and speech, or if it suggests the Eliotian "objective correlative," the poet's emotion realized as the imaginary character's imaginary experience. For Homer his character's inner experience is not for one moment "subjective." It is part and parcel of nature in its own right. This inner experience is, in fact, the grasping of reality, is the process of natural intellectual objectification, and the poetic objectification simply the means to state that natural process. But that intellectual objectification in nature is elsewhere given or attained. This experience's relation to those others can only be stated as the momentary enjoyment of the capacity for all of them, the intrusion of an eternal divine form. The moment of inner illumination is thus conceived as the moment of a man's consciousness of a divine power and of his yielding to it. That power is vividly conceived as external, as abiding. The man's mind is not isolated in his soliloquy; it is, on the contrary, the time in which he relinquishes his isolation. You can not separate the poetic objectification from the traditional theological objectification, the individual case in relation to its own form, man in relation to the divine. Achilles' realization is within himself but it is not singular; it is exemplary. The individual is the locus, but his realization of what is given in his own instance recapitulates what is given in all others, meets the form of that experience in nature.

Athena, in her function illustrated here and often enough with Odysseus, is the capacity to meet a situation correctly, with an accurate estimate of external powers, of the social proprieties, of all the natural and psychological elements that a man in a particular situation faces. The process of realizing her is a process of externalization. The capacity is realized, employed, enjoyed by many men in many cases. It is common, as failure to employ and enjoy it is also common, which for the Greeks, as in Ajax' case, is stated as being deceived by Athena, of being abandoned rather than visited by the eternal form of recognition. Godhead is the bridge, because the form of the experience, between the single and the generic, and the sense of the realization as spontaneously given, or withheld, is inseparably bound with the appreciation of the generic quality of the realization. To realize correctly is to participate in the generic given capacity for such realization, not to assert but to join, to subscribe to rather than deny an eternal form. The realization of deity is the realization of external form as opposed to accidence in a given situation. Achilles himself is a poetic formulation of radiant youth and energy, himself projected in our poem as the form of endowment, of given energy, and we move through his realization of what is the right thing for him to do to a sense of that decision as the local donation of the capacity to do the right thing anywhere in any time. The way to seize a shape of life as given, any special power or capacity, is to seize it as generic form.

But the psychoanalyst, if he can be led to ponder it, should be fascinated by another aspect of the Achilles-Athena confrontation, the two voices. What are they? If there is only one human being in dialogue with himself, why is one voice that of divinity, the voice that restrains him, and the other the voice of man, the man who would slay Agamemnon? The signs are clear enough that both voices are inaudible to all around, are located only within the single self. But there would be no call for Athena and her flashing eyes and grasping hand and swift heated argument, if to the Greek poet one voice did not have to be projected as divine power inhibiting a man's will. Why is that? Our answer may point up again a radical distinction between the Greek and the Hebraic-Christian sense of divinity.

But it were best to approach the problem by an analysis, a breaking up of the constituent elements of the psyche, their possible separation as presupposed by our poem. If there can be self-dialogue, the self is a locus of contrary elements, and will or instinct or apperception separately realized within it. Though like many others I use 'self' and 'ego' interchangeably, here they must be separated, and ego conceived both in its popular pejorative sense and in the sense of the identifiable individual will, the will defined historically as Achilles in anger at Agamemnon. Because the Homeric categories are quite different from the Freudian, I hestiate, even to provide a contemporary point of relation, to equate this individual will to the Freudian ego, though they are partially parallel here. Only partially since will subsumes the desire to kill Agamemnon, an expression of the id. Yet it is parallel in the sense that while both id and super-ego can be projected as divine in Homer, the ego as individual will can not be, simply because those others are generic, and individuation by definition can not be. Achilles as contrasted to, defined by confrontation with Agamemnon is the voice of Achilles here, bespeaking the emotional tenor of that relation while dramatizing that individuation. But the voice of Athena is the projection of his participation in the capacity to stand outside one's self and view dispassionately the elements in the ego's situation. Those two things are at strife within a single self. Achilles first berates Athena, as Helen, we shall see, reviles Aphrodite. "Why," he says, "have you come here to watch me being insulted by Agamemnon?" Yet in that egoistic reaction, in that sense of self and pride voiced in the question, we are following the process of Achilles' externalization. What he rebukes Athena for seeing is what he sees; he is beginning to see his ego from outside, to see himself placed, and one more step in that realization of his place and he will relinquish his instinct to kill. The process of coming to see himself from outside, becoming himself a part of that outside, is, in Greek myth, to be seized by that category or form of experience which is self-realization. Self-realization and self-will are opposed, but whereas self-will is only local, self-realization is the imagination's substantiation of other selves, and a fortiori can not be defined as self, as the identifiable Achilles. If realization of the self from outside comes in and controls, it must be projected in the texture of the poem as outside voice, as compulsion exterior to the individual.

Yet for all that it is conceived as coming from the outside, that pressure must be realized in terms of the individual human psyche. Earlier it was said that the gods and goddesses should not be understood as figurative abstractions of immanent powers; they are formed as human individualities just so that extra-individual pressure or capacity may be focused at the point of human realization, the individual psyche, and that capacity or pressure is projected as "voice," as communicating that extra-individual pressure or capacity to the individual psyche. Athena "speaks", that is, the outside elements are focused to the framework of the locus or battleground where that power of externalization is triumphant, and in that locus speech is the only means of communication. Athena, too, is human in the sense that her generic influence is always exerted formally in individual case. The form for the enactment of divine pressure is determined by the nature of the human psyche. Aphrodite is not Sex or the abstraction of sex; she is the form by which the psyche realizes it is in the domain of sex. So Athena is never wisdom but the form of the psyche's correct externalization projected as generic given capacity. The individual Achilles wills to kill the individual Agamemnon, but he realizes the social situation of Achilles and Agamemnon and all their counterparts and relinquishes that will in favor of that realization. Such realization is his subscription to external reality, but the form of that realization is the voice in his own psyche. As generic capacity Athena is divine, but to be realized she must speak as one human voice to another. The self is the hall of several voices; those which bespeak power and instincts or the forms of action automatically recall their manifold manifestation elsewhere, are immortal forms, the gods. But the local will is only local.

More clearly with Homer's view of the will in the domain of sex or Pindar's view of the will facing extinction, we shall see what it is that our tradition has projected as divinity. The element in the psyche that has given rise to the projection of divine will in Paul, or Calvin, or Dostoevski, is the very element that the Greeks conceived in *contrast* to divinity, enduring powers and enduring forms. The simplest way to grasp this historic antithesis is to analyze the disparate elements in the poetic psyches of Achilles or Helen or Pelops or Tantalus and see which elements are voiced as the realization, in human

31

terms, of divinity and which clearly and always are left as the voice of human individuality itself.

There is nothing in the articulation of the process of the psyche coming to terms with its place in the environment, in this scene of Achilles' abnegation before the power of Athena, which we can not now accept without the slightest bow to the supernatural. But there is one element we can only empathize with, where the Homeric projection for us is simply dramatic. Achilles *sees* a goddess and therefore speaks to her and is spoken to by her, and that originally must have been convincing as a portrayal of psychic experience, just as we have to believe, in order to appreciate Sappho's prayer to her, that she sees an enthroned Aphrodite. Here we are up against childhood conditioning in an inherited symbolic vocabulary. The psychic occurrence we have followed in naturalistic terms had been associated with the independent forms of Greek religion, its statues and paintings, its recited myths, its reiterated names and hence automatic images for the powers or capacities, and Greek poetry functioned as effective revelation of natural phenomena only so long as the defined presences and their names, the vocabulary, and the natural experience flourished in intimate collocation. We can only imaginatively share this fusion, while we recognize its historical accidence, its life and growth and death in a passed society. But I wish to underscore my distinction between the historical existence of these autonomous forms as an inherited vocabulary and my intuition of their existential function. It is not Athena as voice or grasping hand, only as specific countenance, that is any obstacle to our revivification of the Greek poetic formulation. We can not subscribe to the independent anthropomorphic shape, but we can subscribe to the anthropomorphic mode of that power's realization. We are outside the associated imagery of the traditional vocabulary, but we can still appreciate, even seek a substitute for its definition of the psyche's varied relations to continuing powers. It is not simply that the Achilles-Athena confrontation can up to a point be described in our own vocabulary, that we can all agree that Achilles undergoes an internal psychic experience, that that experience consists in his grasp of external reality overcoming his instinct to kill, and finally that his experience participates in the recurrent capacity for just such externalization. I go farther than that. Divinity in this Greek use serves to objectify, that is, to reveal a set of relations for which we do not have adequate terms.

The form Athena binds the projected psychic experience of the projected poetic figure of Achilles into a unity of all such experiences, and that unity, that continuing capacity, the eternal presence of Athena, takes imaginative *precedence* over any local illustration, even in the instance of the supreme man. The single illustration is thereby submerged in our awareness of the abiding form — a form which, as a Greek audience, we relate to in our own right. Scientific study equally insists upon the single case as illustrative, but it illustrates only identical cases; it does not, as this religious or poetic figure does, bring us to rest finally in a sense of the unified determination of all of them. Second, the dramatic process or experience stated as divine presence is the means to apprehend the experience as *given* rather than created by its agent or analyst; it alone makes the individual psyche a locus of force, a spectator — as Achilles sees and feels Athena — of its own· experience, rather than its determinant, its willful master. Lastly, the projection of the given not willed capacity as voice, as Athena speaking, realizes, more subtly and naturalistically than our present vocabulary, the interreaction within a human psyche of discordant elements.

These last points are all essential to my re-evaluation of the Greek mythic mode. Since I have made clear my partial dependence on Freud's tripartite division of the psyche, let me contrast the Hellenic mythic mode to the latter's almost unconscious practice. Having memorized, rather than achieved through struggle, an awareness of their distinction, many post-Freudians conceive of the id-ego-superego division as representing actual parts of the psyche, comparable to the distinction of the cerebrum and cerebellum. They are, of course, purely verbal, that is, poetic means of representing not actual parts of the psyche but psychic fluctuation before variant pressures, and even if we accept its general validity, this poetic literature, that is, modern psychology, never explains the process of that fluctuation, the way in which one pressure substitutes for or overcomes the other. I am suggesting that the

Hellenic tradition of interacting voices is a better poetry for rendering the modality of the interrelation of psychic elements. I am also suggesting that by the evocation of the eternal form Athena — and pari passu of the other eternal forms as divine presences — it better represents the relation of the elements in a specific psyche to their repeated enactment, so that the poetic projection catches the vital, organic relation in nature between one disposition and all others, as our form of definition does not do, so that the case history, instead of remaining just that, unfolds beyond its self the possibility of any case in the first place. In the simplest terms, the case and its accidents become a part of nature rather than remaining separate from it. It is the psychoanalytic attitude, not the Hellenic, which is false to nature. That separation may be necessary for continued accurate study, but it is dangerous in its imaginative result, if when we are done with the case, we remain separated, as in its study, from awareness of the continuous process of which it is isolated example. Modern analytic definitions, for all that they are used over and over, time out of mind, fail to establish imaginatively as single unified phenomenon what they are repetitively used to describe.

And they fail totally to express the relation (as between Achilles and Athena), whether of patient or analyst, between the percipient and the process as summarized. In the use of terms the act of analysis and the process thereby described are insistently coalesced, appreciation and natural process projected as coterminous rather than held in tension. The inevitable result is that phenomenon is not grasped as phenomenon, as given. Greek and contemporary analysis are together as far as Achilles rendered as realizing the intrusion of the external on him; they must part company when that realization is pictured as Athena's self-expression, a man realizing the capacity to grasp his situation as itself phenomenal. That is the deepest point of difference. From the Greek point of view the intellectual failure is a religious failure: the religious failure is always a failure to grasp the structure of nature and man's perceiving position in it.

I must also register the sharpest possible dissent from the current psychological view of the type of projection illustrated by the Hellenic poetic use of the Greek gods. In their case, projection—simultaneously religious and poetic— means to me the creation of images for natural powers or processes conceived as unities, not the projection of human wish or will on to the process of nature itself. That, to me erroneous, view originated in the 19th and 20th century study of primitive religion, Tylor, Frazer, Robertson-Smith, and was adopted uncritically, because it so beautifully fitted his predilections, by Freud. I mean the view of the history of the maturing mind as equated with the withdrawal of the human psyche from phenomena, the series that is often said to begin with animism moves through systematized anthropomorphic deity finally to emerge in the 'objective' scientific viewpoint. It is noteworthy that while such men, Frazer most particularly, were skeptics as regards their own inherited religious beliefs, these early anthropologists were usually content to let them stand by implication rather than direct assignment in the series, and Freud in anti-Semitic Vienna warily essayed an Hebraic but not a Christian integration within the scheme. Awareness of this evasion is essential, because the whole schema is based on a silent appreciation and rejection of the projection of human purpose and beneficence as omnipotent purposive deity.

But this anthropological and later Freudian series is profoundly misleading, as the application of the latter's own tri-partite division of the psyche, had he ever used it in this context, would at once have made apparent. It is a misreading of animism, human subscription to the presence of anima or animus in both the organic and inorganic objects of nature. At least we know from dream analysis the way in which animals, artifacts, and natural forms, such as mountains, caves, are still used by the mind as imagistic definitions of its own emotions and affects quite beyond its will or control, objectification, that is, realized through as-if autonomous forms, of uncontrollable given urges, not as projection of human will over animal life or objects in the landscape. As our dreams will forever show, we can not live without psychic projection, in the naturalistic sense, for realizing the elements of our own nature as independent of our authority. Projection can, of course, mean the reading of the individual or social will, the self as triumphant in the process of nature; or it may mean an imagistic mode of relating the forces, processes, and objects of the environment, internal as well as external, to the human psyche. The first is not only pre- but anti-scientific, the latter a mode that science sadly lacks. But what concerns me is classical Greek religion as expressed in its poetry which contradicts the Tylor-Frazer-Freud theory at its root but also lies athwart the Hebraic-Christian concept of deity which, I hold, produced that theory in the first place.

In the confrontation of Achilles and Athena, as of Helen and Aphrodite, which we shall next take up, there is no fulfillment of will, no wish-fantasy, no projection on to deity whatsoever. Deity is purely a form of thought, the symbolic figure of given pressure. Achilles does not pray for Athena to come or in her presence invoke her aid; Helen fights the presence of Aphrodite and pits her own will in vain against the goddess' invasion. It is true that Achilles is elsewhere presented in this poem as par excellence the triumphant will to power, though that is always qualified by showing that he has been endowed with, given the natural vigor and energy which can substantiate his will. In this instance his will is to kill and is relinquished by the process of self-realization symbolized by Athena. In both Achilles' and Helen's instances the individual will is thwarted, in the one case by instinct, in the other by focused fact. There is absolutely no projection of the psyche or will into the environment to govern or determine its sequence, to effect the purpose of the man or woman who is the field of active force. Nor is the form of divinity—to say the same thing from the point of view of the opposing dramatic figure—a form for the projection of the individual psyche. The realization of that form is the definition of the limit of individual will, and its further purpose, as I have already said, to connect the specific instance of such limitation with all similar cases.

And what is true of the nature of Hellenic deity in these two chosen examples can epitomize their deployment in the whole length of Greek poetry from Homer through Euripides. Now it is certainly true that men do will, and given the law of averages, their natural energy or the contours of their situation, their wills should in many instances emerge triumphant. Men may ask for Athena's help, and she may come—or she may not. She spurns the plea of the assembled Trojan women for the security of their city and of their men. Granted Achilles' endowment, the divine figuring of his history should simply figure its natural course, and even he is not immune to doom and destruction. Because Odysseus is a consistent projection of Man Who Realizes the constituent elements of confronting fact, Athena will hearken to him time and again. He is her favorite, which is to say that her capacity is his inherent companion through life. But Ajax is the counter symbol, the man who fights against the facts: Athena curses him. Patroclus perishes when Apollo, the symbolic representation of male fighting strength, deserts him, and that same strength in confronting men is stronger than Patroclus' own: their combined strength rather than a single man's, Apollo, slays him. Thetis asks Zeus for what Achilles' strength can substantiate. That is all he claims and all he gets. Divinities figure the very real powers which men in their time illustrate, but human will is successful only when it coincides with the independent will of the power expressed in the natural process.

And a fundamental definition of Greek tragedy might be the destruction of human will: Agamemnon, Ajax, Hippolytus, Heracles, Hecuba, Cassandra, Clytemnestra, Phaedra, Pentheus: roll-call of defeat. A religion that glorified human will or created deity as its projection would not have issued in its last most complex expression *as* tragedy. It is true that many Classical commentators, raised in an antithetical religious tradition, have consistently tried to undo the implications of that Hellenic starkness. They have tried to recast the Zeus of the *Agamemnon,* inexorable natural order, as beneficent pur-posiveness, have claimed transcendent value for Sophocles' characters beyond disaster so as to dissolve the Hellenic recognition of the quietus of disaster itself. Man is wonderful: that is Greek enough. He is never triumphant; he is always subject to death. That realization alone forever divides the Dionysiac theatre from Christianity.

Man's aspirations do not change, and for that reason we must guard against equating Greek poetry with Greek religious practice. Since men wish to triumph both individually and as societies, they will use whatever means lie to hand to achieve

37

those wishes, and we know perfectly well that the Greeks, like everyone, tried to bend the symbols of natural power to do their bidding, that they prayed to their gods for personal security and happiness. Poetry, in fact, *represents* them as doing just that. But the Greek poet in his great day was as limited by his appreciation of natural fact as much as the contemporary scientist, and he did not represent them as getting their wishes or teach them to expect to. Nor was man or city taught by the poet that by present sacrifice or self-abnegation he might win a later triumph. This aspect of "morality" is totally foreign to the Hellenic certainty of the continuity of expression of established impersonal merciless powers. The Dionysus of *The Bacchae* oversees Pentheus' destruction as easily as Zeus looks down on Agamemnon's.

The anthropological and Freudian thesis, then, of projected will in animistic and anthropomorphic religion is not applicable to Hellenic deity. The reasons for this mistake are probably many, including a failure to understand the symbolism of animal and human imagery in religion, but it might have been avoided as regards the Greeks in purely psychoanalytic terms by distinguishing between individual (or social) will and the forces in the field of force where it is only one element. Either the triumph of the id or its explosion through subconscious repression is as clear in Sophocles and Euripides as in psychoanalytic theory, as, in a different context, Freud recognized. The war of ego and superego, the disaster of the first in challenging the second, or the fragility of the latter under the first's attack, is also dramatized. Nor does Greek poetry fail of appreciation, often as not symbolized by divine forms, of the purely external elements which threaten or destroy human security and concomitantly the will for that security: fire and flood, the sea, earthquake, volcano, or the subjection of individual will in the conflagration set off by the human psyche itself, of which war is both pattern and apogee. Divinity asserts environmental power, just as it asserts the elsewhere-determined elements in the individual psyche and its destiny. Instead of being projections from the psyche of its hoped-for magic powers, the Greek gods denote the projection into that psyche in recognizable form and accent of all that determines its history; they are the mode of its realization of its own form, its own elements, and their place in the natural environment.

The lack of just such a complex vocabulary of the modality of the human condition in natural situ weakened, I hold, the great 19th century poetic restatements of a parallel appreciation of man in his necessary environment, leaving them as simply individual poetic positions. The consequence was their failure, on the one hand, to illuminate the poverty of appreciation inherent in scientific categorization of process, aimed at understanding structure and its sequences in order to control them, while failing to unify repetitive process as simultaneous irresistible phenomenon, or, on the other, to challenge successfully a religious tradition which saw human will as dominating the powers and processes of nature rather than as one of nature's products. The result has been to leave science in its isolation to assume an ever greater role in determining thought as well as in manipulating that environment and, for the most part, to leave the effective religious tradition still bound to its defiance of the natural history which science categorizes and manipulates—with ever greater danger from the unrealized predicament of that human psyche.

Those two fashionably opposed forces, science and our traditional religious doctrine, have played into one another's hands, as man has increased his technical powers and to that extent increased the deployment of his will. The illusion of our traditional religion has been fed by that which in its own exercise ignores it. And from the Greek point of view that is the prelude to disaster, with the species in civilization rather than a great king representing the pinnacle of human will, as the protagonist. In purely Greek terms our culture is godless. It fails to realize the natural propagation of the human psyche, the relation of the will to the other elements in it or to its total environment, and their combined natural, not human determination. It can not understand the psyche as expressive of the powers that determine its history; it can not accept its subjugation to given power in life or its definition by death, its natural course. It can not accept human defeat, so it can not accept nature. To insist on triumph is to defy nature and at last to be willing to sacrifice life itself for that hoped-for triumph of the will. But triumph it can not. It is nature that will endure, not man—unless he bows to nature.

While Achilles, because of his endowment, is projected as the figure of the temporary triumph of human will in the *Iliad*, he is also projected in that poem as the great consciousness of the limits of that or any will. He is the intellectual center as well as active hero of the poem. And when he slays Lykaon mercilessly, making him cheap by comparison with Patroclus or his own glorious life, he is not in the Homeric sense being blind or cruel, except, of course, as he voices the cruelty of life. The failure to remember that Achilles is purely the projection of the poet's consciousness and that Achilles is our representative for facing and announcing the facts at the heart of reality, is one of the reasons this passage has been misrepresented in our tradition as the poet's rejection or denigration of the Achillean consciousness, though it is the poem's and realized for that purpose. Nor will we accept the fate of Lykaon. But the Homeric consciousness does—and there is the deeper source of our failure—accepts it in the same way as the poetic consciousness that saw in its imagination and described in ferocious imaginary detail the sinking of the *Pequod* in the face of natural challenged power. Achilles unwillingly in one instance hears his horses prophesy his own destruction but on other occasions states it as simply and as instinctively as he exults in his temporary power. For such a poetic consciousness, his imaginary Achilles, the image for the most glorious of men, is saturated with the sense of imminent death. The tragedy of lesser men dying at his hands is only comparative; if Ahab drowns, Stubbs must drown too. The great moments of peace in Greek poetry are like that Pacific sea after the mast, the claw, the beak, the hammer have all gone down, and its rippling surface resumes its rhythm over the grave of all effrontery. So through the day and night the fires burn for Hector's funeral, and calm claims the plain of Ilium; so Oedipus firmly walks into the innocence and freedom of natural dissolution.

But there is no better way to challenge Freud's thesis of what deity projects than to see, in Freud's own terms, the Hellenic view of the relation of will to sexual instinct. And there is no better way to see what our religious tradition deifies, individual will, than to see its view of the correct relation of that will to sexual instinct contrasted to the Hellenic view. There is surely no greater contrast than seeing submission to sexual desire, even when unwanted, as submission to divinity, its negation as insult to deity, as opposed to the subjugation of sexual desire by individual will seen as a service to deity and unwanted submission to it as sinful. And we can thereby see how necessary and inseparable a part of the 19th and 20th century reassertion of the primacy of natural predicament is the worship of this instinct and rebellion to the overarching religious proscription of it, why Whitman and Nietzsche and, later, Lawrence were searching for its ancient relation to religion.

The basis of the quarrel is once again best seen in a simple analysis of the elements of the individual psyche when in the domain of sex, and which elements any religious view emphasizes or projects. Let us examine Helen's confrontation with Aphrodite in Book III of the *Iliad* as a companion piece to Achilles' confrontation with Athena as the realization of the capacity the goddess represents for the individual psyche.

After Aphrodite has whisked Paris from the battlefield and Menelaus' vengeance — a miracle which serves the purpose of the poet but not, as far as I can see, the will of any character — she comes (3.383f) to summon Helen to his bed, a Helen full of social consciousness after her conversations with her father- and brother-in-law, Priam and Hector. Aphrodite's desire-provoking breasts and glistening eyes shine through the sagging haggard body of an old-woman woolcomber of Helen's suite. Youthful sexual attractiveness in that aged frame serves like Athena's invisibility to the assembly surrounding Achilles to insist upon the complete internality of Helen's subsequent experience. Aphrodite calls, commands. She presents to Helen the to-her desire-provoking image of the radiant Alexander in the scene of previous sexual response, the chamber, the intimate bed itself. Helen recoils at this inner vision of her own desire and its specific shapes and reviles the power pulling her. "Dread one seducing me over and over again, you will yet no doubt take me to serve some sex-inspired man of Phrygia or Maeonia. But I see a way out. Narrow your power. Serve Paris alone. Stop being divine, turn away from the path of the gods, go no more to Olympus, but become the symbol and slave of Paris himself. For I shall not go and serve that bed. I would be ashamed before the reproaches of the other women of Troy. Already I have suffered enough shame on this score."

Helen has suggested no less than that Aphrodite stop being the power in the world she is. Helen has bid sex stop asserting itself in the world as divinity in action. And that divine power in its wrath answers her, "Without me you are nothing. If I abandon you, the result will be terrible for you. The Trojans and the Greeks together will turn and slay a woman for whose sake they die the moment you are deprived of your sex-derived power. Remember that." And Helen shuddered in fear at her speech. She covered herself in her veil to escape the glances of the reproachful women of Troy and in silence sped to Paris' side. "The goddess ruled," *êrche de daimon* (3.420). The divine power had its will. That is the close to the confrontation of the mortal woman and the divine form for her own sexual instinct. It is a phrase not to forget.

Aphrodite's voice, it is perfectly clear, is the voice of Helen's own desire to join Paris, and the images Aphrodite uses to beckon are the images of past experience in Helen's own mind creating desire, that is, eliciting Aphrodite's power. But Helen, the poet's human representative for sexual attraction, bespeaks her awareness that her instance of desire is just that. It partakes of the ever-coursing power of sex. That is why we can not say, for all that Aphrodite voices an instinct within her, that Aphrodite is Helen. Helen herself is her identity, her singular will, conscious of her social place, and that individual will, instead of being consonant with, is pitted against the pressure within her of eternal desire. Though this passage, this confrontation serves better than any in the *Iliad* to epitomize Helen's own symbolic dimension in the poem, desirable woman desiring, the poetic consciousness that projects her as this symbol does not equate but sharply divides the will of that woman and even the role he has assigned her. The whole issue here turns on the distinction between mortal will and divinity, and the shape of Helen's answer to the divine power — that it cease to be divine — has never encouraged comment.

As theology, godhead as form for the individual mind to realize supra-individual capacity or instinct, this passage parallels, of course, the Athena-Achilles confrontation. But the elements within the psyche and hence the pattern of their inter-relation are quite different, and once again the oblique not parallel reflection of modern terminology can serve to objectify the ancient illumination. Athena bespeaks external reality and hence enters the psyche as the pressure of the super-ego, so that her voice is the voice of reason and objective fact. What she says will be argument. But Aphrodite bespeaks id or instinct, first asserting the images of satisfaction, and when those are challenged, refused, speaking as if in anger, just as, of course, denied instinct is felt in the psyche as irritating, provoking pressure. So the confrontation of denying will and denied instinct turns into the well-recognized shape of a fight. Athena persuades by evoking present and future situation; Aphrodite overcomes by asserting the primacy of instinct in Helen's own destiny.

Yet at that point the role of the goddesses becomes mixed, because Helen's own role, whether considered symbolically or historically, calls to mind her precarious situation. Helen's ego here subsumes the super-ego, the reproaches of the Trojan women, just as, contrary-wise Achilles' ego subsumed the id, the instinct to kill. But whereas the super-ego and its rationale serve the fate of Achilles and win the day, that super-ego in Helen, which has momentarily coalesced with her will, is shattered, not only to obey the call of instinct but to establish her own external place and fate as the human shape of that very instinct. Submission to desire is her only way out in the larger grasp of her own situation. Aphrodite at the last takes over a part of Athena's previous capacity and thereby shows us, in modern terms, the limitations in the natural environment not only of the individual will but of its subscription — the super-ego — to the social scene. Super-ego no more than the ego is determinant, i.e., recognized as the final and success-establishing form. The consciousness here is far more flexible than Freud's, because the natural world itself is made finally determinant, not a hierarchy of purely human values. Even the hierarchy of the bourgeois genius of Vienna seems willful in the face of the Greek poetic consciousness.

And the reason, I reiterate, is the Greek poetic ability to avoid seeing id or instinct isolated by the case and thereby of necessity responsive, if there is to be success, to a pattern set up as the form of success by the individual within that isolated case, for seeing 'success', that is, as the reconciliation of specific human will to its own social sense or its singular appreciation of its social situation. Here it is Aphrodite as the determinant of Helen's own destiny as sexual, who establishes her 'duty', not Helen's respect for society. To the Greek, Freud's ultimate if unhappy claim for reconciliation with social sense would be irreligious, because it locates solution or salvation in the human awareness of singular situation and not in realization of determination by given power. "The divine power had its will," and that alone could lead to success as 'Helen'. The claims of intimate society, the Trojan women whom Helen avoids, are broken down, just as much as individual will or pride, and that can be success in Helen's case as in Helen's time because with this Greek consciousness it has a religious sanction.

The final voice of Aphrodite is the angry voice of instinct shut out by its human host, not, as in Athena's case, of dispassionate assertion. Now as the voice of instinct in the psyche this is accurate transcription, even as far as the modern psychologist is concerned. But he would boggle at that being given image as divine will, rather than simply defined as the voice of instinct within the single mind. Yet he, not the poet, insists upon the finality of a man-projected form, the isolation of the case. It recapitulates a million others, as he will have to agree. How, then, express the completely generic quality of the single experience, simultaneously with the psychic awareness that the instinct is given, represents not the sufferer's will at all? If the psyche is realized as locus, and as representative locus at that, and its will as not determinant of the force deployed in that locus, its apperception of the universal determinant of its own experience is, to the Greek poet, the human realization of the divine.

And in this sense and this sense only divinity has "will." Will is simply voice, human psychic recognition of presented power.

It need not be purposive or beneficent. And since it does not point to purpose or moral form outside its own exercise, it is never engaged in moral testing either. Apollo's will for Oedipus is simply the life he leads. It proves nothing at all. It is not a glorification of Apollo himself or the marvel of his oracle, as Christian-determined commentators would have it. The only thing Oedipus cannot avoid is the only thing Helen cannot avoid: his own or her own life. That is why a Greek poetic representative of human fate can be openly angry without blasphemy at divine will. Helen is no more or less angry at Aphrodite's power than Ahab is furious with the whale. For the Greek to assume in our sense the reconciliation of human and divine will is to assume at some level or other, extra mundo if not in this, that the two are coterminous. It is to assume, in the long run, either that man should want to grow old, wither, and die, or that he never does. For the Greek the natural determination, sex as death, has to be accepted, but not for that reason blessed or enjoyed. At the intense moment when that acceptance is least desirable, divine power is most clearly established.

The power of the sexual drive is, then, to be worshipped, bowed down before, whether we like it or not. The human will must be subservient, if it is to recognize godhead, and the claims of society, of the super-ego, our own social consciousness may, in harsh cases, as in Helen's, have to be submerged along with the individual will. When the priest counsels the lusty boy, "Pray God to help you resist temptation," is he not suggesting that the individual will, presumably subsuming social situation, be strengthened to overcome given, endowed instinct? Is the God so addressed, then, anything but the projection of that individual will as itself a power in the universe greater than instinct? Is the godhead denying nature anything other than will denying nature, and the religious service of such denial anything other than service to the idea of the supremacy of such will in nature? The priest's advice is equivalent to Helen's desparate sarcasm to Aphrodite to leave her alone, to desert her place on Olympus, to cease to be a god. If we follow the analysis of the elements in Helen's situation, her denial is the will of the identity, Helen, and its social connections. And at least we see that her subjection in the Greek sense is, literally, the rule, the command of divinity. Divine will and natural power are synonymous for the Greeks, not divine will and human pride.

The form of Aphrodite derives, of course, from the form of woman as desirable, but I think that Helen's, a woman's submission to this form, points up beautifully my earlier distinction between such a form's as-if autonomous existence in a traditional Greek vocabulary and its existential function. Helen, as woman, is not, that is, drawn on the path of her instinct by the shape of amorous woman as projected in Aphrodite but by the images of Paris invoked by Aphrodite's voice, instinct in her own psyche. The form of the god is in no way the form of her desire. The godhead, then, is clearly the symbol of power as exerted against her will, not the casting into the environment of an inner wish or wished-for form. Clearly, for Helen, she does not exist even as abstraction of desired form in actual life. The same distinction must be made for men worshiping Aphrodite, as in ironic fashion it is made by Plato in the *Symposium,* where the power of Aphrodite is locally or in nature expressed in the form of the young male. Normally, of course, such a distinction—between the autonomous form of the god and its existential function—is blurred from the male standpoint, but its clear articulation in these other cases means it can be made there, too. In Helen's case, too, the female voice of Aphrodite is closer to the woman she is and that points directly at her function: the divine form as the psychic formulation of received impression, not the externalization of inner desire. This distinction must serve for Sappho, too. Aphrodite is not one of her girls writ large; she is the determination, the giver of victory or defeat—Aphrodite without her power is inconceivable—for Sappho's own sexual instinct. The form of the goddess, the sense of divinity, then, for men and women cannot be conceived as projection in the modern anthropological or Freudian sense, of giving local desire a magical power over the natural environment. It is rather the form presented to the psyche, for good or ill, denied or accepted, leading to success or failure, of the need of man for woman, of woman for man, or even of either for one of the same. Aphrodite is not the projection of desire onto the world—it is already there!—but the formal presence of the power of desire, which exists everywhere, in the individual psyche in a mode of human recognition. To pray to that form for victory is, of course, projection of the will. The answer, however, is always Aphrodite's to make, and that answer is only made known in the play of instinct itself.

Aphrodite is, then, a form both of relation and realization for the individual, of the individual relation to the ubiquitous manifestation of the same subjection, absorption, and fulfillment elsewhere, and of the individual realization of his or her desire or performance as given, not willed. Divinity is power known in the self, not power determined by the self; worship is the acceptance of the natural terms of that relation.

It seems a strange thing to say, but the Christian cannot adore the propulsion and process of sex itself (I do not mean as mysteriously representing some other all-powerful power but as representing the power defined by its own expression) for the same reason that Freud rejected godhead altogether: neither can grasp the radical locus of the divine as the individual apprehension of the blast of the given. The one glorifies purposive will, the individual will with its moral and social contours become the arbiter of individual destiny, while the other conceives of such purposive will for human success as the tenor of divinity. For either the defeat of such purpose, in individual or social case, argues the absence or failure of divine support. Freud's pessimism is the measure of the continued hold on him of that old form, the Mighty Fortress of our fate.

"It seems not to be true that there is a power in the universe which watches over the well-being of every individual with parental care and brings all his concerns to a happy ending. On the contrary the destinies of man are incompatible with a universal principle of benevolence or with—what is to some degree contradictory—a universal principle of justice. Earthquakes, floods, and fires do not differentiate between the good and devout man, and the sinner and unbeliever. And even if we leave inanimate nature out of account and consider the destinies of individual men so far as they depend on their relations with others of their own kind, it is by no means the rule that virtue is rewarded and wickedness punished, but it happens often enough that the violent, the crafty, and the unprincipled seize the desirable goods of the earth for themselves, while the pious go empty away. *Dark, unfeeling and unloving powers determine human destiny;* the system of rewards and punishments, which, *according to religion,* governs the world, seems to have no existence." (italics added)

That was not written by a bitter Herman Melville, though it is again the "wickedness" that limns the drama of *Moby Dick,* nor is it, as it could also be, a sound modern commentary on the world-view presumption of all Greek tragedy, *Oedipus* or the *Septem, Hippolytus* or the *Trojan Women.* It is, of course, Sigmund Freud in a late summing up (*New Introductory Lectures on Psycho-Analysis,* New York, 1933, trans. W.J.H. Sprott, 228), revealing the ineradicable equation in his mind of divinity and the God of Job and Jacob. The working of nature which he has defined, in the first clause italicized, as *contradictory* of religion, is, of course, presented as its valid base in Greek theology. But there that view is not pessimistic. It is pessimistic only when contrasted, a contrast simply and beautifully expressed by Freud, to the belief in benevolent determination, the triumph of human will, the will not only for success and security but for justice. When there is no such contrasting presumption, the dramatic enactment of reality and the theological definition of its extant powers may be stark, but it is not downhearted or pessimistic. That is why the *Illiad* or the plays of Sophocles are so radiant, not because they are reaching in some mysterious way for a "faith" that contradicts their own enactment, and certainly not because they glorify the terror, the precariousness of the human situation, but because they seek to set in the full light of consciousness the forms of destiny and the perpetual, inexhaustible powers defined by them.

# CHAPTER 2

## THE NATURE OF DREAM IMAGE: FREUD, LANGER

For convenience we may consider apart from the previous chapter a theme integral to it, the function of image for art and religion expressive of its instinctive functioning in dream imagery. The sequence of what I conceive to be error is instructive. With the widespread acceptance of the Freudian theory of dream analysis, any theory of symbol formation for religion and art is, of course, bound to reflect it. But originally, I hold, the Freudian theory in regard to dreams goes back to a religious misapprehension as to the place, actual or putative, of the individual will in phenomenal experience.

Now Freud saw perfectly well the results of the conflict of sexual desire and individual will, particularly as the latter subsumed social situation. His practicing medical life was spent trying to heal the wounds of that struggle. But just as deeply as any Jew or Christian he predicated civilization itself on the determination of the struggle by the human will. Yet while he saw civilization as built on and bent on the repression of sex, the Greeks from Homer through Plato saw it built on its expression. Aphrodite (or Eros or the Graces) is not only the congress of the sexes, but the congress of the elements, the congress of citizens in celebration, the congress of the mind and the phenomena of its environment. And in a most practical way Hellenic urbanization probably increased the possibilities and varieties of individual enjoyment.

Nor did this Greek view of erotic effluence blur the realization of the most bitter predicaments and their conse-quences, the clash of instinct with the taboos of family and society, as with Oedipus, Phaedra, Jason or Haimon. But it is to be noted that the religious symbol always expresses not the will destroyed by instinct but the instinct itself. Aphrodite's will destroys Hippolytus and Phaedra as it forced Helen to submission, Apollos's oracle is for Oedipus' incest and murder, and Haimon's rebellion to his father elicits Sophocles' great ode to Eros. Nothing could be more unChristian or more unHebraic, either, and the heart of the matter is not sexual activity or expression but the relation of individual will to it, the realization of divinity in the subjection, not the dominance of will in its domain. Freud was painfully, pessimistically aware how his analysis of sex perpetually threatened his view of the correct relation of sex and society, but he remained quite unaware that the latter was simply one more attempt to substantiate the Hebraic-Christian conception of individual will and its glory. Through his analysis he came directly to the Greek realization of the precarious situation of the ego between the demands of society and the demands of instinct, but whereas the Greek religious sense accepted and dramatized that situation, Freud, like any 'true believer', emotionally fought against it, hoping that it could eventually be overcome.

His instrument for that victory was the human intellect and its continuing will, not the will of God. He saw those two as antithetical. In fact, he had stumbled on the source of the very religious symbolism he rejected. That intellectual position is curious, reinforcing the active effort, individual thought and its willed determination of the expression of instinct in society, while denying the religious symbolism of that local, active endeavor as completed in all its parts in all places, the triumph and domination of the human will in nature. Freud hoped for just that, while rejecting the religion or philosophy which presupposes or anticipates it. Freud's pessimism stems from the conflict of his experiential grasp of the Greek view of the necessary (and hence for them to be accepted) position of the individual ego with the hope which was born of his native religion. What precluded him from recognizing the extrapolated form of his own intimate hope?

Freud quite misconceived the nature of art and the function of religion, and his erroneous view of the nature of their imagery underlies his denigration of them. If their underlying imagery is to be established on a valid basis, his denigration must be met; and the argument must be pitched in the area where he first built his theory of symbol structure, the imagery of dreams.

The first problem is the form of Freud's own thought. It is because of the nature of his own statements that it should not be surprising that a literary critic should challenge Freud's theory of dream imagery. Freud's *attitude,* like that of any modern historian or philosopher, may have been scientific: respect for accurate impression, honesty in its integration into theory, the use of a series of examples or cases to substantiate supposed theory. The mode of his thought, however, was not scientific at all. Freud's creative insights were stated as imaginative verbal hypotheses, not as mathematically or exper- ientially testable theorems, as discoveries in every science must be stated, including medicine, on whose technique he thought his own was based. He borrowed analogies or figures from science (and I shall point to one instance where I feel such analogy or figure was erroneous), but his constructs, his theories with their science-analogous figures have no testable or even locatable existence within an independent sign-system, the continuing modality of any exact science; they are purely individual and imaginative. A scientist works in a sign-system which can reject or accept a theory depending on whether presented data can be integrated according to the rules for the manipulation of those signs. Freud's own imagination, disci- plined by reason or common-sense, was the only control of his own insights. He may have been honest, but the only test of the validity of his propositions is their acceptance or rejection by other imaginations before similar experience. And given the nature of his material, the biologist or medical practitioner instead of being at an advantage is at a disadvantage in comparison to poet or literary critic in testing those assump- tions.

For his material is instinctive symbol formation of which in individual life dreams, as in social life poetry in its largest sense, provide the richest examples. His data or material is something which has already been highly structured, given human form, in quite a different mode from his own. Right here he fell into a second error which, for our appreciation, cannot be separated from his first, the delusion that he was a working scientist. He misconceived radically the relation of the mode of his material and his own form for restating it, an error by no means limited to Freud, the view that abstract verbal statement alone equates "truth" about the previous symbolic or figurative mode. Freud compounds an error as old at least as Plato with the further assumption that the relation of his thought to his data is analogous to the relation between chemical formulae and sensuous liquid, gaseous, terrestrial experience. He thought, that is, that he was concerned with the relation between a provable sign-system and unformulated experiential process, whereas he possessed no such sign-system and his data are already formulated to the highest degree. Freud is everywhere concerned with the translation of symbolic figures or images, visual as well as verbal, into abstract verbal statement.

Freud's delusion of being a scientist may have been quite harmless, but his error in the relation of his own form to his material has done — and is still doing — real damage. Convinced that "truth" was abstract verbal statement, in turning imagistic form into such abstract pattern, he felt he was wrestling with blindness. The imagery, of poetry or dreams, does not, of course, automatically translate itself into his preferred mode of comprehension. In its resistance to this act it became for him, in fact, motivated by its relation to his own system! It became a mode of disguise. We are concerned with the significance of dream imagery for religious and artistic symbol. Let me present the crux of the Freudian error in the words of an avowed exponent of the symbolic mode in art, Suzanne Langer *(Feeling and Form,* New York, 1953, 244).

These principles (to mark the basic distinction between discursive and non-discursive thinking and presentation) seem to govern equally the formation of dreams, mythical conceits, and the virtual constructions of art. What, then, really sets poetry apart from dream and neurosis?

Above all, its purpose, which is to convey something the poet knows and wishes to set forth by the only symbolic form that will express it. A poem is not, like dream, a proxy for literal ideas, intended to hide wishes and feelings from oneself and others; it is meant to be always emotionally transparent . . . The process of poetic organization is not a spontaneous association of images, words, situations, and emotions, all amazingly interwoven, without effort, through the unconscious activity Freud called 'the dream work'.

Mrs. Langer's distinction between poem and dream is a false one. The nature of dream and poetic image is the same. But Mrs. Langer's juxtaposition, if for contrast rather than comparison, of the poetic synthesis of images and the instinctive symbolism of dream imagery serves our purpose perfectly, as does its reference to religious myth (which I should never characterize, however, as 'conceit'. A conceit may last for the life of a poem; a religious symbol endures as long as a given society uses it to express a given power).

"Dream as proxy for literal ideas." There is the heart of the error, Freud's; for this is perfectly acceptable shorthand for his basic theory of dream formation which Mrs. Langer assumes, as do I, most readers will know, that the dream imagery is a "manifest content" or figurative disguise for thoughts, unacknowledged wishes, urges. Dream censorship, the nighttime agent of repression, keeps the hidden direct thoughts or "literal ideas" from expression but, in some unexplained relaxation from day's conscious repression, allows a garbled expression of that hidden intent, the literal idea, in the form of symbolic, that is, intent-ful acts, personalities, imaginary war and love.

Such a theory of dream formation is contrary to experience; it would make Freudian dream analysis itself impossible, if it were true. It is a beautiful example of intellectual projection, for its reads Freud's purpose in reverse into the process of dreaming itself. It is easy to see why Freud invented it and continued to find it useful for his own purposes, but I do not see how anyone who holds the imagistic mode to be revelatory, in instinct or in art, can accept it for one moment.

Freud has transposed his own struggle to render images as logical or discursive analysis as the repression of an anterior, discursively grasped psychic intent in the process by which the imagery of the dream is created. The theory evolves from the tension between the analytic or discursive mode, in which the analyst *wants* to understand the dream, and the symbolic form in which the dreamer dreams. The dream does not speak directly to the analyst in his own language; it must at every point be translated from one mode of expression into the other. This continuous tension, this sense of barrier to the analyst's analysis is then read as the motivated disguise, the "manifest content" of the imagery of the dream. Ergo, the dreamer is hiding something, keeping something away from both himself and the analyst.

But by what right does Freud or any Freudian posit, in Mrs. Langer's term, a "literal intent" prior to or "behind" the dream image? Such "literal intent" is the abstract or theoretical grasp by its victim of given instinct, an intellectual appreciation. But no experience, daytime or nighttime, shows that such abstract grasp precedes the imagistic formulation of precisely the same urge. Lust in the day is aroused by images and as images, as of the self or others, for biological response to assume its sway. The grasp of such urge as "instinct" and the realization of its social predicament − and hence repression − does not in active life precede but follows such instinctive imagistic apprehension as its response. No one represses a blank; *the repression of an instinct by day is the repression of images* enabling biological response. Similarly, there is no warrant to posit the sleeper's "literal" grasp of an instinct prior to its dream symbol. How does he know that urge except through that image? Or feel it? The dream image is, in the instinctive mode, the expression of that instinct. It, too, is formulation, and the formulation that in daily life, as in cultural history, always precedes the "literal" grasp of intent.

Nor should the man on the couch, whose relation to his dream is in some ways analogous to the analyst's, be coalesced with the dreamer. As patient he may well be hiding or repressing many things, portions of the dream imagery itself or his own connection between dream imagery and daytime experience. But the dream imagery the patient *does* reveal is what the analyst is dependent on for his analysis of the dream. Therefore, if that analysis is valid, the dream imagery has, in fact, been expressive. The analyst's understanding in the discursive mode is dependent on the imagery of the dream in the symbolic mode; the symbolic mode has expressed *in its own way* everything the analyst later grasps in his own way. The dreamer is the maker of meaning for both, though in his own right a maker of imagistic not analytic thought. But it does not follow that the symbolic form in which the thought content of the dream resides is to him a form of disguise. It is, on the contrary, his instinctive mode of revelation. Freud is working on the unargued assumption that thought is discursive grasp or statement, and that such grasp or statement must lie "behind" symbolic imagery rather than, as experience teaches us, be derived from it. His quarrel is with imagery itself. To him it does not tell the "truth"; only discursive statement can do that. If it does not tell the truth, which is "literal" grasp, it is hiding the truth. There must be a motive to such hiding of the truth, such imagistic expression as opposed to literal grasp or statement in the first place. That motive is repression.

Individual experience could have taught everyone of us that the "dream-censor" or dream repression are fictions of Freud's own making, fictions to bridge the gap between dream imagery and dream "intent" defined as discursive statement, the gap between symbol and its interpretation. Whereas he posits the intent as anterior to the image and the image as its disguise, they are, of course, simultaneous; in Mrs. Langer's words for poetic symbol, the one is the *only* symbolic form which will express the other, the only form in which the dreamer, like the poet, even knows the intent. The dream image instead of being disguise is instinctive form of expression for urges, wishes, fears, psychic reaction of all sorts.

I have said that the possibility of Freudian dream analysis, which is the rendering of dream symbols as discursive statement, itself contradicts the Freudian theory of symbolism as concealment rather than expression, since the symbols contain altogether what the analyst reads out of them, that the error springs from assuming that such "direct" appreciation preceded the symbolic formation. But Freud himself contradicts yet further his own notion that the dream imagery is the concealment of wish, that the wish meeting the barrier of the censor expresses itself in the veiled form of visual symbol. In case after case he points to the revelation in the dream of facts of psychic dynamism — at least he regards them as facts, as he regards his analyses as valid — which are concealed in daytime life, of hostility and its object unacceptable to the dreamer awake, of channels or object of desire inadmissible in social context, of previous psychic wounds whose recollection the man awake will avoid at all costs. Wish-fantasy in the night, if we are to follow his theory, discloses pain and hate, and the psyche bleeding at their call, day's most unwished-for recognitions, or lust in mode or person it will not heed or obey in the day. The wish-fantasy symbols, that is, reveal what Freud would consider psychic reality as opposed to the craved delusions of the day. Dream symbols reveal both the situation, the precise locus of the individual psyche and the polar personalities or experiences of its environment. Dream imagination reveals the truth, though its whole purpose was to tell lies! Only the analyst's intervention turns those lies back into truth, though his material, his data for truth deceive their very source, the experiential spinner, the dreamer himself.

We might sum up the contrast this way: The dream imagery for Freud himself creates his appreciation of the psychic situation that daytime experience cannot disclose. Truth for him, too, comes only in imaginary, that is, symbolic form. But it is most important to remember that the patient in the day is bound by his wishes, ambitions, hopes. He is subject to *will* and *conscious purpose.* In that day mode of will and conscious purpose he cannot disclose to himself the determinant pressures of his psyche and its history. In the dream the images that somehow come into being do reveal, beyond his will and desire, contrary to ambition or social purpose, the determining pressures of his real psychic existence. The natural conclusion, then, would be that the dream formation, instead of being the product of wish-fantasy, wish meeting the barrier of the censor in the night, is precisely the opposite, the disclosure for the will or self of its precarious position as merely the focus of elsewhere determined pressures and their elsewhere determined objects. Dream imagery as disguise arises from the Freudian temporal transposition of discursive statement and symbolic process, but that the impetus to the imagistic formation is the dreamer's will or wish takes us to an even deeper Freudian error, his cherished illusion of the autonomy of individual will.

Whether individual wish or will does or does not propel dream imagery is the crux of our quarrel with Freud, and we shall return to it in a moment. His error in regard to the formation of dreams represents for me his misreading of the phenomenon of life, his refusal to accept the individual as the locus of planted powers, expressive in his symbolic appreciation, in dreams and art, of their determination of his history. But our dissent from his theory is consistent as well as radical, denying not only wish or will as the propulsion to imagery but repression or censorship in meeting it as explaining the specific shapes of dream images. While delaying the main argument, let that dissent touch briefly his theory of "displacement" as one of the forms of repression.

Dream images, as often as not, are metaphors for literal facts, not literal facts themselves. Since Freud's theory of dream disguise is based on his theory of sexual repression, let us use the most ordinary sexual examples. If a man or woman dreams of the male member in the form of a mouse or a bird, that to Freud is evasion for the phallus, a covert way of accepting as removed image what the censor will not allow to be expressed directly. And what is true of mouse or bird is true of swords or guns, or in other contexts, of gates and caskets, mountains, caves, the plethora of sexual symbols. But what for Freud comes into being through repression as displacement is for me expression as metaphor, and it seems to me that everyday experience should easily challenge a view that is now almost universally accepted to explain the image of one thing as if something else.

Who are the members of society who richly use sexual metaphor or symbol in their instinctive unpondered speech, a use I would equate with the spontaneous promulgation of parallel symbols in dream imagery? They are, of course, the uninhibited and unrepressed (I do not, of course, deny the actuality of social sexual repression, barriers, conscious and unconscious, not only to overt sexual expression but to initial sexual appreciation, the formation of instinctive image response). In Italy, the bird, as in American slang, in Spanish, the mouse, are used consistently and alternatively for the literal designation of the male member — among many others - and precisely by those who have the least inhibition against direct designation. It is the bourgeois repressed — Freud's own milieu — who avoid ordinary sexual metaphor in their conversation. The wider and deeper the direct experience, I would hold, as well as the more easy and profound its acceptance, the more automatic and the more inclusive the *sexual appropriation of related forms and shapes.* I do not understand the mechanism of the process, but I can posit as easily as Freud a figure for it — for that is what "displacement" is, a figure from biology giving a specious scientific aura to an erroneous imaginative insight. The figure implies that instinct, like a coursing liquid, meets a barrier, is turned from its course and issues in a new channel. But the relation of the created image to its source is not at all that of a channel to a coursing liquid. The image is sprung from, grows from its impulse, and that impulse can still be located in the new shape, or else there would be no *sexual* symbol. The strength of the impulse, I hold, is directly proportionate to its insistence or capacity for turning parallel shape into its own expression: not repression but freedom for response accounts for the rich helter-skelter of appropriation of analogous forms. The correct biological figure would not be displacement but metathesis, or metabolism, or in chemistry, the reformation of old as new substance. Any theory of metathesis or metabolism would have to account for both the pressure — the food to be turned into enzymes — and the process of the change.

But we are dealing, in fact, with psychic, not physical phenomenon, and our traditional analogy would be drawn from the given or instinctive form of psychic recapitulation, speech as it reveals the process of image formation. We usually call the process creation, the product metaphor or symbol, and assume that the metaphor or symbol expresses its reference or intent. The terms, admittedly, beg the question of the process, but they do imply that that process is purely imaginative, and that its goal is not the disguise, enforced by repression, but the expression as sharper, clearer impression conveyed by removed analogous shape, of the impelling experience.

What, in fact, is the psychic resonance of the metaphoric substitute in speech which, I hold, is parallel to symbol formation in dream imagery? Objectification, separation from controlling or observing psyche, and magnification as participation in ubiquitous manifestation. The image is the thought; the man realizes the member *as* bird or mouse, thereby moving it outside himself to lead an autonomous existence, magnified by its relation to all others. In referring to it as mouse or bird he unconsciously fails to distinguish "whose" and thereby makes it generic. It becomes phenomenon, unwilled fact or experience, by taking the shape of that other form. As the bird or mouse lives outside himself and his instrumentation, the shape drawn from one or the other becomes his intuition of his psychic relation to his hitherto undisclosed participation in the member's *otherwise* determined functioning. The metaphor is not evasion but realization. The man uses the animal form to realize his own need as separated from his psyche or its will. That psyche then becomes the spectator, precisely as the psyche is always the spectator to the dream. The mode of the dream is quite as much revelation as its imagery, for it discloses the relation of the individual to the instincts those images figure. It is perfectly clear why Freud would fight against such revelation. Dream imagery does not distort or disguise instinct; it realizes and reveals it in symbolic forms and also reveals the relation of the psyche to those forms, *its own lack of control.*

As I have said, I do not understand the psyche's automatic mechanism for the apprehension within its field of objects or animals as the forms of its own pressures, but Freud can shed no light on this problem, since he can not accept dream image as instinctive realization rather than as the later disguise of literal statement. Once understood, however, this mechanism may recast our interpretation of animism, as well as of the symbolic functioning of the Greek gods, as of the figures of more primitive religions. For example, Demeter's sexual life, it seems to me, should never be interpreted as symbolic of the life of the grain. It must be the other way round. The life of the grain concerns man only as it sustains or reflects his. Its life-giving property can, then, figure human procreation and nourishment. Natural forms are appropriated by the imagination as realizations of its own instincts or predicaments, their objectification as phenomena. The phallus is not "projected into" the mouse or bird with the narcissism of the childhood of the race, as Freud would have it; the latter are appropriated as the forms for the psyche of the instrumentality of its own life. In fact, the phallus as symbol is itself such another form, the expression as shape of its own function, and when viewed separately, expressive of the psyche's relation to that function.

The whole catalogue of visible objects, man-made as well as natural, is a vocabulary for psychic appropriation as the images of self-realization of invisible instincts and intangible relations. Freud may have pioneered a partial translation of that symbolic vocabulary into discursive statement of those instincts and the pressures of felt relations, but Greek religion and poetry, like any primitive art, used them, without benefit of such translation, just as our dreams and uninhibited metaphorical speech may use them all the time with transparent clarity – to echo Mrs. Langer's phrase in regard to poetic image.

For the dreamer dreaming does realize his psychic predicament. This is so obvious, it would not need statement, except for Freud. How often love, fear, hate and their specific objects are either felt more deeply or revealed altogether in the dream. That predicament has, of course, no clarified relation to the obfuscation and repression of daytime experience. A man can enjoy a deep recognition of his condition without deriving from it any clues for future action. Poets are not necessarily legislators. The dream is just such a figurative recognition of coursing powers and their individual polarity, spontaneous formulation as visual shapes and their action of confronting instincts and felt relations. In the dream the psyche is the spectator of its own endowed powers and enforced history.

To deny the censor in image formation is not, of course, to deny the pressure in dream imagery and its action of repression and inhibition. I see no reason why these tensions should not realize themselves imagistically too. Our prime concern is not psycho-analytic theory but the nature of image as metaphor, whatever its expressive content. My point is that the image itself is not the dynamic product of the censor confronting instinct but the realization of varied pressure and its predicament in the given psyche, that imagery is not disguise but expression, that the imaginary picture mode and its pictures operate through a mechanism Freud never pondered for a moment, since his psycho-analytic pattern was itself projected as an effective dynamic of form rather than, as it should have been, left simply as the analysis of a part of the product of an unexplored dynamic.

It is on the formal or "ontological" level that I challenge, too, the basic Freudian thesis that the dream image is the individual's wish fantasy. The sense of the nature of dream image for anyone is grounded on his view of the living predicament; the definition of dream-imagery as wish fantasy springs from the assumption of the autonomy of individual will; its denial is based on the recognition that the will, itself an endowment, is endowed as agent of given powers whose enactment, if individual in mode, is generic and enforced. Destiny is expressed through the individual but its governance, in active as dream life, is supra-individual, metaphorically "beyond" or "outside" the individual. The enactment of instinct in the dream accurately defines the relation of the will to it and can lead to an appreciation of the relation of will to daytime action or achievement, its agent or guide, not its ruler.

For Freud all dreams express wishes, their imagery the distorted or refracted (censor-contrived) product of those wishes. Apart from his later independently postulated death-wish, they are all, too, the products of erotic desire, since hostility and fear, proceeding from thwarted love, are directed at one or the other jealously viewed parent (or later surrogate) or rival (or its surrogate). Such a simplification of emotional motivation, *as contrived in the dream,* is, of course, strictly dependent on the postulation of the censor as blocking direct (revelation of the impelling experience) and enforcing oblique representation. Without such a censor all imagery and its accompanying emotive affects will be the *expression* of the varieties of pressure and their polar personalities realized in those active visual symbols; the variety of revelation will correspond to a variety of motivation, just as varied reactions, hate, fear, lust, are realized as differing glandular response or differing motor affect. (Long ago William James argued that emotion derives from such response or affect, not vice versa; similarly, I hold, the image initiates knowledge and its emotional contour, not vice versa.)

Let us limit ourselves, however, to those dream images which everyone would agree express erotic desire and so avoid the problem of pluralistic motivation. Such erotic dream images, whether psychic or physical, Freudians describe time and again

61

as wish-fantasy. The images are not only a substitute for the satisfaction of the day, to which anyone must agree, but deception willed by the self in defiance of reality. The psyche in the dream then becomes something quite different from the psyche limited by daytime barriers, whether accidental or social, familial or self-imposed taboos. Its simplest and most dramatic form, the male dream resulting in physical satisfaction, can serve as paradigm for such erotic imagery, stark enough to avoid any quarrel as to the relation of image and its motivation and posit the issue of wish fantasy in its clearest terms. Such designation stands unchallenged by even the many anti-Freudian or Freud-qualifying schools in analysis of dreams.

I am challenging the basic pattern of this seemingly self-evident theory. I claim that the psyche in the dream does recapitulate the situation of the psyche by day, clarified and focused, that the dream imagery likewise recapitulates, clarified and focused, the status of instinct by day, often obscured in the confusion of daytime experience, that the imagery unrolling to the dreamer reveals the status of individual will even in daytime action, and that the relation so disclosed, of individual will to planted power, holds the key to the validity of the imaginary experience of art and of the imaginary figures of ancient religion. To me the Freudian theory and its phrase are yet another expression of the belief that the individual will can and should rule instinct, is the potential master of the given; and the whole practical purpose of Freudian analysis is to make the will seem triumphant, even when in active experience it is merely the agent.

The word wish-fantasy as applied to the dream implies that the individual will creates the imagery, and that the imagery is false and deceiving. I claim that the individual will does not create the imagery at all, that the imagery like physical satisfaction derived from it is the realization of given energy. What to Freud is deception is to me insight into nature: will denied the illusion of its own governance of instinctive enforcement. To Freud the dreamer wills his satisfaction in defiance of the barriers of life; to me vital, coursing, unarguable instinct creates or, rather, is realized by the imagery. The dreamer can not express his will to the slightest degree; he may have practical —

i.e. willful, reasons for denying satisfaction, and yet as "successful dreamer," in our stark example, pitched to fulfillment against his will. He can not create the imagery – it is created for him – nor call or dispel the instinct which the imagery actualizes. A man of seventy can not summon what a boy of seventeen can not send away. Whatever an old man's longings in the day, whether retrospective or contemporary, he will not dream to satisfaction; he will be haunted in the dream as out by the nostalgia of irrealization.

*The erotic instinct wills its own satisfaction.* No one will deny the organic, material reality of the instinct that creates the images. What, then, are they? The recapitulation, the image, in the literal sense, of that instinct itself, and the deeper the held experience, needless to say, the more vivid the erotic imagery. Distorted imagery should imply an oblique daytime relation to experience. The distortion of dream imagery may express accurately an obfuscated relation to vital instinct. There is no place for a dream censor; the modality of the day, the dreamer's daytime relation to instinct, repressed, confused, or clear and uninhibited, is directly reflected in the modality of dream imagery. The dream fulfillment runs not only its biological but its psychic course as a precise recapitulation of daytime potentiality. It is not the dreamer, the will, that postulates its enactment at all, but his instinct. He is merely its field of force. The imagery can not then be, as Freud says, the projection of the will, wish. No one goes to bed and wills the images of his dreams and no more wills the pressures realized in those images. They are the formulation in visible shape of vital *self*-propelled desire. To deny the genuine articulative nature of those images is to deny the reality of the instinct they realize. It is only "real," says Freud, when it is subject to your will; its will-less enactment is deceit. Reality for Freud, then, can be simply defined as the substantiation of individual will.

I am aware, of course, that erotic dream imagery is not erotic action, just as I am aware that a conversation postulated in a novel did not in fact take place. But the only relevant question is whether the imaginary conversation accurately recapitulates active psychic motivation, as whether the dream imagery recapitulates the potential psychic or physical pattern of reality.

We have said that the greater the man's active sexual experience, the clearer and more likely to be satisfying his erotic imagery. His "fantasy" will be the juster appreciation of the actual which it substantiates accurately without the delusion of his will as its determinant. Between the dream image and daytime action falls the enactment of will in given circumstance. That will can accept or deny its own instinct, accepting it can be successful or frustrated in its deployment, failure or success dependent not only on its own strength but the response of other will. But if I do not deny this distinction, I do not, clearly, think it very important, anymore than the daytime distinction between frustration and satisfaction—the very distinction, in both its parts, which is all important to Freud. Frustration announces desire as poignantly as satisfaction and more clearly dramatizes the relation between will and instinct, which is blurred to extinction, in satisfaction, in our culture. What is and what we effect through it are not the same thing, and the first does not depend for its existence or its realization or take its importance from the second. The message of the Woman Taken in Adultery is as much anathema to Freud as to any proper bourgeois; a sense of divinity and a dedication to individual will are always antithetical in their definition of "reality."

Freud's dream theory, and its giveaway phrase, wish fantasy, are subscription to the glory of the individual will. I am trying to show that the glory of the dream is the absence of will and what that absence in dream imagery can tell us not only about the propulsion of instinct but the relation of the daytime psyche to it. Freudians can not conceive that in successful action, too, sexual instinct is not the instrumentality of the will, though will may coincide with it. The 'healing' to which Freud looked through psychoanalysis was the integration of will and instinct. To the Hellenes, from Homer through Euripides, from Helen to Phaedra, this is wish fantasy itself. Even in those cases where happily will and instinct coincide, such a view fails to distinguish between Aphrodite, who is all powerful and immortal, and her transient worshipper. Yet so blind are the Freudians to their own purpose, that they can tell us that Aphrodite and the other anthropomorphic Greek deities are themselves the "projection" of human wish or will, dream fantasies, too. The dream fantasy Aphrodite is what sends the wish fantasies of erotic dreams!

Instead of defining a dream image as wish-fulfillment or wish fantasy, I would define it as instinctive, and hence, *given desire realized as imago*. The radical difference both in motivation and result should be clear. Desire is not individual will; individual will stands often against it. It has a will of its own, and we see that better in dreams than anywhere else. I call that autonomous extra-individual will desire. Our paradigm is erotic but is applicable to all instinct and to the pressure of all affective relations. All the variety of biological and emotional propulsions I posit as self-propelling and see no need, with Freud, to limit their kind or radical source in dream expression. (Yet language itself uses the erotic paradigm for other instinct. We say, A man *wanted* to kill. The Spanish *querer*, to love, used in similar case, is even more pointed, and it may be that such metaphor deceived Jung into his overall theory of libido. Homer, and most early poetry that I know, will not say that a man wants to kill. It will say that the power of a god or his infatuation is leading him on to kill, thus distinguishing the individual and his instinct.)

I say imago, not image, both to separate the definition from what is being defined, the dream image, but also to suggest the nature of the latter as an entity, an abstract formalization or visualization to realize the contours of hitherto unfocused pressure or instinct. There is, in this definition, no more separation between desire and its imago than between the sounds of a word and its meaning. The imago is the 'meaning' of the desire, but the desire is also the 'meaning' of the imago, its imagery the only means to that desire's psychic apprehension and appreciation, whether for active rejection or active implementation, for the daytime intervention of the will. And I understand the mechanism of such spontaneous apprehension as visual symbol of given biological or psychic instinct as little as I understand how the sounds 'doll' or 'table' create for my or any other mind the pictures of such. I hold that the instinct in dream realizes itself as picture of the individual's appreciation of its actual course, indirect or distorted, direct and popular, as the psyche appreciates experience. Any repression or censorship took place long before the dream was made. It is expression pure, if not always simple.

The mode of the dream is quite as important as its imagery: the psyche as passive spectator of the enactment of instinct. [1] In the dream the will for a while is quiescent, and the given world unrolls as planted powers evolve it. For the self that while even its will is a helpless puppet. It is not always helpless by day, but there is a necessary conclusion from this new way of seeing dream formation. If the dream propulsion is actual given instinct and the dream image simply its imago, then the psyche in the dream quite accurately recapitulates the position of the psyche in life. It points not only to its precarious position amid its instincts and their place in its environment, the pressure of all relations as the poles of insistent unwilled power; it also points to its position even in their *successful* manipulation as focusing agent, not governor of those instincts and powers. The triumph of the will is an illusion produced by the agent's skillful management.

The dream, said the Greeks, is from Zeus (*Iliad* 2.26,63); the dream, said Freud, is from the individual. The whole quarrel can be pitched there: the dream-image as the enactment of divine, not human will. The message of the Greek way of putting it is to me still valid. It was against that message that Freud pitted his great mind and its great will. But the psyche is the created locus for the passage of given, that is, divine power, its will the hazarding, intermittent arbiter of those powers, and that arbitration, even when momentarily triumphant, successful surfing of given waves. Without the given there can be no fulfillment either in action or image of action. The ancient respect for dreams, as prophecy as well as recapitulation, is based on the belief that in the dream, in a state of will-lessness, the pattern of force is more clearly focused and realized. But such a respect is inseparable from a sense of divinity, in every instance transposing the experience as phenomenon, as given; it is inseparable from acceptance of the precarious situation of the will. That is not, however, to be shunned, or even wished away, since the psyche as focus or agent of instinct comes into being just as the instinct itself. Its focusing capacity, too, is given, as is the relation of its will to what it focuses.

Art and religion are as much the work of the imagination as dream imagery, but if our sense of the status of the latter is sound, that does not mean that they are, as the Freudians conceive it, the projection of will or wish. Rather, the images of psychic realization in art or the figures of power in religious myth formulate in visible verbal shape the otherwise unapprehended governance of natural event, the otherwise invisible pressures in human relations or to human acts. That is not true, of course, if the religious symbol is the pattern of the triumph of human will, or if the picture in art is the picture of triumphant individual will. Such a view denies the validity as religion of the 23rd Psalm, as it denies the validity as art of the Hollywood ending or the later end of Job, while it subscribes to the pictures of Oedipus and Ahab, the apprehension of the fate of Agamemnon as the will of Zeus. In true religion, to borrow Santayana's phrase, the symbols will be shapes of actual powers. And for such religion the dream is true in a sense that was simultaneously perceived and rejected by Freud: it realizes dramatically the relation of the psyche to those powers, the subjection of the individual to the given, not his dominance of it.

It might seem that Freud in insisting on the ubiquitous revelation of erotic desire in psychic response says just that, and in a way he does. Yet this never led him to any intuition of phenomenon as given, to realizing that the analyst like the dreaming psyche simply bears witness. We should not forget that Freud's perception of the plangency of natural power led him not to praise and joy but pain: the psychic predicament is an awful thing; he would it were not so. And we are all too apt to overlook or at least to separate what he presents as analysis and what he is attempting to do with it.

That interrelation, that veritable coalescence of "analysis" and its purpose, is well caught in what we now mean when we say colloquially, "someone is undergoing analysis." We do not mean that he is to yield to analysis at all. We do not mean that he is simply to become aware of his individual pattern of subjection to instinct, which is what we would mean, if Freud had accepted the psychic predicament as given, if we or he accepted the meaning of the *Oedipus*. We really mean that the man has hopes of preparing to govern his instinctual career, overturn Apollo's oracle. That popular transposition of the term, analysis, is perfectly sound; it shows that we can not separate, in discussing Freud, what he claims to see and what he claims to do. Nor did he. Freud could not worship power, because he sought to possess and control it: he was jealous of the gods.

He has many partners in this attitude, but it is not universal; and if he fell into one of the commonest of psychological fallacies, reading his own motivation as everyman's, we can hardly, in his case, put it down to psychological naïveté — for all that he equated "health" and ambitions such as his own. It was for Freud, surely, the correct social attitude, ordained, prescribed, extra-individual, and so could be read as everyman's. I think, in terms borrowed from Freud himself, that it was the way in which he maintained a precarious peace with his father, the way, that is, in which he preserved his religious heritage while seeming to renounce it. But to keep such peace, like any of his patients, he had to deceive himself. He was forced *not* to recognize that his goal for his own thought and 'medical' practice was the attempt to resubstantiate, in a new mode, the religious view he pointedly rejected.

It is the deep preservation of that seemingly rejected heritage that at one and the same time accounts for his pain at his own revelations and his misconception of the nature of symbolism in art, religion, and the dream.

Freud grasped symbolism at its most radical point for him or anyone, its shape for divinity, for ultimate Power. But that shape in his case was projected will, the cosmic picture of human will sometimes for justice and benevolence but always for self-substantiation, the triumph of given identity. But this symbol, like any other, also points to an intimate habit of mind in its holder's own right, his own life, and that is the habit of mind of the putative "analyst," Freud, who in point of fact is teaching his patients how their wills may dominate, achieve the mind-determined goals for their instincts. To dedicate your energies to this local purpose is to hope, at least, that the purpose will eventually everywhere prevail. To pray that an overall Will, guided by your own intuition of what is just or good, may rule the social and natural world is to do the same thing under the aegis of the symbol for such purpose. To say that it has taken place may be arrant self-delusion; to desire it cosmos-wide as the rule of a willful God is the extrapolation as image of the impetus to the local effort. Very very few would claim that the larger purpose can be substantiated without the intimate effort, but most will likely agree that the intimate effort is propelled, if unconsciously, by the larger hope. Such a divine will is that effort pictured as if running its full course, as if it had triumphed.

But Freud's mind, as a result of his own analytic revelation, balked at that parabolic projection. His pain and pessimism spring from realizing the probable, nay necessary, contradiction between that as-if and the psychic predicament, the cockleshell of aspiration tossed on a sea of instinct. But there would have been no pain, if that as-if had been rejected altogether, if with the symbol the intimate habit of mind it inculcates had been let go, too. Freud could deny his God in symbolic form but not in intimate hope. His late pessimism is the price paid by the dutiful son.

One need only contrast the joy of the close of the *Colonus,* written by Sophocles in his eighties, with the bitterness of Freud's later essays, such as *Civilization and Its Discontents,* to get the measure of the one man's acceptance, without blinking, of the most terrible facts of natural life as opposed to the other's war with them. One had behind him not only the Zeus of the *Iliad* and the *Agamemnon* but the realization of Apollo in his earlier *Oedipus*, while the other is pointing out not the irreconcilables of any civilization, as he thinks, but the irreconcilability of the predicament of the psyche as he perceived it, and whose conditions he defined in terms of Sophocles' dramatic patterns, with the assumption, but not the symbol, of the supreme benevolent Ruler, the impossible reconciliation of the Apollo of the *Oedipus* and the God of Isaac and Elijah.

But that early and radical appreciation of symbolism in his own life, the Jehovah from whom he, singularly, thought himself quite free, had another result, and this one quite misleading for this century's appreciation of art and religion.

That shape, Jehovah, was projected will, and all his life Freud read other symbolism with it as paradigm, in dream image, in art, in all other religion. His influence here has been in confluence anew with a stream that can be traced back to a common source, the naive 19th and 20th century interpretation of Greek or other ancient religion. A contemporary Freudian critic, quite as much as a 19th century Anglican divine, reads the "will" of Zeus or Aphrodite in terms of the will of Jehovah, not as the plangent power of natural sequence or erotic instinct.

But the myths of Greek religion do not teach that individual hope will triumph, that any identity, national or racial any more than individual, is ensured to safety or eternity by divinity. The relation between the individual and divinity in Greek theology precludes the possibility that the shape of the second is a projection of the will of the first. Nothing, perhaps, teaches this more violently than Apollo's oracle for Oedipus, and a *reason must be found,* I hold, *why the contemporary mind which used Sophocles' play as the dramatic epitome of his primal male psychic pattern completely ignored it when he defined religion or the use of art.* It is that contradiction which I have tried to clarify here. No more than a Christian could Freud conceive that the terribleness of Apollo's will (which is not will at all, but impersonal accident) is the measure of the play's religious resignation and revelation. And for the same reason as the Christian, if without the Christian symbol — God, because of his instinctive belief that the individual will *should* triumph.

Similarly, Freud attempted to give a new "scientific" basis to the Judaic-Christian glorification of will in the domain of erotic instinct. He was, if not the last, one of the most subtle-minded of Puritans: they, as much as he, "see sex everywhere," and he, *au fond,* as much as they, was troubled by its effluence. Quite unlike them, of course, he bowed to his obsession, dutifully, honestly studied the patterns of its apparition; and, in his great productive period (his intuitive penetrations were realized before the First World War; thereafter he became an increasingly baffled and baffling theoretician), the problem of value was, quite innocently, ignored. Yet in the long run he could not reconcile those intuitions with what, from another source, he unconsciously, held *should* be, and to join them evolved the theory of civilization as the product of repression. Again the dutiful son was saved, the central role of will restored. Like his theory of dream imagery it substantiates "displacement" for "metathesis" or "metabolism," the law of repression for the evolvement and availability of oblique forms for instinctive expression — the glory of human complexity beside animal simplicity, the realm of *charis*, "celebration which makes things lovely to men who must die," in Pindar's words. You will seek in vain through Freud for the celebration of that without which, he himself claimed, the forms of civilization could never have sprung into their historic shapes. He could never move from Jerusalem to the coast, openly to offer worship to Astarte or Aphrodite.

Nor in all his subtle apprehension of the variform manifestation, so often indirect, of eros, does he ever approach the intuition of the *Symposium,* the step by step ascent towards an ever more complex, an ever more constructive if ever more indirect expression of the power of Aphrodite. Nowhere do we find the simple faith which from Sappho to Mozart exploits for human self-realization the loveliness of the vagaries of erotic expression. With these singers the achievement of complex modality in their art forms is itself fed by erotic impulse. That impulse is not fought but cherished, led by its servant, art, to ever new rhythms, melodies, affects. *Visse d'arte, visse d'amore;* Tosca's cry yokes what artists have always joined, for expression, not repression. Nor for all the psychic paradigms Freud, drew from Sophocles, could he have subscribed to the first or last lines of that poet's ode to eros, "love unconquerable in battle . . . unfightable plays the goddess Aphrodite" (*Antigone* 781, 800). For Freud civilization evolved from fighting her who, Sophocles declares, can not be fought, *amachos.* The metaphor, fight, goes to the heart and core of the difference: the fate of the individual will. Its glory Freud will not relinquish; for him civilization derives from its enforcement. To the Hellene this view itself is impious, a refusal to bow to deity. The evidence of Greek poetry can be brought to bear with fresh force in direct contradiction: art and religion disclose the predicament of the psyche, not of its own choosing, in a world

71

it did not make, and so replace bitterness before love and death with their acceptance and celebration. For the *charis*, the gratitude which Pindar bespeaks for life's effulgence, Sophocles at the last brought to bear on death itself: "Cease your threnody, my children. Those things for which the celebration beneath the soil, night, awaits, there is no need to mourn. For so it is established." (*O.C.* 1751-3)

Let me restate in closing, in answer to Mrs. Langer, that as far as imagery is concerned, our dreams are perfect poems, perfect in the sense that the imagery is directly expressive of the emotion or instinct for its formulation, the ideal of the artist. However fast or violently the dream imagery changes, its propulsion is the expression of the successive layers of self-realization within that propelling emotion. But they are perfect poems only as dreamed, and they are usually private poems, even if their imagery is sometimes generic. There is no such thing as a daytime recapitulation of the organic unity of a dream, organic not only in the connection between the pressure and its objectifying images but in the emotional interrelation of the successive, changing images. There is by day merely the discursive translation of a few separated salient images.

The important point is that the mode of objectification in dream is the mode of objectification in art, the realization of pressure or felt relation as visual or verbal shape. The dream as dreamed is as "emotionally transparent" as the poem, though as with the poem its discursive analysis remains apart from its sensous appreciation. The dreamer 'knows the meaning' of his dream while dreaming it, precisely as the reader first grasps the meaning of a poem as its words and images, that is, the dreamer realizes the emotional affects of these images of his dream, even though he is not thereby enabled to place them in a discursive pattern which illuminates their relation to daytime experience. Like the reader he either dispenses altogether with or awaits the translation of the imagery. The unconscious creation of the dream is the prototype of poetry; the poet is great to the extent that he can consciously apply the organic rules of image synthesis the dream spontaneously fulfills. The dream is our natural exemplar of image creation: from nowhere to here, unity in variety, instinct and emotion realized as figure.

And the mind dreaming realizes the action-blurred relation of the daytime psyche to experience, the role of spectator; it is the artist's consciousness which restores to our appreciation the psyche's natural location. Poets have always been known as dreamers; that is their strength, not their weakness. For as artificer, as maker, the poet must let his psyche approach the condition, the focus without will, of the dreamer's psyche.

The important difference between dreams and organic art is one of social usefulness, and the ancient art of dream interpretation was an attempt to make the transition from individual revelation to social purpose. It may not have been often successful, but its intent is meaningful, and its assumption clear, that the dream as much as the poem is a descent into the realm of primal organization rendered imagistically and, if seen correctly, a way to revelation for daytime action.

# CHAPTER 3

## SAPPHO'S *HYMN TO APHRODITE*

Glittering-throned deathless Aphrodite,
child of Zeus, seine-weaver, I beseech you,
do not by disdain, by turning away, damn,
    Potency, spirit.

But come hither if, in another time,
my cry hearing afar
you hearkened, leaving your father's gold
    house you descended,

chariot yoked under your power. Lovely,
quick birds bore you near to the dark earth,
thickly throbbing their wings, from heaven
    through the mid-aether.

Of a sudden they came and you, Blessed,
smiling with deathless expression
questioned, What now again I suffer, What
    now again call for,

What to me most I wish to have happen
mad-hearted. "Whom now again do you yearn
Seduction to bring your embraces? Who,
    Sappho, contemns you?

For if she flees, soon shall she follow;
if gifts accepts not, soon shall she give them.
If she loves not, soon shall she love,
    even unwilling."

Come to me likewise now, from harsh — oh free me —
cares, and all to accomplish
heart longs, accomplish. Do you yourself
    be fellow-fighter.

Our rough Hebraic-Hellenic contrast can serve another purpose. If religious thought is the attempt to direct or control the will so as to ensure individual or social triumph, then the religious thinker, watching the course of events and searching for the pattern of enactment, will try to decide what individual or community will is good or bad, what intent right or wrong. He will want to know whether individual or social will coincided with appreciated sequence, and if not, why not. Religious thought, if the correct exercise of will is its focus, will take the shape of passing judgment, judgment on events as fulfilling or failing individual or community goals, judgment on men's actions for helping or hindering such triumph. There is no room for mythic image, for that is image created in the psyche of felt unwilled power, just as there is no call for art, for that is the systematic rendition of such psychic appreciation. If will is the center, what should you *do* is the religious question, how should your will take shape and find its religious realization. For I am talking not alone of the king with his practical answer, but of the prophet with his religious one.

On the other hand, if religion is centered in the psyche's appreciation, by its focusing faculties, of given power or recurrent relation expressing such power, the religious search will also be a search for the nature of appreciation and should issue in successive formulations of that appreciation. No one ever argues the extraordinary way in which Greek civilization expresses itself formally in the arts, in striking contrast to Israel; and those Hellenic artistic forms classically are primarily religious, architecturally temples to the gods and their approaches, in poetry the choral hymn, the Dionysiac theatre and its enactments of the relations of gods and mortals figured as heroes, and the vase painting or temple sculpture of the same myths. Art, of course, in any medium is formalization, and for the Classical Greek that art is religious, finding or creating the form of the expression in the psyche of divine power.

And the question is, What or How you see. In logical discourse such a search is the attempt to answer What do we know, How do we know it, How does what we say register what is, How do we know that the form in the mind accurately presents what lies outside the mind, epistemology. Such questions are the articulating skeleton of Plato's early virtue dialogues and of his central illuminations — *Protagoras, Symposium, Republic* — quite as much as of technical formulations like the *Theaetetus.* But the artist, the worker in images, is ask-

75

ing and trying to answer similar questions; the choruses of the *Agamemnon* and the dramatic unfolding of the *Oedipus* are such "epistemology."

That is, the poems are both trying to answer not only what do we know but how we know it. How do we see and comprehend the ground of the expedition from Greece to Ilium, Iphigeneia's killing, the murder of Agamemnon? The answer is all mythic projection, event rendered as the imaginative creation of event, and that imagination posits the divine, the given pressure issuing in the event. Even the night of Troy's fall is presented as purely imaginary, in this case Clytemnestra's vision, and that imaginary character's imaginative picture is an epitome of the whole poetic process for conceiving Troy's ruin and Agamemnon's death. Likewise, the dramatic tension of the *Oedipus* is an imaginary character's coming to see what has happened to him. Once again, as in Clytemnestra's Troy vision, the creative process of the play — the creating imagination of the poet — is formalized within the drama as the mode of its own realization: Oedipus' search and knowledge. The Greek poets, in other words, are "epistemological" in the imagistic mode, seeking to show in art the means of art as a mode of knowing.

So Helen's encounter with Aphrodite in the *Iliad* is the Homeric formalization of the power of sexual instinct realized in the psyche of woman. The moment dramatized is the moment of realization, the imaginative seizure of the form—Aphrodite — which clarifies, realizes, symbolizes the pressure, the given pressure issuing in the event. In the lyric mode — the ego mode — Sappho's *Hymn to Aphrodite* is another such formalization, realization, unfolding imagistically, of the given pressure that issues in the act of love.

I approach this poem as an example of Greek religion, the psychic apprehension of the traditional figure for erotic experience, and thereby deny that it can be criticized from a purely "aesthetic" or "literary" viewpoint. Experience is so totally felt and expressed within the traditional terms of the Greek religious vocabulary, that the exegesis of the poem must ipso facto be an analysis of that traditional mode of seeing. Not realizing this, current Anglo-Saxon interpretation is by and large misleading. C.M. Bowra, it is true, attempts to interpret it as a religious poem, or at least the so-called epiphany within it as a religious experience, though even that as a private vision. But the religious terms in which he tries to explain it are alien to it, though he has seen fit to kill in the 2nd edition of *Greek Lyric Poetry* (1962) the earlier reference (1st ed. Oxford, 1936, 195) to St. Teresa's vision which served, at least, to reveal the premise of his interpretation. But an 'epiphany' for a Greek poet is not the least private and at the farthest pole from mysticism. Mysticism implies an unknown god—deus absconditus—revealed ineffably in the rare psyche by exotic means. A Greek god is a figure, and a community-wide figure, of daily experience open to everyman. Aphrodite is Helen's own instinct which speaks to her directly, as that instinct can and does to everyone; their dialogue, as we have seen, is the dialogue of self and instinct. Sappho's case is identical. The apparition of Aphrodite instead of being private or singular is the private or singular become communal and communicated. No hidden being is revealed. A very real pressure is announced in religious form. We shall return to this point later.

D.L. Page (*Sappho and Alcaeus*, Oxford, 1955, 4-18) sins far more grievously than does C.M. Bowra. With naive ethnocentricity he reduces this paradigmatic Greek religious expression to the sophisticated private banter of some Lesbian London hostess communing either with herself or her own small circle on the waywardness of sexual aberration in playful self-mockery. But the privacy as well as the humor of the poem are, I am afraid, all Mr. Page's aberration. He not only fails to grasp the poem in its historical setting, in terms of Greek symbolism; he violates the simplest canons of modern literary criticism.

There is nothing I shall say about this poem that will seem strange to readers versed in contemporary methods. For the usual Classicist it will be altogether original, if not wayward, simply because of his failure to apply that method to ancient poetry, Latin as well as Greek. He would be startled to hear that you can learn nothing of his love life from Catullus' poetry, that Vergil's *1st Eclogue* concerns the art of poetry not landholding, that the choral "I" or "ego" of Pindar's verse is the choral ego of Aeschylus' or Sophocles', the choral personality. By and large the ancient poet is read as if expressing personal bias or feeling on politics, society, his private amours. Yet the moment a contemporary mind moves into the orbit of classical form, of classical objectification, of classical symbolism, the subjective heresy must be shed.

Before analyzing the imagery, the religious symbolism of this poem, let me state its status in the simplest terms. The *Hymn to Aphrodite* is as much a hymn for public performance and recitation as any in our hymnbooks. It is an address to a publicly worshipped divinity of Hellas that any worshipper of that divinity can use for her or his own parallel predicament. There is no private vision, no mystic apprehension in it: the vision of Aphrodite is the clear conscious apprehension of the communal form of erotic experience. The poem is dramatic from first to last, as is most great lyric poetry, and drama always insists on the individual voice, but the individual voice objectified. It is the social concretization of generic individual experience. Sappho could not, of course, have created this "objective correlative" with conviction without individual experience, but neither can we re-experience the poem with conviction without such individual pathos ourselves. Our experience meets hers in the poem, because our momentary realization of such experience is dependent on her objectification of it. The 'Sappho' of this poem is as much a dramatic projection for generic experience as the 'Helen' of the *Iliad.* The realization in a stringent metre of traditional Hellenic symbolism for erotic pathos should of itself prove an insuperable barrier to any simple view of 'self-expression'. The ancient critic who preserved this poem adduced it as a model of formalization, as smooth harmonious synthesis (Dion. Hal. *Comp* 173f). He was alive to form in a sense Page and Bowra are oblivious of. Theirs is the view that has wondered why Eliot in his twenties describes himself as "an old man in a dry month" or at thirty as an "aged eagle," the view that has refused to accept Whitman's assertion that begins all his poetry in all his editions, that the chosen mask is the mask for everyman, not his alone, the view which coalesces "Walt" and someone christened Walter. The persona of a successful lyric poem is always a mask, a poetic, that is, literally, *made* personality, used directly by its creator as

"Walt" (later a mask for life, incidentally) or 'Sappho', or quite distantly, through a borrowed poetic idiom, as with Horace and Catullus. Catullus' unfinished exercise— *ille mi par esse deo videtur*— bespeaks his appreciation of the mode of the Sappho poem it imitates and has not one thing to do with his own personal experience.

Here that mask is the subject of a prayer and is a parallel in the monodic lyric mode to the created character in the imagined situation of prayer in epic, choral, or tragic verse. Any Hellenist can provide his own list of parallels. Here is a limited arbitrary selection simply to illustrate breadth of parallel poetic exposition: *Iliad* 5.115; 10.284; 16.233-8; Sophocles' *O.T.* 163f (with its echo of elthete kai nun); Pindar *O* 12.1; *P* 8.1; *N* 10.; *I* 6.42f; *Paean* 6.3. These artists created these prayers as imaginary expression of the psyche before imaginary or the imaginative recreation of historical situation. The 'Sappho' of our poem is a projected character and is used as theirs to illustrate the generic relation of an individual's immediate success, in this case, in love, to the everywhere power that is exercised in such success, or marked as failure by its absence. The 'Sapphic' predicament can become anyone's. The generic, the repetitive quality of the experience is insisted upon in the hymn. It can, then, become, as much as a prayer in the Book of Common Prayer, a form for anyone's realization of parallel situation, and so, I assume, it was used in Classical Hellas. If the reader bristles at the parallel, it is because we bristle at the notion of public prayer for amorous success, at subscribing publicly and religiously to the power of sex. That is a problem of a different order.

Implicit, though often unrealized, in the contemporary canon of the lyric personality as mask or projection is the modality of everyday psychic phenomena, experiential and linguistic. That is, all experience if individual in mode is generic both in source and in biological and psychic expression, a posited someone stands for all others in a given situation. Secondly, all language is the means of rendering that existential commonality, is itself the transformation of the individual experience into its communal or objective statement. What is true of language is true of its metaphors and religious symbols; they are the means whereby the experience, still rendered in its individual contours, can reveal its generic source for community apprehension.

The measure of our poem's objective use of the lyric mask can be seen in yet another fashion. In the Homeric picture of the women of Troy (*Iliad* 6.297f) praying to Athena – to add yet another to our list of parallels – the epic poet states directly (311), from the never disclosed position of the omniscient narrative point of view, Athena's rejection of the prayer, thereby marking the limit of the will of those who pray and the narrator's detachment from that will and its situation. Sappho in the lyric mode achieves the same expression of that limit – a point which will concern us as religion shortly – and of the creator's detachment from it. The poem as a whole discloses the limit, the situation simply as beseecher of its posited dramatic personality. There is no illusion of necessary victory, no sense that she who prays exerts her own will, even if, in the god's donation, she obtains it. The prayer, then, is simply the objectification of situation, as in a narrative or tragic texture. To that degree can Sappho be said to be writing, quite literally, dramatic verse in the lyric mode and 'Sappho' her character. She as creator stands outside the creation of the subject of the prayer and thereby discloses the relation of her character to the power for her fulfillment. It is not merely mastery of metrics and simple diction that marks her sense of form; anterior to these is her sense of the prayer itself as the form to be fulfilled. To fulfill that form she must dramatize, which means objectify, the relation of her who prays and the power to which her prayer is addressed.

Yet I do not think she could have obtained by art this degree of objectification without her inherited conception of divinity. Greek religion as well as Sappho's place in it are necessary for her sort of creation. I myself have pointed to a Christian as well as ancient Greek parallels for her prayer situation, and from one point of view that parallel is appropriate. All prayer is the projection of wish or longing of some sort; to deny prayer is to deny the need expressed by it, to expect or even desire that the species cease from praying is to want them to stop needing. But to assume that the local wish or will in prayer by invoking divine power compels the outcome is quite a different matter.

Here the ordinary Christian conception of prayer is merely the obverse of the modern intellectual denial of its efficacy, and both must part company radically with the Greek poetic objectification of the psychic predicament in prayer (I do not say the Greek practice of it, but its poetic objectification), and that because of a radical distinction between the Greek poetic and the ordinary Christian conception of divinity, the distinction between the unifying figure for acknowledged, to this day acknowledged power, and the Christian God as a projection of individual will. Even if prayer is the projection of wish or will, and this whole poem is such a wish, such a projection of will, it is clearly seen as such a projection, but the arbiter of that will's success or failure is realized dramatically in the poem as quite separate from it. The immediate, the local will and the eternal, abiding power for sexual fulfillment, in which it can and does participate, of which its need, in fact, is a manifestation, are here juxtaposed, not coalesced. There is nothing in this poem that a contemporary sensibility free from all superstition or belief in supernatural will cannot accept as the reiterated pattern of psychic experience.

From the opening vocative forms of address to the closing adjuration, the poem is built on the tension between the local will and the eternal power, between 'Sappho' praying and the Aphrodite who while in her and sometimes with her, is forever elsewhere, who comes and goes as desire dictates. The only effective will is will in nature, not the will of the individual. This contrast closes the first stanza in the juxtaposition of the power, *potnia*, the ruler of men and beasts, and the one who prays as a will, *thumon*; it is dramatized in the dialogue between that rendering power and its suppliant and provides again the polarity for the final stanza, which like the first is prayer direct.

But the contrast between Sappho and Aphrodite is not the only one. A tension is also built between the two aspects of Aphrodite herself, as locally manifest and ubiquitously powerful. It forms the contrast between the immediate concretization of her presence, and her unrealized but posited presence elsewhere. This contrast is struck off immediately in the two opening adjectives, glittering-throned and deathless, the significance of one of which is apt to be denied, of the other passed off lightly as a stock-epithet. They are, in fact, weighted and weighted by contrast as signal for later analogous divisions.

The injunction against "idolatry" is still with us, at least in literary criticism, and the first word of the poem, *poikilothron*, "goddess of the throne of varied or shimmering color" (or "of various materials": chiaroscuro effected in some fashion), is interpreted in every possible way except as the forthright notation of a seated goddess. The inlaid throne at Mytilene where the smiling goddess sits, the cult image for cult rite, should stare at us as it does for Sappho for every line of the performance of this hymn. To read it away is just another part of the attempt to seclude this poem in the closet of private expression.

But the Greeks, of course, did not, as their Judaic or Christian critics sometimes conceive, think of the idol as the god, who is always a power in nature, but as a local concretization of that power, just as a local enactment of love bespeaks the same everywhere capacity for love. The immediate throned statue is contrasted at once with 'deathless', which recalls the natural pressure to which the cult image is related; with the easily slipped over "immortal" we pass from the local need to the everywhere donation of it. A mortal is praying to an immortal; her fulfillment is simply the exercise of immortal power when given. But just as she, in her limit, is contrasted to that deathlessness, so the power in its defined appearance is contrasted to its own continuity and ubiquity. The Aphrodite who sits in sculpturally realized form before the performance of the poem, like the character of Aphrodite within it, are momentary imaginative forms — and both surely known to their artificers as such — for coursing power which lies forever beyond their definitions; they are simultaneously concrete and abstract, concrete as shape, abstract as sign.

The exercise of that power is always in the individual mode, in nature prior to art; it is always formulated as person-to-person, however much those persons vary. It is perceived only as the individual psyche perceives it. There is no such *thing* as sexual instinct at all; our own form of abstraction deceives us, as the Greek anthropomorphic deity cannot. Once again, (as in Helen's encounter with Aphrodite) the limiting aspect of deity as anthropomorphic is essential; it is the way to see the power defined as it impinges on the individual mind.

So it is the personality Aphrodite who 'weaves the trap' *doloploke*. The implication, incidentially, is not of deceit, the usual English "weaver of wiles." That takes us again to the notion of independent and motivated will on the part of deity, when the intent is to render the effect of sexual attraction for the Greek. Sappho's third epithet foreshadows Aeschylus' chain or net for Paris in adultery (*Ag.* 358), and later she uses Peitho, Persuasion, Seduction, the movement from psyche to psyche that compels the unwilling girl to Sappho's arms, the same word that Aeschylus will use of the power of Helen's beauty over Paris (*Ag.* 385). "Grave the vision Venus sends of supernatural sympathy."

Once we have the constant figure, the goddess, as the intra-personal power, as the shape which resumes the affects of both psyches involved, it can dramatically figure the reactions of either one. So with *asaisi* and *oniaisi*. They are not to be translated or interpreted as griefs or pains, distress conceived as the goddess' willful affliction — that perpetual Job-like reading of Greek deity. If they were to be figured personally in our poem, they would be assigned as active adjectives to the recalcitrant girl, for both words imply revulsion, a sense of annoyance, the girl's grounds for rejection of Sappho that lead to the latter's consequent frustration. But they are not attached to either active participant. The girl's response is figured as Aphrodite's and simultaneously combined with Sappho's re-action to it. The divinity, the image of love for our poem, contains the psychic response on either side. And this is intrinsically naturalistic, since the power of one for another is simply the evocation of her own need, the power of sex in herself defined by confronting person and psyche. Proust's perplexity is dissolved; the subjective delusion announces the extrapersonal power that has brought it into being, and we close the stanza, as I have already noted, with the second antithesis between the single will or spirit and the Divine Power exercised through it, *potnia, thumon*.

In her predicament the suppliant enlists for her present the memory of past success in love. This is the apparition of

Aphrodite and her dialogue with 'Sappho', the 'epiphany', and our explication of it is as an exemplar of the nature of Greek religion.

The evocation of Aphrodite in this poem is a conscious imaginative creation; we might keep two parallels in mind. It is the poetic equivalent of the sculptor's creation of the statue of Aphrodite before which the hymn is performed. And its poetic counterpart, surely conscious to this poet, is the confrontation of Aphrodite and Helen in the *Iliad*. It is the formalization of past amorous experience.

Just as Helen realizes that it is Aphrodite in her which is drawing her to Paris' bed, so Sappho declares that it was Aphrodite who brought a girl to her before. Sappho's vision of Aphrodite working for the victory of her will is of the same nature as Helen's vision of Aphrodite announcing its defeat; the dialogue in both cases is the externalization, the concretization of psychic history. This is not in our sense epiphany. There is no place for such in Greek religion, for there is no hidden deity to break in on the real world. There are only the actual powers of that real world realized by psyches in moments of acute stress from those particular powers.

Who would argue that the ever practical Odysseus was the psychological sort given to mystic trance? Yet he sees and converses with his Athena impulse or component more often and more variously than any character in Greek poetry. Who would claim that the great Achilles, who swears by his right arm, has ever sought divine converse by fasting, prayer, or a probing of his own soul? Yet godhead comes and speaks to him. The Sappho of our poem sees Aphrodite just as those epic characters see their special deities.

The apparition, I will be the first to agree, is convincing, but did not the 6th century sculptors of our extant stone-carved goddesses see her too? Did not the 5th century sculptor of the east pediment of Zeus' temple at Olympia see Apollo? There is no more convincing purely visual rendition of anthropomorphic divinity than that peace and order loving countenance and all embracing stretching arm. Would the sculptor after realizing this shape in stone deny that his hammer and chisel had made every square inch of its surface, rendered the light of its eyes, the stance of its chin and cheek, the weight of its whole form? The vision in all these cases is experience realized within a particular traditional symbolic vocabulary. The Olympian sculptor has experienced law and order compelling peace from strife and sees that as Apollo. Sappho has known the course of love that brings a fighting girl to her arms and sees that as persuading, seducing Aphrodite. The conviction of the rendered vision in all cases springs from the depth and conviction of the experience and its precise historical meeting with traditional symbolic forms for that experience. In this historical period we can suppose that many men and women could form their experience of their gods simply by an awareness, as by us with language or borrowed psychological concepts, of the powers working in their persons. Any actual experience of love could be said to realize the presence of Aphrodite.

Note that there is no union with deity here, no emotion passing as between power and its suppliant. Sappho's Aphrodite laughs as she stands apart, as Helen's Aphrodite threatens and compels her. Any love is between actual persons, psychic as well as physical; the tenor of the character's dramatic attitude to deity figures the tenor of the human response to the possibility of love, necessary but hateful to Helen, wanted but unsure to Sappho. Note again, too, the relation in both cases of the human will to the divine ground for the human emotion; Helen's will is bent, broken for the enactment of love, Sappho's victory is the deployment of Aphrodite's power in an unwilling girl.

These simple points are underscored to contrast this apparition to any Christian or other mystic experience. C.M. Bowra did a service in once bespeaking the parallel to St. Teresa in her ecstasy (*Greek Lyric Poetry*, 1st ed. 195), for he simply crystallized what most commentators hover around, the equation of a Greek divinity to an unknown and generally unknowable God, issuing mysteriously from nowhere into the known, in an intimate personal relation to the believer who has successfully summoned its presence. St. Teresa's ecstasy is the sex act sublimated as union with the divine, and Bernini's visualization of her position and countenance a faithful representation of her own woman-experienced psychic account.[1] But that account, like its marble image, can proceed only from a religion whose projections are hypostases of human aspirations, not, as with the Greeks, a vocabulary for coursing powers in nature which no one may deny.

The Greek religious form, the goddess, simply realizes for consciousness what is: the act of sex totally dependent on given energy and a given centering-consciousness for the deployment of that energy. The singular act not only rehearses all others but the common capacity for them, that energy and its centering-consciousness. That, as I argued in the first chapter, is one of the reasons that divinity is figured in human shape, the immortal form for the human seizure of its own capacities and their use via the centering consciousness. Sappho objectifies her singular portion of need or delight by relating to it, seeing it under the form of the same power as realized, as we shall see, by all men as well as women.

Commentators would be helped, nay authorized, to comment as they have come to terms in their own minds with what is expressed in variant religious projections. That something vivid, overwhelming happened to Teresa is undeniable; the Bernini statue merely visualizes it. Is that a representation of the apparition of godhead, or merely the illusion of its intrusion derived from the absence of love in human form? The Ecstasy can be grasped as image either way, but appreciation or interpretation will radically divide. Ultimately that division will depend on allegiance to or rejection of a *deus absconditus amans*. Similarly, the interpretation of Sappho's vision of Aphrodite is dependent on the relation of the symbol, the figure of the deity, to its local ground, to the experiential validity of the coursing power for which it stands.

To us the vision of Aphrodite in Sappho's hymn is a paradigm of the relation of an immortal process to local success in love, and the conversation between the Sappho of the poem and Aphrodite, like Helen's converse, the individual in dialogue with the power in her that makes seduction of the desired object possible. What makes it possible is never her own will — but the beseecher's fortuitous position defining or meeting another's sexual need. What brings the defying girl to her embrace, when the girl's will is set against it? The girl's own generic need; it is Aphrodite working through her. She refuses, as Helen refuses, and then accepts, as Helen accepts, because a power greater than that will is exercised on her. She who fled will pursue; she who would not take gifts will give them to get satisfaction she now owns and demands. She will love against her will. This happy reversal has been experienced in the past; the present hope is that it will be experienced again.

That past experience itself was generic, momentary, one of a series. The instinct speaking to the individual, Aphrodite to Sappho, asks, who on this occasion, who again. That three times 'now again', *deute*, is not humorous or frivolous. It is characteristic, of love as an experience, a repeated experience. Helen says the same thing. Whither now will you lead me, to what new man of Maeonia or Phrygia? (*Iliad* 3.401). Plato establishes this repetition in the *Symposium* as the path to the grasp of the nature of love itself, to the realization, in earlier terms, of the ubiquitous Aphrodite. It can be bitter, as with Helen, or in the *Phaedrus*. But it is a Greek formulation of quotidian experience, of one individual through time or of many individuals at any time. It points to the resilient and coursing nature of desire itself, formalized, seen apart from any one of its subjects. Like the 'immortal' and 'Seduction' of the invocation it objectifies local experience as yet another of the manifold expressions of the same given power. In the term Aphrodite uses in her conversation, the reiterated 'now again', she describes the repetitive nature of her own apparition; the poet, be it always remembered, conceives those terms, and thereby defines the natural history of love figured as Aphrodite's power or presence.

Sappho's victory in the past has not been an individual's victory but the power of which she is agent working on the girl's mind and body against her will. Her prayer is simply that that power be exercised through her again. There is nothing supernatural here at all, suggested or dramatized. This poem can stand in the lyric mode as an epitome of Greek religion, of the objectification of the relation of the single will to the alltime everywhere power of sex, the immortal one who can come on occasion to the defined self. The 'Sappho' of the poem is that perpetual self; the Aphrodite the perpetual power of its fulfillment.

There is another and even simpler way to grasp the fact that the Aphrodite who appears through this hymn is a conscious artifact comparable to a cult statue, not for a moment the poetic verbalization of a private vision. Her apparition in the poem is built up out of a careful accretion of traditional epithets or attributes. A conventional vocabulary of communal significance is as determinant of the images of this poem as the parallel plastic conventions would have been for the cult statue before which it was sung. I was instructed in Sappho's verse, as many others, in quite a different fashion, in this instance by Mr. Finley, to remark the simple direct tactile or visual sensuousness of her language, the delight in sparrows and dark earth in this poem, as in flowers and perfumes in others, the "feminine feeling" for the literal, the unique, the personal. But Sappho, in this poem, at least, is not concerned with the literal or the unique or the personal image; she is concerned with conventional signs. I will review this inherited vocabulary of the vision only briefly, but it could be read in relation to many other instances of parallel — hence communal and traditional — uses of the same vocabulary in Classic poetry.

Aphrodite is borne to the earth by the incessant throbbing of the wings of the *strouthoi*, sparrows. That is the Latin *passer*, Spanish *pajaro*, Italian *uccello*, the 'bird' of contemporary American slang. The sparrow or bird (and they are clearly interchangeable in this connection) is not some vague symbol, as Mr. Page would have it (*Sappho and Alcaeus* 7.8), of wantonness or fecundity. These multi-lingual references are all metaphors for the virile member, a universal dream-image created by shape and movement, exemplified to this day by the winged phalluses sold at Pompei or in the streets of Rome. The bird's own love life is of no more importance than that of the mouse or snake used with similar significance; it is the bird as shape or image that is significant. The Italian by *uccello* means precisely what the collegian means by 'bird'. The image metastasizes the human attribute as an animal form and thereby objectifies all enactment as a unity, outside the domain of individual will — a point made in the previous chapter. In Sappho the incessant throbbing of the winged birds bespeaks in one phrase the omnipresence and repetition through nature of this carnal process as clearly as Lucretius' invocation of alma Venus opening the *De Rerum Natura;* nor is his juxtaposition of Venus' power and that title inapposite to her poem. We may recall, too, Catullus' two *passer* (or sparrow) poems which are the metaphorical statement at different stages (the death of the *passer* is the *post coitum tristitia*) of the sex act. Those male signs in Sappho's poem wing near to the dark earth, immemorial sign of the receiving mother, earth which is dark as the new-plowed soil where Demeter and Jason copulate (*Odyssey* 5.125). The power signed in its male form in approach to the female form is the power which will bring the girl to Sappho's arms, her love-making, *philoteta*, a word for amorous embrace weighted for Sappho's sense, as for ours, by its manifold uses in Homer, to mingle in *philoteti*. Sappho's embrace yields its isolation in being seen to proceed from the everywhere power signed first in its male form in Aphrodite's carriage into the human scene.

But this power, as in Lucretius' poem, is under the roof of the cosmos, the sky from which Aphrodite comes. She has left the house of her father, Zeus, symbol of the order of the natural world. That house is of gold; gold is the sign of the summit of the everlasting, the divine, as we shall see again in Pindar. It marks the crest of power, the keystone of the arch, the pediment of the world. Even Aphrodite's power is seen to be exercised within a natural order symbolized by her father in his gold palace. That worldwide power has now hearkened to one voice, catching up the previous collocation of *potnia thumon*, potency and one will, the singular individual and the immortal presence. The objectification of Sappho's own love-making can go no further.

But the power of sex is awful as well as benign. Aphrodite's carriage is the war chariot, *arma*, the sweep of horses clanging into battle or in the chariot race. The chariot used symbolically always implies its steeds; nor is there any contradiction here to the birds as the bearing power. Bird and horse are symbols of identical power; neither is literal. The wild stridency of those carriers is echoed in the horse metaphor used by the imaginary Sophocles in the opening scene of the *Republic,* the horse from whose traces his old sexless age has at last freed him. This metaphor for the sex drive attains its subtlest and fullest deployment in Plato's *Phaedrus* with the black and white steeds. But the sexual power signed as the horse power conceived as *arma*, chariot, also suggests victory as its outcome in this instance. The *quadriga* could be used simply to sign triumph, as in Gelon's use of it to celebrate simultaneously his victory at Himera and in the 480 Olympian chariot race on the *Demarateia*, and in our poem the past instance of the exercise of Aphrodite's power is recalled because it has led to success.

Yet before the victory is obtained doubt reigns. We must think of that smile on the goddess' "countenance divine" not, with Page (ibid. 15), as humorous but as terribly ambiguous. It can suggest the Tyger as well as the Lamb. Sappho's phrase is the same as Blake's not because, as far as I know, of any interrelation between the two poems, but because the post-Enlightenment poet is free again, like the Greek poet, to come to the expression of *impersonal* divine power.

We must, then, dispel any notion of imagistic simplicity, subjectivity, or "femininity" in Sappho. Her every image is communal and conventional, a means of expressing the local or experiential in a structured world whose pattern is thereby disclosed. For us the vocabulary begins in Homer and is deployed throughout the whole history of succeeding Hellenic and Latin poetry. The references in Sappho are of the briefest compass and are left momentarily.

But to transform amorous experience by that inherited and continuing vocabulary is to render it totally public. The Sapphic vision of Aphrodite is, therefore, the farthest from the private, as it is the farthest from the mystical. It is rendered not as of the chamber but as of the society where this vocabulary is the means of communication. Sappho is translating experience into mythical form, as Homer does with Helen, or Pindar in the amorous dialogue between Pelops and Poseidon in the *1st Olympian*. We should, in fact, think of the encounter in this poem between 'Sappho' and Aphrodite as its myth, as much its poet's creation for the sake of objectification as these others. And myth is always expression in traditional terms. Personal experience communicated is experience transubstantiated by symbols viable for all those who appreciate the references of its vocabulary. Aphrodite and her attributes, her voyage, her dialogue, is the image of a whole society realizable by every one of its members. So the poet's, Sappho's, intent and result in creating that myth with all its references, far from being a sounding of self and its inner emotional resonances, is the objectification of experience for society in its language. When she has done with her poem, as much as the sculptor with his statue at Mytilene, or at Athens or Olympia, she has created an artifact which those who come after may use as they see fit as an expression of similar situation and its posited power.

We have been concerned to give this hymn a new but simple historical exegesis, to see it clearly within a Classical Greek religious vocabulary, as exemplary of a Hellenic conception of divinity, to see as conscious artifact its apparition of Aphrodite and her dialogue with the subject of the prayer, parallel with a sculptor's imaginative visualization of a divine shape. Sappho's imagination, we hold, is responsible for the vision and speech of the goddess.

But such a realization is convincing, is possible only at a time when it is felt that the 'truth' about divinity is imaginative, when, historically, imagination rendered in a conventional sign system is trusted as the means for the actualization of consciousness. The center of Sappho's hymn is the conscious- ness voicing itself, crying out its own appropriation of its own pressure. There is no point at which you can separate the religious and the poetic, the dramatic confrontation of the subject of the poem with its own pressure, its assertive consciousness of its dominating environment *and* the ritualistic or religious symbolism of it. Aphrodite is simply the greatest of the images, the greatest of the 'ideas'. She is the final cry of the consciousness for the pressure experienced, the pressure to the situation expressed as our hymn.

But she, too, is logos, she too is Word, her naming, describing an intellectual act, an assertion of consciousness. Sappho's use of her inherited symbol of erotic pressure is no whit different from her use of each word in the text as the appropriate assertion of given shape or substance, gold or dark earth or whirring wings, and all these others, as we have pointed out, are means to assert the specific hierarchical position in nature of the pressure before which the subject of the poem asserts itself.

The social valence of the poetic symbol can hardly be overemphasized. The poet was the religious teacher and thinker *par excellence*, the *sophos*, the wise man whose mastery of language, myth, and religious meaning could not originally be distinguished. The mastery of poetic form is mastery in religious pronouncement.

But power, divine power, must be revealed through poetic speech for poetry to perform the task of religion. We can, perhaps, state this contrast as two views of "revelation." For Whitman, as for Emerson, revelation is now, never as clear and salient as in the present. There is no validity to Whitman if one does not accept this claim of contemporary revelation. But a similar claim — usually passed over in silence — is made by Greek poetry; Aphrodite, a goddess, talks to Sappho, as Pelops talks to Poseidon, a god, in the present tense, and in both cases the poet composes every word of their dialogue. Dionysus is beheld by Pentheus as well as the Bacchants, Artemis converses with Hippolytus, Ajax with Athena. The "revelation" of these gods, their power, intent, or relation to mortal experiences, is newly conceived by the living poet in his own time. This is also the distinction between the Gospels and post-Pauline Christianity — a point which will concern us largely later — between revelation in a perpetually evolving present, at the point of the future, and revelation conceived as sealed in a unique past.

The disjunction between poetic and religious appreciation, separating instinctive linguistic response from its natural intuition of divinity in action, may be said to derive from the hypostasis of a putative Conciousness quite different from ordinary human consciousness which is, of course, the ground of the voice of poetry. That putative Consciousness may descend, if very rarely, on rarely located psyches. It is, strictly, ineffable, because it is, self-contradictorily, defined as the recognition of what can not be known. This is as much a denial of the Hellenic deployment of art to reveal the divine powers, divine personalities in act and speech, as it is a denial of the Whitman-Rilke-Stevens faith that the word can go beyond itself to reveal the thing in its natural location. "The one integrity ... To which all poems were incident, unless That prose should wear a poem's guise at last."

Greek poetry is such a guise, as is the post-Enlightenment poetry which squarely upheld the new faith setting the new task:

Hear the voice of the Bard
Who present, past and future sees.

There is nothing startling in one more critic ascribing to the claims of modern prophetic verse. What is new is relating that claim to the unargued assumption of Greek religious poetry and seeing their common ground as a *theological* assumption, athwart the traditional epistemology of Christianity as "revealed truth." As I have said before and will repeat, the status of the two—Greek verse and modern prophetic verse—is quite different. For one the poetic claim is at war with traditional religion, and in the other is the expression, the fullest expression of it. There are, I am well aware, a congery of other differences, that Greek poetry precedes while modern poetry follows the claim of logical discourse to ultimate validity, that Greek poetry had to hand a communal visual vocabulary, while modern prophetic poets have either had to create a private system of symbols or, eschewing symbolic evolvement, make the imagination which creates and uses them the subject of poetry itself, and there are others. But the one word 'status' can pull all the differences together: there are very few now who believe in dream imagery as a revelation of divinity, few who believe that musical assertion, a given mode of reaction to the environment, internal as well as external, can reveal it more subtly and more naturally to the centering consciousness than any later, intellectually constructed form of discourse, few who believe either in given power or in the instinctive modes of its appreciation.

We can not ever separate the allegiance to given mode of reaction and the allegiance to given power. Art flourishes when instinct is accepted, and Sappho's musical mastery is inseparable from her worship of Aphrodite, the elaboration of reaction inspired directly by realization or appreciation of plangent power. It is only in terms of 'status', in terms of its public musical formulation, that we should discuss 'Sappho's attitude toward sex'. Within her poems—our only possible source—there is no such 'attitude' at all. All discussion of such a non-extant quantity for Sappho is the product of societies where there is, nay, has to be such an individual attitude because of the communal rejection of the given as divine. Sappho's hymn to Aphrodite can not be torn from the context of a society's public worship of Aphrodite: and such public worship of sexual power-for-performance is the measure of our distance from the normative attitude of the individual hymn. It is not a question of sexual practice, but of social worship and therefore of the nature of divinity. Practice, as with us, can be blatant in its defiance of religious prescription or proscription, since that prescription is not for submission to felt pressure. We shudder still at the public worship of Astarte as deeply as the Hebrews from whom her coastal rite was but a few miles distant, shudder at the birds of Hera and Aphrodite, at the lingam of Shiva,[2] shudder at centering consciousness on the vivid signs, the instrumentality of sexual potency. Yet music, a hymn to Aphrodite, is but such a consciousness formulated, and formulated for social participation. It is the worship of given power, and the worship of this formulation of power is not to be separated from all others. Poseidon's worship, too, was, in part, sexual, symbolically in the phallus of the horse; he is the boy Pelop's lover in Pindar's *First Olympian*. But he is also the plangent power of the sea, and the worship of the two forces need not even be separated in their common symbol. Nor is submission to sex to be separated from submission to death, to the acceptance of the will-less human condition in all its aspects, and the road to immortality, in a different religion, can be paved, among other ways, by the will's victory over given sexual instinct.

Nor with the Greeks is submission to sexual instinct in its homosexual aspect separable from subscription to its unified power. Aphrodite in Sappho's "Lesbian" poem is borne to earth, we have seen, by the symbols of male instrumentality. There is, however, a social-psychological factor expressed in the religious sense, the status of woman as related to man expressed in religious symbol which I can only treat most briefly here.[3] Homosexuality can be publicly sanctioned only when it can be religiously sanctioned, and it can be religiously sanctioned only when the role of woman as mother is religiously glorified. Psychologically, homosexuality is the accompaniment not of

94

the debasement of woman, as is so consistently and erroneously stated in regard to the Greeks in full defiance of the result of Freudian analysis, but of her exultation in her role as mother. Disrespect in the male for homosexuality is concomitantly always an expression of belief in the unarguable inferiority of woman. Modern psychology substantiates rather than contradicts the social attitudes of classical Hellas or the Mediterranean generally on this matter. The male homosexual response in the Freudian analysis is the exaltation of the mother at the expense of the father in the son's psychic pattern, and Hellenic homosexuality, to the degree to which it was socially acceptable, is never for one moment to be separated from the worship of the Great Goddess in her manifold Hellenic forms. The opposite is, of course, equally true: the razing of Sodom is the necessary price for patriarchal hegemony. The figuring of deity as female was social and familial, and hence religious blasphemy to the Hebrews. Their religious proscription of homosexuality is ours, but so also is their patriarchal psychology—at least until quite recent times. But the invading Hellenic tribes absorbed this worship of the mother goddess and the psychological patterns, social and individual, that went with it.

The result was a position for woman qua woman far higher than with the Hebrews or with northern European patriarchal societies—with its consequent effect on the male psyche. (The assumption of masculine status as the sign of feminine equality is psychologically an altogether different matter, is in fact a statement of the inherent superiority of the male role. Women enjoy far more male rights in North Europe, but woman qua mother or mistress is more significant in Southern Italy and Spain even in the present day.) It is obviously not directly relevant to our present point, which is earlier Lesbos, but the position of women in 5th century Athens has been radically misread by German and English scholars in the light of attitudes toward women in their own societies—which has always been one of radical inferiority. Though Athens as Hellenic was patriarchal and, of course, predominantly heterosexual (the predominance of homosexuality is another strange misconception), the margin of male hegemony was very narrow. We need only remember Athena's deciding vote in *The Eumenides* on

95

behalf of the superiority of the male principle, and remember that single vote was Athena's, a female goddess. We might also remember the great roll-call of heroines in Athenian tragedy, Clytemnestra, Electra, Alcestis, Antigone, Hecuba, Phaedra, Medea. Where in their myth or legend are the Hebrew counterpart for these? Plato was in birth and upbringing a 5th century Athenian, and the presuppositions of his place for women in *The Republic* could only have been drawn from his social and familial experience, and the putative position of women in his ideal state is equality at the highest functioning level, intellectual as well as political. It is the sort of equality that we are at long last pursuing, as a not altogether impractical goal, in American public and social life. That this vision of complete male and female equality — no matter its contradiction of many of the actual social conditions in which it arose — was first and last projected, in the history of thought, by a fifth-century Athenian should give us pause. Even as an ideal picture, just for such an ideal to have arisen in a man's mind, should of itself have overturned the usual clichés of the comparative status of the sexes in Classical Hellas.

But above all we should never forget the public worship of Hera, Demeter, Artemis, Athena and Aphrodite and at that point pitch Sodom's fate in a society which could brook no female image alongside Jehovah's, the father principle. Christianity, in its larger Mediterranean, not its Judaic form, revived the great Mediterranean Mother Goddess, of course, in the worship of Mary whom the northern patriarchal societies rejected in the Reformation. Athens under the aegis of Athena worshipped the divinity in female aspect as deeply as medieval Europe in the form of Mary.

Lesbos, as I see it, took on the hues of Crete even more deeply than Athens, and the Mother-worshipping and hence male-loving males found, in a society where physical and psychic need were of themselves accepted, their female counterpart in love such as Sappho's for unmarried girls. Both would have been accepted as social forms for the fulfillment of given need. Though I do not understand in detail the social-psychological dynamic of Sappho's situation — it surely deserves further study — it might well deflect us from the basic religious assumption repeatedly emphasized in the phrase 'given need'. There can be no problem of conformity here, which so divides the commentators on Sappho's sexuality. Conformity, as much in Freudian as Christian terms, implies the exercise of will to attain prescribed goals. But conformity to the Greek is conformity to the given pattern of instinct, no matter what its propulsion. The definition of the 'natural' is pari passu contradictory in the two viewpoints. To the Christian what is natural is what fits a posited goal; to the Hellene what is natural is what is presented to the psyche. Once again the distinction made in opening this chapter, between will and appreciating psyche as the center of religious expression, must be made, if we are to confront Sappho's worship of Aphrodite in a prayer for a young girl's submission to her own need, of which Sappho herself is only the momentary agent. Aphrodite is the divinity; both Sappho and the girl are mortal, not only death-bound, that is, but submissive in individual will to presented power. For the contemporary consciousness the unembarrassed homosexual content of this poem can only be appreciated by contrast, by its innocence in the midst of our self-consciousness. Only so do we penetrate to the difference in its religious base. Only so do we see why Gide and Djuna Barnes must remain, for all the sympathy in the world, rebels. But they are rebels in our pattern, ironically, because they do not rebel against presented psychic pressure, which alone, as in the instance of Hippolytus, would make them rebels to the Greek. "An action demanded by the instinct of life is proved to be *right* by the pleasure that accompanies it." The emphasis is Nietzsche's own, the religious affirmation Greek. A Sappho would have been bewildered to think it a question to be argued. The unarguable is faith. Her hymn to Aphrodite is the expression of such a faith.

97

# CHAPTER 4

## *The First Olympian*

Greatest:  water, or gold a blazing fire
flames in the night out of mighty riches.
If to cry out the fights
you long, dear heart,
beyond the sun behold
no hotter star day-shining through clear aether,
nor shall we declare a greater game than Olympia's;
our storied hymn is a victor's crown wreathed
by a poet's design: loud to laud
Cronos' son as we come
                              to the bountiful
blessed hearth of Hieron
who raises a righteous wand over Sicily, many flocks,
commanding the top of all valor and art;
arrayed now in the finest fleece
words and music we dance
young men stepping close round his table.
From the wall take the Doric lyre,
if Pherenikos' form at Olympia
has stirred your mind to sweet celebration
when by the Alpheus he ran
rippling unspurred flanks in the race-course
and in power bound his master,
Syracus' horse-lover king. His fame shines bright
among glad men in Lydian Pelops' new home:
him mighty-muscled Earthholder adored, Poseidon,
when from the cleansing cauldron Clotho raised him,
and ivory gleamed his fitted shoulder.
Yea, wonders are many, and somehow some men's
speech, beyond the true account,
intricate craft of shimmering lies, myths deceive us.
Joy of form, which molds delight for us who die,
bestowing status, many times contrives
                              what is wrong to believe

to be believed;
the rest of days
most knowing witness.
It befits a man to say fair things of radiant power.

Less the censure.

Son of Tantalus, you I shall sing contradicting earlier men:
when your father called the gods to beautifully-ordered,
his own lovely Sipylus,
setting them thanksgiving feast,
then did Radiant-trident seize you
overpowered in his heart by lust, and on gold horses
to the highest house — far-honored Zeus' — made you climb
whence in a second time
came likewise Ganymede
for Zeus meeting the same need.
So you were no longer seen, nor to your mother anxious

searching men bore;

straightway some envying neighbor behind his hand swore
how from the water's fire-seething rush
with a knife they morseled your limbs
and on set-tables the delicious flesh
of you took each one and ate.
For me it is impossible to call One Blessed cannibal.

I stand aside.

Their rewards falls often enough to the evil tongued.
If ever, indeed, some death-bound man Olympus' watchers
gave status, that man was Tantalus. But digest
great happiness he could not, in satisfaction clamped
self-delusion, arrogance; so Father above
hung a mighty stone over him
which always warding from his head he wanders from heart-easing mirth
and grips instead this unshakable life, perpetual pain,
with three fourth labor, because from the Deathless stealing
to fellow-drinkers of his age
nectar and ambrosia
gave wherewith his perishing
They'd stayed. If the divine watch any man
hopes to escape in any deed, he fails.
Wherefore the Deathless sent back again his son

into the swift falling race of men.
Before the push of blooming growth, when
down wreathed dark his cheek,
he turned his mind to marriage now,
from her Pisan father fair-imaged Hippodameia
to tear. Close to the grey sea, alone in the obscure
he cried to deep-rolling
Fine-trident, and He to him
before his feet shone near.
To Him he said: "Love's gifts,
the Cyprian's, if ever, Poseidon, to thy joy
fulfilled, bind Oinomaus' bronze spear.
Me on the swiftest chariot ferry
to Elis, drive me to power,
since three and ten men slaying,
suitors, he puts off the marriage
of his daughter. Great danger hires not the impotent.
Die we must: should someone, then, nameless
old-age, sitting in darkness, futility pursue,
of all good things without his share? For me this fight
is laid down sure. Grant the performance I desire."
Thus he declared nor handled words
without power. In his illumination god
gave the gold cross-board, the winged tireless steeds.
He clamped the might of Oinomaus and virgin in his bed
who bore six leaders, warfare striving sons.
Now in blood offerings
radiant he mingles
on his back by Alpheus' ford,
owning a tomb of service beside the pilgrim-crowded altar.
Fame afar looks down on Olympia's courses —
Pelops' — where speed of foot is fought
and brawn's harsh-labored climax.
The victor the rest of his natural life
owns a sweet good day
for his fights. The ever new day's blessing
latest comes to each in turn. Our call to crown
the man before us in 'the cavalier measure',
in Aeolic song and dance.

I am persuaded that of the living no patron
more knowing of beautiful things, in power more lordly
will we exalt in artifact
                        as the announcing hymn unrolls.
God being propitious minds thy concerns,
this we see His care, Hieron.
If not swiftly He depart,
yet sweeter fame I trust
with rushing chariot to raise, finding purveying way of words
as we come before high-visible Cronos' son. For me when due
Poetry her most potent shaft nurses in strength.
In other matters others grand: the ultimate
crests kings. Look not beyond.
May you tread your time on high,
may I as in this song with victors
walk so being shown through Hellas for all poetic knowing.


And not through Hellas alone, one is tempted to add, but to
any awareness on which Hellas may impinge, not only in its
own language and poetry but in the recrudescence of the
impulse to that Hellenic poetic imagination, even to its figure,
poetry as light, the illumination provided by the poetic
consciousness.

> The Poets light but Lamps —
> Themselves go out —
> The Wicks they stimulate —
> If vital Light
> Inhere as do the Suns —
> Each age a Lens
> Disseminating their
> Circumference —                                    (883)

Everything is different for those lines, music, social sense,
background of belief and poetic causation, everything, that is,
but the renewal of full poetic responsibility. That is no accident. But in contrast to Pindar it comes in an aftertime of religious belief.[1]

> Those — dying then,
> Knew where they went —
> They went to God's Right Hand —

101

That Hand is amputated now
And God cannot be found —                                    (1551)

And the poet must lead the search party. For those who would conceive that the connection between Dickinson's use of the light figure and Pindar's is wholly fortuitous let me point out an even more striking Pindaric resemblance to a theme of modern verse, the use in line 105 of the verb *daidalosemen* which I have translated as 'exalt in artifact'. But Hieron, the patron of the arts and lord of power, is the direct object of this verb. Literally it is to make an elaborate artifact of him, to construct of him a shape as Daedalus might. It is the theme of *Sailing to Byzantium.*

> Consume my heart away; sick with desire
> And fastened to a dying animal
> It knows not what it is; and gather me
> Into *the artifice of eternity.*

> Once out of nature I shall never take
> My bodily form from any natural thing,
> But such a form as Grecian goldsmiths *make*
> Of hammered gold and gold enamelling
> To keep a drowsy emperor awake . . . .

This poet, too, is aware of poetry as the artifice of eternity, of the poet as the artificer, of poetry as the *alathe logon,* true revelation's statement. "Who, if I cried, would hear me from the Angels' orders?" Poetry is Announcement, and the poet the Announcer. This sense of poetry is the revival of the sense of it in which Pindar composes, for him a social tradition, an inherited tradition, as opposed to an assayed role for these modern poets. Pindar's religious imagination and poetic practice are coterminous. He does not "use" poetry for religious ends, nor "use" religion as the content of his verse. He conceives poetry as illumination, and illumination as the religious view, the awareness of the human as phenomenon, as the given, the temporal aspect of deathless divine presence. Perhaps his most famous lines are those of the close of *Pythian 8* which could stand as an earlier brief summary of the theme of the ode under consideration. It closes: "Men of a day. What is someone? What is someone not? Dream of a shadow is man. But when the god-given radiance comes, a shining light is upon men and a honey sweet life." Those lines are the correct gloss for the significance of the relation of much and little in the following quatrain. (There should be no separation in our mind between them; the poet's own mark is rhythmical, metrical.)

In this short Life
That only lasts an hour
How much – how little – is
Within our power                                    (1287)

In neither case, any more than with Rilke or Yeats, is the poetry a meditation on a religious theme, a comment on or illustration of belief. The poetic statement is *itself* the religious realization. The process of the verse is the religious exercise, its held picture the presence of divine power in the mind. The poetry is inseparable from the awareness it elicits. And so, too, with *Olympian 1*. Its own performance in time is the moment in time when godhead shines. It is our present task to show how that moment is situated, some of the elements that enter into it, the process of formation that becomes a process of transformation.

The scene of our performance is the megaron or hall of Hieron's palace on the island center of Syracuse in Sicily. Hieron was, in effect, the last and most powerful of the Deinomenids, brother of that Geloan general who, like some early 19th Century Latin American or contemporary Arabic military, seized the rule from a waning monarchy. That Gelon had already conquered Syracuse whither he moved his capital, and in the year of our poem, 476/5, Hieron's rule stretched from Gela on the south coast past Kamarina, pivoted at Syracuse itself and stretched past Leontini and his new Etna to a leige lord straddling the straits at Messina and Rhegium, through whom as well as the allied city of Locri it was exerted in South Italy. (A Locrian was this very year inscribed 'Syracusan' on the Olympic victors' register.) I am also one who claims that after the summer of 476 Theron held both Akragas and Himera in fief from Hieron, who had won a bloodless victory over him on the Geloan plain. For roughly a decade Hieron held sway over more land and more men and greater revenues than any classical Greek ruler. This poem's denotation of his power and wealth is not flattery; it is accurate statement.

So is its bow to his, which might include his family's, artistic patronage. At this moment the two greatest poets of Hellas were at Hieron's court, and I like to think that Aeschylus was present as admiring critic at this great ode's performance in Hieron's hall, and that Pindar a little later held a front-row seat for the performance of the *Women of Etna* celebrating Hieron's new foundation of that city under the mountain's slope, a foundation celebrated by Pindar himself in the *First Pythian* in 474. These two supreme poets, almost exact contemporaries, trained together as boys at Athens under the same teacher, Lasus of Hermione, and their careers, as I date them, close roughly at the same time, Pindar's with *Nemean 10* for Argos in 463, Aeschylus' with the *Oresteia* at Athens in 458. Lifelong they must have heard and pondered each other's verse, knowing in each case that the single other was his peer. It is fashionable to contrast them, and since Pindar's 17 tragedies have perished, they seem to be working in only distantly related genres; but neither the political nor religious gulfs imputed to their work find objective substantiation, and the unsounded similarities are, in any case, paramount: the temporal transposition of narrative sequence in choral myth, the mutual trust in the revelatory power of imagined act or mythic abstraction, the same announcement of the divine ground of human act or achievement, for good or ill. Simonides and Bacchylides also may well have been in Syracuse at this same time. We have report of the uncle's presence in Sicily the preceding summer, of the nephew's later. It is at least possible that all the major poetic voices of Hellas were gathered at this hour in one room.[2]

On the plastic arts as well the Deinomenids lavished their splendid sums. Sometime after the Himeran victory of 480 Gelon had struck the most beautiful of coins, the Demarateia, the quadriga, the victorious chariot of war and the Olympic races of 480 on one side, Arethusa and Syracuse's dolphins on the other. Though he was now dead, it may be that his offerings at Delphi were still in progress, completed only as Hieron's for the later victory of Cumae got underway, tripods and statues, gold and bronze. Every reader assuredly knows, and while reading this poem should bring to his vision, the Delphic

Charioteer, Gelon's offering posthumously superscribed by one of his brothers. His Syracusan driver most likely stood model, and he can stand model in our visual imagination for the pride of stance and glance, austerity of dress and devotion to function of the young men who are singing this hymn two or three years later in Hieron's hall. If that driver was not one of them, perhaps his younger brother or cousin was. These performers are drawn from the athletic aristocrats of Syracuse's first families, their self designation as men (line 17) marking the contrast to a chorus of boys. Just as that young driver of the chariot race had turned artifact by the sculptor's hand, an artifact Pindar, of course, would have seen, so Hieron is made artifact by his celebration in this hymn in a line already referred to. The interrelation of the arts is a recurrent theme in Pindar. In *Olympian 6* and *Pythian 6* he is an architect building the temples or shrine "treasuries," in *Nemean 5* the sculptor once more transforming his subject into an enduring artifact. He claims in all cases that his work is more effective, more widely realizable, more enduring. But for us the comparisons should point to a common source and function of the arts, the transformation of natural form as imaginative or mythic form in defiance of physical dissolution.

But the Deinomenids, we may be sure, did not spend all their wealth for display at Olympia and Delphi alone or have their architects, sculptors and engravers exercise their skill only away from home. There is no account of their Syracusan palace, but there, by all logic, their greatest treasures shone, on walls or ceiling, on columns, lintels, on altar, tripods, tables—gold. Gold as adornment for display but gold also in wrought shape in the service of deity, bespeaking its power, gold the ancient sign of the eternally fresh, the divine, the contrast to human transiency.

The opening of this poem is not a conglomeration of arbitrary figures; it is the careful poetic statement of the elements of the scene of its own performance, beginning with the physical scene, moving through its human components to the focus of achievement and power. It is night and the fire of the hall elicits the sheen of the gold that decks its walls and utensils and the ornaments of the group in power, who alone have been summoned for this act of self-congratulation. Gold in the room is a sign of Hieron's wealth and power derived from lands that stretch far beyond it, all the tribute of tributary states. The local substance reflects the power that has compelled its collection. And it shines; it is reflected in the human mind. Such apprehension is bespoken in a poem which is just such another act of apprehension. The poem is the formalization, the subconscious made fully conscious by a traditional social mode, of the instinctive psychological process of the men in the room who are either its performers or audience; it is the way to appreciate the actual. The fullest appreciation of the possibility of just such a focused scene must lead at last, through poetry's function, far beyond the men and their pride who listen to it. We shall come to that in time, but it were well to note at the beginning that the import of the myth is bound to the opening image of gold which, like a fire, shines in the night. The poem in its earliest performance amid those men in that hall does not have to say, given their physical perceptions of the moment, what we must supply, that when the chorus says 'gold' — uses a word for what is already visible — that act of formalization in another medium exemplifies human registry, verbalization that turns physical affect into significance. The audience can then move, without a break or conscious adjuration, to follow what the poet believes that significance signifies. That is not tautology; the gold signs wealth and power; that wealth and power for the focused host only last an hour, it is his sign or his transient expression of divine power.

It leads at once to Olympia and Zeus, to victory at Olympia which is to shine in all the Greek world, and to the deity of whom that sort of ultimate shining is the momentary donation. What gold means for the immediate audience, the achievement at Olympia means for the larger one, and the poem, most precisely, is the 'gold', the signing system, the exchangeable currency of that larger luster. The poem itself is gold because it does for the man what his displayed wealth does, and in both cases the glamor points to the power that makes it possible. The use of 'gold' in our poem must be sharply distinguished from symbolic device in modern poetry. It takes off from actual gold outside itself but builds a set of relations parallel to the instinctive use of gold socially as a sign to show what that sort of sign itself signs. The function of gold as social symbol at the beginning is reflected in the end by the function of the greatest poetic skill which has disclosed that Hieron "walks on high" with divine favor. The performance of the poem this night is the means to realize formally in the mind what it means to be within these walls this night.

But the poem does not begin with the apostrophe to gold but to water. This choice has troubled commentators as has its direct juxtaposition with gold.

Water has a physical base in our scene as clear as gold and just as immediate and parallel a symbolic reference. Around Ortygia stretches the sea. If it was not visible in the hall, it was just outside, and every man who had come to the hall that night had looked at it and felt it stretch from Syracuse to Greece, the sea over which had come not only the poet but all Hieron's stable, trainers, riders, Syracusan athletes in the other contests and their entourages, half the audience, likely, and of the chorus probably even more. We shall note many of the aspects of sea and water, but I choose first that of communication, the means to the all-Greek center, the way to fame and acclamation.

And like gold it shines itself; it catches the light and casts it back in men's eyes. Pindar had used this common bond of water and gold in an earlier poem, in the opening of *Isthmian 5*. "Mother of the Sun, many-named Radiance, on thy account men value mighty-strengthened gold beyond other things. And the racing ships in the sea and horses under chariots through the status you bestow, Lady Power, in the swift-wheeled contests are wondrous to behold. And in the athletic fights fame makes that man an object of sexual desire whom the gathered wreath has bound for his victory with his hands or by his speed of foot. The might of man is determined by the radiant powers. Two things alone with blooming wealth husband the loveliest unfolding of life, when a man who enjoys good luck hears its blessed report. Do not seek to become Zeus."

Once again, as in even briefer compass at the close of *Pythian 8*, the whole of our ode has been summarized in those lines. Aspects which are touched off in brief phrase in that summary are singled out in our poem for emphatic or mythic elucidation, but the first parallel is clear enough. Ships racing with their beating oars create the pattern of light or radiance from which gold obtains its value. But achievement in the games is metaphorically just such radiance. The anonymous victor here is related to the sheen of gold and water just as Hieron is. But that radiance of achievement as seen through a victor makes him a sexual cynosure, *potheinon*. Achievement and the desirability that leads to love are quickly juxtaposed. In our poem one is a metaphor for the other, or rather in the myth they are coalesced.

For the sea, of course, is Poseidon, Pelops' lover. The substantiation of that love is Pelops' victory at Elis or Pisa, which serves as the mythical paradigm of Hieron's later horse race victory in the same place. That we shall analyze later. And Poseidon, of course, is also one of the patron deities of horsemen, himself worshipped in the form of the horse and its phallus. The interweavings here are of such a nature that logical analysis despairs of clarity while violating the interrelations in its very effort. The sea by Syracuse is a means of communication to Greece and social recognition, social radiance, but water as substance produces radiance, the physical standing for the psychological experience. That shining is the apparition momentarily of deity, which can be figured as loving divinity's expression, just as personal radiance is almost always cast in amorous metaphor. The flowing of water is an age-old dream symbol of the coursing of sexual desire. All this can be gathered in Poseidon, and to top it all, we have his connection with the horse where a horse victory is being celebrated.

But Pindar uses flowing liquid catching light, whether wine or water, in a number of instances with another reference, for poetry. In *Olympian 7* (1-11), the pouring of a toast is the metaphor of the poem as celebration. Our poem is not only gold, then; it is also water. It, too, is a means to radiance, to registry of the shining object; it too, like sexual yearning, makes its subject a pole of appreciation. Furthermore, water is life-giving, on land in stony Sicily, on sea whence then as now the fishermen drew food for Syracuse. Nor is the life-giving property to be separated from its power as love, which in turn is revealed as the power to achievement. Poseidon, that sea, drives

Pelops to power as in the form of the horse he smashes Hieron to victory.

These multiple references are implicit rather than at once expressed by the initial acclamation of water; only as the poem unfolds will the interconnections, never analyzed or logically constructed, reveal themselves. And it was not, I suggest, intellectual critical ability on the part of the audience that brought them these multiplex realizations but their suspension by music at a level of consciousness where water could recall radiance or sexual power, horse power or physical and psychic communication.

At the outset, as with gold, only the actual natural substance is acclaimed, and that is never forgotten: it is this, I reiterate, that so sharply distinguishes Pindar's use of substance in nature for its psychic, even its dream resonances, from any arbitrary symbolic term in modern verse.

But it is acclaimed, it appears as word, not as substance. Within two lines the poetic activity (*garuen*) which has brought water and gold into recognition is applied pari passu to Olympia and the whole social situation set for present acclamation. They are of one piece. The word is not the substance; it is part of the hymn, and consciousness of the function of the hymn forms, as usual with Pindar, a major part of its onset. It is not only that the physical substances are signs of the powers gathered in the social scene; that substances have become signs, are recalled as word, is itself theme for the hymn. We can see what is true in the small, word replacing substance so as to create the possibility of its significances in elaborate verbal contexts quite beyond substance, more easily, perhaps, in the large, the chorus as part of the hymn proclaiming the importance of the fact that they are performing a hymn.

Once more the physical basis is there. In the center of the hall stands the altar to Zeus Xenios, Zeus guardian of guests, focus of the host's moral world to whom libations are poured before the song and dance are performed or the banqueting can begin (Xenophanes 1). The hymn is the extension of the ritual libation; *formally our ode is simply the worship of Zeus.* As the chorus makes its religious self-declaration of function in the opening strophe (9,10), so it closes (110) with the hope that it may at Olympia itself, where Zeus is 'high-visible', perform a similar rite after horse loving Hieron has won the even more honorific chariot victory there. The so-called ode is always a part of divine ritual, a hymn, its only classical definition. What is relevant of political, social, or familial fact in the minds of the audience is absorbed into this ritual. Recent athletic victory is just such fact and is so absorbed. But there never was an "epinician," which is simply an Alexandrian library category, and other social or political fact often stands ahead of athletic fact, as in *Pythian I.* Nor is there in the logical or abstract sense a "subject" of the hymn. The only unity is the poet's imaginative integration of disparate fact under the aegis of his religious purpose.

Creative power is the imaginative power to see events as phenomena, to see what happens in a certain pattern of relation, and the architectural strength to sustain and exhaust that vision of pattern. It is shown by skill in subordination which is another term for the transformation of the experienced in the key of the particular vision. It is well exemplified in our poem by its first social denotation, the Olympic games. The poet's imagination does not permit their entry into his poem except as they take their place in relation to the complex connotations established in the use of water and gold, physical substances that reflect light to men's eyes, thereby figuring the communication of honored identity to men's minds, which is the function of this hymn to Zeus. Between the desire to cry the games and their announcement falls the figure: the sun, the day-shining star bringing heat through the radiating ether. Olympia enters in the chosen aspect as source of warmth and light to men, both to those who win and those who appreciate their victory. Without directly saying it, though later in the choice of words for Hieron as well as in the myth he will ring the changes on this theme, the poet equates fame and light. The more famous the man, the more he is spotlighted. It is the equation of *Isthmian 5* and *Pythian 8,* a commonplace in Pindar, Greek verse, or any.

But to call this simile or metaphor is not quite accurate; for Pindar the processes of physical vision and intellectual realization are not separable. The phenomenon of light is not the figure for the realization of achievement but its ground in nature. Just as with the substances, water and gold, used as 'symbols', where the contemporary term is misleading, so with this equation. The physical ground remains at all times part of the intellectual event. It goes back, of course, to the Greek verbal identification of seeing and knowing, but just as much as with Plato, that inherited verbal synthesis is explored, crystallized, set forth itself as theoria not merely used unconsciously. How without the eye and only behind it, the mind's eye, is the acclamation of particular identity possible? How without the sun are the races run or the victor distinguished? How is there any knowing of a man or his position without in one form or another a seeing of him? One form or another does imply that he, while physically invisible, can be made visible, by word, by such a hymn as now being performed. But the process and function of that hymn, even in a later time, will take its ground from the natural fact of a man's clear resolution in daytime seeing under the sun. Our hymn springs directly from given conditions, so when it says "whence," *hothen* for its own enactment (8) it is referring not only to Olympia and Hieron's victory and to the overall phenomenon of that victory at Olympia, which is a man's status as victor realized by the minds of other men, but also to the divine ground for that or any achievement, Zeus' power and presence. That is why the reference to Olympia is preceded by the acclamation of the sun's heating light and that in turn preceded by the acclamation of the function of water and gold as carriers of radiance. Pindar has insisted, before bringing in Hieron himself, that Hieron's achievement be realized as phenomenon by the audience celebrating it. Such realization is formalized by the process of the poem itself. Let me try to show how as an architect of public choral verse Pindar felt this claim in intimate concrete detail not simply as theory.

The audience in Hieron's hall reflected in their eyes the sheen off gold on walls and tripods which to their minds signed his wealth and power. Their awareness of Hieron, the pride of their summons and their awe in his presence, are figured in physical display transforming the physical being of the man into the compelling presence of the king. But to know who he was and

111

what he had done, to know the facts and the facts as creating social status, they depend on quite another mode of transformation, words. The facts lie outside the room, in the sweep of grain and flocks from Gela to Leontini, or in the applause at Olympic's race course. But young men dancing and singing before them concentrate those facts in a few words, and the listeners' minds then absorb achievement verbally as they have wealth visually on behalf of the man at the center of the room. In their status-yielding minds his figure is now centered in all its illustriousness by the successive strophes of the hymn.

But it is the creating poet who has consciously programmed this realization. It might be diagramed in this way: (a) A man or men and the facts of his or their life > (b) a hymn which bespeaks them > (c) listening men > (d) their realization of (a). (d) is the realization of (a) but it is not (a) itself. The hymn has intervened; it is not the facts but their poetization. Without it there can be no realization on the part of the audience. Though man-made, requiring the most conscious craft, as far as its final end — the audience's focused realization of its source of acclamation — it functions as a natural mode of illumination, and its sounds and music are just as physical as tripods, altars, walls. That the silent creator of this functioning was deeply impressed by it we can gather from his building into his hymns, over and over again, for their immediate performance, the awareness of them as if they had already taken place, a sense of their process as enactment.

The process I have diagramed we, of course, take for granted. But we should make it conscious, since it is held in the mind of the poet at every moment. It is in a way the overriding 'subject' of his poetry. His hymns are forever telling us what is happening *in* the hymn as event and using that as the pivot of the 'meaning' of whatever is declared in the hymn. The 'meaning' of the declaration is simply the phenomenon of its declaration.

It is well to stress this, because in Pindaric criticism this insistence on the part of the poet on the importance of his poem is so often put down as a species of self-advertising. If so, Mallarmé's sonnets are such advertisements, and so is *The Man with the Blue Guitar*. But it is not advertising if, in quite a literal sense, *Gesang ist Dasein*. There is no other way for the facts of

112

Olympia and Sicily to enter that room for their appreciation. And unless you realize the means, you cannot understand the nature of what is presented through it, what it is for there to be social acclaim. This is a poet who walks with victors and with kings, who oversees libations in a room filled with gold, and through his poetry victors and kings are brought into relation with what has made them kings and victors: god-in-action.

The whole weight of a social tradition, a historic role backs the poet, the highest possible claim is made for poetry, as high as Rilke or Whitman ever made, yet that claim is made and realized in public performance, so that magnification itself is functional, spotlighting the social religious end the hymn is built to fulfill.

On the physical side the autonomy of poetry in antiquity was far and away more marked than with us. Choral poetry, like the tragedy that issues from it, is formal religious service. The men in that room, or any ritualistic *temenos*, are "called to attention" and "lose themselves" in the physical performance of the chorus before them. For the moment they are watching an elaborate artifact, simultaneously musical and intellectual, separated by its formal orders from their daily lives, the formlessness of their approach to and departure from that room, or from the eating and drinking that follow the hymn. It is in that state of suspension, time imposed by musical time and imagination shaped by poetry's words and pictures, that they subscribe to the purely imaginary events in the myth and its understanding as the will of divinity.

I want to insist on separation, in all its intimate personal aspects for the audience, for the place and enactment of poetry as the "made," the created, the imaginary, a separation as insistent as the separation between the street outside and the performance of the mass at an altar within a church, before turning and claiming that such separation is purely formal, and that the function of the form is to relate all that takes place in the street to the focused pitched psyches of the men who experienced the outside events. The function is autonomous: creating poet, enacting chorus, religious form. But that formal autonomy is deployed as public social function, and so what was before and what comes after is gathered in the religious

113

exercise. It does not relate us to a different world; it gives form to this one, or better, the 'other world' is the realized form of this one. "Without conscious artifice" we may breathe and live but we do not know that we breathe and live, and without artifice we can not be said to achieve at all. Act assumes social significance only as it is "related," in both senses, told or celebrated, in reference to ends. The key is order, or in Pindar, music. The hymn not only makes a man famous but discloses what fame is, realization in other men's minds. And achievement itself? Divinity-in-action, the realized form of given power.

The hymn makes that juxtaposition in literally successive breaths. Its function is expressed as a purposive infinitive dependent on the word hymn: to proclaim Zeus before the hearth of Hieron who . . . . His wealth and power are at once proclaimed. The performance for and before Hieron is gathered as an active participle agreeing with the infinitive, to proclaim Zeus. There is no separation, no break, not even a hierarchy, man-hero-god, Hieron-Pelops-Zeus, as in the famous opening of *Olympian 2*, though there as here the other two are forms for seeing the man. Religious appreciation, then, is the formalization of given or presented experience, and poetry is *its* form. The hymn, we are told, is the "choice fleece" (15) of the poetic realization of what Hieron's achievement is, a garment whose glittering array will be unfolded in the myth whose wealth of words is foretold, just as the function of the whole ode is proclaimed as the prelude to the functioning (8-11). What they are doing and their means of doing it are the chorus' verbal accompaniment of their musical march to the altar or hearth — *hestian* — in the hall of Hieron.

But such a self-declaration is made so that the audience may appreciate and thereby enter the experience of the choral enactment: its whole point, after all, is their illumination. And if that functional aspect is realized, then the autonomy of art, the whole formal religious exercise reaches its climax in its own dissolution as the experience of its listeners. What it does consumes it. The insistence on art is not for art's sake but for its fulfillment. The circle is completed; the formal act, as in drama, has itself become event for its audience, though in this case that event is simply the realization as phenomenon of previous event. Our event is now a knowing, and we can turn to ponder what such knowing is. That is made a point of as the introduction to the presentation of imaginary event, the myth (28-34). Myth, too, then, will be presented as part of poetic knowing, as part of the present event. Poetry as knowing is the final claim (116) of this poem, and throughout it has been a rigorous exercise in presenting as its own form the relations between the elements in an act of poetic knowing. It is governed at every step by an awareness of what is seen, who sees, and the means of that seeing.

We are right up against a constant problem for every artist: how what one psyche realizes or imagines becomes in every nuance another psyche's appreciation. We call it the problem of communication, but it might be considered, in dramatic terms, the problem of transference or metempsychosis, one man becoming another in his psychic reception. All Greek poetry is built on the need to come to terms with this problem, and drama is its last solution.

There, of course, the actor is putatively the hero, one individuality expressed as quite another. But anterior to the actor's assumption of the role is the poet's creation of it, his relinquishment of his identity to take on imaginatively an inter-related variety of others. And posterior to it is the audience's imaginative assumption, with every line of spoken drama, of the identity of the speaker, the momentary assumption of his position, personality and viewpoint. Creating poet and appreciative audience as much as the speaking actor assume other personalities, other masks, for the duration of imaginary personality's self-projection.

We should not forget that tragedy evolved from choral poetry, and that the same metempsychosis is at work in the latter's creation, performance, and appreciation. The range may be smaller, but the problems are as sharp, and there is one element, the relation of given historical identity either to its direct poetic or indirect mythic expression, which can be avoided in tragedy. By and large this problem has never been studied in Pindar; laggard 20th century criticism follows an already — as far as contemporary art was concerned — outdated

19th century assumption that Pindar is talking *in propria persona* for individual ends to an audience equally incapable of self-transformation into putative personality. If this were so, myth could never have functioned at all, and choral poetry as much as tragedy in an enactment of myth.

Even at its simplest level the gravest error still holds the field. All Pindar's verse is choral, of precisely the same formal nature as the choruses of tragedy. The speaking voice is always the choral personality. Anything the poet expresses he expresses in the assumed identity of his chorus. Here that chorus are Syracusan young men, elsewhere Theban, Argive, Aiginetan, etc. Anything that Pindar says even of the poetry he has created is *as if* by that chorus. The transference, of course, works both ways: the chorus bespeak the poet's viewpoint, announce his intuition and appreciation. Socially they remain, unlike the tragic choruses, *in propria persona,* but both ritualistically and poetically they are agents, in the ritual song and dance, for poetry, a means of knowing and appreciating even what it is to know and see. Between them and the creator of their lines and their trainer for the singing of them we have the same relation as between the tragic chorus and its poet — and both members of the relation relinquish their own personal place to their poetic role.

And as with tragedy this interchangeability of person for both poet and and chorus is carried over into their relation to the audience. The latter must be divided on some occasions into two parts, the man or men who are being celebrated and the ones who enjoy that choral celebration. When a whole city is the major focus, this distinction for practical purposes is dissolved. The chorus, here, for example, not only speaks to but of Hieron, both directly and in the myth, and when he listens, he must view himself through their voice. He, too, momentarily relinquishes his given self and becomes that self as poetically appreciated, as, in the myth, a form of destiny. As much as the poet from the other side he imaginatively muses or dreams *as if* from the viewpoint of the chorus member singing about him.

But that is not all. The chorus members all sing the words of Pelops' prayer to Poseidon. At this juncture they become, as the tragic chorus or actor in tragedy (the two have not in this form

116

been separated; their separation is, in fact, the moment of the 'invention' of tragedy), a purely imaginary personality, as has the poet in creating the lines or Hieron or the rest of the audience in listening to them. For a few minutes everyone's psyche in that room is 'lent out' as the psyche of the youthful suitor and would-be warrior. At this level of dramatic projection, a common psyche has been created and is functioning for everyman, and only with such a common psyche can myth itself function. Before we analyze the content of any myth we must grasp its psychic ground; before it gives us a 'meaning' we must see how it can have meaning at all.

Let me reiterate parenthetically here an earlier theme, that myth is purely imaginary and recognized as such by its creator. True, the myth of Pelops and Poseidon becomes by means of this poem a quasi-event, and the original listener no doubt thought of it as fact, though not as history in our sense. But for the moment of the poem we do the same thing ourselves; for us, too, it can only be grasped in the semblance of event. There is a distinction between that original reaction and our own. To it Poseidon is not symbol but force in being; the Greeks, that is, believed in the existence of the form not just in the power it concretizes, just as they believed in the mythic 'historicity' of Pelops. To us they are both imaginary forms, and once the myth has run its course, we resume our disbelief (though surely we do the same with *Lear* or *Hamlet*). Because both figures are terms from a continuing vocabulary for the Greeks, as not with us, they could carry as a perpetually renewable affirmation the image of the love of the god for the boy as divine illumination through physical achievement at Olympia.

But nowhere surely has Pindar made it more clear, even before he tells his story, that it is purely imaginary. It contradicts earlier myths; those are labeled lies. His word is new, nor does he claim added 'research', a new exploration of the facts as his warrant. His authority is his own imagination or rather the poetic mode working through him. He tells the truth, but it is the truth of the new dream, and no one in that audience would have been disposed to quarrel with the basis of his claim. Pindar merely dreams more truly or can more truly tell what the images of dream mean.

But we must not separate *his* imaginative projection from its particular position in that psychic nexus where are bound together the psyches of the creator, of the singing chorus, of the man addressed and of the audience. The myth takes its life as the objectification of the dynamics of that pattern of relations. We cannot think of the poet's dream, his myth, as in any sense an arbitrary individual dream.

I have already pointed out how the audience's visual realization of Hieron's power and wealth in gold artifact itself becomes a part of the act of the hymn which celebrates Hieron as ruler and victor, man seen under light. Our myth is the heroic example of achievement realized religiously as emergence in full light. Furthermore, the chorus of younger and socially subordinate men sing that celebration, that centering of the king. Their act in the hymn recapitulates the process of Pelops' attainment of luster. Their position as celebrants is re-expressed mythically as the voicing of acclaim for Pelops. Their 'mythical' function is nothing more or less than the attainment of generic status for their actual position.

The same is true of the king. He is denoted specifically for his political power and Olympic victory, but never as the idiosyncratic individual. (And that is true of every single one of Pindar's victors or patrons; not a shred of personality or individuality in our sense is expressed in his poetry.) It is the status mask through which Hieron lives in the poem. That status is unique, historical. But for him listening to the chorus' words the same transformation takes place as for them: the myth via Pelops' victory turns his individual rank generic, his achievement seized as the appreciation of what any achievement consists of. The listening audience attends this process on both counts: their sons become generic in their roles, as the king becomes generic in his power.

The poet's creative role is simply the imaginative plotting as reiterated pattern concretized as myth of the psychic positions of these other men. To fulfill that role his psyche most of all must become the non-individualized vision of marked place, dramatic awareness pure and simple. To fulfill his technical role, without glancing aside at problems such as 'point of view', 'subordination of personality', 'dramatic projection', his psyche is automatically consumed in the formulaic projection ·of given position. Is it any wonder that he claims that Poetry itself, the Muse, suckles her most powerful bolt on strength (112)? Again strength is not metaphor; it is the psychic flow of his graphed grasp of actual strength, his poetic realization of the power of Hieron and all others such as he. The others participate in the common psyche which is his imaginative creation. His imagination — but not his personality — stand at the center, at the nexus of all the other interrelated psyches, its very process a flood of light for these others. When he hails radiance it is working through him.

But the form of the common psyche, for him, for the glamour-center, for the celebrants, for all who listen is always individual. It can only be expressed as an individual and his appreciation. The poet's vocabulary for such individuation are the figures of myth. The myth is the means of individuation, the mask for the common psyche absorbing, enfolding the position of each of our posited participants — expressed as putative history. It is as if the poet dreamed the actual scene in another time and place, filled completely, as dreams are, with the emotional integrity of its own tensions, unbroken, as the scene in the hall needs must be, by the warring egos of many men.

Let me point out how everyone, in this instance, at least, not just the king enters the myth. It covers an entire life-history. It starts with a beautiful boy who is still his mother's son — a point that will call for psychological comment later. It sees him as the adolescent beloved of a great male god. It carries him through the *rites de passage* to emerge as successful warrior and husband. It turns him into the patriarch with six heroic sons, gathered not unto his fathers but established as a founding father. Finally, it remarks his perpetual posthumous fame.

His achievement at Olympia is paradigm for our king, but at one or another of the stages of his history everyone in that room is fitted into the chain and sees his part as only a link in that chain. From continued Mediterranean as well as Greek custom we can assume cupbearers and general errand runners as the counterparts for his youngest appearance in myth. Then we move on to the level of his victory at Elis which bespeaks such as the Delphic Charioteer. Hieron did not ride Pherenikos, but his jockey would likely be present at the celebration, as also his — this time around — defeated charioteer, as well as the other Syracusan victors in the games. They may not be mentioned outside the myth, to keep Hieron undiminished, but their training, labor and fights are expressed directly (97-99), and they can all find place in the myth. The older men, some victorious, can look back on just such struggles and now feel as the patriarch Pelops the pride of sons. And between some of them and the pre-victor class there were likely such relations as made myth in the *amor* between Pelops and Poseidon.

And the poet? He comes to the heart and center in Pelops' prayer to his god, the hero's awareness *which is the poet's,* of the ground of his power. It is the use of Achilles of the *Iliad* again, as of Oedipus later, as of any supreme hero in myth. The supreme hero possesses the supreme consciousness of the powers, of the stake, and of the role of the man with the god-given powers in attaining it. The words, of course, of Pelops' discourse are the poet's, and the words are sent forth by the singers from his "knowing" (8,9), his command of meaning in music, the claim rehearsed again at the close (116), which is simply the celebration in song of the divine donation known to men as individual achievement.

Myth is not an autonomous substance, like the walls of Mycenae or the records of the Civil War — though critics often treat it so. It is the substantiation, the arraying in music, as Pindar says, of the mind's vision of the actual. Only by it is the actual realized. "Gesang ist Dasein," or, to replace Rilke by James this time, "It is art that makes life." Myth is realization; myth is understanding. The facts are in the rooms, on the street, in the agoras, at the race-course, on the battlefield. The poetic consciousness of them is summarized in image as myth. At the center of the myth is the heroic consciousness, the individuation of the myth realizing its strategic predicament. That heroic consciousness, from Homer through Euripides, is the center of Greek poetry. *But the heroic consciousness itself is the external form of the poetic consciousness.*

We must, however, give our detailed attention to the prime interconnection between historical actuality and our myth, between Hieron's horserace victory, his political power and Pelops' victory and its consequences, remembering, as just pointed out, that this specific parallel is also paradigm for the athletic, battlefield, or political prowess of any of the other illustrious figures in that room. The illumination of such achievement as myth is the crux of this poem. As celebration it is itself just such illumination as it conceives fame to be, like light playing off gold and through water or a man visible under the hot rays of the sun. Yet its mythic message is illumination in a further sense, seeing in the mind what it is to achieve such place, realizing the given or divine power for individual achievement. The awareness of phenomenon, achievement as divine illumination, is the final light; the poet's illumination, too, is divine donation in the intellectual sphere. In the immemorial terms of the Western tradition, first Hellenic and then Christian, to be filled with light is to be filled with the awareness of the human as the manifestation of divine presence.

In our myth the divine donation emerges from the love of a god for a man. It seems, on the face of it, proto-Christian, just as the next Pindar poem, both in time and fortuitous indexing, *Olympian 2,* seems proto-Christian in its mythic picture of the Western Isles as the reward for abstinence from sinful acts. There certainly is an inter-relation, but let us consider it in an Hellenic context.

The love of Poseidon for Pelops is of quite a different nature from the encounters of Helen or Sappho with Aphrodite or of Achilles with Athena, which we have analyzed. In those instances there is no love of the goddess for the poetic personality. The goddess is a symbol either of sexual drive or of the capacity to grasp a situation correctly, and the confrontation of the human and the divine the dramatic modality of immediate seizure of the everywhere instinct or capacity. But Poseidon is pictured as passionately in love with an individual, and that love is eventually substantiated by the power of Pelops exercised in other relations, in his triumph over Oinomaus and his conquest of Hippodameia. And it is perfectly clear that the Poseidon-Pelops love is a figure for the divine power realized in the king's political power and Olympic triumph.

The love of Poseidon and Pelops, and its precise obverse, the sin of Tantalus, is the myth of *Olympian 1,* and I shall proceed to explicate it in the immemorial if misleading fashion of turning concrete dramatic relation into abstract 'meaning,' hoping that my comments on the myth as presenting the necessary individuated mask of the common psyche of all the participants in the act of choral poetry have made clear why the dramatic mode alone could have served that original audience's need. The nature of our comment, in short, must needs violate the nature of the material under consideration.

But we face another difficulty. There is no extant term for the relation between the love of Poseidon and its expression in Pelops' victory over Oinomaus and marriage with his daughter, or for the relation of that substantiation to Hieron's status as victor and political chief. And no purely aesthetic or critical term could serve our purpose. The problem is a problem of 5th century religion. The term would have to be theological. We talk about the *doctrine* of the Incarnation. One may believe or disbelieve it, and one may believe it as myth or claim it to be historical fact. But no one has ever argued that the Incarnation can be explained as a literary device. Similarly, there can be two views of the authority of Moses descending from Sinai in his promulgation of wrong or right for Israel. Either he is the spokesman for tribal custom or the voice of Yahveh for Israel's functioning. But in neither case will the relation of the Commandments to their authority be understood as 'literary'.

The love of Poseidon for Pelops is not, then, a figure or metaphor for the relation of the gods to Hieron's power and glory. For Pindar it is the mythic *form of belief.* Similarly, within the myth the love of the god is not a figure for his effecting Pelops' will in his own struggle. Pindar need not have stressed the amorous affair in such detail, if that were his purpose. Within the myth itself the love of the god is fulfilled in the heroic achievement, it is not the elucidating image for it, just as we have seen that the play of light is not a figure for but the physical ground of the glamour of athletic victory or kingly recognition. *The young man's strength is the god in being.* The god's expression and the human achievement are simultaneous, coterminous: Pelops' victory is god expressed through man.

Pelops' power is Poseidon's. He has Poseidon's gold chariot and horses in winning his victory. The god does not bless him or will his will; the god gives him his own instruments of power at the very moment of his victory; he does not look down from on high; his donation is the hero's instrumentation, his mastery and strength are for a moment the young man's.

Nor is it ever said that Pelops loved Poseidon and for that love and piety received his reward. On the contrary, he is rewarded as having been loved. The 'figure' for which with our Christian training we instinctively grasp is clearly irrelevant. Pelops at both stages is purely recipient and instrumental and one donation or instrumentation is somehow the natural outcome of the other. How should that be? It will be necessary to explore the psychic tenor of the love affair to realize its theological intent. That psychic tenor is completely taken for granted, and hence its automatic illumination for the original Hellenic audience is lost for strangers to it.

The aristocratic Hellenic view of pederasty from both participants' standpoint must be clearly understood. In and of itself it represents fulfillment, expresses love, only from the point of view of the older man. Hence it is that Poseidon is expressed, fulfilled, made apparent in Pelops' achievement, finds himself glorified. On the other hand, it *leads* to manly fulfillment, heterosexual and self-assertive in war, for the younger man.

Poseidon finds and falls in love with Pelops when he is still a mother-bound boy. It is not to the father that the search party is to bring him but to the mother. But it is from the exercised masculinity of Poseidon that he takes the image for his own assertion either over Oinomaus or Hippodameia — that double assertion, military and amorous, expressed significantly in the Greek by a single verb. The god teaches him what it is to be a man both in bed and on the battlefield. That combination is a Hellenic commonplace, a social norm. It is expressed in Plato as the compulsion for the beloved to achieve in war to gain the lover's respect (St.III.178E-179B); it is echoed in Vergil in the relation of Nisus and Euryalus (*Aeneid* 9. 176f.). Its social side does not directly concern us here, but it is the Hellenic recognition of the Oedipal tension, of the barrier of strife

123

between father and son preventing the father's implementation of the male image. In patriarchal Israel such displacement of the father would be sacrilege. The razing of Sodom is the necessary counterpart of the jealous Yahveh, both 'images' of the assertion of male right in the family as against the mother claim so poignantly, if briefly, expressed in our myth. So it is from the lover, as in Melanesian society from the maternal uncle, that the boy draws the pattern of his masculine expression. To repeat, the ultimate sanction for male homosexuality in historic Hellas derives not, as commonly claimed, from the submergence but the exaltation of mother-right.

But if this social setting is merely background, its intimate details are necessary for the religious understanding of this hymn. For the very physical motions of Pelops, as of his loins or fighting right arm, bespeak the motions of his lover Poseidon. His acts are a reflection of the god's own gestures. His acts are his lover's acts renewed.

Pelops' will, his assertion of his individuality, are of the first importance, and that will is freely expressed in his prayer. But it can be seen at once that there is no question of will in his relation to the god. He has only to call on that which is in him already, Poseidon. He has to bring back to his mind in all its clarity and overwhelming presence the Poseidon-derived pattern of his being. The god never answers him, never blesses him, never declares any purpose whatsoever. "He handled words not without power." His act of invocation, which is the invocation of his love affair with Poseidon — and all that we have sketched in Greek terms — succeeds. His relation to, his absorption of the deity is then made manifest in his double victory. He realizes whose chariot and horses he is using. He recognizes in the act the source of his power. His piety is not self-abnegation. Quite the contrary, it is the fullest self-assertion, contrasted to obscurity, darkness, famelessness. The relation of man to deity could not be more brilliantly contrasted to our own. In his fullest egotism he declares the godhead which has given him the command, the proper functioning of that egotism. His piety is recognition, not abnegation. Given the Hellenic social ground for the mythic image — the psycho-sexual relation expressed in the donation of the gold chariot and winged steeds — there is no way in which in self-assertion and action he can fail to recognize the lineaments of his mentor, guide, and lover. His action is his piety.

Human achievement, then, in Pindar's myth, is not in our sense love of god but the presence of god in act itself. The love affair is the medium for the transmission of skill, understanding, the deployment of strength, not a blessing from on high, a supernatural moral sanction of individual will. The will acts of its own accord with its own motives of social illumination. It expresses itself and nothing else. Deity is the instrumentation, the actual coursing strength and its pattern, the power of fulfillment, not the choice of goal. Divinity is energy and its pattern, not the selective fiat for willful enactment. There can be failure, of course, but except as pitiable contrast that is not the concern of a poet celebrating success. His function is to see what success is. It is the momentary announcement, the flowering expression of divinity. The deep waters roar, the gleaming-trident shines on the shore; the gold-cross board gleams; the tireless horses rush. Every one of these Pindaric images is immortal energy in motion, manifest. These powers are perpetual, though not their temporal vehicle, unstoppable, though not the death-bound will that employs them. A man claims them only at the peak of his natural powers, no more. Pelops grows old and dies. He has won through to momentary illumination, but his will is transient, measurable. His victory is self-assertion, but that assertion has its natural limits. He achieves no miracles. There is no denial of nature in his brief triumph, no proclamation of an individual's moral victory over natural power or pattern. In victory he expresses the divine endowment and recognizes it. His will is fed by his god-given life force and its god-given modality, but that will must follow the natural history of that force and its modality. This myth is an exploration of the ground of success and a clear announcement of its divine source. It is bound to natural phenomena.

Any denial of the human limit, of the purely human prerogatives in the exercise of god-given power is sin. The sinner contrasted to Pelops is his own father. That in itself is a wry unconscious comment on the psycho-sexual and social gulf between Hellas and Israel, the father as the epitome of the sinner in contrast to the glowing nobility of the son. In Israel's legends that would never be endured. Fathers may be meek and obscure, sons rebellious or prodigal, but no moral paradigm could be made of a son's virtue against a father's sin. The father's role is not, to say the least, glorified in Greek poetry. We need think only of Agamemnon at Aulis, Heracles and his offspring, Laius-Oedipus and Oedipus-Eteocles, Theseus and his son, to glimpse the cloud of father-hate and destruction that dogs the Hellenic mind. Right there we have sufficient reason for the choice of lover and youth rather than father and son as the Pindaric paradigm for god's relation to man; Pindar is not at war with his society's sense of psychological patterning.

But apart from psychic pattern, as the theological concept of sin the contrast to our own view could not be more complete. Sin is not given instinct nor self-assertion. Sin does not spring from nature but is the failure to see and come to terms with it. Sin is blindness, self-infatuation, the refusal to realize the given as given. Salvation is consciousness and celebration.

Pindar in the image of the history of Tantalus speaks blasphemy to Christian ears while emphasizing as a Greek the sinfulness of the human denial of mortality. I know no better way to dramatize what is taken in one time and society as rebellion and in another as religious appreciation than to quote as a gloss on the myth of Tantalus a terrible paragraph of Friedrich Nietzsche.

> Paul, with that rabbinical impudence which distinguishes him in all things, logicalized this conception, this *obscenity* of a conception in this way: "*If* Christ was not resurrected from the dead, then our faith is vain." And all at once the evangel became the most contemptible of all unfulfillable promises, the *impertinent* doctrine of personal immortality. Paul himself still taught it as a *reward*. (Italics Nietzsche's. *The Anti-Christ* 41, Walter Kaufmann trans., *Portable Nietzsche* 616.)

*The impertinent doctrine of personal immortality.* To assail the doctrine seems to the Christian to spring from an attitude grown from sin; to believe in it to Pindar is sin of the highest degree. To Pindar as to Nietzsche it is a terrible impertinence; Pindar's view is as much at war with Christianity as the modern philosopher's.

We would not know this from Classical commentators who still rearrange the Greek poets to dovetail with traditional religion, not its blazing 19th century foes. To Mr. Finley (J.H. Finley, Jr., *Pindar and Aeschylus*, Harvard, 1955, 50), Tantalus' sin is a form of frivolity, "the ties of common gregariousness," preferring the lesser company of drinking companions of his own age to the demanding converse of the gods, the gay young man in taverns who will not study the lessons prescribed by his elders which alone can bring him honor in their ranks. But this is to reverse the Pindaric intent under the pressure of a perhaps unconscious Calvinism; instead of good times with friends being any sin to the Greeks, that is what Tantalus is *deprived of* in his punishment, *euphrosune,* Milton's 'heart-easing mirth'. What he loses to Pindar is the good, and that to Mr. Finley is his sin. The gloss could not more clearly contradict the text.

What Tantalus is punished for is stealing nectar and ambrosia, that which keeps the gods' veins forever coursing with youthful blood, and giving this instrumentality of immortality to his human friends. He is punished for acting like Paul, for attempting to bestow the prerogative of divinity on men, for being the evangel of immortality. For Pindar it is a terrible form of impertinence. It epitomizes self-infatuation, *ate*, to the highest degree, *huperoplos*. Pindar's picture of Tantalus is the mythic form of Nietzsche's stricture on Paul of Tarsus.

In his last hymn for this same king, *Pythian 3,* Pindar says it directly to Hieron himself. Hieron had been ill for a number of years and was to die within months or even weeks of this poem, as its composer must have known. The poet starkly addresses him on the eve of dissolution, "Do not, dear soul, grasp for immortal life" (61). In that poem the myth of Tantalus appears as the myth of the great healer, Cheiron. Bribed by gold he tried to save from death a man already in its grasp. For his effort to make a man immortal, Zeus from his own hand sent the terrible blast through the chests of both him and his patient. The gleaming brand of Zeus, who is the natural order in all its majesty, destroys Cheiron at once. For his impertinence in attempting to give another man the gods' own privilege he meets with nature's own answer to his aspiration, his obliteration. Pindar's words in the *Third Pythian* are quite as terrible as Nietzsche's, and he goes on to point the moral of Cheiron's punishment. "It is necessary for a man to seek in his death-bound heart what befits him from the radiant powers, knowing what is before our feet, knowing the prescribed fate we live within" (59,60). That 'knowing', *gnonta*, is all important. It makes sin a failure of awareness, a failure of consciousness. And it makes sin an exaltation of will, the will for immortality, against natural, given condition.

There is no more sense of sin in that poem than in this in glorifying the great and achieving life. Hieron is praised even more extendedly for his high place in mortal existence. Only he is told without apology that it is a mortal condition and no further presumption is allowed.

Tantalus was even more blessed than Pelops. By the gods' will, not his own, he was given nectar and ambrosia. But he made the mistake of confusing donation, the god-given, with possession, over which his will held sway. He tried to bring within his own power, to exercise as possession what had been simply given. "He could not *digest* his great blessing" (56). He could not *assimilate* the presented *food* of life simply as individual *sustenance.* He tried instead to make it an expression of will, to act like a god. The gods can give and take. A man can only receive or be deprived. To make his gift a gift to others is not generosity; it is to misconceive his relation to it.

Tantalus' punishment too, is emblematic, the perpetual psychic price of his pride. In Pindar he does not roll a stone up a hill; he tries forever to keep it from crushing his skull. Like the other eschatological symbols that Pindar uses, as in the myths of the *2nd Olympian* or the *10th Nemean,* his state is the expression of a continuing psychic or moral attitude. What is that? The fear of his own obliteration. The price of making the individual will the center of the phenomenon of its own efflorescence is perpetual concern with its extinction.

Throughout the poem Pelops and Tantalus are played off against one another. Their familial relation is not of dramatic importance itself. It is a means of juxtaposing two attitudes, and Pindar is less interested — and this is a general rule of choral verse — in the temporal unfolding of the myth than in pressing the contrasts of the two significant shapes. Poseidon's love of Pelops is proclaimed before Tantalus is introduced as the still pious host of the gods at the banquet where the god first meets the boy. We have the love affair in progress, and the boy out of sight in heaven, before coming back to Tantalus' symposium sin. We then pick up the victorious aftermath of Pelops' submission to the god's presence and the description of his memorialized end. This ababa (Pelops a, Tantalus b) presentation of the two aspects of the myth, their careful inter-locking, makes emphatic the indivisibility of their significance. On the surface the two fates seem almost irrelevent to one another, their inter-connection fortuitous. The Pelops theme is expressed over and over again in Pindar in its own right, as noted in *Pythian 8* and *Isthmian 5,* just as the Tantalus theme is presented in the guise of Cheiron in *Pythian 3.* (That latter interchange, incidentally, is a beautiful example of what I have called the vocabulary of myth, the flexible lexicon of mythic figures for interpretative images of actual existence. Cheiron's use springs from the same intuition or evaluation as Tantalus'.) Pelops is our mythic example of the radiance theme of these other poems, the gold of his borrowed chariot picking up the gold first acclaimed in Hieron's hall, connecting his race with the Syracusan king's, but also echoing the use we have seen in Sappho of the denotation of Zeus' house as gold, his achievement simply his part of the natural order of which Zeus not Poseidon is keystone. To make the Sappho echo sharper, Pelops, be it remembered, was carried in the first instance on gold horses to Zeus' house, and the parallel with Ganymede reinforces the Poseidon-Zeus interchangeability.

Pelops is presented, too, as the successful user of power. His words to his god are 'not powerless' (85), and his prayer is to be brought directly to power (78). That term is used precisely of the effect of Pherenikos' victory in the race for Heiron (22). There is a conscious verbal replay. In both cases winning physically enmeshes, binds, coalesces the individual in *kratos,* might, the force for victory. This verbal echo binds Hieron and Pelops' status together more firmly, perhaps, than any other lines in the poem, and that status as radiance discloses its divine source.

It is easy enough to see Tantalus' punishment simply by way of bitter contrast to Pelops' glory. But that of itself has no theological significance. I have already made consciousness, the recognition of the divine gift as such, as opposed to the individual's willed appropriation of it, the key to the mythic contrast, but even that by itself does not exhaust the interrelation insisted upon here between the ultimate of natural self-expression, the social triumph of the individual seen as god's gift, and the social extinction of the individual, wandering from *euphrosune*, seen as divine punishment.

The first point to make is that both mythic pictures are forms for the actual and not at all instances of supernatural manipulation. This is hard to understand for those who insist on reading Judaic-Christian 'divine will' into Greek divinity. There is no reason or divine purpose either in Pelops being loved by Poseidon and glorified through that love or for Tantalus' sinning. There is no anterior cause given in the myth for either predicament, and no divine motive posited for their comple- mentary, if contradictory, enactments. Tantalus' punishment is automatic, simply reveals the psychological nature of a man with his blindness to divine donation. His constant fear of death is the inevitable concomitant of the misconception of human will; it follows as the night the day. That punishment is now and everlasting, because myth is paradigm in image, not history. Tantalus' punishment is the concrete image of the psychic state of the man who faces life as he does. Concomitantly, as we have already said, there is nothing supernatural about Pelops' victory. It is his conscious enlistment of his actual god-given endowment to serve his immediate will. It parallels Achilles' triumphs in the *Iliad*. Achilles, like Pelops, never forgets the source of his tremendous power, nor does he forget that he will die. Because he *faces* his own death so completely, and pari passu everyone else's, Achilles is presented as the man who least *fears* death. It is the ultimate secret of his self-confidence, the spring to his total as opposed to others' partial absorption of given power.

What is psychological nexus within the single character of Achilles — acceptance of death and total expression of given power — becomes the pivot for the two complementary mythic images, and their significance, in this hymn. It accepts death as a means of glorifying life. It exults in individual self-expression as momentary radiance while condemning as everlasting punishment the misconception of will governing that expression. Tantalus' attitude toward death and Pelops' self-declaration of the divine are the two sides of the same coin.

"Death is the mother of beauty." Or to use the family figure of Pindar's contrast, "Only the acceptance of death would be the blameless father of achievement grasped as divine radiance." Death alone provides the definition of will which can disclose its source even in its most glorious expression. How can will in its very enactment disclose godhead, if it governs its own unfolding or can resist its own destruction? That Poseidon's chariot was the means of Pelop's victory can be grasped only when we appreciate the dimension of Tantalus' sin in setting men nectar and ambrosia. We should also remember that the 'love of the god' is mythically simply a way of stating the boy's natural beauty, in a supreme case, just as the 'god's steeds' are a mythic image of natural strength, in a supreme instance. Both bloom in nature and both fade. That fading is a declaration of natural condition, and when it is appreciated the efflorescence in time is a parallel declaration of unwilled donation, not self-assumed power. Tantalus is Pelops' father: I have already pointed out that this has no dramatic but a purely symbolic use in our hymn, and Stevens' metaphor for the genesis of appreciation has picked up its tenor: the one appreciation must precede the other. That is why Tantalus' punishment is described prior to Pelops' lasting glorification. Acceptance of death is the avenue to seeing life as phenomenon, as the disclosure of divinity. Full psychic submission to extinction is the preliminary, the father, of the appreciation of the living moment as donation, the son as god's paramour. Only so is the predicament of the will disclosed. To defy or deny death is to misconceive will, and so the will's enactment can never reveal the gold of divinity, Poseidon's cross-board. With the psychic subscription to death begins the intellectual appreciation of life as phenomenon. And to say phenomenon, that which appears or shines, simultaneously implies the physical seeing and the mental limning of the viewed being, the realizing of its transient status as well as of its present sheen. That for Pindar is the specific function of poetry, simultaneously celebration and revelation of the precariousness of what is celebrated.

The great error for Pindar, then — and it is simply the Pindaric expression of a continuous Greek poetic theme — is to make any claim that you are not entitled to make, to claim as your own what is not your own or more than the order of nature establishes for you. Theologically, it is the sin of pride, psychologically it is the delusion of the autonomy of the will, intellectually it is simply the failure to see, to recognize the facts.

Yet Pindar glorifies the individual will, though no more than Homer or Sophocles. There are no more self-willed characters than Achilles or Oedipus. Pride shines with breathtaking innocence in the poetry of Pindar. He is par excellence the poet of success, of the celebration of military and athletic triumph, of familial and political eminence. He shines the floodlight of poetry on wealth and family lineage, on a city's geographic or economic sway, on man's physique. How do we reconcile this acclamation of success, of fully willed and self-congratulatory expression with his condemnation of willfulness, of the sin of pride, or self-infatuation?

Our problem is theological, not linguistic, though it is clear that we use quite a number of words — self, will, pride, etc. — in quite different, even opposing senses. One can only trust that, if the different theological points of view are made clear, so also will be the uses of those words in their differing contexts. The key to Greek theology, in myth and anthropomorphic deity presented within it, as much as in moral judgment or conceived human drama, is the formalization of the organic, the establishment of terms for given appreciation, nature, as far as possible, recapitulated in language, of which religious or poetic form is the extension. It is this which sets it off from all the religions of denial. For it is as clear to a Buddhist or Christian as it is to a Hellene that all men are ego-centric. It is their nature. And given the nature of social symbolism as simply the expression of organic response, men extend that naive ego-centricity to their families, their states or cities, their entire culture. It is clear, too, that naturally the individual — or the family, or the state — prefers success to failure, renown to obscurity, wealth to poverty, youth to old age, and life to death. Greek religion not only accepts given instinct and egocentricity; it exists as, consists of an elaborate symbolization for given desire and the individual modality of its expression. The Greek sense for form in any of the arts is inseparable from the sense of momentary individual expression and even self-congratulation. A sculpture, for example, does not come into being, is not initially prompted except as the recognition of natural self-expression.

To recollect 5th century sculpture and its exaltation of perfect physical form is to place the Pindaric artistic celebrations in their Greek religious context. It is hard for us to conceive of those 5th century sculptural forms of athletes as religious, so hard that some art-historians still tell us that they represent the triumph of secular appreciation — their unconscious reflection of a contradictory religious assumption. In the 5th century — the 4th is another matter — physical perfection or worldly triumph *as* realized is religious apperception. Religion, in fact, provides the form for the recognition and celebration of the natural expression.

Religion as the formal seizure of the natural is to be sharply set off against secularism, whose pressures already at work in Greek culture in the 5th brought its creative life to a close in the 4th century. Nor is that secularism to be distinguished from our own, or any other, for the simple reason that secularism must always be the same, since it is incarceration in presented objects and their idiosyncratic aspects, in specific greeds, lusts, or ambitions, a failure of appreciation of beings in their natural context, a failure to realize them as phenomena, which is why it can live happily side by side with vulgar superstition, as it did in Greece for several centuries. But such secularism is never to be confused with naturalism, least of all with an elaborate symbolic structure for the seizure of the events of nature, their propulsion and their form, which classical Greek religion provides from Homer through the 5th century.

For this view, striving to approximate realized pressure, never sees the individual being in isolation but in the context of its total history, juxtaposing triumph and its "sure obliteration," the nowhere before and only the memory after of any achievement. The individual is always grasped in process, seen under pressure, revealing gravity or instinct, always conditionally, a form the temporary definition of those necessary conditions. Secondly, the individual is always grasped generically, as the exemplar of repetitive form. That is why there is no portrait sculpture before the end of the 5th century. Each and every triumph, as well as its actor, is the repetition of every other. Lastly, though the will or its enjoyment is frankly self-centered, it wills neither its own existence, its endowments, nor its termination. Seen from inside it is total and perfect in its egotism, *seized as temporary generic form in process* it is simply manifestation. Only as manifestation does it reach its acme, disclose the everlasting in its brief span, ride the gold chariot of a god to its local victory.

There is, then, no contradiction between the glorification of individual existence and the exhibition of its ultimate will-lessness. Pride is innocent as the realization of self, sin as the failure to realize that self in its natural predicament. Will is right as self-assertion, wrong if the will is thought to be eternal, omnipotent, or autonomous. Self is to be celebrated as the only knowable form of the everlasting propulsion to self. The gods love men or women, not the reverse in Greek theology. That is a way of saying that natural glory is given, not owned. Poseidon falls in love with Pelops for a brief while, i.e. his brief span of natural flowering. Pelops is merely grateful to Poseidon for the love-making, that is, he recognizes the nature of his self-substantiation, recognizes his endowment. The appreciation of the god is, in fact, the *form* of that *self*-recognition, and by the god-mortal contrast, on which that appreciation is based – 'This is Poseidon's chariot I drive' – the limit of exultant will is automatically defined.

It follows that self-abnegation can only be a denial of natural form, a denial of the only perceivable shape in which any energy is ever expressed. To deny the self is to deny the everlasting mode of the everlasting energy seized in it. And though the Greeks did not, of course, have to face the problem, their theology points by implication to the motive for self-abnegation, however closely hidden: to make the individual will a paradigm of everlasting omnipotence, to project the self as the propulsion to self. That is hubris, that is sinful pride to the Greek, for it is the denial of the local predicament, natural modality, mortality. In denying nature it denies the radical relationship between the given form and the endowment of that form.

But Pelops beloved of Poseidon and ensured victory by his power — individual beauty and strength realized as endowed form, god in man — is contrasted not only with Tantalus and his sin — the human attempt to conceive life as its own willed and controllable possession. He is also presented in contrast to previous myth, restated in our poem, of Pelops' dismemberment and consumption by the gods. That myth is labeled a lie and is said to have gained credence because of the power of poetry in this society to compel belief. Our singers bespeak the poet's sharp dissent as the introduction to the new myth of Poseidon's love.

Our poet's religious appreciation is not, then, consonant with received tradition. We are suddenly reminded that Pindar is a 5th century poet, innovating, exploratory; we are reminded of Aeschylus' similar stance in the Helen chorus of the *Agamemnon* (757) with that bold, "I stand apart," a direct foreshadowing of his contemporary's introduction of a new view of the process of social or familial destruction, another reminder that these two poets, religiously as well as artistically, are variant aspects of the same evolvement.

Others might be reminded by this dissent of the contemporary dissent by Xenophanes of the whole "Olympian troupe," to use Mr. Eliot's term, the rejection of the man-projected forms of adultery, lying, stealing, squabbling of the Homeric and Hesiodic theogony, and Pindar's dissent would also seem to prepare us for the Platonic rejection in *The Republic* of the entire poetic projection of 'immoral' godhead.

The assumption behind such an explication of this Pindaric passage is clear enough. Pindar is simply part of the later Greek attempt to "clean up" their conception of deity, to purify it, to make it noble, to make it, in fact, as far as possible resemble our own. Plato as the last and fullest representative of this reformation can then be assimilated into Christian conceptions.

There is far too much and much that is self-contradictory jammed into this view of Pindar's purpose in rejecting the cannibal motif in *Olympian 1*. Between Xenophanes' revolution, the rejection of poetic symbol and Plato's later rehearsal of it, the continuity is unarguable. But how can Pindar be fitted into a development which denies the intellectual or moral validity of the anthropomorphic forms of godhead? This or any other poem of Pindar's is based on the conviction of the reality of those forms, here Zeus and Poseidon, elsewhere Apollo, Athena, the entire traditional vocabulary for the recognition of the active powers of nature which Xenophanes and Plato assail.

And as long as that vocabulary was a medium for the recognition of the vital powers and natural event, the gods as symbolizing the variant propulsions of nature must do terrible things. Euripides at the end of this tradition, in the *Hippolytus* and *Bacchae*, makes this formal necessity crystal clear, but it is to be remembered that Apollo's oracle for Oedipus makes inescapable the murder of Laius and incest with Jocasta, that the power of Zeus in *The Trachiniae* commands Heracles' destruction; nor can we overlook the divine sanction of murder in *The Libation Bearers*, or *Nemean 10* or our hymn, where Oinomaus is slain. Pindar is full of the lust of the gods, their tyranny, of their propensity to destruction, as he must be, since nature is full of lust, rules by force, and entails death. His poetry does not in this regard differ from Homer at one end and Euripides at the other of the Greek tradition. That poetry, whatever the developments within it, was for its life the formal expression of the same natural theology.

It might be sounder to approach the myth of the feasting on Pelops, which creates a very real tension in our poem between what the poet wishes to be understood and what he fears many men think, not from the viewpoint of intellectual history but from the drama of the poem itself and the light that is intended to be shed on human psychology.

The motivation for the myth presented as a malicious lie is human envy. In poetry which is celebration of success the peril of envy must be met with every acclamation. It is such a cliché in Pindar that I do not think that in individual contexts we should search, as so many critics do, for specific historical references. It is first and foremost ritualistic. The divine envy, the imminence of fall from the transient height, must be prayed against. The great majority of his victory odes perform this ritualistic averting of the evil-eye. Nor is there any sharp distinction between divine envy and one of its natural grounds, human jealousy, though there are, of course, other natural grounds which the symbolic projection, divine envy, figures, loss of health or strength, of wealth or talent, of anything which leads to or secures success. And when a poem is the appreciation of success, itself the ritual of its celebration, it must also avert envy directed against itself as the formal realization of always imperiled triumph. Needless to say, in our readings, this averting of envy directed at the poem is concerned with its function and content, not with the poet, who is always social in his proclamation, never appears *in propria persona.*

It is to be noted that for all that this supreme ode is a major celebration of Pindar's greatest patron, the envy theme or cliché, rehearsed in so many other poems, enters this only as an adjective, and that apposite of imaginary figures in the myth, not the social setting of the ode itself. But neither the intent nor effect is suppression of this sentiment. For that emotion is here made the propulsion to a myth; here it attains its fullest theological and psychological statement. Rather than being played down, the envy motif is indirectly played up in *Olympian 1.*

Now Pindar gives a full expression of the myth he labels a lie. We know the story through him. He claims to be slamming the door on a deceiving view and then turns and projects the view he is assailing. It might seem that this runs the risk of being the best possible propaganda of it — as our intelligent poet must well have known. Except for that adjective 'envious', and the preceding disclaimer, there is no reason while the false myth is unfolding to give it less credence than his own. When it is finished, of course, he is enabled to make his dramatic disclaimer all over again, "I can not call deity belly-raging. I stand apart." I wonder, then, if it is as much established myth as the present belief it incorporates that has been his incentive. Would he so elaborate not only his disclaimers but his mythic expression of what is disclaimed, if he were not troubled by the immediate hold of the belief expressed in such imagery, a contemporary pressure he sees dangerously submerging the religious appreciation he holds most dear? Plato, too, in *Gorgias, Protagoras, Republic I* gives a past dramatic setting, a past historic mask to views which he is fighting for their effect in his own time. But it is the present danger that elicits the picture of past intellectual history.

If the sinews of the grip of fable is contemporary error how should its psychology be stated? We must go back to our earlier discussion of the correct myth as the appreciation of success, realizing glory as given. The god's love is the mythic image of the boy's beauty which in the story causes the god's love. This is the mythic manner of presenting equation as causal. The classic example is Artemis' anger in the first chorus of the *Agamemnon* at the eagle eating the hare, leading to Agamemnon's sacrifice of Iphegeneia which *is* the eagle eating the hare. The causal concatenation is simply the transposition of recurrent condition as mythical event. The neighbors, however, can not understand the boy's beauty *as* a god's love. The source of envy is the denial of divinity in natural flowering. If the donation is outside anyone's power or control, its presence leads not to envy but worship of its source. The neighbors suffer from the same error as Tantalus, only it is not their own donation — too insignificant to be mentioned — that is at stake, as in his case, but someone else's. They, too, see achievement or perfection of form as simply individual, and they must fight the sense of inferiority which, if conceived in individual terms, such blessed possession imposes on them.

There is only one way to get rid of that reminder of inferiority. It is to destroy, to rend and eat the beautiful, to kill it and take into themselves the special property of what is consumed — the immemorial motive of cannabalistic practice, always a sacred rite. We must keep clear in mind what anthropology teaches us of cannibalism. It has nothing to do with Ugolino. It is the appropriation of the *virtu* of the absorbed substance. Now their myth is a lie: it is not, that is, the true appreciation of phenomenon. But it is an expressive lie, expressive of themselves. Their myth of the gods' eating Pelops is their own desire to rend and eat the boy. It is Claggart in relation to Billy Budd, envy which seeks to destroy that which, with innocence, could be appreciated or loved. Melville has spelled out the same psychic interconnection that the *1st Olympian* posits between the envy of the neighbors and their myth of the beautiful boy's destruction. The appreciation of the true nature of endowment leads to the image of Poseidon's love, of it as individual possession to be envied, to the picture of its annihilation.

There is a suggestion in our poem that such a destructive tendency is present anterior to the true appreciation. Pindar very clearly has kept a part of the "wrong" myth within the "right" myth, and he makes no attempt to clarify the contradiction or the temporal confusion that accompanies it. He has Poseidon fall in love with the boy just as he is being taken from the cauldron which has prepared him for the cannibalistic feast! There could be no better example than this "confusion" that myth is not pseudo-history but the imagery for interlocking psychic states. That part of the envy-produced "lie" is still a part of the "truth" of our poem, only the intervention of Poseidon, that is, the appearance of the form for the recognition of the source of the boy's beauty, saves him from destruction. It is as if Captain Vere had torn Billy from Claggart's lash and vituperation and carried him away to his own cabin, for his punishment, the envious would say, to glorify him, according to those who would celebrate the possibility of such innocence and beauty.

It might seem that Pindar, in comparison with Melville, is radically optimistic, his myth wish-fulfillment, ideal appreciation presented as putative history. And in part such a charge would be justified, though like Plato's parallel optimism, it does not blink envy, malice, and destruction. It does, however, suppose a different relation between sin and innocence from our own, a relation which in most myths of the origin of sin is expressed as their temporal sequence, though the choice of anterior and posterior is an expression of belief as to the paramount. With the Greeks the temporally antecedent is the good. In Hesiod the golden age precedes its successive degenerations, and Pandora's box is introduced into a world which has known innocence before its importation. And even to make the

Hebraic-Christian myth of the Fall a paradigm of *original* sin is to read the happy hours before the apple was eaten as a device to set the stage before the determinant event is enacted upon it, though if sin is an intruder in the Garden, the problem remains whether it can be called original, whether it is nature or the perversion of nature.

But Pindar's answer is fully Greek, sin as the corruption of nature. And on examination it is not far from Melville's view. For Billy Budd is innocence personified, the natural projected in that myth, beauty simply as given, and endowed with a psyche that looks on life and others' motives with an equal innocence. And Claggart is corruption. He is not original nature, Billy is. So in our poem the envious neighbors are certainly in the poet's view corrupt. They can not realize that Pelops has been carried to Olympus on gold horses. They can not realize what the natural, the 'original' is. Sin is their failure of appreciation; it is a failure of consciousness, as the *3rd Pythian* puts it, not knowing, *gnonta*. For Pindar as for Plato sin is intellectual, not a failure of will. Will would just as naturally be for the good; ignorance, infatuation prevent its natural fulfillment. The awareness of divine radiance, to see Poseidon in Pelops, is to know that the neighbors' tale is a lie, even if great poets, great theologians in Greek society, have given it honored credence. "It befits a man to say beautiful things of the *daimones*, the radiant powers." The proper attitude is the appreciation of the phenomenal.

"Blessed are the pure in heart for they shall see God." Pindar, like that teacher, points to innocence as natural, spontaneous, and grants it the same reward. Pindar's belief and its denial of the myth of dismemberment points up the same contradiction as obtains between, "Suffer the little children to come unto me, for of such is the kingdom of heaven" (which is not, "Suffer the little baptized children") and the doctrine that they are damned in nature. "Children", after all, is always the figure, the mythic image of the original, the natural.

Once it is known that Poseidon loves Pelops, there is no room for the story that his absence is the feast of the gods. The natural is a god's love. That is the central myth of our poem to which both Tantalus and the envious neighbors are contrasted.

Destruction comes from the denial of love induced by envy. It is Claggart; it is Iago; it is Ahab. They are all perverse. Billy Budd and Desdemona are nature, and so is Queequeg at ease in bed with Ishmael.

A belief in radical human innocence, then, is enfolded in the Pindaric conception of divinity, as it is in the Gospels. Such a belief lies behind the Platonic Socrates' claim that men will seek the good, if only they know it, the antithesis to the Pauline belief in instinctive inclination to evil. But on the other side, proclaiming an originally sinful nature, lies not only Christian dogma but much Greek myth which anticipates it. I mislead, if I simplify the complexity, even contradictoriness of Greek views on this subject, just as I would be at pains, if I were examining Hebraic or Christian assumptions for their own sake, to cite their local antitheses. Pindar is not isolated, he is never to be considered the strident speaker of a minority. But his work must be treated as eliciting emerging views, contemporary revelation which may have to discount what has gone before or what is actively blocking its appreciation with his audience. It is extremely important to him that the right view be known, that its position as truth amid error be proclaimed. Just as his social and historical predicament as the conscious 5th century innovator, who is also the heir of a great tradition, emphasizes the importance of knowledge, new knowledge, so does his doctrine itself. It is perfectly clear that in it *knowing* is the key to salvation. It is the recognition of what nature really is that is the safeguard against destruction. Sin is first the misconception and then action that proceeds from that misconception.

It follows that *paideia* is all important, education not simply as the indoctrination of the young, though that is important, nor merely the transmission of the valid insights of tradition, where Pindar like Plato is instinctively conservative, but education in the sense of contemporary realization of the given forms of natural life for everyone, whatever his age or achievement. Such learning is always in process, must be experienced and acknowledged time and again. There is no strict moment of salvation − though there is conversion to an original correct outlook − since salvation is that moment's seeing, and other moments necessitating similar insight will be coming up shortly. The spokesman for the good or for the gods is himself always engaged in the same process, the realization of divinity manifest in human achievement.

The sense of this perpetual process and its strategic importance are common to Pindar and Plato but not what that process consists of, for the philosopher dialectic, for the poet the use of myth and anthropomorphic deity to illuminate experience. Nor would Pindar any more conceive of indexing even discarded myth than Plato of proscribing Heracleitus. He excludes wrong myth by making it incompatible with the right one, in this case by emphasizing their temporal coincidence, the absence of Pelops from Sipylus, so that if one is true, the other can not be. But as much as Plato, or any Christian, he is aware that men are prone to err, are forever failing, that sight must be restored, that nature be grasped again as it is, so that sin does not take over. That sight is wisdom and its means in his time poetry.

This all seems simple enough, but I restate it here because of a current critical tendency to downgrade the *knowledge* insisted upon in all the Pindaric references to poetry, in the hymns' direct denotation of their own function. Both in the proem and in the closing line Pindar marks that poetic skill as wisdom, as knowing, *sophia.* It simultaneously means skill in poetry. That second sense has now been isolated and the poetic claim often rendered as purely technical. This is one of the several errors of conception in, for example, Mr. Lattimore's translation of Pindar. But for Pindar, as for any Greek poet, the two senses can not be separated. The strategic task of that poetry, as the core of society's realization of divinity, is implied in that word, *sophia,* poetic knowing as the necessary means of salvation. It fulfills this function simultaneously, inseparably from its function of celebration, understanding and acclaiming human achievement. The celebration of the human must be the realization of its divine ground.

Nor is the process of appreciation to be separated from *its* means. Apollo and Zeus stand behind the enactment of the hymn to Zeus or Apollo. To be left outside such celebration is at once sin and its punishment. The *euphrosune* of which Tantalus is deprived is not to be distinguished from this hymn as an example of *euphrosune,* and the *euphrosune* of the hymn consists of seeing Pelops under the radiance of Poseidon's love. The hymn teaches simply as it is the experience of what is to be learned, itself the model of the appreciation that restores the right view of nature. There can be no envy here. The common psyche, which we posited earlier as between poet, chorus, victor and audience, is the common psyche for the realization of Pelops' victory as Poseidon's gesture. And the common psyche of celebration, its appreciative center, precludes the individuality that alone leads to envy. Those envious neighbors are such as do not participate in such a hymn, such euphrosune and its common psyche. They are the damned. But everyone, so far as he yields to the rhythm of the song and dance and the words of its realization, everyone within that circle at that time is made blessed. Only when it, or moments like it are broken, can the envy of individuality and individuality as determinant reassert itself.

In the blazing proem of *Pythian I* Pindar uses the danced hymn as the epitome of social harmony, of peace as opposed to war. The gold lyre of Apollo is the counterpart of the gold which proclaims Zeus' and Poseidon's existence in our poem. Tantalus and neighbors who feed on images of dismemberment are there the hundred-headed Typhus, the terror of volcanos and the destruction of war. What is assumed here is declared there, that the moment of the hymn, its simultaneous musical and psychic harmony, is the time when the fires of destruction slumber, when the bolts of Ares are charmed to peace. The hymn not only celebrates; it becomes the moment of peace on earth, good will to men. Our poem is the musical restoration of the radiant reign of gold, of water and gold, of love.

143

# CHAPTER 5

## REVOLUTION: XENOPHANES AND PLASMATA

A basic revolution whose barricades are always with us needs must have a name as sign to mark for all time its determination or issue, the voice for later mind of a point of view which sums up the pressures which have led to it, as an exclamation point in history. Xenophanes is such an exclamation point, the Greek denial of the validity of its myths and its forms for divinity, the glory which is Homer and Aeschylus, Pindar and Euripides, Sophocles and Sappho.

Xenophanes is one of the most important names in intellectual history. He represents in Western culture what happens in any when the mythic mode becomes selfconscious. And since the mythic mode is revived now and again or lives on in pockets of now differently oriented cultures, he can stand for the reiteration in independent circumstances of his own appreciation. He can stand for the ever renewed barricades, setting on one side those who intuit deity instinctively in human shape and use myth as the form of its expression, and, on the other, those who posit a phenomenal world without personalized deity or the dramatization of its realization, confining themselves to natural process as confronting not absorbed by the human imagination. To trace not only the reiterated opposition of these two viewpoints but also their insistent interrelation (as in Plato) would be one way of reviewing the poetic vs. the noetic life in Western civilization since the appearance of Xenophanes.

Just to place the Xenophantic revolution and its barricades in our own cultural era can illustrate the historic entanglements crowding the appreciative continuum. In art or philosophy, unlike natural science, expression, if continuous, is not cumulative, one proved fact or successful system displacing a previous one. There are only successive moments of appreciation congealed under the pressures of the given moment. There is no necessary progress; there either is or is not illumination. Each moment is total unto itself, and though it can be related to moments both before and after, it must be criticized as it evolves,

144

as temporary reaction and formalization. Picasso does not cancel Goya, nor Cezanne Poussin; one is not superior to the other, displacing him for future time. Yet what happens in either moment is happening, in different fashion, in the other.

The same law of appreciation applies to poetic or metaphysical statement. It is always socially entangled reaction, not the product of an autonomous discipline. The revival of Xenophanes' appreciation is one of the most signal and dynamic pressures of our own religious and artistic thinking, but its isolation is no simple matter.

A generation ago T.S. Eliot said of Arnold's *Stanzas from the Grande Chartreuse,* another three generations earlier, that they "voice a moment of historic doubt, recorded by its most representative mind, a moment which has passed, which most of us have gone beyond in one direction or another: but it represents that moment forever."[1] Mr. Eliot was both wrong and right, as so often making a generally invalid claim from a valid appreciation of his own poetic or intellectual situation. Arnold bespeaks the recent failure of Christian myth for those members of the English middle class who had become the carriers of culture, risen in a few generations from humble pious unself-conscious stock to peer over the battlements of intellectual history. But they had in their own right merely undergone what the explorers of the 17th century had already experienced. There is no new attitude in *Dover Beach;* it is long out of date as intellectual history. It was, however, valid poetry, momentary appreciation, significant socially as well as personally for that segment of Anglo-American life, including Eliot, which had come to provide the artistic voices for that dominant culture.

Mr. Eliot's critique has not only ignored the isolated explorers of the 17th century; it has unhappily forgotten the widespread revolution, social as well as intellectual, of the Enlightenment which alone made possible the new symbolism of all Romantic poetry, including the English, and led in its American evolution to the flowering of the American Renaissance. All this poetic production must be predicated on the rejection of the myths and faith in them only later mourned in *Dover Beach.* A crux of intellectual history that can be illustrated in the 17th century from Italy to England, from Bruno to Bacon, with wide social application in 18th century France, England and the English colonies (the relation to Christian myth of Franklin, Adams, and Jefferson) becomes a personal English bourgeois problem a century later, only to be adduced by an Anglo-American in the 20th as a decisive watershed for his own generation's sensibility!

Nor does the problem stop there. After his conversion Eliot published his famous manifesto, *For Lancelot Andrewes,* proclaiming himself a Classicist in poetry, a Royalist in politics, and a Catholic (Anglican) in religion. He never was the first; offhand, the second seems contemporaneously irrelevant, but the third is a taking of sides in regard to the Xenophantic revolution. Its opposite side was voiced at once, and intellectual history clarified by the Eliot proclamation in relation to the short, simple, but cogent reviews of Conrad Aiken and Edmund Wilson. Mr. Aiken claimed that Eliot's "curious doctrine that the work of art is an escape from personality" was itself a psychological attempt to escape from personality, that "from the psychological chaos, of the 'I' and 'now' " (which, as we shall see, is the essence of Xenophanes' position) he sought "refuge in a world of canons, forms, and rituals," that his book "seeks a refuge from humanity in Grace, from personality in dogma, and from the present in the past. Turning its back on the living word, it retreats into a monastic chill; and denies the miracle and abundance of life. But can the miracle and abundance be denied in this fashion? . . . The moment is still with us, it is a world to be explored, and there are still intrepid explorers."[2] And Mr. Aiken's voice in 1929 is the voice of Emerson in 1838 or of Whitman in 1855; such are the recurrent moments in history of similar voice.

Mr. Wilson's review is an exploration of the position of the contemporary American sensibility, its need for escape and the various forms of that escape. He closes, "We shall certainly not be able to lean upon the authority of either Church or King, and we shall have to depend for our new ideals on a study of contemporary reality and the power of our own imagination."[3] That last phrase should bring to mind the total work as well as the specific watershed poem, *Sunday Morning,* of Wallace

Stevens. Like *Dover Beach* for 19th century England, it proclaims with greater intellectual power for 20th century America a world without the mythic forms for divinity, a world simply of the natural environment and the human imagination meeting it. It, too, is superb historic statement.

Yet it is not new either. Its dramatic setting, at home when others are at church, with a parallel message, had already been used by Emily Dickinson,[4] as the splendor of bird and beast as *exempla* of the natural environment had already been used by Whitman. But it was not new then, either, if its world had already been voiced by Xenophanes as the 6th century B.C. became the 5th: twenty-five hundred years of layered history in which, in differing rifts or slides, the same perception shines, blurring by its own light an older radiance.

But I have not done with the perplexity of the critic before the complexity of the related statements about which he is to make his.

*Ash Wednesday* had appeared just before *For Lancelot Andrewes,* and a decade later the *Quartets* began, poetic statements with only an oblique relation to the proclaimed dogma, trailing many voices, but most significantly Whitman as well as Shelley, spokesmen for the attitude Eliot declaims and Aiken acclaims, a lovely irony![5] As poet, at least, Eliot, too, is historical; scrupulously faithful to his own motivating emotion, he locates his own place in time by his expression.

There is a further complication in the relation between historical expression and its existential motivation. The responses of Emerson, or Melville or Whitman, to dogma must always be viewed as responses; their reactive freshness is bound to a moment of liberation. The structure has to be there for the rebuttal to come into existence. Furthermore, the liberation is still so tied to its base that the search is for a complete substitute, for a new and cosmic view that may be realized in artistic, imagistic form. Not only does thesis relate to antithesis, but the resolution of the former is carried over as the goal of the latter.

The successive predicament is bound to be different. Eliot's poetry like his historical position expresses the confusion after that experiment has run its course and its point of departure has taken on a wistful, if, from the historical point of view, an anachronistic solidity.

Similarly, in another context, I have already remarked (pp. 3f) the strange historical relation of Xenophanes' attack on myth and Greek divinity to their 5th century use. We cannot date precisely any of his fragments, but he was 25 when the Persians took over his native Colophon about 545 (Diehl 7); his life was spent largely in the 6th century, so that his work may be safely dated before the entire preserved corpus of Aeschylus, Pindar, Sophocles, and Euripides — the apogee of mythic illumination in Hellenic culture. It is easy enough to point to the differences between the Asiatic Ionic naturalistic viewpoint, of which Xenophanes is a descendant, and the more traditional culture of the mainland city states, remembering the fate of Ionia's representatives amid the increasing reactionary pressures of late 5th century Athens. But the intellects of poets are not to be confused with the prejudices of the hoi polloi, and we must assume that these later poets knew his views in toto and in detail, where we have the skimpiest fragments. It is perfectly clear, too, how those views had totally captured the Athenian intelligentsia in the course of that century. Thucydides writing at its close is completely bereft of mythic interpretation, a man who grew up, whose mind and outlook were formed in the very heyday of the Attic theatre. And Socrates, whose life spans the century, was put to death at its close in part because he was in the popular mind a local representative of the godless Ionian position. In Athens' most creative years, before the dissolution of civil war, the most intricate use of myth and intellectual indifference to it live side by side in apparent harmony, Pericles, Socrates, and Thucydides evolving their non-mythical thought patterns in the very hours that Sophocles and Euripides are composing tragic choruses.

We can move to a further element of this seeming paradox. The rejection of the forms of traditional deity in Greece is somehow bound up with the belief in the radical innocence of the uncorrupted psyche, the human consciousness in its natural state. This is the key to the Socratic doctrine that man pursues the good, if only he can learn what is good for him, and Socrates in the conventional Athenian view is a disbeliever in traditional divinity. And Plato's expulsion of the poets from his Republic rehearses Xenophanes' critique of the traditional deities as the projection of man's destructive or evil impulses. These thinkers reject such emblems of man's inevitable nature.

Yet the creative exploratory work within the traditional symbols seems in its own way to be seeking to objectify the same intuition. It is somehow related to Pindar's ascription of the gods' cannibalistic feast to the minds of envious neighbors who fail to realize the actuality of a god's love in Pelops' absence (135-141). It issues in the cries of Oedipus and Philoctetes. Sophocles in his last plays disclaims the traditional religious view of *miasma* expressed in the bitter exiles of those heroes and sharply contrasts, surely for our acceptance, their self-proclamation of their radical innocence. Those who cannot see it have been corrupted by ambition, Odysseus and Polyneices; those who see it and act to establish it are blessed, Neoptolemus and Theseus. Sin is the exercise of will, the lust of domination, the use of others for the will's glorification. Goodness lies in the appreciation of the imposed as imposed. The radical innocence of Oedipus, which Sophocles makes the key to the action and the polar viewpoints it discloses in contingent psyches in his last play, may stand as the ultimate artistic Greek dissent from the doctrine of original sin.

Nor is Sophocles in this regard to be contrasted to Euripides. Where Sophocles is concrete, social, dramatic in the technical sense — eliciting value only in the clash of personality — Euripides is symbolic. His meaning for us must be expressed as the discursive statement for the imaginative projection. His playing off of symbols against one another is inconceivable without the Xenophantic revolution, without the realization, that is, that they are symbols, just as Pindar and Sophocles' moral intuition presupposes the original isolation of the symbol-projecting psyche isolated by Xenophanes. As you cannot come to an appreciation of Oedipus' innocence unless you see the significance of Apollo's ordination in his acts, unless you see his predicament as imposed and the individual's psyche separated from its necessary history, so you cannot realize the innocence of the Bacchae unless you accept the divinity of Dionysus. He who denies Dionysus, for reasons of pride or willfulness, is destroyed, just as he who denies Aphrodite, for reasons of pride, is torn by the dashing of horses, the symbol of sexual drive. To deny given force or discrete forms of such force in Euripides' dramas is to proclaim the individual will – and to perish. Failure of appreciation, in Pindar, Sophocles, and Euripides, is the ground of wrong action, and that failure is usually predicated on individual self-assertion, self-prescribed individual or social goals. Expressed that way, is not a radical relation to Socratic doctrine disclosed?

And the whole purpose of the *theatron,* of course, is to see: the social motive of the art form is simultaneous with the intent of individual dramas performed in it. Salvation for the spectator in his seat is parallel to salvation, or damnation, for the character before him. The Ionic discursive and Attic symbolic modes are different, but they share a common purpose, understanding, and disclose the same radical locus for it, the neutral or uncomitted perceiving psyche.

If you believe in pragmatism as applied to history, that a position will disclose its own motive or pressure by its results, then the great wealth of 5th century statement, symbolic or discursive, which immediately follows Xenophanes', should reveal the pressure to his. In the long run we must face the hard question of what in Greek symbolism for divinity led to its denial. If we regard Xenophanes as historical voice, as the crystallization of pressure to his own expression, we may be able to see it as issuing right out of what it denies. To have suggested what organically developed from it may recapitulate that original pressure. Let us now turn to some fragments of Xenophanes. (The numbers are Ernst Diehl's.)

> (1) For now, indeed, the floor is clean and everyone's hands and the goblets. Someone places the woven wreathes around (the guests' heads), while another places beside them sweet-smelling myrrh in a vial. The mixing bowl stands full of heart-easing mirth. And other wine is ready, which, they say, will never give out, honey sweet in clay jars, breathing its bouquet. In the midst the frankincense sends forth its pure fragrance. There is cold water, sweet and clean.

Alongside lie ruddy loaves and an heirloom table loaded with cheese and fat honey. An altar in the center is crowded all over with flowers. Song-and-dance holds sway throughout the house, and the joy of feast-day. The first duty for men of good will is to perform a hymn to god with myths of good will and clean words, after they have poured libations and prayed to be able to do what is just. These are the things that must first be attended to. It is no shame to drink as much as one can hold and still go home without a supporting servant, unless one is very old. That man is to be praised who when drinking discloses what is handsome as memory and his dedication to nobility's code (prompt). But do not recount the battles of the Titans or the Giants or the Centaurs, the imaginary creations *(plasmata)* of earlier men, or vehement civil quarrels — for there is nothing useful in them — but it is well always to hold the gods before one's mind.

(10) Homer and Hesiod have ascribed to the gods all those acts which are a disgrace and shame for men: to steal, to commit adultery, and to bear false witness against one another.

(11) .... how they have given utterance to abundance of lawless deeds on the part of the gods, to steal, to commit adultery, and to bear false witness against one another.

(12) But men think that the gods are born and have their clothing, speech, and form.

(13) For if cows and horses had hands and wished to draw with those hands or make works of art as men do, horses would draw the forms of their gods to resemble horses, and cows to resemble cows, and would imagine bodies for them of the shape each possessed themselves.

(14) And the Ethiopians (would imagine or draw) their gods as flat-nosed and black, and the Thracians theirs blue-eyed and blond.

(16) For not at the outset did the gods show forth all things to men who die, but seeking in time they (men) found out what is better.

(19) One god greatest among gods and men, neither like those who die in shape or thought.

(20) Entire he sees, entire he comprehends, entire he hears.

(21) For without labor he holds sway over all things with the heart of his mind.

(22) Always he stays in the same place, never moving himself, for it is not fitting for him to proceed from one place to another.

(28) She whom they call Iris, this too is a cloud, purple and red and green to our sight.

(30) So we can see that no man has been born or will live who clearly knows about the gods and all those matters I discuss. And if he should happen to say what has surely come to pass, even so he himself does not know: for all things their revelation is constructed.

(31) .... this is the way things are revealed reflecting what actually is . . . .

(32) .... such things as are disclosed to men's vision . . . .

Our first and longest fragment of Xenophanes has a just reputation for liveliness of sharp detail. It also has a misleading reputation for simplicity. No one, as far as I know, has attempted to relate it directly to the theological fragments, to the insistence on the man-made form of divinity, though a moment's reflection on the concrete texture of modern verse which assumes a similar theological outlook might suggest such a relation. We may preface such a vital interconnection by our definition of the function of the poem. It is the affirmation during its own enactment of the details of a social function in order to create a precise viewpoint towards those details which can serve as paradigm for the place of the perceiving psyche in the natural environment. That formulated relation between mind and its circumambient world will provide the base for Xenophanes' theology.

The locale of this poem is the locale of all elegiac verse, the symposium. The setting is, in one sense, the subject of the first fragment of Xenophanes. Now if we place the affirmation of that setting in that setting itself, we can realize the function of the poem and thus dispel its one dimensional quality as description. This poem is, on its face, setting forth the proper program for the symposium, but we must remember it is establishing that program not only for an audience that must have known it very well but at the very moment when such knowledge or appreciation would seem most redundant, at a symposium. We can from its imagery locate that moment even more precisely, the space before the viands have been touched and thus lose their quality as image, before the drinking which destroys the sense of what the aim of drinking should be, before the descent into the hurly-burly of feasting itself, an accompaniment, like the *1st Olympian,* of the ritualistic libations with which a feast must open (15), as traditionally an Anglo-Saxon dinner was preceded by the "blessing," by awareness of divinity before private pleasure. The Greeks, we may be.sure, did not wait for Xenophanes to learn what Homer had projected in imaginative detail, the right way to conduct a feast. The lateness of Xenophanes in both social and poetic canons should inhibit any sense that his purpose is to teach the procedure of the feast. Even less is it the connoisseur's appreciation of its code and implements.

Both for his original audience, or in its later use by singers at symposia, description is apostrophe, without apostrophe, to look, to see, to listen. Stop now and behold the flowers, the frankincense and myrrh, the gestures of the serving boys putting them in their places, note the carafes of wine, the drinking glasses, the honey, the cheese. Listen to the music and catch the sense of anticipation that spreads beyond this hall to the kitchen and non-participating but empathetic women (12). Before we move on to the moral or religious — but as the proper preparation for them — we are arrested by the scene in which we sit; its detail is resumed as in a circular mirror view to establish the entity of the social performance and the type of response appropriate to it, awareness of simple facts and the calm loveliness into which they blend. One is reminded of the famous Conrad preface[6] of the arrest of attention to gesture and the interplay of light and shade as the basis of art.

I said that the scene is the subject, in the sense of content, of the poem. But the subject of a poem, in another traditional sense, is the dramatically projected consciousness of that content, and the creative consciousness here, the poet's composing the lines, is projected as that of the ideal spectator or participant at the feast. Without a dramatic or mythic subject — which, as we shall see, Xenophanes' intent could not permit — the Greek poetic law of instant communication, the poet's and the listener's consciousness becoming identical, is obeyed. The poet speaks as spectator without an apostrophe that would dramatically separate commander and commanded, so that the audience may spontaneously assume the awareness his poem is eliciting and fulfilling. He does not whip the audience to attention; he makes use of the physical scene they both confront to integrate them all as common centers of appreciation by defining their visual relation to the objects listed in it. They might be composing the lines themselves, so obvious and easy the response they call for. Yet that response, physical and psychological, which they drift into before the noted instruments and atmosphere of the symposium, is for him the core of morality and religion. Its preservation for the duration of the symposium, and beyond it as the symposium is the focus of *paideia*, of learning ends and means, is the purpose of the poem. If only that state can be kept and extended, how safe a place this world would be, and how happy we would all be in it.

The wine jar's gift, *euphrosune,* is what in Pindar Tantalus loses as his punishment *(Ol. I.*58). Not that there is any probable connection between the verbal texture of the poems; it is just that they suppose the same Greek religious commonplace, that social solidarity and conviviality is the paradigm of paradise. But we had best be a little intellectual about "heart-easing mirth," lest we instinctively slip into Christian simplification or disparagement. Nor is it merely that one does not take a little wine for the stomach's sake but a lot of wine for the soul's sake, as not only the great worship of Dionysus but the reiterated ritual of the other gods in the context of the

154

symposium attest. The elixir of alcohol produces physically what the poem with craftmanship is at such pains to instill psychologically, a common consciousness, the loss of singular identity through participation in the common feast. It is not the joy of love or even social paradigm of it, for that presupposes polar suspension between individuals. Lovemaking, like drunkenness and quarreling (that last pivotal here) follow the feast's acme and mark its declension if not denial, the loss of *euphrosune*. True, as symposium members we can discuss love as also the bonds of our political union, the state. Plato well illustrates his appreciation of the psychological basis of the symposium where everything that is said about a common interest becomes common illumination. *Euphrosune* is good intent towards eveyone present in just such measure as resolves singularity and permits entrance into the common joy of being alive. It does not here imply anyone's becoming imaginatively anyone else, but each man's awareness is bound to a common center provided by the poet's imagery, the room and the things in it. Barring myopia or misanthropy, each man will see the same objects and feel the same anticipation before the coming celebration, *thalia,* which fills all the house (12). He will surely hear precisely the same words in listening to the poem. Through it an entity is coming into being in which all its psychic participants are submerged, that brief entity so well proclaimed by the youthful cry, a Party, a Party! To be a part of the Party is *euphrosune.* For its time span there should ideally be one consciousness. Such consensus, even if intermittent, is the basis of society, religious or political; it can become an actual psychological phenomenon at the symposium. Little wonder, then, that in classical Hellas such should be the scene of the promulgation of political, moral, or amorous meaning as between members of society who could be so intimately inter-related. Nor is it to be wondered that symposium poetry, elegiac verse, precedes the flowering of tragedy, which in the precinct of the god of ecstasy and wine takes over that function in a democratic society. When with Plato this form is revived in prose, it is for an aristocratic minority in that society.

For Xenophanes, then, the first function at a symposium is to establish the psychic phenomenon of the symposium. And to guard against its destruction. Its enemy, its destroying curse, is singularity, the reassertion of egoism. The epitome of egoism is the fight. But once again Xenophanes does not apostrophize or command. He does not directly enjoin fighting; he seeks to prevent its imaginative entrance into the scene by banning those myths which establish it on divine ground or its political projection within the society. As the base of the feast is *euphrosune,* good-heart towards everyone, then its poetry must be visions of goodwill. The mind must see in divine projection the psychic base for the feast, not its destruction. Already the Platonic belief in repression has supplanted the mythic or tragic mode of cathartic illumination as the way to avert the impulse to evil.

But let us make a further definition, by contrast, of the type of consciousness elicited in this poem. We saw in Pindar how physical elements in the substantial ground of the poetic enactment, water, gold, even the various conditions or relations of the individual audience members, were absorbed in the poem in symbolic or mythic appreciation. The literal ground was not obliterated in itself, but it became immediately only one aspect of the appreciation of those physical properties or psychic relations. It was not allegory, as with Latin poets, where the literal is a code language for the imaginative intent, nor was it, as with modern symbolism, an autonomous relation of chosen properties which by that patterning disclose the poet's intellectual or psychological meaning. There is, as we have lamented, no current critical term for this Pindaric practice of maintaining at one and the same time the given physical or psychic elements and using them merely as blocks for symbolic or mythic edifice. There is never specific denotation without imaginative reuse, projection into a purely imaginary system.

There is nothing of this at all in Xenophanes. Symbol is as absent as myth. The wine is the wine and nothing more. It is not another expression of the functioning of the poem nor even a sign of the elixir state it will produce. The bread is bread and not the staff of life for a community of men. Goblets are goblets and not, as in the *7th Olympian,* instruments of the toast for focusing social identity. Water is water, not love, or a means of communication, or propulsion to sheen, or figure for the radiance of poetry. Imaginative projection has been abandoned and the systems based on it. No new world comes into being, via the poet's imagination, drawn from the objects or their atmospheric inter-relation in which we sit.

As lovers of poetry we are bound to feel a loss, and this it is, surely, that has given Xenophanes a reputation for simplicity. Yet his very lack holds the key to his power and intent. We are not only denied here the imaginative craft which makes Pindar and Aeschylus so great; we are intellectually denied the possibility of such expression. We are at a point of revolution, which is always destructive as well as liberating. All we may have are the specifics, physical or psychological, and the consciousness of them. There is nothing but the phenomenal world *and* awareness of it. Bear in mind that Xenophanes keeps both those elements alive. His function is not merely to point but to elicit the sense − it is the 'game' of this poem − that he is pointing, to create consciousness of common specifics and conscious enjoyment of them. *The phenomenon of awareness itself is his controlling preoccupation* − without that we should never get Xenophanes' natural theology.

We can see that distinction sharply enough, if we proceed, as the poem does, with the same attitude, from the water and bread and honey to the altar and its flowers. All we have here again is the altar and its flowers and our, the symposium's, awareness of them. The altar does not bear us to Olympus, any more than the water bears us to Olympia, as they do in Pindar. The altar does not even, as in the other poem, bear us to Zeus or Poseidon. There is no imaginative or figurative leap whatsoever. And what is true of the physical altar is true of the religious act before it, the pouring of libations to the gods with the prayer to act justly. The religious act is appreciated as a religious act, but the consciousness is outside it in the room watching its performance and noting its social validity, not becoming a part of it that takes us out of the room, as Sappho's and Pindar's hymns have done. One reason we may fail to appreciate this distinction is that for all intents and purposes we now follow religious performance with the Xenophantic attitude, not the Sapphic or Pindaric, while often assuming that we are capable of the latter projection. Religious practice has become for us, too, a performance outside ourselves to be appreciated, so we may miss the drama of the historic poetic moment when it became such and was realized as such.

To argue here theologically is beside the point. We are dealing with the development of consciousness in history that no one who is honest can do one thing about, and nothing is served by taking one's stand on any theological problem. But perhaps Xenophanes' position can be appreciated, parenthetically, by an appeal to the cinematography of religious ceremony by Federico Fellini. In his filming of religious exercise there is no cynicism or denigration of Christianity; at times there is, in fact, an aura of sympathetic nostalgia. But there is no question of belief or non-belief, either. That has become irrelevant. We are simply spectators of the rite. Our appreciation is psychological, of course, as well as physical. Along with the visual detail, rain on umbrellas in an outside shot or the candles and priestly costumes of an interior performance, we are also made aware of drawn faces in a sombre pageant. We note the human elements elicited or magnified by ritual act, but it is the ritual as visual process to which we are bound, not its own supposed significance. These are the facts which the centering camera's eye is focusing for our consciousness.

This poem is such a directed camera and its centering of consciousness, and there is no attempt here, either, to make those libations and the prayer for justice anything more than libations and a prayer for justice around an altar crowded with flowers. Yet this is a religious poem, the vestibule, I hope to show, to Xenophanes' theology, and the spectator's awareness of the prayer and libation a high moment in that new mode of religious realization. But it is a very different sort of religious awareness from the imaginative act on which it is itself focused.

Now I have previously used the term 'subject' for this poem in two quite different, if traditional senses, the subject matter and the putative personality which is to experience its passing images, claiming that the one is the elements of the symposium, physical, psychological, and lastly religious, and the other the common consciousness of the participants or spectators of that physical scene and its psychological or religious content. These are two different things and must, on the one hand, be kept separate just to give their combination its full value, but they can be combined. The circle of awareness and what is perceived can be closed, can itself become an entity, the poem, as with Pindar, dissolving into what it brings into being. And at that moment the 'subject' of the poem is no longer its ground or content or the generic consciousness of them but both together, consciousness as phenomenon, the seeing, hearing, and intellectual seizing of form.

That which is depends on sight, hearing and intellectual comprehension for its self-realization, and perception, sensuous or intellectual, is simply the moment of that realization. By inhibiting himself to given points, physical or psychological, denying all imaginative projection, any vicarious participation in some postulated independent existence for what is perceived, avoiding taking off from the crux of the intimate inter-relation at the point of perception between what is perceived and the perception, Xenophanes has succeeded in rendering existence as consciousness of its specifics, consciousness as the realization of the forms of existence. Xenophanes' new theology begins in the room of the symposium.

That theology is not, of course, discussed in our poem. It is, however, expressed through it, implicit in it, as I shall further argue. That implication is raised here before leaving the texture of the poem in order to disclose the ambiguity of the last line, the injunction to hold "the gods before the mind." On the one hand, that is merely the last bow to the centrality of the libations to deity opening the symposium, for whose appreciation this poem exists. But Xenophanes in his rejection of previous myth, the *plasmata* of earlier men, which is an essential part of his new theology, has already clearly begun to change that conception of godhead in this poem. The new conception, then, must join the old ritual here. That new conception is derived directly, we shall see, from the phenomenological experience which the audience has just undergone. To appreciate deity is to appreciate the sort of consciousness which has absorbed particulars at the symposium. The one is propounded without any break following the other. That sequence should be absorbed in the final reference to deity which must suggest

Xenophanes' new conception along with the old. That is why the ultimate reaches of his theology are germane to the poem's explication.

I should like the reader to leave the poem — the reiteration serves as the background of the theological discussion which follows — with the two points already made clearly in mind: that it is built from first to last on the dynamics of presented fact and appreciative consciousness, the room and its objects as viewed by the symposium participant; and that it is itself the process for such consciousness to come into being. Those points, if accepted, are enough to reject previous explications of this poem as either a handy guide to banqueting procedure or the personal expression of the author's delight in it.

The act of consciousness is Xenophanes' formative obsession. It lies behind his poetry of social argument, claiming greater value for the thinker than the Olympic victor (2) in the community. A man is to be valued to the degree of his consciousness. It is a key to his classical critique of previous poets in their forms for deity. And his own deity is the projection of the act of consciousness itself, as the 20th fragment so clearly illustrates: "Entire he sees, entire he apprehends, entire he hears." There the experience of the ideal participant of the symposium which we have just followed is expressed as the function of godhead itself. Should not this fragment alone make clear how deeply inter-related the experience of the symposium to its participant and the intuition of deity as total perception are in the mind of the poet who created them both?

But as we approach Xenophanes' conception of deity, his revolution as it touches the nature of godhead, we should bear in mind certain assumptions that are often obfuscated or lost. As students of the Greek tradition generally we should bear in mind that the form of deity is a form of expression, an imaginative projection, not a natural something in itself. What is may or may not be correctly formalized by that form, correctly grasped by that imaginative act, but the form and its function must not be confused with natural existence, nor yet its validity challenged because it is such an imaginative form.

Secondly, we should appreciate and not take for granted —

for it was not only revolutionary with the pre-Socratics generally and Xenophanes in particular but is a precarious achievement at all times — we must appreciate the definition of the elements of *aesthesis,* of the distinction between what is perceived and who perceives and the modality of their union, that what we have are objects on the one hand and the perceiving mind on the other, with perception somehow their interrelation — the difficultly earned realization of the room of the symposium, the point of departure for epistemology.

Let me illustrate the reiterated failure to grasp these two essentials by an essay of G.E. Moore, *What is Philosophy?*[7] Moore is still, I believe, held in respect, at least as a sound point of departure, by a certain English school of analysts, and his American editor here speaks of "the power and purity of Moore's thinking." An extraordinary claim, for note in the following sentences how naively he assumes the quite unnaive intellectual labor that laid the aesthetic foundations of all epistemology, and how vulgarly superstitious he is, in the literal sense, in regard to the nature and function of deity, how unaware of the revolution which made possible discursive statement or of the symbolic thought which preceded and was rejected in that revolution.

"There are," says Moore, "certain views about the nature of the Universe so universally held that they may, I think, fairly be called the views of Common Sense. I wish to begin by describing those views, because it seems to me that what is most amazing and most interesting about the views of many philosophers is the way in which they go beyond or positively contradict the views of Common Sense: they profess to know that there are in the Universe most important kinds of things which Common Sense does not profess to know of, and also they profess to know that there are *not* in the Universe . . . things of which Common Sense is most sure." Common Sense, he then goes on to say, posits simply "(1) material objects in space and (2) the acts of consciousness of men and animals upon the earth." But he tells us there are views which add something very important to Common Sense or contradict it or do both. His prime illustration of the first are "the enormous numbers of people, and not philosophers only who believe that there is a God in the universe: that besides material objects and our acts of consciousness, there is also a Divine Mind, and the acts of consciousness of this mind." He makes a belief in a future life a parallel to the belief in deity as such an "addition" to the Common Sense appreciation of the universe. For his "contradictions of Common Sense" he posits the various, by now classical denials of the validity of perception, sensuous or intellectual, for realizing the actuality of the universe, including the view which — while not denying objective existence — denies the certainty of our knowledge of it.

I am not going to study the contradictions of Xenophanes to this neat thesis except to point out that Xenophanes is part of the Ionian revolution which first posits a universe in naturalistic terms, posits phenomena and perception as discrete for the first time, which assumes no powers or personalities outside that world, yet Xenophanes all the same essays a new conception of deity; and to point out that while he emphasizes the contingency of our appreciation of the objective universe upon our mode of perception, and hence the limitation of that appreciation, he never questions its objectifying function. But I do wish in a few sentences to deny either power or purity to this sort of thinking.

Moore's Common Sense is not, of course, common sense at all, that is, unselfconscious perception and reaction to it, though by making the equation Moore has assumed already what he wishes to prove and can put down as nonsense anything that may seem to contradict those unargued assumptions. But common sense posits no Universe at all, a point to dwell on in a later context; nor does common sense make any distinction between an object and its perception or the ensuing use of that perception. Common sense gets things done and never stops to ponder what is involved in reaching those ends. Common sense never uses terms like "phenomena" or "act of consciousness," and that is not a question of words: common sense is betrayed and paralyzed by such appreciation, inhibited against the coalescence of object and perception for immediate use.

Nor did the Greeks confuse, as Moore does, what "everybody believes" and the careful thought of Anaximander and Parmenides. Did Heraclitus or his audience assume he was talking

162

common sense? Xenophanes, like Heraclitus, lamented (fragment 2) what he thought separated him from others' assumptions.

For what Moore posits as Common Sense is the hard won distinction of the elements of aesthesis, and those who worked for it dramatically contrasted it to the assumptions of unselfconscious, unexamined perception. Furthermore what Moore lists as a hasty, unargued sequence, (1) (2), is no less than the dramatic polarity, the conceptual "room" established by this distinction, opening the way to argument about the relation of the perceiving center to its environment. All that Moore lists as the "contradictions" of Common Sense — here I refer the reader to his whole essay — are historically the evolvement of the problems of epistemology *created in the first place* by the highly conscious, intellectual establishment of what he calls Common Sense. The "contradictions" of Common Sense were brought into being by the use of Common Sense! In fact, not a one of them, no matter how extravagant, is a contradiction of what he calls Common Sense, but its projected, logical conclusion, as the thinker sees it; they all, that is, follow, according to the thinker's pattern, from the revolutionary moment of separating consciousness from what was perceived, a distinction the man in the street never makes. Greek epistemological climbing from Thales to Plato, and, pari passu, its rehearsal in modern times are simply put down as sequent sentences for what everyone realizes.

The same naive ethnocentricity governs the definition of deity as an "addition" to Common Sense. But such imaginative and imagistic concept has always *preceded* Common Sense, we must realize, once we understand what is implied by his mistaken term. The very positing of divine power for given process posits such process as beyond the observer's power, sometimes his power of observation as well as of control. The modality of such relation varies, of course, from people to people and concerns us elsewhere. The important point here is that the images of godhead are the imagistic or mythic mode, before man is conscious that the perceiving center has cast its shadow on the observed process or phenomenon, for abstracting and combining varied impression *as* process, for grasping the unity of form and the unity of the history of form. This symbolic abstraction issues with the. Greeks in a complex system of discrete powers, often intermingling or overlapping but distinguishable as identifiable process or power in action: Aphrodite, Poseidon, Apollo, Artemis. Ionic naturalistic abstraction is inconceivable without the imagistic abstraction or symbolism of two poetic predecessors from Asia Minor, Homer and Hesiod.

Historically, then, the "additions" to Common Sense are its foundation! Just as its "contradictions" can be seen as its historical evolvement. Moore has stated, as if "general truth," the accidental relation of modern materialism to the Christian postulation of transcendental deity, existing in and of itself apart from phenomena, a view of deity that is not expressed in Greek poetry from Homer through Euripides or in Greek philosophy from Thales to Plato.

Further, Moore's jejeune materialism, to borrow a term from Santayana, not only fails of appreciation of the imagistic mode of statement; it is totally oblivious of its own parallel nature and function. Words, too, it could be argued are "added" to things, since they are not a part of objects in nature, quite as unreal or imaginative in their own right as any concept of deity. Definition and discretion or any system which uses them are totally symbolic, too; any theory built of words is an "addition" to natural phenomena, not a part of it. To posit a Universe for perception, as Moore does, is as thoroughly an imaginative act as to posit a God, even if the discursive has been substituted for the imagistic mode. What Moore calls Common Sense is a late product of speech, a human symbolic "addition" to the naturally given, and such discursive distinction between what is perceived and who perceives it arose from self-consciousness in regard to previous mythic or imagistic symbol without such distinction.

Now Xenophanes' god springs directly from the new realization of the modality of perception; his godhead comes into imaginative being at the moment in intellectual history when we are told that all we possess are phenomena and our awareness, as selfconscious man aware that we are aware, of them. The fragments of Xenophanes can stand as an early denial of Moore's assumption of the naiveté of the polarity of phenomena and perception, as well as the denial of his posited contradiction between deity and those given natural elements of aesthesis.

To follow in a distant and differing vocabulary for imaginative flight Xenophanes' intuition of divinity is most difficult, but its starting point we can appropriate at once: the hall of the symposium on which that intuition depends has historically become the room of our consciousness again.

> .... late
> Coffee and oranges in a sunny chair,
> And the green freedom of a cockatoo
> Upon a rug mingle to dissipate
> The holy hush of ancient sacrifice.

Once again the lucid objects in the room and the selfconscious appreciation of them inhibits their unconscious marriage in the myth:

> "The tomb in Palestine
> It not the porch of spirits lingering.
> It is the grave of Jesus where he lay."

Xenophanes is related as Stevens to the ancient sacrifice and its myth. Ionia in the 6th century and Athens in the 5th underwent what different levels of our society have experienced in layered time since the 17th, and it is remarkable that neither the Ionian nor the Platonic attempt to intuit divinity on a new basis has been recalled for service in this reiterated theological crux. It is noteworthy, too, that though we find in both Plato and Xenophanes harsh criticisms of the moral intuitions of traditional mythic religion, we never get a call for a crusade against it. Equally interesting, we never find from Parmenides through Plato any effort to recreate it, either to accept it as it was against a new instinct or reread it in terms of the new dispensation. History and its gifts are not denied. What has been brought is accepted, and work begun at that point.

What has history brought at this point? It has brought the maker of myths the recognition that he is making myths; it has brought to the imagination which conceives godhead the selfconscious awareness that it is doing just that. It is the same

165

point in regard to theology that I would claim as the crux in the invention of tools or naturalistic discovery, the conscious definition of the elements of traditional use which opens the way to their directed and flexible manipulation. It is Xenophanes as poet or maker who has come to the recognition of what his kind's function has been. His inhibition against anthropomorphism springs from his isolation of human awareness from what it perceives. Once those two are separated, the one can no longer unconsciously cross over and give its shape to the other. The moment of recognition of the two elements discloses their previous coalescence and will insist on a new relationship between them.

In the Greek carrier of theology, poetry, this moment of recognition is, perhaps, sharper than with us. Xenophanes, like all the classical Greeks, ascribes to Homer and Hesiod the conception of the gods he is at pains to reject. For him as for Pindar *ton proteron,* earlier men, are earlier poets. Poets are the makers of *plasmata.* The shape and acts of the gods are their imaginative constructs. It is thus impossible for the Greek to appeal 'behind' or 'beyond' the poet for his revelation of deity; the poetic faculty and its exercise are recognized as the source of the shape of divinity. His disclosure was revelation. The absence of discursive discourse separate from myth for theology — that is coming into being at this very time in contradiction of the traditional form for deity — as well as the absence of an authoritarian priesthood over the poet as exploratory social spokesman locate the Greek theological revolution squarely in the poet's awareness of the nature of his own artifacts, his *plasmata.*

Xenophanes' illustrations of the wrong conceptions are all drawn from art, if not from poetry, from sculpture and painting, how the Ethiopians or Thracians would represent deity, or how the horse or cow as artist would represent his god. The argument is concerned with the nature of art, not, incidentally, as representation but as imaginative projection. As Xenophanes crossed the agora in Colophon, the shadow of a man fell across his path; he turned and saw the statue of god. From the moment he recognized the nature of the illusion, the illusion for such as him could no longer work.

The theological revolution, then, springs not from any metaphysical argument as to the nature or purpose of deity but from selfconsciousness before the mode of art. All that had been presented as most external to man and most sharply contrasted to his own capacity, divine power, force in nature, was seen to have been defined or limited by the shape of the imagination responding to it. Man had related himself to the sources of his own being as well as the external phenomena of the natural world by seeing them through aspects of the self.

Though the reader is not apt to accuse the writer of deliberately distorting Xenophanes' meaning in those sentences, they are not his own way of stating his recognition. But at this late date one has a duty beyond the easy rehearsal of Xenophanes' awareness of the human psychic nature of traditional Greek anthropomorphism. If Greek poetry from Homer to Euripides, from whose essential mode Xenophanes is now departing, has valid revelation for us, one must juxtapose with Xenophanes' statement of the nature and limitation of that mode our awareness of its purpose and result, the effective relation achieved by this self-propelled and self-defining imagery to those natural forces and powers, the illumination of Helen and 'Sappho' in relation to Aphrodite and of Pelops to Poseidon that we have already commented on. There is no need to dismiss — and we shall see shortly that Xenophanes never did dismiss — the intent of such imagery, the relation of the human mind to the powers of its own life or the phenomena of the circumambient world, to dismiss the given place of the human psyche in the natural order. Though as the heir of Xenophanes and the Greek tradition generally we may fully subscribe to what may be called the negative aspect of his discovery and thereby define the so-called (and currently fashionable) confrontation with deity, whether of Kirkegaard or Buber, as confrontation with the self — an act of self-delusion made possible by not admitting the Greek awareness of the source of poetic imagery, one could also argue, once the nature of that imagery is fully acknowledged, that the external world and the individual's donation within it can be most dramatically grasped in terms of intimate self-awareness, that self-imagery and self-projection as a mode of poetic or dramatic expression recapitulate the self's place as the registering psyche or center.

We must see Xenophanes as a moment of discovery, not just dismissal, and, like all discovery, opening, not closing possibilities. He is himself filled with such a sense of discovery. "For not at the outset did the gods show forth all things to men who die, but (men) seeking in time *discovered* what is better" (16). And he is talking not just about natural science but about theology; these are not yet, in fact, separable, nor is the nature of the perception appropriate to them distinguished in Xenophanes' fragments. And the same attitude towards revelation in theology obtains as towards revelation of the natural order in what we call science. Revelation is the world seen and the powers within by each new man in his new place. And Xenophanes' sense of discovery in theology, of the continuous process of revelation, is the lifeblood of the mythic mode in its exercise following him, the constantly renewed struggle for perception. It is bespoken by Pindar, "I stand apart; I speak in contradiction of previous poets," in the *1st Olympian* (52.36), by Aeschylus in similar phrase in the *Agamemnon* (757), by the whole aspiration of Athenian tragedy as constantly new revelation of the relation of divine powers to the human scene. The mythic and the discursive modes are different, but the underlying Greek attitude toward revelation is the same in each, and Xenophanes has provided the *locus classicus* of this Greek definition of revelation: that which appears to the human mind. "No man has been born or will live who clearly knows about the gods and all those matters I discuss. And if he should happen to say what has definitely come to pass, even so he himself does not know: for all things their revelation is constructed" (by the mind). *Dokos d'epi pasi tetuktai* (30). Or again, "This is the way things are revealed but like to what they are in their true selves" (31). Or, "All matters as they appear in the sight of those who die" (32).

It is misleading, if not wrong, to read these sentences as an expression of skepticism. Skepticism is the rejection of dogmatism, in the sense of that which is secure or fixed. But these statements are themselves the definition of dogma in the Greek sense, that which appears to the human mind, and so are analytic, not negative. This modern failure to grasp the radical Greek appreciation of modality has often lead to the misreading of *doksa* as 'falsehood' or 'deceit', in Parmenides, for example, as if he were denying the validity of his own carefully constructed views. To the Greeks such insistence upon the modality of perception establishes its limitation not its invalidity, sees it itself as shape, and how that shape arose. Statements about the world, even about deity, are constructs, made by the percipient center and must be seen as such constructs. *Dokos epi pasi tetuktai.*

Xenophanes' words, then, are an invitation to exploration, not an injunction to freezing self-doubt. Here, instead of doubt we have the assertion of the modality of perception, instead of skepticism the means to that modality's use. Que sais-je? is a voice of the 16th century marking, of course, a tentative step towards the position which Xenophanes is so forthright about, but Montaigne's famous phrase is negative, the single voice in a world of dogmatism, ringing with the futility for any creative effort. Nothing can dramatize as clearly for us the gulf that separates Xenophanes from any such negative skepticism as his turning from the location of the mythical base for deity in the human mind to construct a new conception of divinity. He proves in his own right the freedom for creation inherent in his epistemological stand. That he placed the source for all the constructs of deity in the human mind does not inhibit him from using one such mind all over again to bring forth a new intuition of the totality of experience in the form of godhead. Montaigne was precluded from any such endeavor, from any feeling that he had a right to it. Not until after the Enlightenment, which in fact he helped bring about, could such an effort begin again, could the meaning of revelation in its Greek sense, its meaning for Shelley and Emerson, be reborn, focusing again the given position of perceiving mind in the universe.

The radical freedom based on this meaning for revelation obtains throughout the whole history of Greek theology, poetic or discursive; the 5th century poets, we have seen, exercise it after Xenophanes in the mythic mode as clearly as he in challenging that mode. But there had been no hint in Homer or Hesiod that what they reveal had been revealed for once and all, never to come again. Xenophanes is working in a tradition of continuous revelation; the relation of poets who follow him is not different in this regard from his own relation to poetic predecessors. Homer's own freedom is exercised in his statement of the power of Aphrodite in Helen's destiny or of Apollo's in Patroclus'. The poet is free to *imagine* those figures and the ground of their behavior. Theology is a poetic, *made* mode not history. Xenophanes defined, discovered, in the sense of making self-conscious, the imagistic base of that mode; on this count we must separate him and his discursive successors from the poets. But in the sense of the possibility of new revelation we must see his definition or discovery in an unbroken continuum from the Zeus of Homer to Plato's idea of the good, as part of the Greek tradition, imagistic or discursive, endowing each new member in the tradition with the full right for the deployment of his centering awareness. Homer never went up on a mountain and brought down the law; he stood before the symposium and sang, and those who cared to — and historically Xenophanes is that moment of caring and working out its implications — could clearly see the relation between what was said and the voice which said it. Hesiod's Mount Helicon is the antithesis to Sinai, because his experience there is a declaration of modality, of the source of his own revelation. The source of Greek theology is proclaimed in the opening lines of the *Iliad* and the *Odyssey*: it is the Muse, the divine image of the poet's own power of statement.

Yet that traditional poetic background is, from another standpoint, a hindrance, not a help to our understanding of Xenophanes' god. It is a most difficult effort, to realize a new imaginative intuition with an old term. The old term is god, and that term, together with its unavoidable Judaic-Christian intent for us, is in a Greek context, as it was to Xenophanes, the figure of one of the Olympian deities. The term derives from the very imagery Xenophanes seeks to escape, and yet it must not be allowed to carry the full weight of its previous into its new use. Xenophanes cannot escape from vocabulary, from the inherent imagery of inherited words, but he is attempting to transform the old term to render a new presence and a new relation to it. We are called as critics to make a parallel effort and not desert him in midstream, not to look back upon the shore where the

Olympian statues stand in a row and single out the largest as his ideal but look ahead with him to the sky and trees and hills on the opposite bank which he is trying to focus as a significant whole in a new relation to the man who sees them. The term for the relation of that totality to a single mind is borrowed from the relation, wrongly conceived he holds, between any one of the observed statues behind and a worshipping mind. We shall return to this point as the central problem in the critic's definition of Xenophanes' god.

Another critical problem is posed by Xenophanes' monotheism. By and large recent Classical criticism has resisted the equation of Xenophanes' "single god, greatest among men and gods, not like in form or thought to men who die" to the Judaic-Christian God, has strenuously resisted any encroachment on the Judaic-Christian patent on monotheism, for if the equation is allowed, a 6th century Greek, has already proclaimed god beyond any human imagery, any man-form, a god through which the universe can be apprehended by that purely mortal human mind. The resistance to such equation is itself revealing. Furthermore, if my argument of Xenophanes' relation to Homer on the one hand and to 5th century poetry on the other is sound, Xenophanes' monotheism is born from Greek polytheism and maintains an intimate relationship to it, and Greek polytheism, not Judaic monotheism, will have to be seen as first producing the intuition of godhead beyond the form and will of man. For some critics this claim must also be resisted at all costs.

Despite recent criticism, the naive equation of Xenophanes' four statements of the nature of god (19-22) to the later Western theological definitions of god beyond the ken and self-imagery of man is not only perfectly sound; it is the classical statement of the Greek theological tradition which was absorbed in Christian theology and accounts for its imaginative search beyond both specific myth and historical institution. The Greek Xenophanes, not any Hebrew prophet, is the initial historical promulgation of godhead, not knowable in the form of man, which subsumes the universe.

At the same time, the critical view which denies this is also sound and discloses what, in another sense, monotheism historically has meant. I am simply juxtaposing two quite different meanings of the single term monotheism which have lived side by side, as so much in religion, in resolved conflict.

The orthodox Jew worships One God but he will not for one moment accept the equation of Jehovah and Allah, and vice versa the Muslim's One God Allah has only One prophet, Muhammed. Similarly, the orthodox Christian does not accept as a believer in "his" God anyone who does not believe in the godhead of Christ, the only means of salvation. To Orthodox Jew, Christian, Muslim the other's Only God is a mistaken effort at "his" true deity, who is the ward and shield of those true believers and from whose precincts and worship these others, for varied social reasons, are excluded. In each of these cases god is an identity, and hence the continuing need for the capital letter, a will and mind consonant with, if truly appreciated, the wills and minds of his worshippers.

This meaning of monotheism has nothing to do with Xenophanes, but those critics who claim that his monotheism is not the initial announcement of the Western tradition of monotheism as non-institutional theological definition have simply signed their own names to a definition of monotheism as credal integrity, exclusive Identity projected as deity. They have also, paradoxically, signed their names to belief, in however diluted a form, in the anthropormorphism of deity. The popular Jewish, Christian, or Muslim God is in the last analysis anthropomorphic. The first step in the relinquishment of anthropomorphism, after all, is the loss of social identity.

This basic point was made in a different context by George Santayana seventy years ago.[8]

> If we hope to gain any understanding of these matters (i.e. the relation of reason to religion), we must begin by taking them out of that heated and fanatical atmosphere in which the Hebrew tradition has enveloped them. The Jews had no philosophy, and when their national traditions came to be theoretically explicated and justified, they were made to issue in a puerile scholasticism and a rabid intolerance. *The question of monotheism,* for instance, *was a terrible*

*question to the Jews.* Idolatry did not consist in worshipping a god who, not being ideal, might be unworthy of worship, but rather *in recognizing other gods than the one worshipped in Jerusalem.* To the Greeks, on the contrary, whose philosophy was enlightened and ingenuous, monotheism and polytheism seemed perfectly innocent and compatible. To say God or the gods was only to use different expressions for the same influences, now viewed in its abstract unity and correlation with all existences, now viewed in its various manifestations in moral life, in nature, or in history. So that what in Plato, Aristotle, and the Stoics meets us at every step — the combination of monotheism and polytheism — is no contradiction, but merely an intelligent variation of phrase to indicate various aspects of functions in physical and moral things. (italics added)

This statement discloses the essential dynamic of that meaning not only of Hebraic but also of Christian monotheism which stands apart from Xenophanes' intuition of one god. That dynamic is the assertion, in Santayana's example, of national identity, though it can be, as in Christianity, institutional or cultural identity as well. The sin of polytheism is the sin of divided loyalty, and it is a varied empathetic loyalty which Santayana is claiming as the rational approach in our time to all religion. "When religion appears to us in this light its contradictions and controversies lose all their bitterness. Each doctrine will simply represent the moral plane on which they live who have devised or adopted it. Religions then will be better or worse, never true or false. We shall be able to lend ourselves to each in turn, and seek to draw from it the secret of its inspiration."

What may go unremarked in the rhetorical finish of those sentences is their clear foreshadowing of the study of religion, or for that matter any social belief, as expressive symbolic form, the viewpoint which in its technical application issues in work like that of Ernst Cassirer a generation later. For all his own distaste for labored analysis Santayana is a herald of the

173

appreciation of religion as symbolic form, epitomized in his oft repeated dictum that religion is poetry.

But also, with some historical blurring, he has suggested that the Greeks themselves had already assumed their myths and their deities to be the varied symbolic rendition of natural appreciation. He has implied that philosophic monotheism is the abstract synthesis of the differentiating images of poetic polytheism. As his examples, unfortunately, of the happy mixture of such polytheism and monotheism he has chosen writers who all follow the displacement in Greek culture of the mythic by the discursive mode. Now the switch to monotheism is in one sense merely an aspect of that displacement, and we could expect the philosophers to use the key terms of their synthetic systems in easy alternation with the ones they were assumed to replace. Our problem is somewhat different and more complicated, because it must face the problem of how the discursive, to Santayana the rational, develops from the mythic, how monotheism springs directly from polytheism. Plato's "rational" or abstract verbal system in which deity functions comes into being only on the death of myth, but we want to know why Greek myth was peculiarly susceptible to just this transformation. Xenophanes stands at the crucial watershed from which descends the "natural theology" of Plato and Aristotle as, pari passu, their absorption, free of culturally identifying myth, in Christianity. Santayana is, in effect, taking Plato's historical position as his own and taking for granted the historical process that led to it.

Yet his intuition is perfectly sound. If we go back before the revolution in Greek sensibility, the change from the mythic to the discursive mode, we find its own genetic possibility in embryo in that mythic mode. That possibility in myth is well seen in the abstract use of the term god, *theos*. There are two excellent examples in the poem analyzed in the last chapter, *Olympian 1* — "If a man hopes to escape the notice of god [*theon*] in any deed, he fails" (64). "God being propitious take thought for thy cares, having regard for thee, Hieron" (106-8). In neither case is the definite article used, and no specific figure or personality of the Olympic hierarchy intended, no Zeus,

Poseidon, or Apollo. It is the power of divinity not particularized, an intelligent variation in phrase, as Santayana says, which prefers to avoid in these instances the particular aspect of divine power located by denoted personality. These examples are adduced because they come from a poem included in the text, but lest anyone object that I have myself made a great point of Pindar's poetry coming after Xenophanes', be it said that this use is as old as Homer. Agamemnon says to Achilles in the first book of the *Iliad,* "If you indeed are stronger, god in some fashion or other has given it to you" (1.178). Achilles will fight, says Diomed later on (9.703), when god arouses his spirit. Examples could be multiplied. It enters the adjective 'godlike' with which not only Achilles but many of the heroes in supreme moments of power or beauty are denoted. No divine figure enters the imagination of the poet for these references, no cult statute resumes them, they bespeak no hierarchical role. Clearly, too, no question of will is involved when deity is formless, faceless, cultless, without any shred of identity whatsoever.

God and the god-given without identity runs as a minor thread, then, through Greek mythic poetry intertwined with the specific aspects of divine power defined by the major Olympian figures. That easy alternation Santayana remarks in Aristotle and the Stoics is evidenced from the start in Homer, so that by the moment of Xenophanes, when those hierarchical figures begin to recede, the poetic imagination, and its audience, had had a long experience in separating its intuition of divine power or presence from the confines of identity.

Now in the light of the argument of the previous chapters, the mythic or polytheistic propulsion to later unified non-anthropomorphic deity, foreshadowed in myth by the easy alternation between references to defined and undefined divine forms, is reasonably clear, the latter form taking off from the response the two earlier sorts of reference hold in common. The propulsion to both sorts of earlier reference is the sense of phenomena as given; it will be simply the form of response to appreciated power. You might say that the earlier difference is one of intellectual effort, the choice of figure and its hierarchical role bespeaking the more organized response within a clear

175

intellectual pattern. The depersonalized reference is not an improvement on or even a moving away from reference to personalized shape but rather a vaguer way of saying the same thing. But for us those depersonalized references are an excellent means of revealing the dynamic of the organized hierarchical definitions, a salutary inhibition against the delusion of the gods as separate, independent shapes. The undefined references, that is, disclose the defined references as precise imagistic form of the same response as bespoken by themselves, the appreciating psyche's awareness of its own position, its will-lessness before given power. (Undefined) god gave you your power, says Agamemnon to Achilles. The confronting hero sees his adversary in all his capacity as *given* power. But Homer's character speaks from the same point of view as Pelops in the *1st Olympian* in his realization of his capacity to win as the *donation* of a specific deity, Poseidon. And Pindar himself in the (undefined) "god-given radiance" of the end of the *8th Pythian* is clearly saying the same thing as in the Poseidon-defined radiance of *Olympian 1*. Phenomenon is resumed and the located place of the perceiver before it in any reference to god. And if divinity is the formulation or symbolic realization of the psyche's relation to presented power, then a change in the definition of deity will be a change in the modality of the formulation of the psyche's position before phenomena. That is Xenophanes' revolution, the attempt to replace the man-form shape by a formulation based on the analysis of the relation of the percipient center to phenomena.

That is why he may not discard the old term, god, which would for Xenophanes be the equivalent of proclaiming the death of God. And for a Greek that would amount to proclaiming the death of the natural powers focused in the perceiving psyche, which today's sun and the observer's death tomorrow deny. Cultural identities do die, and Apollo was a respected traditional but empty form for Plato and Aristotle, a "symbol" for the hoi polloi. But the natural powers do not die, nor the propulsion to percipient centers. The percipient center does not die except as single shape, which is the mortality of man. Its function is forever resumed as well as the phenomena it faces, and deity is the formulation of one in terms of the other.

From Xenophanes through Plato Greek theology is the struggle for new formulations of that relation. With Xenophanes historically we should first be dramatically aware that a new definition of deity could come into being at all; we should be as aware with him as with Plato that Homer and Hesiod can be cried down, and new formulations take the place of their mythic projections. But the new Hellenic formulations are possible socially and intellectually because the mythic projections sprang from the same freedom of the poet or maker to manipulate the traditional symbols, as best he could, to express his own perceptions. Perceiving man in his definition of deity is describing his own psychic predicament amid given power. And there was no law in Hellas which denied the new man the freedom to construct new ways to state that relation.

And that struggle for new formulations we may always relate to the name, Xenophanes, using it simply as a sign of a revolution possible at any time. In a quite different historical situation, no longer dependent on any direct relation to the intuitions of Xenophanes but sprung from the rebirth in history of the freedom which his name bespeaks, his insight has a new and coursing validity.

Let us attempt a partial explication of Xenophanes' new definition of deity with the help of lines and stanzas taken from Wallace Stevens' *A Primitive Like an Orb*. To resume again, for collective discussion, the fragments on the nature of god:

> One god greatest among gods and men, not like to
> those who die in shape or thought. (19)
> Entire he sees, entire he apprehends, entire he hears
> (20).
> But without labor in the heart of his mind he rules all
> (21).
> Always he remains in the same place, not moved at
> all, nor does it befit him to go over from one place
> to another (22).

Though it should be crystal clear that the emphatic *one god* of Xenophanes' definition carries not a whit of the social self-proclamation of Judaic monotheism, the glorious banner raised on high to float before the marching host, it is still by its

177

position clearly the dramatic word in the first fragment. But the drama of this intellectual as opposed to social self-proclamation is apt to be lost on us because we assume that there is such a *thing* as a universe, forgetting that it is a hard won *conception,* or, if we remember that, forgetting that such a conception, the universe, is also an act of the imagination similar to the projection of godhead. But *eis theos,* one god, reveals both those things: the proclamation of a universe to encompass all separate powers and their manifestation, and in the proclamation of that conceived universe as divine simultaneously revealing its establishment as an act of the same nature as had created Aphrodite as the résumé of the manifestation of given sexual conflict, or Zeus as the symbol of order or necessary sequence, the final reach of the imaginative power of the Muse, "The central poem is the poem of the whole."

But Xenophanes makes a new distinction between god and man: it is the distinction between local perception and the appreciation of the possibility of all organization and its total perception.

The old Greek distinction between god and man is most dramatically the distinction between death and immortality, the gods the recurrence of or the propulsion to the recurrence of the forms of life. It is a far more natural and instinctive distinction than Xenophanes' own, and I have already argued the degree to which the acceptance of man's death is a necessary concomitant of the worship of deity altogether. Xenophanes does not deny that old distinction; his vocabulary reiterates it now and again. But it is not his central point any longer. His central point is that god is not like to man in shape or thought.

The first of these distinctions, that of shape, we have already noted as the new awareness of the old mode, now rejected, of the relation of the percipient center to phenomena, the seeing of those coursing immortal powers which result in human capacities or forms themselves in the form of the human body or mind. The second distinction is a necessary corollary, and we are here concerned with the *activity* of mind, not its outward shape or form, thought, as I have translated it. The human imagination, too, is always local and must be distinguished from

178

its own postulated possibility of an entire view, the "miraculous multiplex of lesser poems." But "the central poem is the poem of the whole, and the world the central poem, but it is something seen and known in lesser poems," that is, local acts of perception or imagination. No single human act of perception resumes that whole, but all of them together may be postulated as a possibility. (We must remain inhibited against the easy temptation to picture Xenophanes' god as a *thing* or *being* outside the universe, listening to it, understanding it, or seeing it, a temptation created by our own theology and its imaginative pictures. There is no more room for transcendence in this new conception of deity than in the old Greek gods. Such transcendence is denied by Xenophanes' definition: the starting point for that definition, after all, is the natural limitation of human perception.)

But how does that local view postulate the single god? How, in Stevens' words, does "one poem prove another and the whole," how does the local act of perception, strictly defined as that and no more, suggest an entity in which it participates but does not encompass, how does it assert what it as definitely asserts it not only does not but even cannot know?

The answer may seem tautological but the patient elicitation of its implications is our only safe road: *by* seeing the single act as limited, and seeing that limit as natural necessity, established, confirmed without escape. By the total commitment to such limitation, the necessary function within the perceived ambience of that endowed capacity, the single act of perception can safely proclaim a totality which can be known only through such limited acts as its own.

It will note, of course, that every act of perception, its own in successive times and places with different viewpoints or others like it from different centers emphatically resumed, reconstructs the same sort of totality, centers everything in its own view, which is its center self-asserted in the perception. It will also, of course, note that everything perceived in that centering view — wine cup or loaf of bread — is itself asserted in its singularity, as a self-centering, and yet that each and everyone of the objects is absorbed, for all its singularity, in the larger singularity imposed by the single view. It may then hold

179

two appreciations bound together, that everything is known only as one by one in one view, but that the percipient center which makes that declaration is not any of the others, wine cup or vial of frankincense, or any one of the other percipient centers, fellow banqueters, who insist on the same singularity of perception and its declaration. *The modality of perception reveals the nature of organization.*

The act of perception leads to the appreciation of entity without which there is nothing at all, and self- consciousness in regard to the modality of perception turns it into a celebration of entity, first in the singular act and then in the possibility for them all.

For the appreciation of the mode of the necessarily limited act of perception is the means of moving beyond it. The self-centering perception which rehearses all others moves on to their combination in its own imaginative appreciation as the Possibility of their total resolution, even if intimately unknowable, in it. That Possibility embraces not only the single night's view by varied centers of singular objects but such Perception everywhere. I use capitals to suggest the totality of such imaginative resolution projected by Xenophanes' one god which is all seeing, all apprehending, and all hearing, the totality of a process that no single human mind encompasses but whose possibility it can celebrate. I know that to some minds to separate possibility from any particular actualization seems like a verbal game, but such appreciation of possibility is the imagination's grasp of the *nature* of its enactment simultaneous with the appreciation of its simple self-centered fulfillment. The act of perception, as Descartes among others insists, is the act of self-assertion, but *as* perception declares modality for *any* assertion, and the distinction between the single act and the awareness of its possibility is simply the appreciation of its modality. To seize modality in the single act is to make it a declaration of perpetual possibility. The single act rehearses but does not encompass the everywhere fulfillment of its own mode; it can declare, however, the total organization presupposed by its singular declaration. And that supposed total organization resides in its own imagination; by its self-awareness and consciousness of limitation it points directly to its own participation in its own declaration of the supposed total organization. It is not 'kept out'; it is allowed a 'window on' the universe of which it is itself the single declaration. There is no reason why it can not celebrate the imaginative totality of which it is the perceiving center while acknowledging that it is such a limited focus. Divinity is not, then, its mind or its mind's act, but it is substantiated by that mind's act, the possibility elicited by its very appreciation of its own limited position.

> The central poem is the poem of the whole,
> The poem of the composition of the whole,
> The composition of blue sea and of green,
> Of blue light and of green, as lesser poems,
> And the miraculous multiplex of lesser poems,
> Not merely into a whole, but a poem of
> The whole, the essential compact of the parts,
> The roundness that pulls tight the final ring
>
> And that which in an altitude would soar,
> A vis, a principle or, it may be,
> The meditation of a principle,
> Or else an inherent order active to be
> Itself, a nature to its natives all
> Beneficence, a repose, utmost repose,
> The muscles of a magnet aptly felt,
> A giant, on the horizon, glistening.
> (A Primitive Like an Orb VII, VIII)

> And still angelic and still plenteous,
> Imposes power by the power of his form.          (X)

> Here, then, is an abstraction given head,
> A giant on the horizon, given arms,
> A massive body and long legs, stretched out,
> A definition with an illustration, not
> Too exactly labelled, a large among the smalls
> Of it, a close, parental magnitude,
> At the centre on the horizon, concentrum, grave
> and prodigious person, patron of origins.          (XI)

>                                            . . . the total
> Of letters, prophecies, perceptions, clods
> Of color, the giant of nothingness, each one
> And the giant ever changing, living in change.     (XII)

Here, then, is an admitted abstraction, poetically given head, arms, body, legs. The giant, of course, is simply figure for the postulated totality of imaginative response to be distinguished from any single imaginative apprehension. And it is an anthropomorphic figure, though the intuition projected is in no way a man. What is so clear in Stevens' use of figure is apt to be lost in appreciating Xenophanes' god, as the usual critical comment so well attests in trying to see it as some sort of magnitude on the horizon. Xenophanes' intuition is, of course, related to his inherited anthropomorphic term, just as Stevens' intuition is resolved in a traditional anthropomorphic figure, but that term, god, must also now be seized as the whole process figured by it as a unity. It can not move, as its predecessors have (fragment 22). This dimension is expressed in Stevens as "repose, utmost repose," just as he rehearses Xenophanes' definition of god who "rules all things without labor by the heart of his mind" as the giant who "imposes power by the power of his form." In neither case does totality so conceived have will or purpose; it is instead a "principle" or "inherent order" fulfilled. Events come and go, just as their perceptions take place one after another, but the imaginative grasp of them all as a unity is dramatically expressed by denying their nature in enactment, the time and place conferred by act and perception. There is no before or after, no beginning or end, no location that discloses sequence or the natural history of natural form. A dramatic shape is conceived in which all existence and perception may be said to unfold. That dramatic shape for Xenophanes is theos, god, though for his contemporary Heraclitus the same fulfillment of inherent order is figured as logos. The difference in terms again marks Xenophanes' immersion in poetry, his instinctive reuse of the symbolism of Homer and Hesiod for his 'theology', a word not yet extant which will coalesce the Xenophantic and Heraclitan emphases of the same intuition. And Stevens as poet has as instinctively returned to anthropomorphic figure for his intuition of the totality of imaginative comprehension, the giant form of its singular man-defined demonstrations.

I say that the nature of act and perception is "denied" by this dramatic projection for the unity of act and perception, and my own term opens the door for the Oriental doctrine of illusion as well as the critical misreading of the Hellenic *doksa* as such illusion. But the overall figures do not obliterate human act or perception; there is no denial in fact. But their total apprehension, or the limited intuition of it does deny that the form of these local histories is the pattern of their mutual enactment. The point of view has been shifted. The kaleidescopic history seen as a unity, "the giant ever changing, living in change" is also a "giant of nothingness," that is, no seizable act or perception at all. Xenophanes' god or Heraclitus' logos is such a giant of nothingness, and in the last analysis no material or even figurative shape satisfies either. The unity they postulate is totally imaginative, completely projected. The symbol, theos or logos, is not a statement of material fact or even of its physical patterning but the attempted appreciation of that physical patterning as unified phenomenon.

In this connection it is interesting to find Stevens, thirty-five years after his declaration in *Sunday Morning* "death is the mother of beauty" — the declaration of the dramatic limitation of form as the very essence of appreciation — extolling the "giant on the horizon," turning from the drama of the single act of perception to that admitted "abstraction . . . definition with an illustration, a large among the smalls of it, a close, parental magnitude." It is clear that Stevens, too, is now obsessed not only with the nature and dramatic locus of perception but with the possibility of all perception. His climb from the oranges and the green cockatoo and their appreciation to the "patron of origins," "still angelic, still plenteous" is the same climb Xenophanes makes from the symposium room and its objects to the projected totality of perception, his god, his definition with an illustration.

We must never lose our hold on Xenophanes' sense of relativity, even when considering his all-embracing single god. Fragment 30 should be borne in mind when considering the definitions of 19-22. "Even if a man should happen to speak justly of what has taken place (in nature), even so he does not (clearly) know." That too can appear only as his limited perception (*dokos*) registers it. And this applies to "gods," he has just said, as well as other matters under discussion. The use of the plural is probably simply the dictation of metre, but to have allowed the metre to dictate it is itself significant in view of his dramatic assertion of one god. There is no necessary contradiction, if we bear in mind that for Xenophanes the totality is postulated, not expressed in the singular view. God as one, therefore, is the postulation as unity, not the appreciation of such limited various perceptions, and such limited appreciations can be expressed in the plural, though they all relate to their common symbolic projection. Stevens expresses the same thing in the last line of his poem in poetic paradox, "And the giant ever changing, living in change." That giant elsewhere is the patron of origins, the sum of all change, not any changing part. But again there is no contradiction. The aspect of the giant seized is always different, and since he is known only in those lesser aspects, a kaleidoscopic giant is made to symbolize the kaleidoscopic history of his appreciation. The giant, which is totality, made to change, is the same as Xenophanes' one god expressed as plural gods.

There is another aspect of the deep relation between these poets' intuitions. Xenophanes wishes to suggest in his figure of divinity that the necessarily limited view comes hard up against the marvelous sense of the universe as unrevealed, the final gift of its own awareness of its limitation. That unrevealed appreciated is the *etumoisi* of fragment 31, Xenophanes' equivalent of the *alethes* of Parmenides, neither of them, in our scientific age, to be translated as the truth. Truth to us is what is *disclosed,* as pattern if not fact, and that for both these thinkers is always *doksa*, what is perceived or registered, whereas these other words insist upon what is *not* disclosed. God will, then, work for Xenophanes two ways. As defined it is purely an imaginative projection produced by limited appreciation, yet that limitation at its crux, at its point of realizing what it does not perceive, dramatically establishes the perpetually unrevealed existence which is partially disclosed in its universe as in all similar but differing universes, and that dramatic relation can be figured as the relation of the mind of man to god. This distinction has, of course, nothing whatsoever to do with our theological hidden mind or will, the purpose of God working itself out mysteriously in defeat for victory, in destruction and death for salvation. No sense of purpose or will enters at all. It is a distinction grounded in the limits of perception, the distinction between what is seen or symbolically realized and other possibilities, never exhausted, of its being seen and recapitulated. It occurs to the self-conscious artist in his perplexity and sense of loss in choosing the particular aspect of act or personality for rendition. And it was a continuing obsession in Stevens, this relation between perception and objects-in-themselves, whether a jar in Tennessee or, in the poem I have been quoting, "the cast-iron of our lives," where the unrevealed substance of iron appreciated in its tactile or visual aspects stands for the substance of our own existences never revealed in our sensuous or intellectual apprehensions, no matter how plangent or varied. Xenophanes has, as it were, coalesced the cast-iron of our lives with the giant on the horizon in his single god, with the result that the single god is at the same time the universe postulated by the single mind, its limited appreciation of totality, and the source for the other universes of other minds, drawing their own imaginative circles which yet come up against the same unrevealed source.

The question arises, Why define the relation of man's perception to what it does not and cannot perceive as the relation of man to God? The answer for Xenophanes must be made in Hellenic terms, though that answer is, I think, mutatis mutandis, valid for our own use of an inherited vocabulary. But let me first say that there is no a priori need to use this term or the sort of relation it has historically implied.

You would not gather from his poetry, except for his rejection of Christian doctrine, that Wallace Stevens was concerned with the problem of god at all, though we know from his statements, in essays or letters, that he was pre-occupied with it in other terms.

"The major poetic idea of the world is and always has been the idea of God. One of the visible movements of the modern imagination is the movement away from the idea of God. The poetry that created the idea of God [note Stevens' Hellenic conception of its source] will either adapt it to our different intelligence, or create a substitute for it, or make it unneccessary. These alternatives probably mean the same thing, but the intention is not to foster a cult. The knowledge of poetry is a part of philosophy, and a part of science; the import of poetry is the import of the spirit." 9

There speaks the student of Santayana, who, in turn, drew his relation to religion from the rational freedom of Greek philosophy which in its climax in *The Republic* could use its own new vocabulary in place of the traditional Greek symbols of the Powers and our relation to them. That possibility, the forging of a new vocabulary, is always open, particularly to the dialectician, though the social duty for the poet, who seldom constructs his own abstractions, is gathered, it seems to me, in Stevens' first alternative, i.e., adapt the idea of God to our different intelligence, or, if he is creating a substitute, make that fact quite clearly graspable by his reader, more than likely nursed in a traditional vocabulary. That was Stevens' intent in his practice, though it can be found only with the greatest labor. His third alternative, make it unneccessary, is rhetorical: he has already precluded it as a logical possibility, though he clearly means, of course, that by the exercise of one of the other options the need expressed by the older symbolism will have been met.

But Xenophanes, unlike Stevens, was not composing for an audience that might be expected to make fine distinctions or guesses at them. He is writing for the intellectual leaders of a whole society, not a preciously educated coterie, whose sense of divinity has been sharply established by the inherited anthropomorphic figures, a traditional symbolism which is to reach its expressive height in the century following his work. Now Xenophanes may have rejected those symbols, but — significant as answer to our posed question — he does not reject for one moment the *relation* they enforce between man and divine power, between the appreciative psyche and the forces in its field of encounters. The sense of the irremediable predicament of that psyche expressed in its relation to the coursing power

Aphrodite, or Athena, Dionysus, Apollo, is carried over into the insistence on the inescapable limits of perception in Xenophanes. The concern, it is true, is quite different. The other poets are concerned with the play of continuing instinct or capacity in personal event, Xenophanes with the structure of intellectual process, but the relation of local endowment to the ever renewed endowing power is parallel. Similarly, we have seen in poetry that the relation of the individual to ubiquitous instinct or insight, Athena as much as Aphrodite, is always expressed in the form imposed by his own psychic apprehension. So even Xenophanes' postulation of god as the ground as well as means of intellectual perception is always defined by the limits of that local act of perception. Always as with these others what is known of the power is known only as that limited self realizes it. Yet that self-realization is never to be confused with what is realized and always, by others, in similar predicament, to be realized anew. The dramatic pattern of Xenophanes' elicitation of individual intellectual life in relation to its continuing source is derived from the traditional Hellenic pattern of the relation of the individual to divine power. Why, then, should he not continue to use the old term?

His practice, I said, might be generally instructive. The predicament of man, biological, social, psychic, created form expressive of and resolved by natural powers whose existence he never wills, presses for its expression, for its realization, and in a way to bring psychic peace in its wake. To move to the source of the imaginative essays of divinity is to realize that only the forms have been invented, that their propulsion is an imposition of nature. The vocabulary of any tribe or even, in our case, long conglomerate culture, carries the history of that propulsion in all its vagaries, the modulations between success and failure in its formal realization. Any philosopher or poet who dispenses with the idea of god is separating himself from his own history, from the richest vein of its expression of his own individual predicament.

Xenophanes' new *theos*, we have found, is consonant with the function of those it seeks to replace. In the denial of human personality or shape as the correct form for deity he is contradicting earlier Greek tradition, but not in the sense that those personalities or images were themselves merely forms of realization. With the Greeks the gods themselves come into being; Zeus has an ancestry. What precedes them is chaos, formlessness. This aspect of Greek myth all unconsciously reveals the propulsion and function of those genetic images. If we stand apart, as Xenophanes by conscious wish did, from the precise personalities, the specific definitions of the natural powers in human shapes, we can see that they are not the cause or purpose or judgement on the natural world but *images for the realization* of its creation, evolvement, and continuing self-expression. Once again the Xenophantic revolution is one of modality, of the form for the intuition of divinity, not a break from the function the earlier forms were performing. In fact, Xenophanes can help us to see what the Greeks unconsciously had been doing all along, creating their gods for the purpose of realization, for seeing the world and their place in it. Xeno-phanes accepts the purpose of the earlier projections while dismissing its modality.

But this point can be made even more dramatic in looking not back from Xenophanes to the poets but forward to the dialectical architecture of the greatest theologian of antiquity, Plato. The ideas or forms are just that, and their capstone, the possibility not only of all existence but of its perception, the idea of the good, is in no way man's, or concealed man's will projected in symbolic shape. Plato, like Xenophanes, we might remember, was bred within the Olympian forms, and his new forms, too, in part revive their function. His revolution is in some ways an Athenian parallel of the Ionian revolution, which in theology we may mark with the name of Xenophanes, because without debate it realizes the earlier shapes *as* forms and proceeds itself to use the term and build its epistemology as well as its theory of natural perception on their necessity: Reality Is an Activity of the Most August Imagination. Or more clearly Platonic — the link, of course, is Santayana — is Stevens' "central poem," his equivalent in that work of the idea of the good: "As if the central poem became the world/And the world the central poem, each one the mate/Of the other." Yet "It is something seen and known in lesser poems," as the idea of the good is made visible in the rays of the sun and the eye's use of them to focus the created objects of its universe. God, then, is a "principle" or "the meditation of a principle," "an inherent order active to be itself."

What might a contemporary scientist or even a "philosopher" make of Stevens' claim that, "The knowledge of poetry is a part of philosophy, and a part of science; the import of poetry is the import of the spirit"? As little, most likely, as of Plato's claim that the engineer or statesman's first knowledge must be of the idea of the good. But if he is an engineer, what would he claim was the nature of the mathematical formulae without which he could not build a bridge that would stand or a plane that would keep in the air? Are those formulae completely in the mind? If so, how does their substantiation insure a stable bridge? On the other hand, does the material or he ever dream that they are in it?

Are they ever postulated as statement of the circumstances of a single bridge? Are they not, as mathematics, the generic rules for gravity and its stress, distance and the weight of materials applicable to special circumstances which, however, always express the same generic conditions? Is he aware when exercising specific formulae that his mind is meditating on generic contingency? Is he also aware that he is hapless without the pattern's expression – that exists nowhere in nature – of those conditions?

Does he ever grasp in a single imaginative unity the mind employing the formulae, the natural conditions they formulate, make manipulable pattern, and that pattern itself? The answer is that he usually takes his local exercise of inherited formulae for universal conditions as complete and autonomous itself, that his will circumscribes his "spirit," to use Stevens' Santayanesque term, that he celebrates his performance, the successful bridge, as the triumph of the will, indifferent to the realization of the relation of his mind to generic conditions or the provenance of their patterning through which alone that will could be effected.

Even more radically, if he is busy, is his spirit circumscribed by his individual biologic and social destiny, blanking out both his own birth and his own death and the immemorial placing they bespeak, unaware that as actor his role is exemplary, its focusing power, himself, totally given, not self-willed, its capacities and their history the enactment of given power. In active existence, too, he is radically rootless, cut off from awareness of divine power; consciousness will vanish without his knowing the Announcement not only of the world but of his own local endowment for announcing it and his place in it.

# CHAPTER 6

## ETERNITY AS FORM: THUCYDIDES AND PLATO

But those who will wish to behold the clear (shape) of what has happened and is yet to be, sometime, all over, in the same or similar fashion, as disposed by mankind's nature — it will be sufficient that they judge this useful. (Thucy.I.22.)

We hold that the divine, apparently, and the human clearly, by the compelling nature running through all, rule those whom they (surpass in) power. We did not establish this law, nor were we the first to use it as laid down, but having received it already in being and about to leave it behind to endure forever, so do we use it, knowing that you or any others who reached the same level of power would have done the same. (Thucy.5.105)

And if we acquire this knowledge before we were born, and were born having it, then we also knew before we were born and as soon as we were born, not only the equal or the greater or the less but all such, for our discourse is not only of equality but also of the beautiful in itself and of the good in itself, and of the just and the holy, of all those, I mean, on which we put the seal, 'self which is', both in the questions we ask and the answers we give in reply, so that it must be that we had acquired knowledge of all these before we were born. (*Phaedo* 75c,d)

These are the thoughts of all men in all ages and
    lands, they are not original with me,
If they are not yours as much as mine they are
    nothing or next to nothing,
If they do not enclose everything they are next to
    nothing,
If they are not the riddle and the untying of the
    riddle they are nothing,

If they are not just as close as they are distant they
are nothing. (*Song of Myself* 355-58, 1855 ed.)

Thucydides' absolute naturalism — to call it pessimism is
already to view it from another land — binds him to his earliest
Ionian ancestor, the poet Homer, and the rigor with which it
informs his history helped smooth the course of obstacles for
Plato's great leap. These men are bound together by their
knowledge of death, death as the end of all that exists in nature,
not only men's flesh, bones, and intelligence, but cities and
empire. And not only cities and empire, but the specific
identity raised and glorified in it. To Homer, Thucydides, Plato,
everything passes away, love, splendor, great action. They think
the unthinkable, or what is unthinkable to the Jew or Roman,
or the ecclesia of Rome and Byzantium.

Urbs aeterna! The Eternal City! For Classical Hellas there is
no eternal city, none whatsoever. But there are eternities,
April's green, *natura,* what is born and dies over and over. And
there is the grasp of its patterns, the ideas of it, of city,
ambition, power, as well as of the grain, the vine, the bull, and
beautiful children, *ta paidia*, child or ephebe. The Hellenic cast
for eternity denies the eternity of identity, but it asserts the
eternity of form, natural and social form reintegrated as
intellectual form. Thucydides' history is not the denial, in this
supreme matter, of earlier poets' imaginative pictures; it is one
of their successors. Nor is it a down-to-earth challenge to later
Platonic structure; it is one of its bedrock bases.

True, Thucydides is a specialist in the first era of complex
intellectual specialization. As historian his projections vary
radically from the philosopher's or poet's, as the medical man's
from a geographer's, or the painter's from the stone mason's or
architect's. Nor can the new historian relate what he reports or
describes to enduring springs of action as the traditional poet
could, with his inherited vocabulary of forms, gods and
goddesses, for just such relating of the specific to the eternal.
The experience, of the Thucydidean text, is altogether different, too, from our experience of the fragments of pre-Socratic
philosophy, the attempted elaboration of enduring forms,
modeled not on natural images but drawn from speech patterns,

for either natural or social phenomena, the Ionian revolution which replaces the human/animal shape of antique divinity by putative verbal models of eternal process.

Thucydides is even further a specialist in presenting the military and diplomatic action of one war, setting up the powers and their conditions, their conflict, its course and consequences. His abstraction, his re-assertion of simple historical pattern, is, by present ambition, reductive, and though his actors, borrowing the tradition of stage or assembly, do voice motive, hope, or despair and disillusion, the warp and woof of Thucydidean narrative is a clear — *to saphes* — carefully integrated, and still irrefutably accurate account of comparatively limited social resources, their military deployment, the consequent external destruction, internal social strain and disintegration. Analysis, always analysis, usually by the simplest system, binary contrasts. Meditation, either on the overall nature of what is happening or on his purpose in recasting those events, is very rare.

But rare in both senses, for when he reveals ultimate program, either of history explicitly conceived as action in being, or history as making such action intellectual entity, he, too, seeks to shape supreme *agalma*, the Hellenic cutting or casting of the monument which can withstand perpetual pressure, outliving natural disintegration.

In his last Assembly speech, as reported by Thucydides (II.64), Pericles drives down to the underlying religious reality of ancient Hellas; it is merciless.

> Know well that our city has the greatest name among all men because we do not give in to disaster, our men more than all others suffering death and pain for her in war, and know well that she has got the greatest power ever known until this moment, whose fame will be handed down to generations coming after — even if we now, sometime, give way, for everything which grows must also fail — because we are the Greeks who ruled over the greatest number of fellow Greeks, confronting one and all in the greatest wars, we who built in all the ways the most magnificient and greatest city.

193

It is not the praise of Athens — that's expected — it is her greatest leader foreseeing her eclipse at the moment of her greatest power.

The thought, if not locution, may well have been Pericles' — we shall shortly see why. But they may not be his at all. The definition of the greatest city at her apex of power echoes the opening of Thucydides' whole history (I.1), as the "fame forever" echoes his bid for *its* immortality (I.23). These words seem inappropriate, too, on the lips of a leader encouraging a discouraged people, after their early reverses, just at the beginning of the great war. Somehow they seem shadowed by the eclipse Thucydides, not Pericles, lived through, as he wrote, for they echo, even better, his own remarkable vision of the disappearance of all Hellenic power, Spartan or Athenian, which also forms a part of his preface (I.10) to the unraveling of their quarter century war-to-the-finish.

"For if the city of the Lacedaimonians were deserted, emptied of all Lacedaimonians, and only the temples and foundations of her civic buildings were left behind . . ." and he goes on to say, in this famous passage, how her power would, in retrospect, be underestimated because of the paucity of her religious or political architecture. Whereas "if the city of the Athenians were to suffer the same desertion (of all living men and women), its power, I think, would be doubled in estimation over reality, from the clear prospect of the city's (monuments)."

It is not the usual Spartan/Athenian contrast that detains us. It is something deeper and more terrible. Sparta was unchallenged military master of Hellas, when Thucydides wrote these lines, and Athens, for all her humiliation, still full of chattering men and women, with renewed prosperity and qualified military power, if not hegemony, around the corner. But the Thucydidean vision, in both cases, is of empty cities, ghost towns, the men who bore the names, Lacedaimonian, Athenian, all gone. And it is a vision that was fulfilled to the last recorded syllable of its enunciation. Just such deserts of their own people both cities became.

This is Hellenic: the greatest historian of the greatest war of the two centers of Classic Hellenic power seeing their end, their

194

destruction, *their only survival their achievement defined.* Can one conceive Livy or Vergil amid the splendor of Augustan Rome, seeing it as its own ruin — for all that that, in fact, is our own image of Augustan Rome? "If there were no more Lacedaimonians . . ." — a thought which was thought when the Spartans were surest of their power. The Roman or Hebrew poet, propagandist of identity, is caught in its web. Since it is his own, he can no more accept its extinction, than know himself gone. The Greek historian, like the Greek poet, subjecting identity to nature, can foresee what we who have come after know as fact: his freedom from identity is his way to look back from a non-real future at his identity gone down.

Thucydides, we noted, put the hint of just such a fate for Athens in Pericles' own mouth when calling on the Athenians to fight even harder for their city's glory, Pericles, too, foreseeing his own deepest love, Athens, going down before the rule of nature, all things which are formed must dissolve. Is that not a contradiction; the appeal to fight and the vision of the end, the term of what one is fighting for? To us, yes, but not necessarily in ancient Hellas. It is a great tradition, a religious tradition. (It is wrong, of course, to think Pericles could have led his people for a generation and not share and act as spokesman for their deepest social and religious feelings, their hopes, but also their clear-eyed awareness of their definition, deathful.) What either Thucydides says in his proper person, feeling it intimately, in his preface, or what, in Thucydides' text, Pericles dares say, while urging on the Athenians to live the Athenian tradition of fighting, "We must bear what the gods give, of necessity, and what our enemies deal us with men's courage. This was the ethos of our city before you, let it not be shut off now — even if sometime we give ground before the law of nature, to lose the height of our great power," what both these men saw ahead, Hector, Homer's hero had said before. (And we should remember, too, that not only Thucydides and Pericles but the men in either's audience would know these lines.)

"For this I know well, as I draw breath and fighting spirit, there will sometime [1] come a day when sacred Ilium will be destroyed, and Priam and the people of Priam of the good ash (spear)." Yet Hector says this to his wife, Andromache, just

195

after telling her it is his duty, not his own ardor keeps him "fighting amongst the foremost Trojans, achieving my father's great fame and my own." He tells it, too, before assuring her that what will likely happen to her — slavery in Argos — is a more bitter vision now for him to carry than his father's and his city's end: such the definition of individual love. (We shall return to this for another purpose in a moment.) Yet he closes this very passage where he — like Pericles at Athens' or Thucydides at Sparta's zenith sees the city eclipsed — beholds sacred Ilium's destruction with a prayer for his son's fighting glory, as stern as Pericles' adjuration to Athens' citizens. "Zeus and the other gods grant that my boy may be as I conspicuous among the Trojans, brave in body, and rule over Ilium in power, so that someday someone might say, 'Why, he is better than his father!', as he comes back from war. May he bear the bloodied arms of his slain enemy, and his mother in her heart rejoice." This is the ethos of ancient Athens Pericles recalls to his people cooped in their city, looking out at their olive trees burned by the now departed troops, having burned their own plague-smitten dead. Yet for the next twenty-five years the men of Athens die bravely in battle, in North Greece, in Sicily, in sea fights off Asia Minor, or in the Aegean, and Hector goes out to run, and then stand to the death before Achilles.

There is no hint, in the Old Testament or Roman poetry, of the religious depth of Hector's preview of his city and his family's — his identity's — abolishment. Religious because such enforced relinquishment of identity is the will of the gods. Those who have made much of Thucydides' remark (II.47) of the uselessness to those in the plague who resorted to temples or to prayer or to diviners, as somehow exemplary of 5th century skepticism, have forgotten another Homeric parallel shortly before Hector's declaration of his certain knowledge of Troy's term. The women of the great families have gone to Athena's temple for the most innocent of prayers, Athena's pity on their city, on the Trojans' wives and little children. They prayed, but Pallas Athena said, No. That prayer, too, was "useless," Thucydides' adjective for resorting to temples in the plague. But the uselessness is the measure of divine indifference, to family or city history, to individual identity. Not divine disapproval or punishment — for divinity is not centered on any identity, as with the Jews — but the ineluctible way of life: what has reached apex must now diminish, what has bloomed must die.

As Hector shows his wife his image of her slavery, he closes, "But before I hear you cry as they drag you, earth poured over will cover me in death." (It is interesting Hector imagines his burial, not the pyre whose burning closes the poem.) Very simple. The dead warrior underground. This view of what happens to the "man himself" is Classic, standard, from the fourth line of the *Iliad* through Pericles' Funeral Oration. Everyone knows that oration, forgetting that its description of Athens' way of life is functional, an appropriate mode of funeral. Nor should we overlook that it is spoken in the midst (what follows the next twenty years is the crest) of the creation of the loveliest sepulchral art, marble carving and vase painting the world has known.

These juxtapositions, Homer and Pericles, and Pericles' Funeral Oration and Attic grave monuments, point both to Hellas' unwavering knowledge of death, and to the mode of relief before it. Death is annihilation — body, mind, presence — (the English word is ordinary, but it is the one chosen by Melville on the beach with Hawthorne outside Liverpool). Everyone at Athens would have crowded to Pericles' speech; he speaks for the city; he is chosen for the task. His view of death must be theirs, and he nowhere murmurs, these men now live a better life somewhere else. (The same, perhaps, could be said of the Gettysburg Address, but Lincoln was not the clergyman for a funeral, as Pericles, in effect, was.)

But annihilation, by contrast, enhances — it does not denigrate — the value of what has passed. It is in prospect of death Hector stamps his love for his wife, and Athenian grave sculptures present the idealized shapes of such as the dead set in *living* act or relation to their closest loves. For all the evolvement of intellect and form in the intervening time, Hector's Farewell to Andromache could stand as epitome of Attic grave *stelai* in 410.

Pericles, of course, memorializes the men who died fighting for their contribution to the city's power, and, through power, its resources and splendor, and hails the ease, the freedom, the variant self-expression in which that power and wealth have been deployed. And he also claims that men's lives are, in the record, morally transformed by such civic deaths.

But cities and their empire, like brave fighting men, are, in time, annihilated. In a later speech, we have seen, Pericles hints it, and Thucydides opens his history with his extraordinary vision of Sparta and Athens empty of living men. He can firmly grasp the possibility of action and achievement, determined in those places by those names, as gone. Everything, that is, except his record of the expenditure of human life and energy in the struggle either to keep hegemony, or prevent another's reaching it. Before the prospect of the death of cities Thucydides places the claim for the immortality of his own work. This is a striking contrast, and must be emphasized. "Thucydides' history of the war of the Peloponnesians and the Athenians which they warred against each other" — his detailed delineation of the action between them which exhausted ambition — can be conceived as a great grave *stele* for both powers, at the height of their power.

But how does either grave *stele* or Thucydidean history stand against death? We will have to see the historian's claim on eternity in relation to the poetic past and Platonic future, but we might introduce it by a word on the sepulchral image.

Fifth-century grave sculpture does not preserve identity or attempt to; that will come later. Those who have died are figured in terms of enduring models, beautiful youth, the virgin or young matron, or the mature but never disfigured older man and woman. Neither the features nor the precise age of the deceased are represented in the carvings. The sculptures attempt to lay bare the essential repetitive forms, either of youth at its acme, or of maturity at its fullest, a different sort of acme. And these forms or models which serve as "receptacles" for the varying personalities and lineaments of the memorialized dead are all descended from earlier models, gods or goddesses. (And it can be debated whether, in fact, this transformation has taken place within the 5th century. For some critics, including this writer, all these models, forms, are still figures of the gods.)

But as we rehearse this commonplace, Thucydides' grave *stele*, the history of the war, does not seem to fit at all.

Thucydides' writing is concerned to present, accurately, he well boasts, a particular event, so many troops under such a named commander meeting so many others at such a time and place, who wins, who loses, at what price, and how the defined event contributes to the growing debit/credit columns of the two sides. Specific geography, dating, military logistics, internal social upheaval (Athens, Corcyra, Syracuse), new alignments, and – beyond his finished work – the end of Athenian hegemony. This, too, must be mentioned, for even the overall drama, as well as specific narration, seems pitched to the unique – unrepeatable – destiny of one city in one time and place. How can a specific war, with its accumulation of lesser specifics, finally defining one center's loss of empire, ever enter the realm of repeated form? How can such idiosyncratic transiency become a shape in eternity?

Yet it is Thucydides himself lays the claim, both to the attainment of form and its endurance, one not enjoyed by man, woman, city, by any natural growth. (Even if Thucydides' "faith" and practice are not compatible, we must come to terms with the first.) In his few, much debated words about the speeches he will present (I.23) – and the speeches are the synapses, the central nervous system of his history – he holds the specific is *determined, enforced,* and hence can reveal eternal human form.

His own memory, he tells us, of the speeches he has heard himself cannot recapture with precision what was said, and those he learned from others are one further remove from the possibility of accurate transcription. To meet this difficulty what is said by his speakers (in the written history) is what the speakers would have been most likely to say, that is, what the situation in which they found themselves required, demanded, as he, the historian judged it, while he clung, as far as he could, to the general intent of what was known to have been said in fact.

The usual quarrel of critics is over the percentile of either element in given case, as well as over the purpose of the first, the putative, the historian's contribution. We are concerned only with that, hoping that, if we see how, from Thucydides' viewpoint, eternal form is attained in putative speeches, we may

199

also see how for him it is attained in the presentation of event, the claim which follows immediately thereafter in his forward.

Now Thucydides had been a military commander for the larger part of the war's first decade, and he must have sat and voted in many an Athenian assembly or generals' council in the field before his exile. No historian (Machiavelli? Clarendon? DeGaulle?) has ever been closer, in a tiny society, to the exercise of power, and the making of decisions, by speech in debate, preceding its use. Thucydides in this passage implies such experience; and he appeals, like a Greek, to the Common Mind, and as a historian to his capacity to set forth correctly the determining pressures within it which issue in decisions, in turn determining the shape of action. It is best seen in reverse: event $<$ action $<$ decision for such action $<$ the words expressive of the determining pressure or pressures for such decision. All together enter the "necessary, the required elements" of the great speeches which Thucydides feels free to compose, not as contradicting accuracy but as its own valid base, the way human speech goes down and comes up with what, in human nature, creates its action, its self-consuming destiny.

Thucydides' abstraction here is purely human, psychological (in its old-fashioned sense), and such abstraction rests on intellection presupposing anterior intellection, what is to be done, calculated and communicated by speech. Thucydides never so much as hints at entities outside the human mind or will shaping action. I refer, by contrast, not to the earlier gods (which are also enduring elements impinging on the human psyche, realized by intellect in specific locus), but to our own 19th century political abstractions in human affairs, determination of action, or decision for action, by greater-than-individual-impersonal-entities (class, economic system, power-transformation-as-process) which are not 'scientific' at all, but variform metamorphoses of Jehovah's will. The contrast is to the Hellenic shaping, as recurrent form, of specific human need or ambition. Nor are the latter instinct, in the animal sense, or as in a fist fight. Purposeful military action or new constitutional system is planned, and their achieved, or missed, shape, to make sense, must follow or reflect in the large the anterior intent. The means to realizing that intent is always speech.

"Determination," "necessary enforcement," as Thucydides sees it, proceed from binding each and every human psyche together, so what one presupposes or intends, in a defined situation, rehearses every other. Thucydides' modality is 5th century, but the presupposition again is as old as Homer, expressed there by the relation of Achilles' or Odysseus' action to the assistance of Athena, eternal capacity of mind. Without this presupposition Thucydides could not himself supply, as he honestly tells us, "what the situation demanded (determined, enforced)" in the minds and voices of his speakers who subordinate his recital of events to the human purpose or ambition expressed in them.

Likewise he assumes his modality of realization is precisely theirs, that his 'logic', as we might call it, the procedure of argument leading to decisions for such and such action, is a rehearsal of what theirs "would have been, as I see it." This double relation, of predictable response and echoing intellection of it, is his "faith" as historian which binds all men together. He calls it quite simply "human nature – *to anthropinon*", and stakes his immortal fame not on unique achievement or unique insight but on his mediation of the eternal bases of human nature which shape social action.

It follows that the sum total of events, determined by such human nature through such intellection, should present an overall sequence that will be repeated forever in recurrent imperial ambition. Our own undeniable demand for aetiological circumstances makes it impossible as historians to follow Thucydides here. Rome wins; Carthage loses: we want to know why. There is no need here to develop this contrast and *its* causes. We want only to relate the overall Thucydidean "faith" in an eternal human nature to his transcendence of identity.

Athens for him is paradigm, even her imperial scope and its loss. For Thucydides the Peloponnesian war is not idiosyncratic, and his very passion for accuracy, which we tend to see simply as the professional historian's, derives from the faith that the facts, and their motive-disclosing interconnection, can reveal eternal pattern. With such intellectual ambition must he not take infinite pains, as he tells us (I.21) he has? Through his work he supposed Athens would become the City of Empire. The extent of her 5th century power is his prompting to the research and writing which can credit the claim. Here he, too, is bound by circumstance. But at last we must see him not as the forerunner of von Ranke and Pastor — bound to identity in life and death — but as Homer's heir: Troy as the Beleaguered City, the Achaians as Imperial Invaders, Troy's first fighter foreseeing his city's end, the greatest Achaian fighter the most fully conscious of and accepting of his own inevitable death.

Thucydides' purpose, then, is not to eternalize Athens, whose eventual disappearance he forsees, but through Athens' course to disclose the elements of imperial command and its loss: self-inhibiting leadership and internal harmony which support, individual ambition and civil strife which undercut the power base, the price — perpetual conflict — to maintain hegemony, the irreversible pressure of imperial growth, the popular hunger for its fruits, the interplay of individual and democratic decisions. We isolate a few elements which have recurred and are recurring now, to substantiate, not as independent commentator, but under the impact of present event — "what is present before us" — the validity, at least in part, of the ancient historian's motive in composition, why his work was "put together": *to reach eternity through Athens, not in it.*

Pattern derived from analysis of the elements and their relation in a given or identified social cosmos which, by that analysis, may be applied to others, whatever their identity: this is, of course, the essence of "political science," which reveals at once its origin in the debates of the polis, the Greek city. When, twenty or twenty-five years into the next century, another Athenian analyzed the elements of various government, in terms, be it remembered, of the constant factors of the human psyche, and then rearranged those elements in the fashion, he held, would best ensure harmony and endurance, he is free, for such rearrangement, free for his play with the form of the city, simultaneously thinking and not thinking of Athens, because, with a different purpose, he is using the "faith" of the Thucydidean preface: the possibility of isolating beyond identity the eternal nature of man or government expressed in any.

202

Here we have entered the realm of idea, both in its ordinary and its Platonic dimension, the repeatable intellection of constant psychological and social function.

The mode of search not only in *Republic* but in the dialogues which precede it come out of the mode of thought of Periclean Athens, as our own sense of intellectual history as an unbroken continuum would make necessary hypothesis. Plato's greatest debt to Periclean Athens is his modality, his search for definitions. The Platonic venture does not start with Greek poetry or earlier Greek philosophy, the only extant alternative formulations; it starts with the attempt to make speech sets of recurring validity which express those modes of individual behavior which coalesce as purposeful or harmonious social action: courage, piety, self-control, capacity for learning, validity of teaching, sexual drive expressed in social cohesion, etc. Soldier, citizen, son/father, student/teacher, lover/lover: these are the roles whose irreplaceable elements are to be isolated, reformulated, and then used.

Why should the roles and their modes have to be reformulated? In terms of intellectual history, because the relation of governance and instance, of enduring form and its local expression had been blurred, where not obliterated, the use of images, gods, goddesses, heroes, as the models of behavior, of psychic expression in society. Thucydides, like Pericles, ignores this older modality, and Plato, who after all is later, is even farther removed from it than they. He seeks to restore its function (as we have seen, Thucydides all unconsciously did), but he never revives it. Dialectic has replaced poetry, which may supply elegant or summary illustrations for it, the slow stage-by-stage assembly of the disparate but integrated social roles and their modes.

The Athenian intellectual achievement must be distinguished though never separated from the Ionian revolution (a distinction Aristotle, like many modern historians, ignores), the Ionian transformation of myth into self-conscious discourse, geography, history, natural philosophy, logic: modalities and their exercise, as the very terms show, which lie at the base of all Western thought. But the Ionians, starting with the great images, the goddesses and gods, which served as "grids" for the natural bases of

203

environmental life and human interaction with it, were focused on process, on replacing the poetic comprehension of overall process by self-conscious manipulable speech-sets. They never relinquished the human/nature interrelation of the poetic mode, where later Athenian specialization begins to make them separate studies. "Origins" or "bases," "the overall system" (*logos*), "the unlimited," "under-lying truth," these are key terms in the Ionian program.

But the specifically Athenian intellectual achievement is focused on, derives from an obsession with modes of behavior, as they may be disclosed in speech patterns, dramatic self-assertion or analysis: tragedy and comedy, Sophistic dialectic, Thucydides' speeches, the Socratic/Platonic dialogue. The social continuity — individual or social behavior 'projected' or analyzed — arches over the peculiarly Athenian monuments in speech. Athenian thought does not start, like the Ionian, with overall process and its systematization, and the attempt to make such a system of Plato's "forms" or "ideas" has radically distorted both their impetus and use.

From *Laches* to *Republic* Plato may be conceived as continuing 5th century debate on individual and social behavior. His dramatic *mise-en-scène* is just such 5th century social debate. On what basis, by what knowledge is a choice of action or behavior made? Not only is the Socratic problem exemplary 5th century/Thucydidean; so also is the mode of approach, the attempt to reach a generalizing verbal structure for a given case; not only the externals — social scene and debate — but the internal intellectual mode binds the 4th and 5th century, the instance generalized. (This, from start to finish, is the practice of Thucydides' speakers, and of Thucydides himself: the instance, the specific historical instance, of what action to take, expressed, as if it set down, the law of action or reaction for every other instance of the same kind.)

As much as Thucydides' or a tragic poet's, Plato's perception is grounded in society-in-being; he does not, in the contemporary sense, need a system — a pattern to unify variant perception — because what he thinks or realizes is at once assumed into, to be deployed by that system-in-being, society itself. From early Socratic aporia to *The Laws* he is concerned with how society 'works', how it can be made successful, what values best sustain it. Plato's assumed "system," society, then, is not doctrinal or theoretical, but functional; a variety of viewpoints, a variety of "conclusions" do not disturb this sort of system, and all intellectual constructs must be subordinated to their end in social illumination. While with Aristotle or Epicurus we face autonomous intellectual systematization, in Plato the social nexus is never loosed, so that his thought, like religious myth or civic architecture, is magnified by its deployment for community beyond itself.

If society itself is our assumed system, it should be clear why Plato's earliest abstractions, courage or piety, temperance or justice, can not be put down as "concepts." Whether men will stand and fight, cheat their neighbors, at law or by force, inhibit ambition or sexual goal are questions as to whether a social order can endure or prosper, questions for an Hermocrates or Cleon, for a Nicias or Alcibiades. How the functional virtues are to be accurately defined in a revolutionary time, so that they may be known and sustained, that is a problem. But not whether "justice is something or not."

But what *sort* of a something? Justice can not of itself be seen, as a tree or a street is seen. Instances can be described, that is, the men and the situation where the instance of justice, or injustice, of courage or cowardice, is presumed to be illustrated. But the virtue itself? It does not lend itself to visual imagery; it exists and exists as a very real differentia of experience, but if we try to define it, for many instances, we can not describe either a shape, or a rule, or a ruling shape — we can only posit one.

That the instances of a given virtue are bound together is assumed by ordinary speech, and Plato in his adumbration of such binding-in-experience-or-fact uses terms appropriate to, if not appropriated from, speech-in-society, *koinonia, metechei, parousia,* holding in common or communion, share in or have a part in, presence. The Platonic terms for the relation of the posited experimental differentiae and their instances send us immediately to the social relationship which guarantees that a word has, more or less, the same meaning for those who use it; or, if the words are seen as a system, the way a word derives its meaning from its place in a common language. The Platonic forms are, of course, all known by the words for them, but the disclosure of the nature of speech, to the degree that it is ever disclosed, is the disclosure of the position of psyche-in-society, not only a binding of all the psyches which deploy a given speech but their binding by common "values" expressed in their use of "moral" terms. That binding is no language game; it is the way society is sustained. The word for a moral differentia is not a concept but a "control" of a continuing mode of reaction.

And just as the members of a society come into it and disappear, so do instances of its moral reactions appear and disappear, while the society or those values go on. The ground for Plato's early distinction between enduring and transient existence is also drawn from society. The continuity is the value, the instance its affirmation or denial. Such distinction is always anywhere known, or enforced, socially.

So deep and strong in Plato's mind is the social nexus whereby first speech and then abstract thought is born, that when he turns to illustrate, by concrete exemplars, his difficult immaterial — if materially realized — moral paradigms, his instinct comes up with human *artifacts,* shuttle, bridle, bed and table, the means by which we weave, control a horse for war or transport, sleep or eat together. In all these cases the man-created social function or purpose is the illustration of the idea, the variant — and variantly shaped — concretizations illustrative of the differing dramatic contexts in which moral distinctions are elicited. And in both cases, both with the artifact and the moral virtue, it should be clear how the singular concretization realizes the function or purpose, while the function or purpose can not be equated to, or made to seem "like" any particular instance or concretization. [2]

The Platonic "world" is purely human, altogether social, a world made by transformation, the use of form, in our sense, to mediate every jot, every iota of the natural world from which it, originally, was constructed. The urban, political, amorous, purely human Socratic response Plato limns at the beginning of *Phaedrus* is typically Platonic, the unbroken mediation of the given by its human resolution as consciousness and the celebration of such consciousness.

First and foremost, consciousness of affect as value. That remains an unresolved "scandal" for much Platonic analysis. How strange and, in contemporary terms, how intellectually self-defeating it can be made to seem. How removed, on the one hand, from the Hellenic naturalism from which it evolves, and, on the other, from the structures, psychological or linguistic, we now use to place it.

Take the erotic paradigm. Plato arrives not at a unifying propulsive center, mythical Aphrodite as new case-defining standard or putative unifying form, nor, for all the wealth of by-the-way illustration, does he arrive at an original analysis of the human psyche in the grip of desire. Instead Plato sums up erotic manifestation as beauty, and then uses beauty as disclosed in erotic context as the natural metaphor for value in a variety of non-erotic contexts.

It is easy enough to see that by isolating in word the affect or impression of desired body on desiring mind as beauty, Plato has created the idea or form he claims to have climbed to and opened for further intellectual use. The word, beauty, *separates* the affect from either its source or recipient, has made it a *something-in-itself* no longer *corruptible* by the sometime desirable bodies from which the impulse to the described affect first sprang, no longer subject to disillusion or decay. *Separation, something-in-itself, incorruptibility*: Plato's terms for his ideas. They are sound "attributes" of affects stated as abstractions.

Or, if we do not dismiss the uses of Platonic beauty as verbal self-delusion, we can study his use of such abstraction, as Socrates' heir isolating the universal, that is, general term, by which many and quite variant images are united; we can posit the "family" of beauty, whose members bear some resemblance to one another, as Plato moves from lovely bodies to beautiful character or habits, to social institutions, and at last to modes of knowledge as beautiful, ending finally – where contemporary analysis leaves him altogether – in the knowledge of beauty itself (*Sym.* 211c). From this standpoint, if Plato was misled into conflating speech and natural phenomenon, at least he began to see and show how speech itself works, how one term serves several occasions, so that mind can control or structure experience, economically, if inaccurately; and by self-consciousness in regard to this misleading economy, by the isolation of the general term and an attempt at the definition of variant application, has begun the careful process of verbal distinction by which the validity of statement is upheld or discounted.

Much earlier, as early as Aristotle, long before the *ideas* were dismissed as verbalizations, or rehabilitated as verbal systematization, they were seen as some sort of mystic progenitors, virile archetypes impregnating supine matter with their own shapes. (*Meta.*987b.)

But for Plato clearly his immortal shapes were more than useful generalizations or hypostasized values and something other than arcane models of the sensible world.[3]

The Platonic 'world', we have suggested, is a social world, seen through, assimilated by individual consciousness; it is a world of one human psyche in relation to others; first and last, it is a functioning world. All functions can be plotted as relations; social functions, the sustaining virtues or values become, in the fact, relations between men; individual functioning is consciousness of relation in action, intellectual and emotional, assimilative or affective. If we define social function as sustained relation, in order to understand or maintain a function we must know the terms of the structure of the relation. In both emotional and intellectual life such structure of relation is most readily and sharply felt as the impact of that relation on the registering consciousness.

Let us then, roughly, define Platonic *idea* or *eidos* as the realization of relation entitized for control or manipulation by the name for repeated affect in the centering psyche, which alone establishes such structures and names them by the extrapolation of just such repeated affect.

We can not ever define imaginative entities with sufficient accuracy to render them in terms of immediate experience; we can only point to what they are intended to do. The Platonic *eide* or *ideai* reassert the absolute contingency of every event without postulating determining fiat or will, personality or mind (though later, of course, these creep back by way of poetic illustration). The Platonic *idea* is the historic crux of two

208

divergent inheritances, Ionian analysis and mythic form, the extraordinary mingling of insistent definition from specific man-mind point of view — the inheritance within which Xenophanes and Thucydides entirely work — and the previous projection of imaginary shape to control continuing process or repeated event as the determining form of that process or event. We have to stress these opposing sides, defined point of view and the extrapolation of unifying image, to realize the originality and grandeur of their conjunction in Platonic *ideai.*

Plato sets up certain conditions for his *eide,* and we may not wish them away. Repeatedly, he uses word for affect, good or beautiful, for the greatest *ideai,* yet we must find some way to see these overarching *eide* as analogous in their nature to the cohesive social disciplines, courage, piety, self-control and also with the primary differentiae in the intellection of sense-perception, large or small, same or opposite, equal or asymmetrical, odd or even, one, two, three, with side glances at sensation divided in similar binary fashion, hot or cold, moving or dead.

Nor can we wish away his insistence that these *eide* are immaterial, incorporeal, not located in time or space, for all that they are repeatedly realized in specific material or corporeal situations in space and time. They can not be seen visually, but grasped intellectually, though they determine the significance of the visible shapes or events which participate in their incorporeal presence. They can not be destroyed; they resist change or transformation, though all else, coming and going in their embrace, is changed, or corrupted. Whatever their nature or function, their recognition is a purely human achievement, a most difficult, most important one.

Anything Plato writes is clearly projected as what one man, sitting and talking, thinks or feels in regard to a postulated problem and tells others intent on the same problem. Dialogue, before it is dialectic, the evolvement through debate of theory, is definition of point of view. Such defined point of view delimits any theory or construct projected by Plato through any of his dramatically limited speakers. All the so-called absolute values, be it remembered, are projected by an individual consciousness and can be seen to be so limited. That individual consciousness has built them, too, from the appreciation of local situations, and they are deployed in such local situations.

Furthermore, any absolute value is projected as itself defining an exclusive relation. Plato, for example, insists on absolute bigness or absolute smallness in a context (*Phaedo* 102) where commentators often attempt to rescue him from his own 'error' by integrating his absolute points of view in an overall — but removed — scale, where size, of course, depends on point of view, but must be realized, within that scale, as degree, not, as with Plato, as ultimate 'form', big or small. But Plato has made it crystal clear that he understands comparative degree — three men of differing height are used — and the use of the same material physical dimension — a man's head size — to establish, on the one hand, the large, and on the other, the small. Yet he insists *in any one of the single contexts* that absolute largeness or absolute smallness determines the relation. He is bent on the drama of relation from the point of view of the defining psyche, and by the inherent situation so defined. The distinction between smaller and larger is definition of point of view, and from one point of view alternation or comparison is foreclosed for the singular relation and its dramatic tenor to be established. Plato has closed the escape hatch some commentators wish to provide him, the escape from location, which is realization of the tenor of relation.

We should be able to place large or large number (megethos or plethos) next to the beautiful (to kalo): in all cases what, large or numerous, or beautiful, is transformed as its impact or affect. Just as Simmias' head length is absorbed into either, the large or the small, so beautiful youngsters are absorbed into to kalo; the singular or particular, that is, is absorbed as it enters a formalized, generic relation defined from the point of view of the percipient or registering center. Every particular registered is contingent on its ordination, the conditions of its registry. As far as possible the world of persons and their situations are codified by a set of primary conditions, the medium of their relation to the perceiving center, in which the affective term, large or beautiful, holy or different, pious or equal, just or uneven, works as the 'key' or 'shutter' of definition in the corridor of specified relation. Significant knowledge is the knowledge of the conditions of relation into which every jot of singular impression, of personality, landscape or action, has anyway to be codified for perception to turn into meaning, or for speech, derived from such generic ordination, to carry or contain that meaning.

To realize the degree to which existence or perception is organized or realized only as realized as contingent on such generic conditions is a difficult — intellectual, emotional, and moral — exercise. But recognition of the original conditions is given, the ability, that is, to make the distinctions on which each set operates — equal or unequal, odd or even, hot or cold. Given, too, is the capacity to build an interlocking set of conditions into a pattern, as in the case of the comparative degrees that distinguish the heights of different men. Plato's famous doctrine of recollection (*Phaedo* 104a, *Meno* passim) is, in our terms, the insistence that intellectual structures are as inherent in our genetic constitution as our organic functioning.

As intellectual structure is inherent, so also is affective, emotive existence; the most intimate responses, when properly understood, lead to the knowledge of their imposition, in all places, in all times, in all useful exercises — the climb from individual amorous fixation to the awareness of the unfolding of all perception, and relation disclosed or established in perception.

The individual, for his time, shares in this continuing intellectual and emotive structure, much as an instance of bravery or justice or beauty shares, as its portion, the everlasting possibility of such response. Individual psychic patterning is the epitome of the instance of eternal revelation of value, and just once (*Phaedo* 106d) Plato equates psyche to the *eidos* of life itself. Such fulfillment has been expressed before, as it will be expressed again, after this one mortal body has deployed it. Psychic immortality in Plato, be it remembered, precedes individual birth quite as much as it follows individual death. A man in his time is realized through a continuum of everlasting realization.

Holding in common or communion, share in, presence (koinonia, metechei, parousia): conscious or sub-conscious these are all ways for restating from the human point of view the older mythic relation[4] of an active instance to an everlasting capacity, organic, intellectual, emotive, Aphrodite, Athena,

211

Poseidon. Though Plato never violates the Ionian canon, delimitation by defined perception, he is involved from start to finish with an abstract verbal structure which will replace the old mythic structure within which every act, of energy deployed, relation attained, or perception defined elicits the eternal donation of just such deployment, attainment, definition.

There is another carry-over from myth which is strategic for an understanding of Plato's thought, a connection that has never been alluded to in modern criticism. An *eidos* or an *idea* is an as-if, just as a god or a god's act is an imaginary as-if. Perhaps because the intellectual nature of deity or of god-act in myth has been so generally misunderstood, or because much contemporary analysis contemns or ignores as-ifs, fails to realize that all "models" as well as words, are imaginative entities — the basic nature of *eidos* or *idea* has been largely evaded. It is an imaginary construct, as necessary as word in speech, as compelling as the realization of natural trope or structure, as illuminating as mythic *eidos* or *idea*.

The Platonic forms are not powers, new philosophic terms for old man-shape propulsions. Plato avoids the ascription of fiat or enforcement to his modalities of realization; in a way they are simply the hypostases of the qualities, values, ends which mind has isolated from their instances. The absence of plotting 'will', the calm impersonality of this functioning Platonic universe, is remarkable. This absence of a sense of will or dictation in process is perhaps as intimate an insight into Plato's fundamental disposition as we will ever possess, his wonder-watching yet analytic psyche. Eros, apprehension, and order are all primary in Plato, yet none of these is propelled from a postulated commanding source, Aphrodite, Athena, Zeus. Somehow the Platonic insistence on building from defined point of view precludes the establishment of such centers, just as Plato's psychic personality is somehow repugnant of ego command, the magnification of individual will.

Yet Plato's *eide* or *ideai* are as made-up, as much as-ifs, as Athena or Aphrodite. Plato has made this perfectly clear by denying them any physical existence, geographic location, by insisting that they are *noeta*, apprehended only by mind not by the senses. What is apprehended only by mind is imaginative; imaginative is a sound translation for *noeta*.

Yet imagination insists on an image, the made-up "image," to "see" what can *not* be seen physically *as if* it were seen physically. Plato's "shapes" or "forms" or "appearances" are *as if* shapes or forms or appearances. The visual term which Plato uses for his non-sensible differentiae, qualities, values, ends — shape or . form or appearance — is neither paradox nor unconscious self-contradiction. It discloses the continuing nature of imaginative thought in abstract discourse, as in myth, as the realization of the non-sensible *as if* sensible. Just as overall process or pressure to event had earlier been "seen" as man-shape or animal shape, so now the devolvement of modality, itself invisible, is "seen" or "realized" *as if* visible.

*Eidos* or 'form' is not the vague, generalized idea — in the English sense — of something we do, in fact, see with our eyes. (That is the still abounding error of English commentary, derived from a tradition which denies the "existence" of the imaginary, and which uses the 'idea of the bed' as normative of the idea of the beautiful rather than illustrative of it.) The "shape," the "form" is the *agalma* of experientially numerous, theoretically numberless cases of relation or realization of relation — established as their quality, value, end — where specific relation or realization has no shape or form; it takes or assumes one only as phenomenalized by its ascribed participation in the made-up "shape."

*Agalma* is an "honor" or "offering" to divine power which. realizes it *as* shape: the cult-statue. An *agalma* of Aphrodite is an imaginary image, now defined in wood or stone, of an everywhere coursing power existentially realized in the coupling of birds, beasts, fishes, mankind, or in the *feeling,* the desire for one another, of boy and girl, of man or woman. This feeling is no more 'in' that stone or wood statue, than the coupling of beasts is 'pictured' by the cult statue of Aphrodite. A marble statue realizes an imaginary shape which in turn unifies all the existential illustrations or variant manifestations and ascribes them to that one *source* or *power.* The made-up image, of the god or goddess, and its purely ascribed power — for no man or woman shape in sky or sea or on land effects, or is 'seen' to effect

213

the coupling of fish, or birds or beasts − phenomenalizes the natural occasions, defines them as local *examples* of the putatively unifying and unified power, realized as unifying "image," god or goddess.

Pari passu, the *eidos* or *idea* of justice, or courage − which it is always safer for us to think of as the realization of a function or relation − is the imagined or posited unification as "shape" or "form" of what, in existential fact, never displays clear shape or form. In situ, spun off the rippling acts of ever moving men, in speech or debate in the assembly or law courts, in battle-line, 'courage' or 'justice' or 'self-control' are realized values; situations, with their changing, confusing and variegated detail, have to be summed and then judged, in order to know whether these values may be said to evolve from them. They are never there as "images," defined or defining models.

If we continue to bear in mind, too, that the god-shape as *agalma* or statue is the concretization of an imaginary "image" which has imposed unity on quite variant material manifestations of the same posited power, that the physical shape of that god form is only obliquely related to the active manifestations, we will the more readily appreciate Plato's reiterated insistence on the separation − *chorismos* − of an *idea* or *eidos* from its instances, from occasions of bravery, piety, etc. An *eidos* as the extrapolation of many instances, of the same kind, as their unity, is *ipso facto*, 'revealed' in any one, but no one of them can be equated to that image-as-unity. The suppressed relation of the Platonic *eidos* to previous divine shape is disclosed in the alternatives, that the local manifestation of a value is made possible by its participation in, its share of the unifying "shape," or, by the "presence," though only partial, of that unifying "shape" in the local situation. As with the previous mythic forms, all significant occasions, acts, expressions are contingent, occasioned by, denotative or expressive of what lies 'beyond' them (the ancient "image" for the unseen control of what is seen) forever finding expression in similar occasions, acts, events. Here in new guise is the old relation of the local act, of energy or capacity expressed, of awareness realized, to the divine energy or capacity for just such act or realization.

Aristotle tells us, in the *Poetics* (9,1-5), that poetry is more philosophic than history, by which he implies the automatic means the traditional poet had to transform the specific as general case, see individual experience in relation to eternal natural pressures and their intellectual forms, always to hand, human character or personality transformed as heroic type, the act of response evoking the god whose eternal capacity it momentarily deploys. But what Aristotle does not tell us is that the "new" philosophy, which he learned at Plato's feet, was made possible only by the demise of the "old," philosophy in the poetic mode, only made possible by history both as lived, and as written by Thucydides. The slow, subtle collapse of the earlier "philosophic" modality, poetry, had to be suffered, before the effort to meet the ensuing emptiness could be made. That effort is, par excellence, Plato's, but the modality of *his* response, we are at pains to re-emphasize, did not arise directly from what had collapsed, but from the "sets" evolved by such as Thucydides in the intervening time in the same society. The way each and every one of the debates to and through *Republic* begin should make that clear: behavioral role unknown because undefined, the traditional prescription examined and discarded as insufficient, the renewed effort, in post-Thucydidean terms, to set up the airtight definition which governs similar instances.

If we were, in the broadest sense, to define the general social reach of Platonic thought, we could do it in the simple but pregnant Thucydidean phrasing, as attempting to establish *ton aiei paronton ta deonta,* attempting to establish the intellectual forms for proper action which the ever present crises of social and individual life require, demand.

We can fetch another Thucydidean crux, his boast for his history, *ktema eis aiei*, into the realm of Platonic meditation. The words might well seem Platonic, an eternal possession, but to claim it for the account of a war for material mastery? Is this not pushing our Thucydides-Plato bond to the snapping point?

Not if we remember that Thucydides claims it for *the effect on his listeners* of his writing, not for Athens and her empire, not for the empire's wealth Pericles had used for the magnificence of the Acropolis, Agora, and Sacred Way. All that, we have noticed, Thucydides could see as ghostly, without its shouting rowers, proud generals or Olympic victors, or morning ecclesia. How does Thucydides' claim tie him once more to Plato, in a related if differing appreciation of the nature of "eternity"?

The quality of Thucydides' appreciation of death answered may qualify our approach to Plato's, at least separate the latter's from its strange historical fate of being read as supporting the eternity of identity.

I am not sure, of course, what either writer means by eternity, even what Thucydides is claiming for his history. True, that work has survived, people still read it, but Thucydides himself does not say that it is the writing per se he thinks will endure. That assumption is undercut by his own contrast: "This work has been put together as an eternal investment for the future rather than as an entry to be heard in a current competition for prizes." Thucydides as much as Herodotus expects his writing to be *read* aloud to an audience, does not think of it as a "book" preserved forever in careful libraries. That latter image, which is automatic for us, could not have existed in his mind. But did he, unthinkingly, like Pindar for his poetry, expect such readings and such responsive audiences, even after their cities were empty of Lacedaimonians and Athenians? That may be; no more than the poet may he have been sure of the mechanical means that would prolong his report and its effect on listening men.

But could he not have felt that that effect itself could be transformed in other places, in other speech or writing, into parallel appreciation of the nature of the struggle for hegemony, and its effects upon the contending societies, long after the pages of his own work had dissolved, in the sands or sea? True, there would have to be a human continuity, and within it an intellectual continuity, leading from one history to the next with its parallel effect, its similar evocation of the psychic bases for decision, their expression, and resulting action. In this way, in fact, Donatello, with an inner recapture of the impetus to Hellenic sculpture, his vision only brushed by a few Hellenistic copies, brings back in full measure the ancient modality. The path from Phidias to Donatello is not only circuitous; the restoration derives from the confluence of pressures which have elicited, mutatis mutandis, the same principles, the same appreciation.

Or Thucydides' imagination — who can forsee the future — may have wavered between the material and evocative survival of his analyses. What is important for our purpose is that in them he felt he had reached not only a set of eternal human pressures for action but the functional pattern for grasping their sequence. In his writing he was related to both these, and *they were eternal.* What he had seen — and that 'see' is intellectual, not physical — would happen again in quite parallel fashion and could be grasped by someone who wanted to see its pattern. This assertion he juxtaposes to his claim for the immortality of the work itself. We should not separate them. His individual mind had been held and illuminated by the same pattern others with the same impetus will forever see.

Our terminology seems Platonic, but does it not hew closely to Thucydides' own phrases? What, to Plato, eternal pattern revealed was quite different, or at least, what he hoped it would reveal. But he, too, pitched eternity to the shapes which human response made of experience.

Those shapes in either case are individual, if emerging from contemporary forms of discourse, and both go back, at last, to the great gods and goddesses, the enduring forms for human recognition of each and every sort of pressure. Those were, in common speech, "tautologically defined," called as a group simply *hoi athanatoi,* "Those who live forever." The contrasting definition, the nominal adjective for man, "he who dies." This distinction was never blurred either by Thucydides or Plato. The forms of experience, fed by organic life and adumbrated by the human need to comprehend it, endure forever. Each and every identity dies.

# CHAPTER 7

## INCARNATION AND RESURRECTION (I): *NEMEAN 10*

Since Castor came to the hospitality of Pamphaes' home,
and his brother Polydeukes, it is no wonder this family
is born to be brave athletes. For
as stewards of broad-plained Sparta with
Hermes and with Heracles (the Twain) oversee the virile rule
    of games,
most zealous in their care for just men. Yea, verily, the
    clan of gods is faithful.

Transmigrating, ever changing, this day beside their father
Zeus they possess and this under the folds of the earth in
    the hollows of Therapne,
fulfilling the same declination. Since
such — rather than wholly to be a god and dwell in heaven —
chose Polydeukes as Castor lay dying in battle.
For Idas angered somehow about cattle had wounded him with
    bronze spear-head.

From Tuagetos looking down Lynkeus saw them in an oak-stump
sitting, for his of all on earth was the sharpest
eye. With swift feet straightway
they reached the scene and a great deed did quickly
and suffered dreadful, sons of Aphareus, at the hands of Zeus.
    For at once
came Leda's son pursuing. They stood opposite beside their
    ancestral tomb
whence wrenching Hades' ornament, polished stone,
they hurled it at the chest of Polydeukes. But they neither
    crushed
nor drove him back. Leaping with the coursing javelin
he drove the bronze in Lynkeus' lungs,
and Zeus on Idas crashed fire-bearing smoking thunder-
    lightening.
On the instant they burned to nothing, deserted. Bitter strife
    for men to meet superiors.

Swiftly to his brother's life-force drew back the son of
    Tyndareus
and found him not yet dead but in the rattle shuddering
    breaths.
Shedding hot tears, wailing
loud and clear he cried: "Father, son of Cronos, what
    loosing
will there be from sorrows? For me, too, death with him before
    me render, Lord.
Value leaves a man deprived of his very own. Few of our kind
    in labor are faithful
to share travail." Thus he spoke, and Zeus came before him
and spoke this word: "Thou art my Son. But this one immediately
    thereafter her husband
in union with your mother death-bound sperm
a hero shed. But, behold, even so, of these things
a choice I give you. If fleeing death and hated age
yourself on Olympus wish to dwell by me, with Athena and
    black-spear Ares,
there is for you of these a share. But if for your brother
you are fighting and all things are minded to portion equal,
half would you breathe being beneath the earth
and half in the gold halls of heaven."
And when he had finished speaking, Polydeukes did not ponder
    decision:
he loosed the eye, and then the voice, of bronze-girt Castor.

                                    (Pindar, *Nemean* 10.49-90)


    These are some of the most extraordinary lines of poetry ever
written, and by a radical claim I hope to begin to lift them out
of their relative obscurity. They have, it is true, within the
confines of Classical criticism, found praise as moving and
sympathetic, though with no hint of their larger import. For the
claim that would raise them from obscurity in their own right is
that in others' use of them hardly better known lines have ever
been composed and sung abroad. Perhaps only *Aeneid 6* or
Plato's *Timaeus,* in Christian transformation, has anywhere near
as deeply shaped the Western imagination, versions of myth
which for later time, their form forgotten, have turned into

geographic Hell and Heaven, or a putative universe and its imagined moral order become the natural mechanics of creation. These lines of Pindar, too, have been transformed, though not beyond recognition; in their own right they are the crucial Hellenic stamping of the myth of incarnation and resurrection.

It took a lifetime of poetic practice to attain this climax of mythic crystallization, and a lifetime of theological introspection to build its intuition. By my dating of Pindar's odes these are the last lines of Pindar's composition which we possess, a hymn to Zeus at Argos in 463.[1] There is also a tradition that Pindar died there, suddenly, in the stadium, so these may well be not only the latest lines we possess but the last lines he composed. In any case, he was, by common agreement, just past sixty at the time of their composition, and they recapitulate all the lines of his we have examined in earlier chapters, the intimate blood clan of gods and men in *Nemean 6*, the divine radiance of *Isthmian 5* and *Pythian 8* disclosed in spectacular human achievement, or the mythic evolvement of that same direct theological statement in *Olympian 1*, in the relation of Poseidon to Pelops' victory.

The first part of our poem, not here translated, concerns the deeds of Argive heroes and the beauty of Argive heroines, the city's pride and the athletic luster of the victor's family. But that recollection of great men gone and lovely women perished is, in the hymn's enactment, expressed in the ambiance of new beautiful girls and proud boy victors, as it is sung by youthful voices; so is the bloom of new life juxtaposed to the memory of life vanished. To catch that dimension of the earliest enactment is better, perhaps, than to immerse ourselves in antique detail without emotional resonance, simply to imagine the splendor of a great 5th century day in historic Argos, the important and beautiful of the hour set against the monuments and inscriptions which recall such life in previous centuries. For this poem's myth is the myth of the nature of life and death when seen together.

What does it mean to say in myth that a hero of myth in the flesh is godhead incarnate? What does it mean for mythic man, dead or dying, to live again? It is hero in myth, god's son, who rises from death, for we are not to suppose that these mythic

220

images represent any change from Pindar's previous poems in their strict submission to the appreciation of the natural bounds of human existence. Pindar's myth of the incarnation and resurrection no whit denies natural facts, naturally appreciated existence, but sees them in relation to eternal forms.

Inseparable, as in later myth, from these cardinal mythic realizations, incarnation and resurrection, is the appreciation of life as love. But the structure of this Pindaric mythic appreciation is disciplined, austere, and intellectual to the highest degree, and the result of that intellectual discipline is most extraordinary. Pindar resolves the nature of love as the human appreciation of human form. He does not in this poem portray love as the instinctual basis to emotional reaction or use amorous response as metaphor for metahuman relation, but ascertains an intellectual basis for the enactment of love and makes that appreciation follow directly from the realization of godhead made flesh. Likewise the realization of the nature of form is the key to participation in the resurrection.

The vocabulary I have been using clearly presupposes that the Hellenic myth of incarnation and resurrection under consideration should, if understood, provide a particular vantage point from which to view later Christian myths with a similar vocabulary. A limited critique of those will be attempted, appraising, from the Hellenic standpoint, their success in expressing a common intent, while trying to define the crises of their error. If that standpoint is revealing, the enduring validity of those myths resides in appreciation of quite a different order from the one to which most of us are accustomed.

For our most serious problem, both for understanding Pindar's last poem and the critical standard it should establish for interpreting later versions of similar myth, is the nature of myth itself, myth as interpretative abstraction not history or representation of natural history. I am not able to define what myth is, but I am very sure what it is not. Instead of advancing any abstract theory let me point to elements in our poem which emphasize the distinction between mythic projection and representation.

The life of Castor and Pollux (or Polydeukes) can in no way be a representation of life in or around 5th century Argos.

Fresh imaginative event in myth, the individual poet's signal contribution, is, by its arcane setting, removed from knowable social or individual scenery. What happens, then, as-if narrative, is opened, as in dream imagery, to the search for the abstract meaning of that as-if narrative; every particle of mythical elaboration is the imagistic revelation of a particular element of the abstract intent which builds them together.

Our myth is of nomadic life, antedating even settled agriculture, let alone the urban civilization of Pindar's own time. The fight is a fight about wandering cattle, and for general readers the anthropological accounts of warring African, Indian, or Melanesian aborigines and their flocks quite rightly spring to mind. This is not the economic or political or military life of 5th century Sparta or Argos, at war or in alliance with cosmopolitan Athens. The weapons and armor are of bronze, not iron; the pictures are scrupulously antique in detail, reconstructed as Eliade's "then." But the life that is given meaning by this picture of nomadic warfare is the life known to poet and audience, the later polis and its politics, its inter-city trade and warfare, contemporary athletic or military acclaim. The only purpose of using the arcane custom and clothing of that time is to give meaning to this one.

Before emphasizing that point further let me parenthetically pause, however, to note the way the antique mask of 5th century myth not only points to Greek social structure previous to any recorded history but also places the origin of the form in which the poet is composing in that pre-historical era. In its own right those recalled mores can be interpreted representationally, as a living memory. Pindar and the tragedians provide an as yet untapped source of anthropological corroboration of the past half century's field studies of primitive society, relational structure and customs. No more than our dreams is that mythic imagery fantasy; both draw on the accumulated detail or remembered experience seen in new collocation. But the only way to account for that living memory in the 5th century is through poetry itself, because the poetic transmission had been unbroken. We have, that is, another sign that the choral hymn goes back to just such nomadic hours of wandering Hellenic tribes, no further advanced when this art form first came into being than their contemporaneously analyzed Melanesian and African counterparts; and since the same social forms and implements often emerge in tragedy, this is another comment on its organic relation to the older tribal danced hymn. Incidentally, in the case of our poem, we have a clear case of that continuing tribal rite's absorption of the independent epic's narrative evolvement in Pindar's rehandling, as the scholiasts tell us (A.B. Drachmann III 180), of the myth as presented in the *Cypria*. Fifth-century tragedy, too, reveals the same disparity between the forms of contemporary life to be understood through the forms of social life used in myth.

But the use of the past time is not to revive or even study it for its own sake. I sharply distinguish, as Classical historians sometimes do not, our interest in its unconscious historical revelations and Pindar's or any creative poet's intent in its use. Some graspable social detail for any dramatic enactment is necessary for the artist, but it is most difficult to use the locally and intimately known except as representation. The imagery for myth must be distant so that any act or attitude dramatically presented reveals the recurrent form for all such acts, not merely its accidental circumstance, and can thereby be fitted into a significant system of such forms, an overall pattern of the dynamic of act. Another world, as in the dream, may clarify the elements of action in the one we know. A remembered but irretrievable past provides such a manipulable scene, but an impossible or unreal present — as with Virgil or Dante — may establish the same distinction between event and its form, or — as in Plato and some Asiatic Indian myth — an indefinitely unrolling future. In all cases the conditions and personalities as if in narrative are abstractions of the forms of such conditions and the predicament of personality. Our dreams do the same thing. The immemorial pressures to action are there realized as images of action in intimate sequence, *abstraction of predicament as if narrative.*

Our failure to come to terms with the mythic mode such as Pindar's is of no little theological significance. That failure may seem now merely an unacquired skill on the part of specialized interpreters of ancient tales, but it is a part of the culture's earlier failure which read the Christian versions of the myth of

223

incarnation and resurrection as history. The current scholarly lapse is a small category of the enduring error, seeing myth as the narration of natural event, when it is the transposition of hundreds of natural events and the figures in them as the forms of figure and event, the attempt to reveal what it means for there to be figures and their histories, not a description of special times and places and personalities.

The mythic figure is never to be equated with natural man, even a remarkable natural man. I have argued this earlier in regard to Achilles. Let me point to one example in this poem of Pindar's which makes impossible any equation of a mythic figure and a definable character as we know narrative. Pindar is at great pains to ·distinguish the ancestry of Castor and Polydeukes, the latter as the offspring of Zeus himself, the former the death-prone seed of Tyndareus. This is a point of such great importance that the poet dramatizes it as the word of Zeus himself. That is the degree of poetic sanction given it, the degree of its emphasis. Yet at the beginning of the crucial scene where Polydeukes is to make his appeal to Zeus as his father, when he is rushing back to his bleeding brother, he, Polydeukes, is defined as the son of Tyndareus. Now the theological significance both of the emphasized distinction between the brothers and of its simultaneous contradiction, the abolishment of that distinction, will concern us largely later. Here I want to point out the contrast to our usual narrative mode which makes possible that theological significance. Polydeukes, dramatically asserted as the son of Zeus in contradiction to Castor as the son of Tyndareus, when himself clearly denoted as the son of Tyndareus upsets completely our sense for identifiable character in narrative. It should show us that the mythic character is no such narrative character at all, no poeticized man, no fictional someone with a fixed place and, in our narrative sense, an enduring identity. The hero is a category or fluid form manipulable by the poet to reveal his intent, just like an abstraction in discursive argument. We do not consider it a contradiction when the discursive thinker tells us that the form of man is always subject to the conditions of mortality but that that form can in its recurrence be appreciated as immortal.

What lies behind the failure to grasp the fluidity of heroic identity — the source of the power of the poet of myth — is the desire to establish historic identity for mythic figures, and to interpret variations in their as-if narrative presentation as the poet's "corrections" of or "deviations" from such established historic identity. The language of the scholium on these lines is most revealing (Drachmann III 182.150a). Hesiod, the scholiast tells us, made both heroes the sons of Zeus, "but Pindar following other historical writers says that Polydeukes is the son of Zeus and Castor out of Tyndareus." "Following other historical writers" — that phrase speaks volumes. It epitomizes not only ancient scholiasts but much modern scholarship. The writers are not named and, as far as I am concerned, are purely imaginary. Pindar's invention here is of the greatest moment, as we shall see, but for the poet to invent his myth and manipulate his mythical identities within it for his abstract purposes, that is what scholiast, ancient or modern, can not tolerate. It destroys their security before myth as quasi-fact. And if Pindar were following anyone, it would not be a historian but a preceding poet as free as he to invent, to manipulate the vocabulary of inherited myth for new revelation, just as all of us can use old words or traditional philosophic terms in new juxtaposition for fresh purposes.

But great as this poem is, there is something even larger than its misinterpretation involved in that revealing phrase, "following other historians." The scholia take us to Alexandria and its libraries, and we do not have to date any one scholiast to know the appreciative failure that stalks them all as far as myth is concerned. Yet there in the 2nd century the likes of Clement the Christian wrote and preached in this ambience which could only read myth as history. Can we not see in the ancient critic's comment on Pindar an expression of the misunderstanding in which Christian myth was promulgated and preached? I shall return to this point later.

But myth is fluid in another sense. The poet's central enduring intuition is forever assuming variant mythic guise, the same significance revealed in differing mythic histories. Let us recall the previously noted parallel of the uses of Cheiron in *Pythian 3* and Tantalus in *Olympian 1* (155). In the scholium on the brothers' fight the few lines of the *Cypria*, Pindar's foreshortened and altered epic source (quoted Drachmann III 180), state that "Lynkeus looked over the whole island of Pelops, son of Tantalus." These are, of course, the mythic figures for Pindar's *1st Olympian.* Pindar, as our poem shows, knew these lines well, and in their wake, needless to say (ancient poets are not that different from their modern kind), rose the myth of his own earlier poem. I do not claim that that recollection informed this poem, because it did not have to. I use the coincidence in another direction: the intuition that was realized in the myth of Pelops and Tantalus will somehow be reformed by the myth of Castor and Polydeukes — the figure in the carpet, the poet's vital source for each and every formalization. The insistent Pindaric pattern of imagination is likely to provide us ruler and compass for our understanding of this one, defining his approach to previous mythic form.

Much of the larger myth of the Pair is clearly irrelevant to Pindar's purposes. The Dioscuri are par excellence the patrons of horsemen. Can they be seen in our imagination apart from those colossal nude shapes leading their rearing mounts on either side of the entrances to the Campidoglio and Quirinale? Those Roman statues quite consciously attempt to imitate archaic figures such as those which flanked the entrance to the hippodrome at Olympia (Pausanias V.15.5), shapes Pindar must have seen but whose significance he excludes from his poem. These heroes fight on foot; there is no suggestion of the horse, inappropriate in any case to our young wrestler victor. The Twins are also the patrons of sailors, their saviors in the storm, but that aspect is also not relevant, though the irrepressible pedantry of one scholiast tries at one point to make it so. But as patrons of athletes, themselves described as Olympic victors, Castor in the foot-race, Polydeukes in boxing (Paus.V.8.4), their might and skill are made the prototypes of the achievements not only of our victor but of his family (38) anterior to the section translated, and this interconnection serves, where we begin, as the transition from family achievement to the myth proper. As Poseidon is expressed in Pelops' triumph and pari passu in Hieron's, so the Tyndarids' prowess (capacity seen as continuous) is expressed in our victor's triumph. The glory and skill and bloom of successful youth are once more the expression of divinity. As the god-given radiance shines in the victor's hour in Aigina, so the Tyndarids are adored in the moment of an Argive athlete's acclaim. Our subject once more is human glory, both natural endowment and its achieved focus, as typified by the successful young male athlete. "As typified" is meant to suggest that such youthful glory focuses achieving man in social response and physical presence; it is simply paradigm and finally becomes in this poem figure for human life itself.

Now it is easy enough to see the Dioscuri, or either of them, as Apollo in similar case, as the divine or semi-divine prototype, the form of the individual instance. With a god's power we usually have a different degree or angle of abstraction, the god not as figure of the instance of capability or achievement but the continuing capacity or power summed as a unity, and the use of that power or capacity in individual instance figured as the *relation* of the individual to divine power. What is the relation of the transient generic individual to the continuing human form of all his capacities? That is the perpetual question of Pindar's religious meditation. It is expressed in the identical clan, with divided power, of men and gods in *Nemean 6,* the god-given radiance of worldly achievement in *Pythian 8,* intimately dramatized in the myth of *Olympian 1; Nemean 10* is his last, most difficult mythic answer. The problem of individual *relation* to continuing form has now emerged as the central focus, not the glory of continuing power or the clarity of individual instance — though Pindar has rung the changes on those aspects. Nor does he lower the grandeur of the divine ground in this poem: it is Zeus clear and clear-voiced. But he makes the mythic pivot the relation *within* the individual of divine power and its mortal frame and turns for the last illumination of his own obsession to the great Greek myth of individuation. It is an extraordinary marriage: the scope of the inherited myth with the poet's primal intuition.

In every imaginative childhood as in the shining childhood of the race caught and expressed in its great myth of individuation lives the grasp of individuality as pure accident which imagination can overcome. A child has no trouble in exchanging the identity of his own genus or species for any other form; he can be glistening white wolf or swooping bird in his mind. He can be born as readily as a chicken from an egg. Within his own species he knows no distinction of age or sex, can, at will, be male or female, young or old. So Zeus appeared to Leda, the Twins' mother, in the shape of a swan; so from the same egg of that union hatched Helen and Clytemnestra.

The Egg from which All hatches is the mythic expression of the realization that species and genera, like the individuals within a species, evolve simply as the discrete or individuated aspects of a common imposition of form. The process can be seen as one, and then all its parts become accidental, interchangeable with every other. Individuation is simultaneously the illusory denial and plangent reannouncement of the eternal one; the myth overcomes its momentary denial of unity by seeing it as the dramatic example of one and thereby the rehearsal of all other ones. Limited to the human species alone, that simultaneous appreciation of individuation as the denial and announcement of unity is the divine Twin. Greek myth, at least in its Classical evolvement, intertwines the myth of human individuation in its own species and the individuation of the species from other animal forms, Zeus as Leda's Swan, Castor and Polydeukes as Leda's Son. The accident of human twins is not essential or even strictly relevant to the Castor-Pollux mythic image, though when that human accident occurs it provides yet another illustration of the phenomenon of individuation, human twins also bespeaking Castor and Pollux, not the other way round.

Psychic ontogeny may perhaps be said to recapitulate — poetically, not biologically — cultural phylogeny. The child become a youth passes from the imaginative freedom which sees Zeus as swan or bull, leaves the dreams of psychic metamorphosis into animal shapes, and lives a while with alter egos of the same sex and age in the simplest, fullest communication, not by an adult mutual understanding but on the basis, in action, laugh, or interest, of interchangeable response, and the adolescent imagination likewise participates in all coeval examples of individual achievement or success. By this time the imagination has lost its power to transcend the individuation of the species but for another while transcends the limit of the individual in the species. Both imaginative possibilities remain open, however, to the adult in his dreams. To Freud, of course, or Freudians, these are all levels of immaturity; to other psychologists they not only reenact our cultural history, they deploy a sadly lost appreciation of the phenomenon of individuation in organic life, whereby self-definition can become appreciation of the self's momentary expression of imposed individuation and the capacities deployed through it recognized as given, not self-claimed.

The Greek myth Pindar uses had established for his society that appreciation of the phenomenon of individuation with greater plangency in statue and cult rite than a few phrases of childhood experience can pretend to revive. Those great figures of the Twins announced in Rome, as in Olympia, One Man as Everyman or Everyman his own Brother. Yet that myth for all its glory and continuing validity is not in its own right the myth of Castor and Polydeukes as presented in our poem.

Pindar takes that myth and uses it to show again, but in a new dimension, the relation of Pelops' achievement to Poseidon's gold horses, and that perversion, as scholiasts ancient or modern might lament, is not an integral part of the original myth. That is why Pindar introduces the divided parentage of the pair and makes the choice of one the climax of his rehearsal of the myth.

The brothers, as we have noted before, appear in Hesiod (fr. 91) as twin sons of Zeus, in the *Odyssey* (11.300-304) as the sons of Tyndareus, in the *Iliad* (3.237,8) as the twin sons of Leda, parentage unremarked. In both Homeric instances the Twins are mortal and emblematic of death at the height of youth, like Herodotus' Cleobis and Biton, another mythic version of the Brothers. As symbols of individuation, the two would normally appear as the sons of the same father, or, if he is ignored, with the older matrilineal sense, of the same mother. Nor would the Greeks have been disturbed by the earlier pre-Pindaric mythic variation between divine and human father. Zeus would establish the divine sanction of individuation which could at the same time be appreciated in its human expression. Pindar's intimately divided parentage does not, as we shall see, contradict the usual Greek appreciation that lies behind the earlier alternation, human act seen from another aspect as divine intention.

But Pindar's emphatic insistence in Zeus' own words on that divided parentage, while it does not, in the Hellenic sense, contradict Homer's or Hesiod's accounts, does reshape the myth to the Pindaric intent, the relation *in* individuation between the human and the divine. The earlier version is submerged in his, like a stream in the ocean, individuation simultaneously pondered as the problem of the mortal relation to its immortal form. The problem of individuation for him is at one and the same time the One in different identity, the old myth, *and* the relation in any one of mortal individuality to its immortal propulsion. The shift in myth for all its dramatic emphasis is a change in point of view, not in any sense the correction of the error of a previous one. Without dismissing the old, a new dimension is added.

The elements of the myth must, therefore, do double-duty, which makes it a most difficult task to turn the dramatic relation of Castor and Polydeukes into what we call its "meaning," meaning by that image as discursive analysis. Nay, triple-duty since in the original myth there is automatically a double reference, one man as another and *therefore* one man as related to another. Castor and Pollux are at the same time the same and divided, identical yet separated, one person and two, and the tension is never let up which must see them as only one person and yet by that very appreciation posit their paradigmatic statement of how in the last analysis one is related to another.

It is in addition to this tension that Pindar introduces his special drama, the relation in the individual between himself as only himself, the mortal, and his immortal self. But once again, as in the older tension, that is seen at the same time as it applies only to the self and that self as related to another. Castor and Polydeukes, then, are aspects of the same person and yet the grasping of that internal relation in the individual governs his appreciation of relation to the closest other. Clearly one can never understand how this myth attempts to recapitulate the phenomenon of individual existence, as long as one is bound to

230

the heresy that a mythic hero is simply some poetic fantasy about a man that you or I, or an ancient Greek, might meet. The mythic figure is a complex abstraction of elements in nature, not a poetic counter for a living counter. To repeat as momentary summation: Castor and Pollux are originally man defined by the phenomenon of individuation, recurrent one and recurrent one as related to another one, but Pindar adds to that definition individuation itself as presenting the dual aspects of human mortality and divine immortality.

Consequently another aspect of the old myth must needs have a new dimension, the alternation of life for the Twain between heaven and underground. Again the old picture of immortality is radically changed without contradiction of it. What Pindar does, in fact, is to take an unrealized aspect of the older myth and make it pivotal in the new one.

Whether as sons of Tyndareus or Zeus (whose sons may die) the Twins had previously been known as mortal, yet their existence in alternating states was immortal, and they were prayed to, honored like to the gods (*Iliad* 11.304), as Homer tells us, though it is to be noted that it is like to the gods, not as gods. Their alternation between heaven and under the earth is, of course, the mythic image of the constant alternation of life and death, as of light and darkness, phenomenal appearance and disappearance. They are man's estate, and youthful man in his full array is paradigm. Now for Pindar there is something not in the least wrong or inaccurate but simply left unanalyzed — or in his mode, without its mythic appreciation — in the old myth, the sharp but unanalyzed distinction made in the old myth between the Twins as emblems both of mortality and immortality, both of them mortal and subject to death yet at the same time figure of perpetual renewal. Pindar's divided parentage serves to see that distinction as the same distinction made for individuation itself, as the *relation* between divinity, which is immortal form, and the human condition always subject to death. Just as the drama of Pelops and Poseidon is the complex imagistic evolvement of the simple statement of god-given radiance in victorious achievement in *Pythian 8,* so the myth of Castor and Polydeukes is the complex dramatic structure expressive of the direct statement opening *Nemean 6* that the clan of gods and men is one and the same, yet the two divided in power. Taken altogether they become an extraordinary 5th century Greek appreciation of how both the divine nature and immortality are expressed in the life of man himself, though he is never a god, never becomes a god, and in his own identity can never be immortal.

That praise may mislead in echoing the vocabulary of our own theology, for this is quite different, its symbolism avowed and clear, its result appreciation of phenomenon, not its denial.

Zeus, the supreme god of the Greeks, speaks to us in this poem, tells us the facts of the Twins' genealogy and sets the vital — in the literal sense — choice on which the drama of the myth pivots. Yet that speech of Zeus is in an intricate metre placed, in a poem constructed by elaborate rules, at a point of climax. The words of the supreme god as well as the craft of their placement are clearly of the poet's making, yet his audience would not be disturbed by full awareness of this poetically imagined and technically emphasized declaration of godhead. What god says, then, is what the poet understands that the form he is using to unify phenomena discloses of its active pattern. Therefore, what "happens" is not event at all — though it is pictured so — but the nature of event.

Zeus declares that Polydeukes is his son, and that a mortal hero shed the seed that became Castor. The seed of that hero becomes, of course the son of Tyndareus, yet that is precisely the designation of Polydeukes himself at the most critical moment of the drama when he runs to the side of Castor. Likewise, when the two are said to spend each other day by "their own father Zeus," Castor, too, is included as the son of Zeus, as Polydeukes is denoted the "son of Tyndareus." Earlier in the poem (38) they are called together the sons of Tyndareus. Three times their parentage is coalesced despite Zeus' emphatic proclamation of Polydeukes alone as his son.

This is not contradiction, carelessness, or confusion. Zeus' and Tyndareus' engendering are the dual aspects of that act, as Polydeukes and Castor are the dual aspects of its result, but it must at the same time be made clear that as identities the two are transposable, so we do not confuse mythic with natural identity but see theirs only as abstractions of aspects of our own. The only way spatially, so to speak, in myth — as-if narrative — to realize two aspects is as two persons, just as temporally, in as-if narrative, to realize the two aspects of their propagation they must be seen in succession. But as total myth, as overall abstraction, such dramatically projected division in time and space is not a way to recapitulate or represent naturally ordained separation and succession but a way to state the related aspects of the same person. Tyndareus' sowing of the seed — myth like dream as visual and dramatic — is another aspect of Zeus' sowing of the seed, since the sons of Zeus or the sons of Tyndareus, as the language of the poem calls them in easy alternation, is the result of that dual propagation. Man is both divinity incarnate and only human: the Zeus-Tyndareus *contrast* like the Castor-Polydeukes *contrast,* like the opening of *Nemean 6,* insists on a distinction between the two; but the Castor-Polydeukes identity like the Zeus-Tyndareus mutual sowing insists, as that earlier poem also did, on the identity of the clan of gods and men. The Zeus-sowing produces the Polydeukes-aspect, as the Tyndareus-sowing the Castor-aspect, but, as the language of the poem makes incontrovertible, that is one and the same person. When the mythic propagation and the mythic personalities are related to man in nature, we must see that man as singular, and we must see the mythic figures as projecting the continuing pattern of man as phenomenon.

The pre-Pindaric myth does that in seeing them as the figure of the perpetual alternation of life and death, of youthful glory and its extinction. They are not any of the individuals in that process but its immortal paradigm and so share in honor like to the gods. Pindar rehearses that old alternation in his own terms. To construe the "gold halls of heaven" we need only remember the gold horses of Poseidon on which Pelops rode to victory or the gold house of Zeus to which he was taken. That gold was the sign of divine donation *in this life,* Pelops' transient, limited participation in immortal capacity in his triumph and worldly renown. So for the Pair we must understand the days on Olympus with Zeus, Athena, Ares as their emblematic expression of human glory as divinity revealed. These heroes are warriors, so Ares bespeaks the human capacity for warfare victory, as Athena ever the capacity of correct situational understanding, and Zeus the whole radiance of the sky and its light, of natural physical and psychic existence. There is no other world. The days on Olympus are the mythic image of human joy in spectacular achievement and the self-congratulation which accompanies it, defined by the discrete capacities most necessary for young men warriors.

Its inevitable price, however, is the rest under the soil. That is where men must end, as Pindar has preached adamantly before. Only Polydeukes "breathes" in that condition: the immortal form of the continuous human enactment, not any one of its death-prone members, breathes despite death's annihilation. That is a most moving verb in its location (87). The 17th century, we know, was obsessed by the "skull beneath the skin." But that is choice in point of view. One could be equally struck by the new breath in immemorial bones. With the living breath of the youthful mythic figure under the earth Pindar has expressed mythically, with harsh economy and poignancy, those long lines of mankind waiting to assume their shape and psyche in Plato's Er myth or Vergil's parade of the birth-expectant in the underworld, the total arc of human manifestation. All the young men in the future who will win games where the Twins are stewards are gathered in the "breathing" of Polydeukes, as their celebrated victory hours are the day on Olympus, their decay and death his and Castor's diurnal declination. The word Pindar uses for the Twins' participation in death itself, *potmos*, is the word he uses for the swift-falling race of men to whom Pelops is returned as punishment for Tantalus' folly (*0.1*.66), as it is derived from the verb Pindar uses of the joy that "falls to the ground shaken by a reversing will" at the close of *Pythian 8* (93, 4).

But in yet another verb Pindar has suggested in the paradigmatic destiny of the Twins the scope of the great myth of the numberless hosts who fulfill the same forms of human destiny, the continuum of existence bound together as a unity, the myth of transmigration. Transmigration is the Latin for the Greek verb, *metameibomenoi*, which Pindar uses for the daily journey ("daily," of course, is the mythic expression of the human span, as in "ephemeral" as well as "diurnal") of Castor and Polydeukes between death and life's full glory. It is a single verb but taken in juxtaposition to the traditional function of these figures it adumbrates that other myth of reiterated existence which Pindar, of course, gave its fullest Hellenic expression in the *2nd Olympian,* the myth of the blessed three times purged from contamination. There as here myth is interpretation of human existence. The suggestion of that other myth is important in our poem, too, because it points to the assumption of natural form anterior to any achievement or its reflection – with which so many of Pindar's poems are concerned – to the putting on of body and psyche, so that a man can see and speak a communicating word, that any one can be that extraordinary creation, an individual human being. In our poem that natural miracle finally takes precedence over even the most radiant of its own enactments. Existence itself, not its partial expressions, has become Pindar's final meditation.

We must turn back. I have claimed that we must first grasp Polydeukes-Castor as the mythic representation of single man, that the inseparable Twins as unity are emblematic of the human condition, a form for that condition's appreciation. We must not let hold of that unity, even as we now proceed to sound the significance of the mythic division as between Castor and Polydeukes and the added Pindaric dimension of their divided parentage.

Life is always individual, always based on a self and the sense of self. But if that self is seen phenomenally, then it is at one and the same time identifiable with and separate from every other self. All selves, by their being a self, are forever divided from all other selves, and yet by their mutual expressiveness one and the same, always confronting, yet that confrontation made possible by their interchangeability. The Hellenic myth – this is not Pindar's contribution – for that simultaneous identity and separation is the Twins. What is implied here is not as obvious as it may seem, for I am claiming that the Myth of the Twins is figure for all psychic existence not, as usually interpreted, figure for any human relation, even that of brothers in the same family. Unless we grasp this, we will not understand the love of Pollux and Castor or the significance of that love for the whole Western religious tradition. The Castor-Pollux love can lend itself as the organic phenomenal base for any form of human love, but it does not itself figure any of them.

German editors have gone so far as to suggest that the personal devotion of the victor-wrestler of the ode to brother or male "friend" prompted its myth, a misunderstanding, still widespread, not of this poem alone but of myth in general. And the old-fashioned English editor of *The Nemean Odes* (London, 1890, 186), J.B. Bury, quaintly sets forth what is still a commonplace appreciation. "In Greek mythology those twin riders ... are engaging figures, tempting us to think into their legend an element of what we call 'romance', especially through their mutual devotion, stronger than death, and their strange double life, passed in heaven and beneath the earth on alternate days.... they were not heedful of the love of women. Such love was replaced by that mystical friendship for each other, which became a type — comradeship here actually overcoming death, through the conviction that 'there are worse things waiting for men than death' in the world."

Bury clearly has no notion of the Twins as signifying death as well as life, but I am here concerned with his implication, shared by many, that Castor and Polydeukes are a paradigm of homosexual love. He does not quite say so, and, as usual, inhibition can easily imagine what is not there. But Pindar was not inhibited. We have seen in *Olympian 1* how he used a classic Hellenic homosexual love as the figure for divine-human relation. But no word in this poem suggests any such relation, neither the denotation of their bond, nor the basis of Polydeukes' plea for release to Zeus — which is all social bond, not any particular one — whereas Pelops, we may remember, spoke clearly of Aphrodite's gifts as the basis of his claim for Poseidon's assistance. Even if we took the mythic relation as representation of human relation, and we should never do so, twin brothers would hardly be appropriate to the Hellenes, who knew the need for difference in physical passion, as lovers. Given the twins' identity we could, in fact, only understand it in such terms as a myth of narcissism. But most simply, we have not the slightest right to bring ourselves sexual suggestions into a poem without them.

Nor are the Twins the divine or semi-divine paradigm of natural human brothers. This may be harder for some readers to understand, though when they have, they may concomitantly develop a more accurate apprehension of the Christian term, brotherly love. The instinctive emotional response of male siblings to one another does not usually provide the basis for the appreciation of love, and you will search in vain in Greek myth for natural brothers as its exemplars. The hostility of brothers is the natural figure, as of Eteocles and Polyneices. The early Hebrews had the same appreciation, Cain and Abel, Esau and Jacob, Joseph and his brethren. Nor should we put down Castor-Polydeukes as Hellenic wish-fantasy contrasted to Hebrew realism.

Yet the word brother is twice used in our poem heavily charged with emotion — as I would be the first to agree. I repeat too, that when, even if rarely, family brothers, or for that matter, homosexual lovers, in natural psychic existence express the pattern of love, they, too, reveal a Castor-Polydeukes base. No pattern, familial or amorous, is excluded, denied by this paradigm. But with Pindar, at least, the bond of the Twins is not meant to figure any specific natural one but the phenomenal base for them all. But because of the word brother and its necessary associational values, it could be objected, he is at least using this bond as a metaphor for all human relations and their possible empathy. The same misunderstanding obtains in regard to the Christian term, brotherly love. Not only our repression and obfuscation about male siblings' psychic instinct but our misunderstanding of the origin of our own religious term is a barrier to our understanding of the bond projected in this poem. Put most simply, we have misunderstood the meaning of the basic term itself, brother.

Pindar uses both *adelphos* and *kasignetos*, which in a way shows that no one term was loaded for him with an emotional reference he was trying to assert but that the relation involved in both terms was his point of departure. The first, *adelphos*, the word, of course, absorbed from Greek into the Christian brotherly love, means "from the (same) womb" or "joined by the womb," and its only verbal compound in Classical Greek, not irrelevantly, is "brother-slayer". Language reveals psychic history. It is the common *origin* the word looks to, not the emotional tenor of those bound by that origin, and, of course, primitively, identity based on origin is established through the mother. The other word, *kasignetos,* means "born as related," "defined at birth by blood relation," defined by knowable social bond. What is that bond? Contemporaneously it is the bond of the small family, but anciently it is the bond of *clan,* Greek *genos,* "those born," in its literal sense, implying, of course, "those born as related." The accurate anthropological definition of *kasignetos,* then, would be "clan-member." It is amusing that Greek dictionaries used to assume that the origin of the term was brother in our small-family sense and then extended, as its constant use showed, to a variety of familial relations. Modern anthropology, of course, has taught us that the opposite is the case. All coeval male members of a clan are brothers, the designation of small-family male siblings a later category. Both words, that is, derive from society's or the parents' point of view and denote not sibling inter-relation but identifiable common or related birth. Their later religious use in myth adds to but does not change the nature of those archaic terms. To be a brother is to be born from the same mother or of the same mother and father or born into the same clan and so recognized by that clan or those parents.

Christian "brotherly-love," then, which is of Greek origin, is not the transference to all other relations of the emotional tenor supposed to exist between male siblings which, in point of fact, is as likely to be hostility as affection. It is the recognition of common origin and mutual replaceability, lastly the recognition of the common phenomenal psyche. It knows no limit of condition, age, or sex, or race, not by some unnatural extension of a hoped-for familial emotion, but because that phenomenal psyche is generic, ubiquitous, offered for our everywhere appreciation. More particularly, the Pindaric Castor-Polydeukes bond is a full 5th century mythic expression of the basis of the Christian subscription to brotherly-love, an accurate rendition of its source.

So, too, with the term *philoi,* those loved *or* loving with *one* word. I have chosen — and all choice is exclusion or loss — to translate Polydeukes' reference to his *philoi* as "his very own," though the connotation of "loved ones," "friends" is certainly felt too. But *philoi,* as its ambivalence between "loved" and "loving" clearly shows, also originally refers to those who are

238

related and recognized as clearly related, and such bond can then express the emotion passively or actively. It means, to use a spatial metaphor, those who are inside the circle, as *xenos* is anyone who is outside the circle, as stranger, guest, or even enemy, as similarly *echthros,* one forever outside the circle. (This primitive distinction, incidentially, obtains in the use of these terms in the *Ajax,* so radically does the language of 5th century poetry reassert primitive social form or sense of that form.)

"Those loved" are those on whom the substantiation of one's own identity depends. The Hellenic poetic use from Homer on, and particularly strong in Pindar, of *philos* as the possessive adjective ("their own father" (55) in this poem, as "his own home" in *Olympian 1.*38) is the original meaning, clearly, of that term, and the emotional affect of that bond or possession springs right from it and employs the same term for its realization. *Philos,* that is, originally marked something as intimately one's own, as identified by one's self or one's self identified by it or him, a sense revived for us by such terms as "possession" in love, where psychic subordination, not physical embrace is meant, or even in the Valentine cry, "Be mine, be mine," where the original meaning of *philos* is reexpressed as the base of its later emotional tenor. None of these words, *adelphos, kasignetos, philoi,* has its origin in emotional affect, sexual or familial, though they all come to carry such affect later; they all spring from definition of relation.

Those original meanings of clan relation or identification are, in our poem, of course, transmuted by their function in the myth of individuation. Its sharpest definition is as complete identity, Castor as Pollux, or Pollux as Castor, one identity interchangeable with any other. As emblematic of such unity, there can be no distinction between love of one's self and love of the other. Expressed in revealing ambiguity it is the love of self, of the phenomenon of self, the realization of entity, of being and its ineluctible form, forever unique, forever common. Whenever, of course, dramatically one realizes this appreciation in nature or society, it will be found in specific relation and its physical or psychic tenor, whether love of parents and children, more rarely of siblings, sometimes of sexual congress in any form, the realization of the wonder of identity, yet knowing very well that identity could be another unique identity, folded into all the forms of human love. It is the overall phenomenon of such recognition we are concerned with in this poem. Let us not say, either, that a "purer" love, freed of its accidents or animal entanglements, is asserted, when we are trying to isolate what, among other things, is found in all of them. Myth is abstraction, and what is realized by that abstraction remains itself abstract. It is a mode of appreciation for the natural, not the substitution of a "higher" actuality. My insistence that Castor-Pollux do not figure either male homosexuality or sibling emotion is not in order to claim that in point of natural fact theirs is a greater kind of love. It is true that the life of the imagination, the seizure of act or event and its personages as phenomenal rather than simply as plangent identities, may, in individual case, qualify emotional reaction, but it is the life of the imagination or appreciation and *its* emotional intensity with which we are concerned in this myth, not the dramatization of specific plangency. For Castor to love Pollux or Pollux to love Castor, then, is to sieze the miracle of being in its only knowable mode, the miracle of individual existence. Never, not even in birth or sex, is that sense of the given form and its given expressiveness more poignant than in death: that he or she should never see or speak again is the most moving definition of how marvelous it is that someone should speak and see.

Let me subjoin two quotations from the richest period of American reaction which seem to me to express the basis of the human bond made mythic image in Castor-Pollux.

> In the last analysis, love is only the reflection of a man's own worthiness from other men. Men have sometimes exchanged names with their friends, as if they would signify that in their friend each loved his own soul.
>
> (Emerson, *Friendship)*

> But I felt pantheistic then — your heart beat in my ribs and mine in yours, and both in God's . . .
> Whence come you, Hawthorne? By what right do you drink from my flagon of life? And when I put it in my lips — lo, they are yours and not mine. I feel

that Godhead is broken up like the bread at the Supper, and that we are the pieces. Hence this infinite fraternity of feeling . . . . Knowing you persuades the more than the Bible of our immortality.

(Herman Melville to Nathaniel Hawthorne, Nov. 1851, *The Letters of Herman Melville,* New Haven, 1960, ed. M.R. Davis and W.H. Gilman, 142, 143.)

Note how in this purely personal context Melville has instinctively reexpressed the dependence of the myth of resurrection on the myth of incarnation, and in the phrase "more than the Bible" also realized that the validity of myth is not as historic event but as the new intuition of its pattern in reiterated experience.

So in our poem the two sides of the realization of the phenomenon on which love is based are expressed together. One apprehends the self, one's own as much as any other, dramatically in the other, but one's own existence, likewise, is dependent on a complementary realization. One lives only as realized — death were better than the failure of that recognition. It is human existence, not animal nature, that concerns us, the existence where to speak a word will directly follow the eye's glance of recognition in creating the bond of community. In human existence the joy of knowing is not to be separated from the joy, nay, the necessity of being known. Once again that interdependency of the Twins can be expressed naturally in the whole variety of human relations, and theirs is epitome not natural illustration. Pindar makes that clear, I have already noted, in choosing to make all intimate social relation not individual bond the basis of Polydeukes' plea to his father, "Few of men are faithful to share labor." That plea does not define unique relation but asserts the necessity of relation for human value. The *philoi* of that plea are loving wife and applauding children, surveying father, age and effort peers who can appreciate one's effort and achievement, all those within any defined bond who share the pain of the individual history. A man has value as the individual and all its phenomenal existence realized in others' minds. This is thoroughly Greek, beginning with the *kleos* of Homer. There is no realization in the "mind of God." Days on Olympus we have already seen are

241

quite a different matter. That limitation to other similar minds must be remembered as we examine Pindar's version of the myth of incarnation. There is only realization by similar form in similar predicament, interchangeable psyche echoed by interchangeable psyche.

Despite Richmond Lattimore's consistent mistranslation of *charis* in Classical Greek by the Christian Grace, the Hellenes are as innocent of the concept of Divine Grace as they are of the doctrine of God's Will. Deity does not "break into" human affairs; it is the realization of what is always there, and the Greek word *charis,* which functions later as Christian Grace, expresses, in one way or another, realization on the part of human beings, not the mysterious intervention of a differing mind. The Greek *charis* is joy and celebration, or thankfulness, human reaction. (The Graces are the formalized unity of that response, as the divine Muse of the process of poetry, another human form of reaction or appreciation.)

The myth of the incarnation will, then, pivot on a moment of supreme realization. Dramatically within the myth it is Polydeukes' knowledge or reminder (in myth that distinction is obliterated, for the particular dramatic event reveals perpetual significance) that he is the son of Zeus, but the mythic figure is the instrument of our appreciation: that which Polydeukes perpetually signifies is as perpetually divine within our own constitution. To recognize the divinity of form is the only way of relating one's self to it in human existence. Such realization, which leads to joy or celebration – grace in Greek terms – is the appreciation not of the mystery but of the *fact* of the incarnation. It is difficult to grasp, but that makes it neither mysterious nor paradoxical; it is a disciplined human appreciation of the nature of existence. What is true naturally is true always, continuing phenomenon. All that is transient is the fixing of the formula for the phenomenal. Myth makes that a dramatic moment, but so was landfall on 12 October, though America had always been there. The moment of incarnation represents no sudden decision or self-revelation on the part of a putative mysterious mind or will of God; it is the moment when through myth human appreciation flourishes.

"Thou art my son": so Zeus from heaven proclaims to Polydeukes. Can any lover of English poetry read that and not hear Milton? Can any Christian and not hear Mark and Luke? This four-word (in Greek, three) sentence rings through history. Do we need even a fifth to mark the extraordinary Western resonance of the Pindaric imagination?

The myth of incarnation, man as god or god's son, like the gods themselves, is with us when intellectual records begin; we know nothing at all of origins. The figure of the divine ruler as god's son never had a fuller social deployment than in the kingdoms of Egypt. But its Christian version is Hellenistic or Hellenistic-Jewish, written or spoken in Greek, and, we must therefore presume, derived from Hellenic models. The Hellenistic Jewish appropriation can not in and of itself disclose either the nature of the modality of the expression or the intent of the intuition expressed within it, can not disclose either the nature of myth or its 'meaning'. If both the intuition and its mode of expression are Greek, what a myth discloses, should, wherever possible, first be studied in that Hellenic setting. Fortunate we are to have a Hellenic mythic statement of incarnation and resurrection at the very height of Hellenic mastery of mythic form.

If the myth of incarnation, divinity in human form, is Greek, then the Greek view of deity is an essential part of its promulgation. Zeus is not a hidden or mysterious Will with its own motives at work 'behind' natural fact and history; he is, rather, 'in front of' all natural fact as a unified form for its appreciation. We may call him the symbol of natural order, but that is postpositive statement of the function of the form apart from that function. It were more accurate to say he *is* Natural Order seized as unity. For Pindar, then, to dramatize his presence and put words in his mouth is not to claim some special priestly capacity to realize, as natural man can not, a mind and purpose behind nature and history but to declare how, as he sees it, Natural Order operates. Pindar is not reading and then dramatizing God's mind, in our sense, but stating the human definition derived from a realization of that Order. Incarnation is, then, the way in which eternal Natural Order is realized in human form, which is, of course, always singular and unique. No motivation is assigned to the working of this natural order. "God so loved the world" presumes to read a purpose into theoretically mysterious godhead. In point of fact it is the hypostasis of emotional affect as determination. We have already seen that even in his analysis of the human scene Pindar does not make human emotional affect determinant but resultant, the offspring of the awareness of relation. Even less, we may infer, would he be disposed to see emotional affect as determining natural structure.

Such myth is not, in our sense, explanation; it were better to say description, if by that we understand abstract formulation of recurrent phenomena, not intimate representation. So nature evolves; so things happen. Why is not even pondered. Descriptively, then, this myth states that from one point of view human form, body, and psyche and its history is divine and immortal, though seen in another aspect it is purely human and subject to death. Only mythic figures can recapitulate both aspects, because the Zeus parentage is itself mythical, that is, recurrent, not individual, phenomenon grasped as a unity. In this myth the two aspects as inseparable are insisted upon by the language of the poem, which declares the seed of Zeus, Polydeukes, the son of Tyndareus as it has Castor the seed of Tyndareus living by his own father Zeus, yet that double figure equally insists on the differentiation of the two aspects, Polydeukes alone as the son of Zeus and Castor as the son of Tyndareus who may die. Why my or any attempt to render this disclosure in non-mythical terms is bound to distort is due to the lack of words which could define a given individuum in its non-historical, non-individual dimension, which recapitulate the purely phenomenal aspect of individual history apart from social identity. Yet such a distorting attempt must be made, if only to reinforce in contemporary appreciation the absence of the supernatural in the Pindaric statement of incarnation.

Form as given is purely generic; the sense of individual will and destiny is always substitutable. Pollux and Castor as identical or interchangeable is the older mythic statement of that. But we must not be satisfied simply with our grasp of recurrent form, of seeing all natural organisms hatched from the same egg, from precisely the same possibility and enactment of unifying singular form. This is part of the later appreciation, though even it is seized not as multiple echoing recurrence, but as the ultimate sense of form in that recurrence, grasped alone, sense of form apart from specific exemplars. But equally important, the form is *given* to any of its actors, singularity imposed, uniqueness donated: that is the crux of the human--divine relation. To appreciate the form as divine, which is always a human statement, after all, is the appreciation of the total will-lessness of the located center even in the most active enactment of will or destiny. Divine will is simply that enactment realized as given, not a purpose postulated for its enactment. The natural order is realized in but not under the control of each of its active creations. The human is not the substantiation of a divine purpose; it is the momentary participation in a process wherein the very form for that participation is granted, absorbed, fulfilled, and abandoned by the consciousness of the immediate history. But the achievement of that history — the hours on Olympus — quite as much as the form of its enactment is the transient experience of the totally un-self-evolved modes of its own deployment. It lives and achieves not only as it participates in divine form but in divine mode for that form's flowering. The son of Zeus makes possible the son of Tyndareus' mutual delight in the company of Zeus, Athena, Ares, as the son of Tyndareus' limitation insists on the son of Zeus' mutual bondage to human extinction. Polydeukes' realization that he is the son of Zeus and his choice, as dependent on his form's only means of historical fulfillment, to go underground, are as nearly simultaneous as myth — as-if narrative — can make them. Man is divine as the enactment of given immortal form and related to divinity as he is related to that form's independent history. Its independence of his will is the measure of its divine determination, his sonship of Zeus.

Now remembering always that Pollux-Castor are one, whatever the significances of their distinction, the divine parentage of the myth does not cancel the human parentage. Zeus breeds and immediately thereafter the human father — though even the latter as hero is paradigmatic of human process rather than simply representational. The Greek myth insists on the interrelation of the two engenderings, just as it conceives Zeus' own act of conception in natural terms. That too is myth of natural engendering. We are without a blush to picture Zeus in the act of love as man in the act of love, because Zeus' act is the appreciation from the human standpoint of that act itself as immortal form and given form. We are back again to the moment when Dawn brings light simultaneously to men and the gods in the 5th book of the *Odyssey*. It is perhaps because there has been a weakening in the sense of an act of Zeus', the transposition of event in the key of its determination, (as witness Xenophanes and the assumed 5th century influence of his thought), the constant deterioration of myth towards representational history, that Pindar here sharply distinguishes while as sharply juxtaposing the acts of Tyndareus and Zeus. That is, Pindar is re-insisting in his myth on the same double aspect of the same natural act as disclosed in the *Odyssey,* but, perhaps, fearing that the Zeus aspect in his time has begun to lose its distinction from natural representation, by bringing it into intimate collocation with the natural engendering of Tyndareus he emphasizes again that distinction, the divine dimension of the purely natural process. Man engenders and is likely in the act to delude himself that he is determinant. But at that very moment the Natural Order for that act has been enacted, and he only its instrument, and so what will be born, while being his son, is simultaneously the son of that Natural Order. And since he has not by will grown or summoned his capacities, even in his enactment it is divine power as well as human energy that has been deployed, just as it is divine form not simply its human participant that is realized in the birth and subsequent flowering. The separate engendering of Polydeukes-Castor is the dual aspect of the act of engendering in nature; to realize Zeus is not only to realize its immortal recurrence but the momentary relation of the human man to his given form and process.

But it is the Polydeukes aspect, for all that he is purposely designated as also the son of Tyndareus, which "chooses" death with Castor, who takes upon himself to be simply the human aspect. Here is the final drama of our myth, and it is even harder to state in non-mythical terms this use of as-if psychic drama to disclose perpetual theological meaning. The scene is filled, of course, with the emotion of human awareness of interdependence on other human beings. But in myth as abstract formulation of recurrence that drama must be the image of the apprehension of divine ordination.

The "choice" is the earlier Hellenic mythical form for that part of the Christian myth we have already criticized as an attempt to read human emotion as determining natural order, that "God so loved the world he gave his only begotten son," or in another widespread Christian version, closer to the Greek original, as Christ's (who mythically and only mythically is simultaneously his own Father) concern for suffering man which leads him to take on human form and endure the utmost of human affliction, which is, as for the Greek myth, as for Polydeukes, to suffer death. And at that juncture, in both versions, the myth of incarnation evolves as the myth of resurrection.

The first point is to understand "choice" in mythical context, understand phenomena transposed as psychic drama. Since myth is descriptive of form, not explanatory, mythic sequence or mythic cause and effect are not a scientific sequence postulating *post hoc propter hoc*. The *locus classicus* for me is always the "anger" of Artemis in the first chorus of the *Agamemnon* (135f) which "causes" the sacrifice of Iphigeneia. She is described as angry because the eagles have torn and eaten the hare with its unborn young and in requital sends the calm on Aulis that leads to Agamemnon's sacrifice of his daughter, her natural offspring yet unrealized. There is, of course, no cause and effect in our sense. Menelaus and Agamemnon are those eagles and Iphigeneia that bleating leveret. In a temporal narrative sequence Agamemnon may be said to have done what has already taken place, the slaughter of the innocent. But this is myth, not narrative, and Artemis' "anger" itself the mythic image for that befouling of the proper regard for the process of marriage, childbirth, and the nurture of the young which is Artemis' governance. Artemis' "anger" is a way of objectifying as image the terrible psychic dislocation of ambitious Agamemnon.

In similar fashion, Polydeukes' "choice" is mythical event, phenomenal procedure pictured as if human drama, the "choice" appreciable image of what takes place now and always. Polydeukes "chooses" what is naturally enacted, but the drama of such choice does stop us and make us see what it is that is always happening. What is always happening, of course, is that the son of Zeus lives and achieves only as the son of Tyndareus, though to make that choice, he must also realize himself as the son of Zeus. The human form and act is only participation in divine ordination, form and capacity only given, but the immortal form and its deployment is lived and appreciated only under human limitation. Polydeukes "chooses" what is in fact the eternal relation of the divine to the human, the eternal relation of the son of Zeus to the son of Tyndareus. If the son of Tyndareus is to dwell in the gold halls of radiance, the son of Zeus must endure the dark depths of annihilation. Death is the mother of beauty realized as divine manifestation. We have now within a single myth the Tantalus-Pelops sequence in the *1st Olympian:* the very awareness of the human limitation leads to the realization of its living achievement as participation in divine order. The image of Polydeukes' "choice" pinpoints the "decisive" issue of phenomenon, the situation of the human condition.

But since Polydeukes makes that choice in his human capacity, as the brother of Castor, as, in fact, himself the son of Tyndareus, but after the proclamation of his divine sonship, aware of Zeus' being and his own relation to it while related on the human scale to another, his choice is the dramatic *acceptance* of the human condition, accepting death when he fully knows he is the son of Zeus. For us, the mortal audience, Polydeukes' choice is the image of reconciliation with the terrible-glorious lot of suffering, loving man, the image of our reconciliation to our own condition. Mythic figures and their acts, which are totally imaginary, are projected for our understanding but also for our possible happiness. Polydeukes chooses our lot — such another one as Castor's — and can thereby be our means to its acceptance.

The result of that acceptance, first and last the acceptance of death, should mean that we, too, thereafter, like Castor, can live with Zeus temporarily, can as mortal know in time the eternal, which is free from death, and, harder to grasp, know ourselves as, will-less, expressing supreme power. We can not overcome death in nature; quite the contrary, the very acceptance of that natural limit, taken together with our appreciation of what life as phenomenon in ourselves is, is what makes possible our celebration of immortal living. Polydeukes must go underground for Castor to dwell in heaven. As Polydeukes chooses *death* he brings to *life* the eye and voice of Castor. Castor, too, will henceforth alternate between death and the full converse of Zeus and Athena. Reconciliation with the natural condition, meaning death, was dramatized mythically as "choice"; the consequence of that acceptance, meaning death, is dramatized mythically as "resurrection." The two can not be separated, the acceptance and its reward. Dying Castor opens his eyes and speaks to his brother. What his future life will hold we have already been told twice over, so that our last and most moving image in the poem may be the moment of his resurrection. It should move to joy and tears as the image of the most wanted human miracle; it should resolve itself in tears and joy as the image of the wonder that a man looks and speaks at all. Pindar has used that great hope to render that great impression.

Pindar in the last line of his last poem has Polydeukes raise from the dead his mythical brother Castor. The myth is clear enough, and I have already invited the reader as, I hold, Pindar did his original audience, to identify with Castor and hence with his new life, as with Polydeukes' realization of his sonship of Zeus. How is this not an invitation, then, to a belief in personal immortality? And if it is not, how does it have any effective meaning, add, as this myth surely once did, to human happiness, the celebration of existence?

The relation of the natural individual of any audience to the mythical figure, for which we use the term "identify," is not, however, a one-for-one relationship, not even for poetry where the figures are under the same natural limitations as ourselves. We say "identify with," but that does not mean that we confuse our individual histories or situations with those of Lear or Oedipus, Ajax or Hamlet. They describe for us, better than we can descry as isolated elements in ourselves, aspects of our or any nature and provide histories of the enactment in given circumstances of those elements. The ground of all sympathy, the common psyche, creates our relation to poetic figures as it does to living human beings, but "identify" with does not mean the enactment of a parallel history.

Even less, in our individual condition or history, do we imaginatively become ourselves those figures in myth which abstract total recurring condition, as do Castor and Polydeukes. They live and die and live and die again, as no individual man does; their own immortality is purely mythical and does not deny nature, in so far as they perish as often as they figure living shape and achievement. We identify with that mythical arc by placing our own condition in it, but as we do so we subscribe to the total effect for many individuals, not one self alone. They figure each of us only as we see each of ourselves as exemplary of the natural process of recurrence, the blooming of the individual psyche alternating with its extinction. A mythical figure 'stands for' us as disclosing our location in natural history, not as prototype of our individuality.

In *Nemean 10* the resurrection of Castor consists in the son of Tyndareus becoming the son of Zeus, enjoying the privileges of his brother, that is, of his other self, the son of Zeus. That transformation, that resurrection is also in the poem the direct and immediate result of Polydeukes', his other self's realization that he *is* the son of Zeus, yet totally dependent on Castor, who is both his mortal self and the substitutable self of another — such is the compression of mythic statement. We must appreciate Two as One but also One as Two. The first appreciation means that Castor's resurrection and Polydeukes' renewed awareness of his parentage are the same thing, the realization for Polydeukes-Castor as the son of Zeus; and hence for anyone to 'know his mortal existence as expressive of divine power.

The second appreciation, One as Two, makes it clear that this realization of the self and its participation in immortal power can only arise in the awareness of relation to another, to awareness of the common psyche as opposed to individually seized existence. By the separation of the Polydeukes-Castor aspects in myth, which never occurs in natural existence, we also understand what it means in the single individual for there to be the son of Zeus *apart from* the son of Tyndareus and his mortality, that participation in immortal form is to be distinguished from the fulfillment of individual destiny. Resurrection is the imaginative moment of moving from the second to the first.

It must be stressed that the myth of Castor-Polydeukes, Castor's resurrection as god's son's twin, is not a poeticization of 'natural recurrence': no myth of resurrection derives therefrom. The instinctive reaction to natural recurrence does not lead to celebration of existence but rather to mourning for it and can not explain the joy of the Dionysia, the Adonis festivals, or the sense of immortality conferred by initiation into the Eleusinian mysteries, all of which are core-kin of the myth of Castor-Polydeukes. Confinement to life in one's own dramatic right is *accentuated* by contrast to other, particularly younger or more flourishing form, by the perception of the renewal of life in and through other natural centers. Suicides, we are told, are more frequent towards dawn, more frequent on sunny days than rainy, and a sensitive man who has taught himself that value depends on individual self-awareness and self-assertion in action will, when life's natural energies are drained, fear death as the complete answer to that self-awareness and, perhaps, in his panic, like Hemingway, seek to end its terror. Not only fear of death but irreconcilability with it are the price of immersion in individuality. The myth of resurrection is the myth of reconciliation with death, and that means imaginative escape from organic individuality.

The partial reconciliation that many men and women effect with death is dependent on partial psychic transposition, not in the abstract, but with *ton philon* of this poem, "their very own," as I have translated it. The suicide, whether he has parents or brothers or even, like Hemingway, sons, does not transpose his psychic existence in their right, dramatically blur his own center by imaginative existence through others, but many men are partially reconciled to the life-death contrast by "the very own" who have died before them and "the very own" who live on after them; they are partially reconciled to death, we say, by love, though we should in that term grasp the

251

necessary transposition of psychic centering as well as its emotional affect; the clarity of the former rather than the quality of the latter is determinant. This is the point realized dramatically in our poem by Polydeukes' cry to Zeus to free him from man's sorrows, man's loneliness, the pain of death. Its answer is Zeus' proclamation, "Thou art my son," and the consequent revival of Castor with that son's privileges.

That is resurrection, and it is dramatized here by the momentary separation of the immortal form, the divine sonship, and its mortal constituent, though they live as the single person. That mythic separation is, however, decisive, though we must apply it, if we turn to nature from myth, to the single person.

Ordinary human experience, even in intimacy, of partial psychic substitution is such a limited step that the drama of all the forms of the myth of resurrection is pitched to a step beyond it, realization of a sort that submerges the bonds of intimacy along with the individuality dependent on them. It is not usually supposed to arise in ordinary existence; its extraordinariness is the very mark of the festival or initiation which produces it. Such a festival was the Dionysia, and the worship of Dionysus is par excellence the momentary suspension of individuality to live as the common psyche. The relation between Castor and Pollux is the putative relation of all the worshippers of Dionysus to Iacchus, the source of their own being defined as young godhead. No man, surely, in the *teleusterion* at Eleusis was to be considered the same man who went into it, else nothing could have happened by his initiation. Such initiation into immortality by submergence of individuality, the assuming of a single psyche on the part of all worshippers is the Greek half — the antithetical Judaic half will concern us later — of Christian membership in the body of Christ.

That separation from the individual act leading to appreciation of its immortal form can be realized prior to death in living experience. The expressiveness of sight and speech and the inter-relation they set up to all other living phenomena is as strategic a part of the realization as the appreciation of the eternity of the form that exercises them. The celebration in the single act of perception or assertion that such perception or assertion exists at once turns it into appreciation of divine capacity as opposed to its singular dramatic fulfillment, the drama of Castor's eye moving again and his voice speaking his recognition of his brother, the image of immemorial perception. Once I have used, in contemporary discourse, the abstraction, perception, in place of one man's seeing, I have set up the possibility of the dimension that is mythically realized as divine capacity, the fiat of Zeus' son for Castor's glance and speaking. The single act of the eye, whether in recognition of the lilies' effulgence or of another human being's, its daily service, once one steps outside its enactment to celebrate it, is its enactment of divine form, the human capacity now recognized as god's son seeing. Castor opening his eyes and speaking has become in his new life the son of Zeus seeing and speaking.

It is to be noted — and it will be contrasted shortly with the earliest statements of the Christian myth — that the immortality conferred on the paradigmatic Castor-Polydeukes does not deny the natural death of either. What it gives, however, is life with Zeus when living, the realization of life in its efflorescence as the expression of divine radiance, the intuition that Pindar has lifelong dramatized. What is or should be abolished by such appreciation is the distinction between life and death, that is, the definition of achievement or perception by its mortal frame rather than as expressive of immortal power. Once that conversion is made, the man dying celebrates the expressiveness of immortal form just as much as in his living.

Nor is it his death as the prelude or announcement of others' living. In his death itself he defines his natural human limits but just as dramatically announces the separation of his will from their determination, announces the realization of divine power. Castor and Polydeukes are not denied or deserted by Zeus as they go underground, though Lynkeus and Idas are — a distinction that will be made shortly. Underground or on Olympus they reveal the natural order for the human condition, a natural order to be subscribed to in both its parts in order to grasp the relation between the human and the divine. Their sonship of Zeus is acknowledged in their declination as in their shining on Olympus.

Men, after all, soften the blow of death by the sense of how important they have been and how important they therefore are to others as they die. It should, then, prove an even greater reconciliation, if it is known, as they die, that the son of Zeus is going underground. It is also the son of Tyndareus going underground, and this myth, as the Christian in some men's minds, insists on that distinction. The mortal identity has perished, but so momentarily has immortal expression. The totality of life has been expressed in that example as clearly and dramatically as in any other; we do not have to wait the next one to know that it is divine power as well as man that has perished, and though it is god, not mortal man, who renews existence, he will be renewed in the same presence. And in the terrible contrast between his mortal will and his present condition man in death most fully reveals that what once seemed his own will and its governance of his capacities must always have been divine determination. The experience of death discloses more fully than any other the degree to which all living is purely expressive, and the moment the self-conscious center of that imposed form seizes his relation to his expression, he realizes, in mythical terms, that the son of god is his inseparable twin, that he himself defined individually is the son of man while simultaneously dependent for his expressiveness on the son of god.

Death then becomes the most plangent announcement of divine power, death, natural death, the sign and seal of resurrection, for, so understood, it makes hitherto unsounded living, the unconscious enactment of given existence, the celebration of divine ordination. The myth of resurrection is such celebration: the son of Zeus will die, and once we know it is the son of Zeus who perished, the son of Tyndareus may live in intimate converse with Zeus and Athena.

One portion of this myth we have not yet examined: the conflict between the Twins and those other, mortal brothers, Idas and Lynkeus. One purpose it serves, of course, is to account for the necessary death of the hero in battle. As such it is only prelude to the death scene and its significance. But the instrumentality of Zeus, the contrasted pairs, and the vocab-

254

ulary of its conclusion insist upon their share in the theological pattern. That portion, as in the Pelops-Tantalus inter-relation, should be the obverse of the meaning we have already pondered. Such it is.

Pindar dismisses the cause of the fight between Castor and Idas as "something about cattle," clearly not intending that any issue between them enter our imagination or carry any moral or theological meaning. According to the scholia (Drachmann III 178), Pindar was following a version in which the Dioscuri had carried off the brides of the sons of Aphareus at their wedding and killed them as they attempted to recapture their own women. This account does not and should not concern us; I recall it to make wider than the Pindaric version the absence from the myth of a moral distinction, in our sense, between the two sets of brothers. Pindar, it is true, eliminates any act of aggression on the part of Castor and Polydeukes, but he does not turn and make their opponents guilty of any, either, and so to be justly punished for their "wicked" attack on "our side." Our instinct, to put it bluntly, is to read the thunderbolt of Zeus as the wrath of Jehovah breaking through nature to give victory if not to the good at least to those with whom he is identified as against their opponents. That is religion that makes divine will expressive of identifiable human will and explains their discrepancy, in the bitterness of defeat, as the lapse of the faithful from their allegiance, the punishment for their sins. Among the Hellenes divine will does not figure human will, individual or social, and human will or even aggression is not necessarily either holy or sinful (and a religion which reads it as one is likely to read it as the other, depending on who is employing it). Nor is deity used to identify the parties in a conflict, the morality of their acts determined by their respective allegiances.

We should always bear in mind the umbrella for all Greek poetry, Homer, where the gods of the Greeks are the gods of the Trojans, and no moral distinction is made between them. The difference between the theological interpretation of the battlefield of Ilium and the theological interpretation of the battlefields of Jericho and Armageddon is a sound measure of the distinction between the Hebrew and Hellenic views of divine ordination. In Greek poetry neither hero nor people stand and battle for the Lord, and where that happens, it is clear enough that the Lord is the will of those who stand and battle.

Idas and Lynkeus are not guilty of any evil acts; they are not punished by a supernatural guardian of morality for any guilt. And since they are quite as Greek as Castor and Polydeukes, they are not distinguished morally in their employment of force by differing tribal or religious identity. What, then, is the meaning of their swift extinction by the weapon of Polydeukes and the blast of Zeus' power?

Along with shedding an antithetical theology we must pass again the barrier to myth. The scholiasts with their usual misunderstanding describe the account of the fight as "history," and so instinctively we take it, conceive, that is, the mythic figures as stand-ins for human figures, the mythic events as stand-ins for natural events, the "moral meaning" the poet's contrived outcome of such human figures in such circumstance. That is not the case. This part of the myth has, indeed, a heavy theological significance, but it is not an intent "behind" the figures or one drawn from their acts. The figures and what happens to them are themselves the images of a theological state and its result, theological meaning *pictured* as men and events, abstraction as-if narrative.

Castor and Polydeukes I have presented in their relation to man in nature, a single man in any audience, as mythically realized aspects of himself, his mortal and divine sides seen both together and separated. Idas and Lynkeus similarly are aspects or attitudes on the part of any man, attitude which is antithetical to that realized in Castor and Polydeukes, the denial of the realization of human nature and its two-fold aspect which the Twins sign. This myth is a unity and only as a unity is related to natural man; it does not distinguish between "us" and "others." Idas and Lynkeus are us, too, if we do not understand ourselves through Castor—Polydeukes, if we do not realize the relation of the son of Zeus and the son of Tyndareus, the divine form of human expression.

Their sin is *not* to realize Polydeukes as the son of Zeus. It is not that they have done wrong or worship another deity than Zeus: they are never told or learn why what happens to them happens: they are paradigm for any man's failure to recognize divinity in human form or act, whether their own or another's.

Lynkeus with "the sharpest eye of any man on earth" is the forerunner of riddle-solving Oedipus and his mind, the man who seems to see who can not see at all, sharpest in human faculty, blindest to the nature of things. And as Oedipus' true state is at the last signed by physical blindness, so Lynkeus' sharp eye "burns to blankness" (72) in Zeus' fiery blast. When divine ordination is revealed in its full glory he has no sight left at all.

Now, as I have said, the destruction of these brothers is not *caused* by anything they do. Their "punishment" is the revelation of their sin, the mythical image of the state they live in. The punishment figures the sin; the sin is disclosed in the punishment. We are to make no distinction between them. Mythical event is the revelation of a state in nature. I point again to Artemis' "anger" as figuring Agamemnon's derange-ment of the natural order of procreation and child-bearing, or Polydeukes' "choice" as the dramatic picture of how godhead must be defined by mortal appearance and disappearance. Mythic drama is the way to state as-if human action what in our discourse would be pure abstraction, recurrent conditions synthesized as images. Lynkeus and Idas are damned; their extinction at Zeus' hand both reveals and is their damnation. And like the damned always, they never know it. They perish "on the instant."[2] If we conceive of Idas-Lynkeus as our other possibility or state opposed to our undergoing the Castor-Polydeukes realization, then their "punishment" is how we live as well as die, undergoing extinction in blindness, just as we have exerted our active natures with no knowledge of our own or anyone's nature as grounded in divine power.

Similarly that punishment is made symbolic of what is disclosed by the knowledge of Polydeukes as the son of Zeus. The Natural Order is figured in its highest lambency and clamor. That bolt is expression of the reality of Zeus, visual image for our grasp of his power in any life as in any death; it is quite literally the *aigla diosdotos,* the god-given radiance in *Pythian 8,* the realization of divine order in human achievement and triumph. We, as members of the audience, grasp the reality of that divinity in blind man's extinction, as Polydeukes, as our representative, the measure of our appreciation of Zeus' presence in our lives, does in the myth. But that is precisely what Idas and Lynkeus do not know. They perish not knowing what they are up against; they perish not knowing Zeus in Polydeukes. It is not identity against identity, one wicked, the other good, but the paradigm of the entirety of human nature that is elicited by the myth, the apperception of divinity as opposed to the failure to recognize it. Nor is it even made exemplary of moral choice; these heroes are not given a chance which they fail. Like Cheiron and Tantalus they are simply mythic images of blindness of the divine dimension of human form and act. Their state or fate, which are synonymous, is anyone's godlessness.

As myth is not natural, the blast of Zeus is not natural, but as mythical imagery, as the interpretation of nature, it is not the postulation of supernatural direction of human affairs. It is simply the sign of the perpetual Natural Order. Its exercise, we have seen, is not brought about by guilty act or wrong moral choice; its exercise, that is, is not brought about by act in history and its moral determination of nature. It can only be understood within the context of myth itself and its demand for image as illustration. It is the momentary illumination of the divine order, the sky a moment shimmering white light as thunder rolls, everything for that moment visible. But it is divine order that is illuminated, and that order is forever and eternal; only the demand for the gathering image in myth makes it temporal. Its confines are those imposed by appreciation, not by natural fact, as the moment of triumph in *Pythian 8* elicits the appreciation of god-given radiance. We should not confuse mythical time and natural time. The mythical image is of the moment, as is a chemical formula's use, but what it discloses abides beyond the image, as does the nature of the substance beyond the time-span of the formula's illumination.

Likewise, the last and most significant word Pindar uses to describe Idas-Lynkeus, *eremoi,* is, in the myth, temporal and the result of act, the blast of Zeus, but its intent is the final and strongest definition of their case: deserted, abandoned, isolated, deprived of the company of men and gods, like Tantalus. Once again, too, the sequence of cause and effect in myth, as in the first chorus of the *Agamemnon,* sharply reverses our usual narrative sense. Logically or narratively, these brothers are punished for what they become; mythically, the result of their punishment simply figures what they are: abandoned of god. The word and its use should be well noted. We shall come upon it in the New Testament; its poetic theological use rings down through history, to San Juan de la Cruz, to *The Wasteland* and *Ash-Wednesday,* the desert of spiritual desolation. Once more in this myth Pindar has established the classic 5th century example of a term for the continuing vocabulary of Western theology and has given it as heavy a theological burden as it will ever carry. The damned are those without god; the event, the quarrel about cattle, is the narrative frame to transform as picture the state of damnation. No human will or act or its punishment is relevant to such mythical abstraction.

The myth taken as a whole is the picture of blessedness contrasted to the state of damnation, the same polarity as established by the contrasting pictures of Pelops and Tantalus in *Olympian 1.* Blessedness consists in the realization of the incarnation and the subsequent joy of resurrection. Damnation consists in the inability to recognize the first and thereby to be excluded from sharing in the second. They are both, of course, in our sense, forms of appreciation, damnation the failure of such appreciation. In a way nothing happens in our myth at all, either in the part concerning Lynkeus-Idas or that concerned with Castor-Polydeukes alone. The heroes and acts of this mythic narrative are abstractions for what is always and forever true, not historical event but recurrent pattern. Castor rising from his death-wound is no more a natural man coming to life again, than Lynkeus-Idas blasted by Zeus' thunder-bolt are natural men in history destroyed by supernatural intervention. One is man realizing divinity in his life; the other man blind to god's power in it.

# CHAPTER 8

## INCARNATION AND RESURRECTION (II):
## GREEK AS CHRISTIAN

It might help us to take an overall view of the problems involved in this second section to look upon Western theology like Western sculpture (or painting) as a succession of variations within a continuity of form. So we can see all sculpture, for example, from the 6th century B.C. to the 20th A.D. and, more particularly for our purposes, from the 5th century B.C. to the 4th century A.D. as a unity. Once the unity is grasped, the differences demand, of course, an analysis of the relation between each stage and its predecessor and successor: What intent or subconscious purpose in each instance accounts for the new expression? But there is another and different question to be asked: In what way is the continuous form radically present in any expression, and what is its particular tension in relation to the momentary one? Not just careful historicity, the preoccupation with dating, the relation to style immediately before and immediately after, but relation to the abiding capacity of the central form and its definitive statement.

In order to make my analogy clearer I shall indulge in unargued dogma in regard to plastic form, qualifying to some extent the usual current assumption of the equal validity of all honest expression within one form. Our joy in the Ravenna mosaic of the Good Shepherd not as iconography but as form is because it maintains, late in time, the expressive capacity best defined by the 5th century use of form. I revive the earlier critical view of a norm, the original meaning of classic or Classic, which implies not simply a concern or feeling for form but the critical decision as to that form's apogee, its fullest revelatory statement. Before we analyze the specific qualitative expression of the great Roman or early Christian sarcophagi, we should in our imagination hold seven or eight centuries as a unity and appreciate that, whatever their variations from it, later sculptural forms are in some way related to and dependent on their 5th century definition. Even medieval sculpture is defined by its denial of the principles at work in its own ultimate models, and that 5th century definition was also determinant of the standards of the second Western apogee, the Italian Renaissance.

Viewing antiquity as a unity, there is also a strict theological parallel of the two basic drives conditioning the transformation of the expressive norm in plastic form, the one beginning in the 4th century B.C. and progressive in its effect, the other beginning in the 2nd century A.D. and likewise progressive. The first is the turning from the statement of the generic conditions of natural form to description, surface articulation of natural identities, the second the gradual loss of the formal recognition of generic conditions altogether even in specific articulation, the first the loss of idea for the sake of surface representation, the second the loss of the awareness of the imposed place in nature of natural forms. The art historian may yield to the critic who concerns himself not with the continuous evolvement of form but with the problem of what the formalization of nature as plastic form is intended to achieve, and if he answers that problem to his satisfaction, he may have to claim that some formal expression in the last analysis denies the vital purpose of its own inherited effort.

Now the parallel to plastic form in theology with which we are concerned is myth; more particularly how myth in the 5th century B.C. is transformed in the 1st and 2nd centures A.D. I claim that Western theology is unified by myth as form as clearly as sculpture by its own form, that myth's expressive capacity can be defined by Classical Greek expression, and that later variation depends for one aspect of its understanding on being related to that definition, that it must be seen as fulfilling or denying that form's revelatory purpose. Myth's 5th century expression is of the same relevance to Christian myth as Classical sculpture to early Christian sarcophagi. Every art historian studies them, of course, in terms of their own expressive purpose, but the local expressive purpose can only be defined by its relation to the inherited sculptural form, which takes us at last to the 4th and 5th centuries B.C. That there be such articulation at all does not derive from the immediate expressive purpose but from an earlier one; they do not account for their own possibility. So Christian myth does not disclose of itself the nature of its own form or that form's intent. What it does to inherited form to satisfy its own purpose is of the greatest interest, but the inherited form itself can only be understood in terms of its original intent and fullest expressive statement. Christian myth is not a beginning but a later variation, and, more importantly, not definitive in its own right of its own form.

By the 5th and 4th centuries Greek plastic form had become, too, a matter of individual achievement; what Praxiteles or Scopas or Myron created was definitive sculptural form through all antiquity, their imaginative work, in the original or copies, present for comparison by all those who labored afterwards. And I am quite as specific in my claim that Pindar's *10th Nemean* similarly became one of the definitive and hence for later time determinant expressions of the combined myth – its parts always inseparable – of incarnation and resurrection. Key words of Pindar's vocabulary as well as the key dramatic pronouncement by Zeus reappear, as we shall see, in Christianity. The Christian version goes back in the last analysis to a number of previous expressions such as the Pindaric version. The Pindaric version, however, can very easily be seen to be original. The epiphany of Zeus in *Nemean 10* is as clearly the poet's handiwork as the epiphany of Poseidon in *Olympian 1*, and as the appearance of Zeus, so, too, his definition of his relation to Polydeukes. What Zeus says to Polydeukes and what Polydeukes does for Castor are clearly of our poet's imaginative fabrication. One can not claim that other poets did not treat other myths with a parallel appreciation. No Greek myth, and no deity, either, is exclusive in its function or imaginative intent. The same situation can appear with variant mythic figures, just as specific natural powers can be symbolized by variant divine shape. The vocabulary of myth, while creative, was fluid. One can not claim, then, that the Pindaric myth of Castor-Polydeukes is the ultimate source of the Gospel myth of incarnation, but merely that it is one of the determinant ones. Nor can it be held that it was a direct source.

I do not understand how or in what later form the Pindaric myth was absorbed by the New Testament writers. By their

262

appropriation and transformation of it they all unconsciously assert, what we so often forget, that Greek mythic poetry was theology, not belles lettres. To a later time, too, myth as theology can live quite apart from the accidents of its original poetic projection, its careful metres, public ritual, and specific social references. Such myth could, perhaps, have been reworked in a later, simpler poetry, attempting to state in contemporaneously comprehensible form inherited mythic statement, or even in prose as illustration of abstract theological statement – though I can not in this instance provide any examples.

Here a different sort of sculptural analogy might be useful. Copies or reproductions of great 5th century originals are often in quite different dimensions for atrium use, but "atrium suitability" for poetry, needless to say, poses additional problems than those for sculpture, whose language and terms are accessible to all viewers. Copying simply for later comprehension, quite apart from historical evolvement of form, will imply omission and transformation, the disappearance of the pride of Argive families or the great games of mainland Greece, the geographic locale of heroic achievement and death. The new writers might well realize that what is strategic is the appreciation of Polydeukes as the son of Zeus and the consequent return of Castor to the land of the living. Lastly, the mythic events can be separated from their original figures and either ascribed to others or stated abstractly as the incarnation and the resurrection of the son of god.

It is clearly at this last stage that the Christian writers appropriate the Greek myth for purely Christian figures. Those Christian writers are at once faced with what, if we maintain our grip on the unity of myth as form, is an extraordinary problem, none the less hazardous for being unconscious. God in Greek myth is, of course, god in its Hellenic, not its Hebraic significance, and the son of god is a purely mythical figure, not a natural man in history. We shall find that the transformation of the myth of incarnation-resurrection in Christian terms is governed by these two radical contradictions of its own nature. The form and its later function are not compatible; the attempt to coalesce them has resulted in misunderstanding which is still operative.

263

I do not, then, hold that Paul and the Gospel writers read Pindar, any more than they read Plato, though they used a mythic vocabulary, whose original function they could not know, which derives eventually from Pindar, just as Paul and John, at least, used Platonic distinctions, whose original function, even before their use of them, had been radically transformed in Hellenistic thought and writing. Whether we call their use in either case misunderstanding or new function, it should be remembered that it could not have come into being at all without the Classic functioning both of myth and discursive discourse, and that its own expression can, from one point of view, be defined by its relation to that earlier functioning. The degree to which the original Hellenic intent is, as I see it, still operative, still determinant of the Christian expression, may startle some readers.

Therein lies the wider significance of this limited attempt to point out the relation between one poem of Pindar's and the earliest extant Christian statements of its own most vital dogmas. The relation of Christian to Greek thought is hardly a new subject, but its basic assumption can be stated in over-simplified terms as Judaism-derived religious intuitions taking their *later* dogmatic shape through the lens of Hellenistic learning and theology, most particularly through the Greek Church Fathers, with John's Gospel, perhaps, an earlier exception to purely local religious intuitions of Hebraic origin. With that post-Pauline and post-Gospel transformation I am not at all concerned; I am concerned with the kernel formulations themselves found in all the Gospels as in the authenticated epistles of Paul. I profess to see in one instance that the basic Christian formulation is clearly Hellenic, that Christian myth at its earliest inception, the account of the life of Christ and his significance, is a late variation of Greek myth, inconceivable without it and to be understood in relation to it.

It must at once be clear that I distinguish between Jesus of Nazareth and the Christ of the Gospels, but I do not thereby hold to any 19th century assumption that Christianity is to be purified by such separation, and its essence distilled as the former and his teachings. On the contrary, Christianity arose only when Jesus of Nazareth became the Christ of the Gospels, when his "historical form," if you will, was determined by his "mythical form." The accounts of the ministry and teaching are, after all, accounts, and those, too, always at the mercy of the appreciating lens in every iota of declaration. Every tale and every quotation is what its writer's intent and form make it, and while one can critically separate Jesus and the idea of Christ, can even for purely critical purposes separate a writer's formulation of one from his succeeding moment's formulation of the other, one can not in either case separate the formulation from its intent or know any facts, any personality, any teaching outside them. Christianity is what Christians thought. It does not have an autonomous existence. (Those who claim it does betray themselves by their insistence on indoctrination and correct education.) And the simplest definition of Christian thought is the definition of Jesus of Nazareth as the Son of God who rose from the dead. If you separate the historical figure from that definition, you may have religious intuition, but you do not have definable Christianity. Though the elements of the two aspects are critically separable, then, the intent of the myth always governs the presentation of the life and the ministry. *There never was any Christianity without Christian myth.*

The only contribution I can make to New Testament scholarship must be derived from the self-defined task of pointing out a hitherto unnoted relation between a particular version of Greek myth and its Christian appearance. Yet in touching its new situation and the sea-change it has undergone, one is bound to point out, from the standpoint of Greek myth, what one presumes are the pressures determining that change. One will, that is, be judging Christian intent. Nor will one attempt to explicate Hebrew prophecy even when, similarly, noting its effect on Greek myth. There is the possibility, however, of a further contribution.

Through this work I have been attempting to criticize form, and my use of that term now coincides accidentally with the term "form-criticism," a study rich in results in Biblical scholarship. While the collocation is accidental, my own use does, in fact, extend the term to an area "form-critics" have tried to exclude from it. Their whole effort has been to establish an element or essence in Christianity beyond "form," residual as "faith," posited in the last analysis as "mystery." I deny that mystery. It is operative myth. Their own motive, for all their learning, is as apparent in their criticism as it is in the creation of Christian myth: exclusive identity. That motive has led to the most extraordinary, because the most critical lacuna in all New Testament scholarship.

No one has defined—because critics have felt they should not define—let alone illuminate the critical moment and its process creative of Christianity. I have already said that I do not know how or in what form Hellenic myth was appropriated by Christian writers. But now looking backward from the earliest Christian texts one is up against a startling phenomenon. They all take for granted the appropriation of Greek myth, the significance of Christ in Greek mythic terms. Paul, for example, never argues or explores those Greek assumptions; they are used as if everyone knew them and took them as self-evident. He uses them as assumed for his own new purpose. Every one of the Gospels announces parallel mythic assumptions, again without argument or elucidation. If Paul's (or Mark's) mind or writing were the moment of creation, surely he would be at some pains to make clear to his readers the mythic assumptions he is using. Since he does not, we must assume that the readers are accustomed to them. Their creative historical moment, the creator and his preaching or writing remain in total darkness. We shall keep running into this problem: the creation of Christian myth. Its place, its time, above all its mind are quite unknown.

Let us turn to one of the most pregnant texts of Christianity, the salutation of the epistle *Romans.*

> "Paul, slave of Christ Jesus, called missionary who has dedicated himself to glad tidings of God which He had proclaimed through his prophets in holy scriptures, concerning His own Son, born of the sperm of David according to flesh, defined as Son of God in power according to spirit of holiness proceeding from resurrection from the dead, Jesus Christ our Lord, through whom we receive thanks and mission for the obedience of belief among all all races on behalf of his name."

Here is Greek myth given false derivation and reversed sequence, to new purpose.

266

First, the myth itself, unargued by Paul, as if his readers understood it without explication. As we shall also see in John, Paul maintains the Hellenic inseparability of the myths of incarnation and resurrection, though he reverses the operative sequence. Secondly, he clearly reiterates the Greek coalescence of mortal and immortal son. For Paul—and this, too, will be found in the Gospels alongside its own contradiction—Christ in the flesh, as the product of biology, is human, the offspring of the seed of David, a genealogy that proceeds through *Joseph* in both Matthew and Luke. In Paul, of course, there is no suggestion of what passes, among Catholics and Fundamentalists, as the basis of the incarnation, the immaculate conception of Mary and the virgin birth of Christ. To Paul, as to Pindar, human birth and divine sonship are complementary, not contradictory. But the Greek myth has also been clearly determinant as to the human genealogy. The Christ must be the son of a hero, and David fits better than any other Hebrew historic figure that mythic role. Hebrew king and mythic hero are not the same thing, of course; historization has begun in making the paradigmatic mythic hero a part of Hebrew history. But the double-parentage in Paul is more significant than that partial historization. It revives the double aspect of the mythic hero, subject to death as the son of Tyndareus, immortal as the son of Zeus. In all his arguments, even in his quite un-Hellenic briefs for personal human immortality, Paul never lets go of this Tyndareus-Zeus distinction, first as applied to his paradigmatic figure Christ, and then to those who believe in him and can thereby be identified with his history. The popular dogma of the Virgin Birth would logically make impossible Paul's use of Christ as the means to natural human immortality, the believer's parallel assumption, perforce humanly born, of the immortal sonship. Christ as somehow the physical offspring of God excluding human procreation and birth never enters Paul's imagination.

Now I have claimed that Paul's use, in this case as elsewhere, is of Christian myth not of his own making, else he would have argued it or detailed it or illuminated it for readers to whom—if this were its inception— it would have seemed altogether strange and new. This is as early a statement, be it remembered, of the

Christian version of incarnation and resurrection as can be safely, if only approximately, dated; the Gospel parallels, which we shall shortly consider, in the state we possess them, at least, are later. Yet its writer could not possibly have been the point of this myth's Christian absorption and transmission. The creator of the Christian myth can only have been a mind which was seeing new figures in the pattern set by Hellenic myth, must have known that pattern with other figures before he substituted his own. That presupposes a knowledge of Greek myth in its own right prior to seeing Christ's nature in the light of that received form and its interpretative message.

Paul, on the other hand, is quite unaware that he is using Greek myth; for him the source of the divine nature of Jesus is Hebrew prophecy, that which God has proclaimed through his prophets in (Hebrew) holy scriptures. I am not concerned with the critical problem—fascinating in its own right—of the use of Hebrew prophecy for Christian purposes, from the Judaic standpoint motivated misreading, though it is good always to emphasize the distinction, still widely blurred in New Testament criticism, between the Son of God, a Hellenic concept, and the Hebrew Messiah. My own point is more confined, though being new it has unsounded implications. It is this: Paul's use of Hebraic tradition to account for Christ's divine nature must separate him incontrovertibly from the time and the process which first read Christ as the Son of God, making him a figure in quasi-Hellenic myth. Paul, like Mark, without argument, makes that Greek concept Hebraic in origin, whereas the creator of the Christian myth was intent on turning a Hebraic religious figure into Greek myth, the precisely *opposite* dynamic. We are forced to conclude that a distance in time and a radical distinction in outlook separate the creative mind which postulated Jesus as the Son of God and the equally determinant minds, such as Paul's and Mark's, which then reread that Hellenic transformation as Hebrew tradition. The clear result of the later effort is to obscure or deny the source of the earlier, its motive antithetical to the one which created the myth they are using. This has nothing to do with conscious literary fraud; on the contrary, so deeply is Paul's appreciation of the myth governed by the dynamics of the Hebraic divine-human relation that it is impossible to conceive that he knew it in any Greek setting. But this view does propose a startling new relation of our "earliest" Christian writers to the basis of their own promulgation of the divine sonship.

But Paul's clear assumption of the source of the myth he postulates does perforce radically change both what it is intended to reveal and its relation to the believer. His misunderstanding was itself creative in the highest degree, but it is the perversion of the Hellenic myth he is so using. As he is himself the "slave of Christ Jesus," so the revelation of the divine sonship sets a "mission,"whose object is "obedience" in faith of those to whom the mission is promulgated.

Greek myth has become a means to enforcing human will. And hence the source of the myth as wrongly understood is all important. It is Yahweh's will in new guise, as defined by anathema to the Jews, the sonship of Christ. The old covenant is denied, but a new and larger one proclaimed: all races must bow to Christ, as one had submitted to Yahweh. It is not the Natural Order which is proclaimed in the sonship, an order about which one can do nothing whatsoever, which one neglects at one's peril but which never argues its reality. It is the old will of Yahweh for his people's allegiance: many men of many tongues are to fulfill the new mission with the old end, submission. The Greek myth of the sonship of Zeus, individual revelation of the immortal form and all its capacities, given temporarily to but never possessed by any of its individual participants, has been grafted onto the Hebraic conception of the allegiance-demanding Will of God, as-if human will beyond nature and history working through them for its own glorification. The myth Paul uses is Greek; his use of it a proclamation of the whole prophetic Judaic purpose with a new international scope. For Paul's purpose his ascription of the myth to the Hebrew prophets is altogether correct. We can understand his message only under the aegis of his conscious heritage, not his unconscious borrowing.

Not only the intent of the myth but the user's relation to its figure is transformed, a relation dramatized by Paul's self-definition as the "slave of Christ Jesus." As the fruit of the mission is the submission of others' wills, its prelude is the missionary's

269

submission of his own. The relation of slave to master thereby provides the tenor for the relation of any worshipper to the central figure of tne myth. The divine sonship is purely Greek, but the postulated relation to it is purely Hebraic. The relation of his people to Yahweh is the paradigm for the new relation of the individual to Christ.

The slave of a god to the Greeks is he whose own will is forfeit to his expression of the natural power symbolized by particularized deity, a slave of Aphrodite an individual whose sense of self or destiny is determined by sexual satisfaction— or if he is a master of making others submit to his desire, he can be said, like Paris in the 3rd book of the *Iliad*, to make Aphrodite his slave. We have seen in earlier chapters how the will of a man is broken or bent by divine power, but that is not usually to his happiness, and surely never to his glorification. To glory in the term slave is to glory in the exercise of will, and the slave's knowledge of the master's will and his pleasure in it derived from his imaginative recapitulation of his own transposed submission the means of triumph. Koestler's *Darkness at Noon* is a footnote to the Nietzschean analysis of the Pauline psychology. To rejoice in slavery is to rejoice in the glorification of will, and Paul makes it clear enough that the slave by his identification with the master shares his glory. Such a master-slave relationship has nothing to do with the relation between the imaginative appreciation of the significance of a figure in myth and that figure itself. Will never enters the process of illumination, whether for the scientist using formulae in a laboratory or a man seeking the disclosure of the location of his given psyche in a given universe.

Paul, I said earlier, maintains the inherited inseparability of the incarnation and resurrection, but his new use for the myth must needs transpose their sequence. In Greek myth the knowledge of the divine sonship, the realization of the immortal form in its temporal manifestation, leads to the imaginative integration of that temporal history in its divine history, the appreciation of the incarnation leads to the awareness of resurrection. With Paul the divine sonship is proclaimed as having been established by — "proceeding out of," "from" the resurrection from the dead. Divine sonship is established by "proof" of will triumphant over nature. Myth at once becomes the miraculous, and the miraculous is always the proclamation of the triumph of individual will over natural sequence. By defying death natural man proves his sonship of deity; the resurrection establishes the incarnation.

It would seem that turning the myth of the realization of ultimate individual will-lessness into the image of triumphant individual will would end its revelatory power for Hellenic purpose altogether. Strangely and marvelously that is not the case. The original myth worked and worked deeply in Paul's imagination, though at the very point of its deepest saturation and new personal expression, it is defined anew, tormented by the purpose such illumination must now serve.

The myth of Zeus and his dual son Castor-Polydeukes I have defined as the myth of the integrity of life and death when they are both realized as phenomenal aspects of order quite beyond the individual participants in that order, and the reconciliation to death the seizure of that individual relation to its own enactment. The words in the salutation of this epistle reviving Greek myth in the dual parentage of Christ and the collocation of resurrection and the sonship of deity are not to be separated from Paul's plangent statement, later in the epistle, of the human condition seen in the light of that mythic illumination. The sharply limited quotation which follows is the personal appreciation bespoken for Pindar's audience in their individual appropriation of the myth of *Nemean 10:*

> For no one of you lives unto himself, and no one dies unto himself. For if we live, we live to (or by) the Supreme Power, and if we die, we die to (or by) the Supreme Power. If we live, or if we die, we are a part of the Supreme Power. For to this end Christ died and lived, so that he might have supreme power over the dead and the living. Why do you judge your brother? Or why do you account your brother nothing? For we all stand at the altar of God. For it is written: I live, says the Supreme Power. So that before me every knee will bend, and every tongue will make acknowledgement of itself to God. So each of you will give the statement (or realization) of himself to God. [1]

271

It will be noted at once that a further element in the Greek myth we have analyzed has been re-established, the relationship of "brother," which occurs, of course, in many other Pauline contexts. Paul has made the relation "brother" in this passage precisely what it is in the Pindar myth, the substitutability of one man for another, the metaphor, or more precisely, the mythical statement of common relation to identical power in life and death. Seized in that dimension no man is defined or even realized to himself as his own individuality. As substitutable he can only be defined by relation to the common source. So each man is here adjured to render the logos of himself, the way in which he is realized formally, as a gift to god. Though Paul is not intent on sounding the significance of the word, logos, by its use he has for himself as well as any user of Greek reasserted its basic meaning, "realization in the medium of speech," and the use of "tongue" as repetition or parallel in the construction seems to suggest his own awareness of that derivation. Self-realization in the last analysis is not the insistence upon individuality but its submergence in the awareness of its determination. If this passage were to stand, as, alas, it can not, as Paul's resolution, in discursive discourse, of the myth of resurrection, derived from the appreciation of the incarnation, it would not contradict Pindar's mythic drama.

There is, of course, a significant variation. We are left in Pindar's poem with the final impression of the wonder of defined human existence, individual speech and sight now seen in the light of its perpetual enactment of divine form, the son of Tyndareus risen as the son of Zeus. We rest at the last with the appreciation of phenomenon, and the myth of Zeus' own statement to Polydeukes, "Thou art my son," caught up but dissolved in that appreciation. So even the concept of God resolves itself in its function as the mode to the final appreciation of given actuality. Paul can not rest in such appreciation as ultimate. That is Hellenic. His close by contrast is stirringly Hebraic. Knee must bow; will must be celebrated. Not the appreciation of divine power as realized in phenomena but the celebration of greater will by individual will. That final note which bends, though it does not destroy the effective human self-realization of this passage, when isolated for our reaction, will become, however, dominant in Paul's further *use* of the myth of resurrection.

But that distinction — between a total centering on the process of illumination and a shifting to the human will involved, thereby losing grip on the modality of illumination — can be illustrated parenthetically from another angle. In Pindar's poem the "sin" involved in regard to the illumination of the incarnation, and its consequent reward, participation in the resurrection, is simply the failure of recognition, and the "punishment" for it, as we have seen, that failure in and of itself. This is why it is important to understand that Idas and Lynkeus do nothing, in their social and moral life, which leads to their mythic punishment. They do not realize god in man: that is all. I trust I do not have to quote to readers the lists of moral and social errors, some grievous wrongs, some natural instincts read in the lens of the writer's traumatized psyche, which loom large in Paul as sources of eternal death, as obstacles to resurrection. In Pindar, as in Plato, as, by and large, in the whole Hellenic tradition, the sin that prevents sight is the failure of sight, and if resurrection is just such a recognition (as the immortality of the soul in Plato is such another), other moral failings are to it irrelevant, however justly to be punished in their own social contexts. Mind you, we are not concerned with the myth of Heaven and Hell, for all that, by the time of the Nicene declaration Christian syncretism has enmeshed that, too, with the myth of incarnation-resurrection. The myth of Heaven and Hell, also, of course, Hellenic, not Judaic, is the myth of the absolute irreversibility of act or attitude and its effect on the actor himself as well as in the life of those affected by it, if for the good irreversibly good, if for evil, irreversibly evil. As myth, as image which is not fact but the appreciation of decision and act in natural history, it, too, became in the Graeco-Roman world confused with such history, but it resides in Pindar side by side with strident insistence on natural death, just as it is expressed in Homer and Vergil with clear recognition of the "unreality" of its imagery, with no claim that physical death is not final for actual human beings. The myth of resurrection, on the contrary, is the seizure by man of his own immortality, and is clearly its own reward. Such illumination is living beyond one's singular definition by appreciating what that self is phenomenally. But all Paul's "fornications," literal or metaphorical, imply that even without such illumination the natural man is rewarded or punished for his acts or attitudes by participation in or exclusion from the boon of resurrection. It becomes, thereby, subject to will, the man's will in determining his acts, divine will in determining his reward or punishment for them. The reason why such a divine will, which after all is itself a mythic image, does not operate in Pindar or Greek myth generally is because there is no belief in determination by human will, which it figures. There the myth of resurrection depends for its own effect on the appreciation of that will's own essential will-lessness, its otherwise determination. The myth, then, is made useless, leads to no resurrection, once the individual will is again made determinant.

Part of the problem Paul presents is the way in which he lives in myth and outside of it in history and confuses the two conditions, as well as the way in which he makes his interpretation of society in history the ultimate meaning of myth itself.

This two-sided indivisible problem is well illustrated by his relation to and use of the mythic figure of Christ. The figure of Christ was overwhelming in Paul's teaching, but the essential nature of that figure is for him mythic, Hellenic to a great degree. No theologian was less interested in the historical Jesus, and the parables and the human psychology of the Gospel Jesus are almost ignored in Paul's immersion in his own intuitions. Yet his interpretation of the historical Jesus determines his final use of the mythic figure. To see how Paul uses the figure of Christ is one way to understand what happens to Hellenic myth at Paul's hands.

A mythic figure is a symbol for an aspect or condition of natural man, as mythic separated from the natural contours and limitations of any appreciative member of the myth's audience, anyone who is listening and watching to find out what it "means." But by its separation from his historical condition, it can perform a remarkable service for him who does want to use it: he sheds his own identity in the appreciation of the aspect or condition of his own life realized by the symbol. To the degree he lives imaginatively via the symbol, he lives generically free of individual identity, seeing in his own right the *nature* of his own history rather than its specific accidents.

Just so, of course, the symbolic figure of Christ can and has been used by many Christians, and this symbolic employment never better illustrated than in the writing of Paul. Yet this service has been contradicted at its heart and core by an antithetic use of the figure as the very sign of identity, and by no writer more than Paul. By one of the ironies of form in cultural history the mythic figure which is par excellence a means of transposing historic identity into appreciation of eternal imposed condition was made the means to insist upon a new historical identity. The very term "Christians" is an easily grasped result of this reversal of symbolic process. It is the sort of term we use for members of a city-community, of a nation, of a tribe or people, Athenians, Romans, Jews. There was, however, the worship of Dionysus without any "Dionysians," or Demeter, without "Demetrians," no "Apollonians" and no "Castorians" or "Polydeukians," either. There was no reason why the same natural man could not appreciate varied aspects of his natural existence in the light of these varied symbols, and others beside them, Aphrodite, Athena, Zeus. To the Jew, of course, deity and social identity are always and forever coterminous.

Though Paul, as Hellenistic, uses Christ as the paradigm of his interpretation of the ends of natural existence, he uses the figure simultaneously — and the strands are never separated in his highly confused writing — as the key to the creation of a new community, the establishment of an exclusive identity for those who are to use this same figure appreciatively. Paul is bent on substituting Christian exclusiveness for Hebrew exclusiveness. The seed of Abraham (*Romans* 9.7) is to become the seed of Christ. Nor is Paul's metaphorical use of the term essentially new. Jewish identity, too, was established as the children of God as well as the seed of Abraham; it is perfectly clear that "God" in such use as "the children of God" is to insist on exclusive identity, not to appreciate relation to the natural order and its creative process productive of all men. The new key, Christ, is, in fact, an attempt to deny the ultimate validity of the old identity-key, God, though Paul's God and His Son are as passionately exclusive, as determinant of identity, as the old Hebraic Yahweh. All other gods must perish, their altars wrecked, their inspiration denied. Christianity like Judaism was to become the exaltation of identity, baptism replacing circumcision as the sign of membership in the new community. (The sign of membership in the old community reveals its patriarchal structure.)

It is wry understatement to say that much has been written on faith, *pistis*, in Paul, not least as it applies to *Romans*. In all that wealth of literature the dynamic of faith has been assumed, by Luther as by Barth, with no apology for its contradiction of what any Hellene, philosopher or free man, would mean in his definition. And by free, I mean free of the claims of identity, for Pauline faith at its core is individual subscription to his identity as Christian. It is not, as Hellene or philosopher might have it, subscription to the natural order or to its symbolic statement, mythical or discursive. "To live in Christ" is not simply to use that symbol to realize human destiny in universal natural order — in which case, of course, another symbol might be substituted — but to insist on unique identity as the only means to such appreciation. The psyches of all worshippers are exalted by their participation in unique self-affirmation. *Christus regnat*, and no other.

The highest claim for this sort of faith, for this unique self-affirmation, is to be free from death, and, in the last analysis, that is the doctrine of resurrection as preached in *Romans* and *Corinthians,* that unique identity, community based on Christ, is the irreplaceable means to immortality. It is the farthest reach from the appreciative insight insisted upon for the audience imaginatively consumed by the myth of Castor and Polydeukes, or by the myth of Demeter-Kore. *Yet the myth is the same one.* Here is the crux of our problem for the myth of resurrection, that the myth which is based on the seizure of the totally generic and totally given condition of man, all men seen as One, in his nature, his life and his death, and the seizure of that phenomenon the means for the individual to appreciate himself in his immortal aspect rather than in his individual history has been transformed into the "belief," the "faith," *pistis,* that only by means of a specific communal identity does he live beyond death. Needless to say, the nature of that state of immortality is thereby transformed. In the original myth his resurrection is possible to any man who can appreciate himself as imposed being rather than as the dramatic individual result of that natural imposition, in its later Christian form, only as he becomes "joint-heir" with Christ of a miracle, open only to the baptized and believing, of a miracle that denies natural history. Only as Christian does he share in resurrection, only as the child of an exclusive God does he participate in that God's reversal of the natural order. So does resurrection become victory (*Corinthians* 15.54), the triumph of the will over natural circumstance. The military metaphor is strategic for revealing the psychological dynamic, the new community's triumph not only over its communal foes but its foe in nature itself. Even nature is made subject to the will of the new believer. The old myth is the appreciation of nature which man in his individual instance is all too apt to forget in self-enclosure in identity, enclosure which excludes him from the joy of resurrection. In the new myth resurrection becomes the final sign and glorification of identity, which is the obstacle to resurrection in the old. The Hebraization of Hellenic myth has turned it upside down.

Yet it has not obliterated it, not even in Paul, nor the old symbolic or paradigmatic (as opposed to identity key) use of the mythic figure. Paul, like the Gospel John, is on this score much closer to Hellenism than contemporary Christianity, particularly in its popular Catholic or Fundamentalist forms. As regards identity itself it is important for Paul that the human Christ, as we have seen, be of natural birth, and equally important, of honorific Hebraic birth, of the seed of Abraham and Jesse, as of the religious tradition of Isaiah. This insistence on natural Hebraic birth, which is, for all intents and purposes, dissolved in popular contemporary Christianity, is for Paul the sign that Christianity is old Judaism with new scope. But it also makes possible the distinction between the natural human Christ and his divine aspect, symbolically, not naturally related to all believers. The sense of identity is never forgotten, but within it a neo-Hellenic tension can be realized.

Very clearly for Paul the worshipper via, it is true, a new religious identity, not through an appreciation of the natural order, can undergo the process whereby the human Christ, humanly conceived and born, becomes the Son of God — the incarnation — and rises from the dead. The "uniqueness" of Christ for Paul is as the key to the new community, the new identity, not as in popular Christianity as "better than" or "different from" all natural men. He is unique as Abraham and Moses in the old dispensation, uniqueness their continuing symbolic command of the identity established through them. The new figure, of course, has added symbolic valence which is Greek, derived from the myth we are here concerned with of the incarnation and resurrection. For Paul each man is to realize himself as Christ and thereby live forever. To a limited degree this is paralleled in Pindar as the audience member sees his own aspects both as son of Tyndareus and son of Zeus.

Yet in addition to differences already noted there is one which reveals how foreign the mythic mode of thought is to Paul. As Pindaric audience we realize our mutual inseparable aspects as simultaneously sons of Tyndareus and Zeus, but we are natural men and Castor and Polydeukes mythical heroes. They are paradigms not of us individually but of aspects of us. Our resurrection, therefore, is our appreciation of our own continuing aspect which is not defined by our individuality, *not* as individual men. But mythical incarnation and resurrection were likely inconceivable to Paul as they surely are to men nowadays who have no experience of the mythical mode. He saw correctly, that is, Hellenically, the paradigmatic use of the symbolic figure, as he certainly did the distinction between the natural man in Christ and the Son of God, but he conceived our *relation* to the mythic figure in individual, material terms, not the relation of natural man to mythic abstraction. Said another way, in Hellenic terms, to realize our individual self as Christ would be to participate in incarnation and resurrection as the Son of God realizes our nature in the deepest degree, as the figure abstracts and dramatizes that our nature is donated and withdrawn beyond our will, revealing the immortal will of that donation. It would be easy to argue — taken out of context many Pauline passages can be made to reveal the critic's intent, which

278

accounts for much of his theological influence — that at times Paul expresses a similar intuition. But in the last analysis resurrection is to him supernatural, that is, material (belief in the supernatural is always belief in the material as subject to human will hypostasized as divine will), a new natural organic being in a "different" mode.

> If Christ is preached because he arose from the dead how can some say among you that there is nò resurrection of the dead? If there is no resurrection of the dead, then Christ did not rise. If Christ did not rise, then, indeed is our preaching (*kerugma*) vain, and vain is our faith. We are found out false witnesses of God, because we bore witness against God that He raised the Christ, whom He did not raise, if, indeed, the dead do not rise. If the dead do not rise, Christ did not rise. If Christ did not rise, vain is your faith, and you are still in your sins. (*Corinthians* I 15.12-17).

We have already seen in an earlier chapter how these lines set Nietzsche's teeth on edge and how, in so far as they are the statement of a belief in personal immortality, they also stand opposed to Pindar's equally stern disavowal of that belief in *Pythian 3* and *Olympian 1*. But Pindar's imagination gives us the life of the Blessed in *Olympian 2* and the resurrection of Castor in *Nemean 10*. That the incarnation and resurrection can be purely mythic forms of the appreciation of natural life and not a belief in a supernatural existence should be clear from Pindar's texts alone.

These lines from Paul, then, are *not only his statement* of belief in personal, material, supernatural immortality. They could never have come into existence without the paradigmatic use of the figure of the son of god which is derived from Greek myth. That appreciative mode they may pervert and thereby contradict its intent, but they are built upon it. Here lie in verbal solution two radically disparate elements, and our comment on this passage is an attempt to resolve that solution and see the elements separate again, and, as with the Gospel presentation of these doctrines, see that Paul's intent depends on his misunderstanding of the mode of the very myth he is using.

Let me paraphrase what I assume to be the Pauline intent in these lines and then contrast it to what alone made the Pauline vocabulary itself possible.

In Paul's view one natural man in Hebraic history became by means *not disclosed* the Son of God (remembering that in Paul there is no room for the myth of the Virgin Birth, and that the putative historical parentage is of the highest religious significance), and as Son of God was supernaturally raised from the dead as foretold by Hebrew prophets. His life and death made possible a community of believers who could identify with his supreme history, "faith" making possible as the "first fruits" (*aparche*) of that identification their parallel escape from the bonds of nature in some sort of life — not even poetically adumbrated — after natural death. It is to be noted that this privilege of a supernatural existence in nature (the paradox is intentional) is exclusive, limited to those who identify with this unique historical man. All others, Jew or pagan, lack "faith" (in my terms, "fail of identification"), live in sin, and are doomed to the finality of natural death. (The Pauline eschatology is, of course, incompatible with Heaven and Hell.)

From my point of view, the principle of identification, the community of believers, is an attempt to change the way in which any mythical audience is related to its mythical paradigm into a neo-Hebraic community, the Greek mythical son of god become the key to a new Hebraic exclusiveness, a new special dispensation. "The chosen people" have become Christians rather than Jews, with the result that the mythical son of god has had to yield power as the revelation in human form of the given natural order on behalf of historical identity. Similarly, the resurrection of the son of god has to lose its power to reveal the given immortal form disclosed in disparate phenomena — all men signed as One — on behalf of the supernatural, material resurrection of those exclusive believers.

*But the materials for Paul's intent were never derived from or created by that intent itself.* This Hebraic use of a Greek myth contradicts Judaism radically. Let it never be forgotten that Christ as the Son of God was blasphemy to the Jews. This is perfectly understandable, since Hebraic belief is always historical and material, not mythical. Given the premises, that historical Hebraic denial is perfectly valid criticism of the doctrine of incarnation. I simply claim that the Greek mythical figure can not be reconciled, if true to its original nature, with those Hebraic premises, and that Paul is attempting in this and similar passages such amalgamation. Yet the very belief Paul is preaching in this passage, that the resurrection of all men is dependent on the resurrection of Christ, is derived from the relation of a mythical audience to its mythical paradigm. Greek myth alone makes possible Paul's attempted Hebraization of it. This passage from *Corinthians* owes its base — the nature of the Son of God — to Hellenic myth. That original mode may be contradicted by the Pauline intent, but to understand a passage historically we must realize that the Pauline intent of itself would never have brought it into existence. There had to be Greek myth in being for Pauline intent to work its will on.

If *our* intent is to understand the continuum of Western theology, not exult in Christian exclusiveness, what in Paul's own writing Paul himself has failed to understand is a very precious part of our heritage; and he, like the Gospels, has been a valuable instrument of just such transmission. Furthermore, Christians still can and historically have been able to appreciate myth in a way closed to Paul of Tarsus governed by his drive to create a new Judaic community. Christian glory is Christian myth *as* myth, forgetful of social identity, simply using its own figures as anyone's for their illumination of the human condition. The mythical illumination of the plastic arts in both the Middle Ages and the Renaissance is second to none in any culture's history.

From the mythical point of view, then, Paul's insistence on the interdependence of Christ's resurrection and his followers' is the dynamic bond of the relation of natural man to mythic paradigm. Similarly, he was quite correct in the earlier passage quoted in insisting on all the individual participants' relation to one another through the mythical sonship. One can say that he wrote truer than he knew, that he misunderstood the nature of the very bond he reiteratedly insists upon, because he draws an erroneous conclusion from it. Mythically the resurrection of the believers *is* the resurrection of Christ. Their appreciation of his resurrection *is* their participation in immortality. That Greek meaning alone made possible the Pauline preaching of immortality through Christ.

For the mythical figure exists *only* as an abstraction of themselves. He *is* the realization by themselves of their interconnection, themselves seen as unity; he *is* simultaneously their image of *what* they are, will-less expression, totally given. They can not in their natural identities become sons of god, because the son of god is an abstraction not only for all of them together but of their aspect as given expression, not individual self-will at all. Without that figure for the entire mythic community they can not appreciate the purely natural fact of their intimate substitutability, and once realized each in his own right as substitutable, replaceable form and that form given, they lose the delusion of dramatic individual will and seize their own aspect as expression of divine will. That, too, is an appreciation of natural fact, but it is never disclosed in motivated action, in the exercise of individual will. Immortality is not the supernatural prolongation of the individual will; such relation to eternal form is only set up when the isolated consciousness withdraws from the individual dramatic delusion in favor of the appreciation of the substitutable self as given expression. Mythically resurrection is the privilege bestowed by the appreciation of the incarnation, the appreciation of the individual as expressive, not self-defined, and as expressive sempiternally, commonly expressive. The abstraction is singular, though existence is many. The incarnation and resurrection are mythic means for the individual to grasp himself not as individual at all, and that grasp requires the *singular mythic figure* outside himself to express all others simultaneous with its expression of himself. The Greek mythical meaning exists plangently in the Gospels, of course, in discursive discourse, as it does not in Paul, that only he who loses his life will save it. The life he "saves" is clearly not the life he "loses," and Paul, in the last analysis, I am afraid, equates them, holds that by strenuous enough self-discipline a man can save his own natural, individual existence.

Now I said earlier that Paul never stops and explains how the scion of David becomes the Son of God. The transposition of Hebraic history as Greek myth is never argued. This has already stood sign for Paul's coming after the transposition. His silence may also stand sign for his ignorance on the point. The transposition took place in the still completely dark interregnum of the creation of Christian myth. Its earliest stages are still vividly apparent in the Gospels, but even before those reached their present stage, later clearly, on mythic grounds alone, than Paul's epistles, the problem ignored in Paul had become quite conscious and led to the creation of the tales of the supernatural existence from the very beginning for Jesus of Nazareth, in conception, birth, in childhood, and after death. These are all clearly needed as "explanation" of incomprehensible myth in being, the myth of the incarnation.

Before turning to the attempt in the Gospels to turn myth into natural history, perhaps the point I am trying to make can be seen in the small, in a sharper historical context, in the Pauline confusion about what the life of the "spirit" consists of.

He uses, of course, *pneuma,* not *psyche,* as "spirit," and it might seem at first glance that he is doing in his own right with the first term what Greek culture had already long done with the second, transforming physical respiration into a sign or symbol for organic consciousness, and then for awareness or appreciation. The term *psyche* in Paul has become by a strange reversal synonymous with body, *soma,* though not only historically with the Greeks but still with us it is the Greek word for soul as contrasted to the body. Paul's ignorance on this point is not at all irrelevant, for in the small it discloses his whole relation to his Greek inheritance; it is the same ignorance that allows the misconception of the nature, the mythic nature of the son of god to take place. The distinction *between* body and soul, *soma* and *psyche,* which Paul uses as synonyms, was, after all, a Hellenistic commonplace, no longer presupposing any direct knowledge of or insight into the Platonic or Pythagorean base for this distinction. For Paul to coalesce the two should make us most distrustful when he assays to tell Christian readers what a Greek mythical concept, the son of god, means. But he then sets up a new distinction, let us say between *pneuma* and *soma* (as synonymous with *psyche;* the distinction he consistently makes between *pneuma* and *psyche* is almost indigestible to a Hellenist). Wherein does this distinction consist? What is the exercise of the *pneuma* or spirit? What is its mode as distinguished from the body's own?

In Paul, the spirit, *pneuma*, is first assumed as a natural substance in itself, and then for his purposes becomes a supernatural substance, disclosing the privileged nature of him who exercises it. Not only is the earlier nature of myth, abstraction via human figure, denied, but the later mode of abstraction, discursive terms which combine natural elements into an appreciative entity, the reflection of the relation of given phenomena in the mind as words, is similarly violated. Paul is quite unaware that *pneuma* is a word, and a metaphorical word at that, drawn from bodily process, and useful only as that word illuminates a non-bodily process he intends to diclose. Instead of being a word, it becomes a substance, an ens, a supernatural something in its own right.

Nor is there any call here to argue at length the nature of terms. A very simple explanation lies to hand, and one that ties Paul's use of *pneuma* directly to his unargued statement to his readers of the assumptions of Greek myth, the quite unHebraic, the totally Greek concept of the son of god, the figure of man in myth as incarnate deity privileged with immortal life. In both cases, in the small as in the large, Paul is using a vocabularly which he does not understand as functional but as "given," as objects or animal forms in nature are given. So terms become things in themselves, and mythic constructs natural personages and events. This is peculiarly the psychic response induced by a foreign vocabularly and its terms. To a remarkable extent Paul's theology is the result of using a vocabulary, mythic and discursive, which was not his own. So Ezra Pound suffered from the delusion that because of its original pictorial nature Chinese was more "imagistic" than Western languages, holding actual shapes in its expression. Any lengthy exercise in ideograms would have dispelled such an illusion, else they are unusable as symbols in discourse. Just as Pound never came to realize the purely symbolic use of ideograms, so Paul did not understand the symbolic use of figures in Greek myth or of terms in Greek discursive argument.

*Yet every word we have he ever wrote is in Greek.* We can
not argue simply in regard to the Pauline intent in the
employment of a foreign vocabulary; no man is free from the
implications of the vacabularly he uses. More than that, his own
thought is in the first instance created and formed by the terms
or images he uses. What is Paul's thought without the image of
the son of god or the distinction between the *pneuma* and the
*soma?* Paul no more invented those terms and their valence than
he invented the concept of the son of god. As with Christian
sarcophagi the forms Paul is using are Hellenic, and realization
of the new use can be grasped only in relation to the old. In
theology, as in art, we must understand misunderstanding.
Instead of trying, as so many valiant commentators have done,
to explain what Paul meant by *pneuma,* spirit, it is far more
honest to say that he himself could not know and could not
know because he derived his *meaning itself* from the delusion,
in using a term or a word or an image, that it had a natural
material existence in its own right, and such a sense of words
comes from using a language that remains forever psychologically foreign, outside one's self, not simply the instrumentation
of intent but an autonomous hierachy of meaning. Symbols
have taken on an existence in their own right. It is not
accidental that Christians substituted the contrast orthodox:
heterodox for the Hellenic contrast *aletheia:doxa.* In the one
form is means, in the other an end in itself. That essential
Christian failure to understand the nature and use of form stems
in part, I hold, from the necessary historical relation of
Hellenistic Jews to traditional and to them seemingly independent Hellenic form. Illuminating myth turns to fixed dogma,
mythic figures to historical identities, discursive terms to
substances, all demanding ego-subscription from historical
community.

Let us now turn to the Gospels and see if we can locate there
remnants of the Hellenic form of the myth of incarnation and
resurrection.

The relation of these Gospel remnants to Pindar or a later
evolvement of his version of this dual myth is, for this critic, far
more dramatic than anything found in the Pauline texts.
Whatever the date of the final composition of the Gospels as we

285

now have them, they all contain elements from that dark period preceding Paul when Christian myth was forged, when local biography and teaching were read in the light of Hellenic myth, giving birth to the very doctrines for which Paul himself was missionary. The myth of the incarnation comes closest to its Hellenic source in Mark, though there is an integral part of it (the genealogy) rehearsed later by both Matthew and Luke, omitted by Mark. It is perfectly clear, too, that large portions of Matthew and Luke are composed to elucidate, give credence to this aspect (the incarnation) of the misunderstood Greek myth. The myth of resurrection in any approximation of its Pindaric form, however, resides only in John. From the point of view of myth, then, elements in Mark and John would seem to present the earliest versions of Christian myth and hence of Christianity as a new entity—old myth forever stamped by one identity—and must precede many of the human tales in Matthew and Luke simply to account for their composition. Yet anyone who treasures the preaching and parables of Jesus of Nazareth will value not only Matthew but the grab bag of garrulous Luke ahead of Mark and John. The extraordinary Nazarene consciousness does not concern the present criticism, but I can only remain perplexed, for all modern scholarship, why the two earliest Gospels, by the test of myth, the definition of Christ and his religious role, contain the least of what one assumes to be the teaching of the historical Jesus. It is perfectly clear to this critic that Matthew and Luke — or their sources — have constructed biographic tales to account for earlier myth, but the scandalous plangency of the teachings one can only suppose them totally incapable of creating; they could only have diluted or distorted. On these grounds elements of even late Luke should have existed, in an earlier state, anterior to the formalization of Christian myth found in Mark and John. (Put technically, the question is why Q is used so much more by later than by earlier Gospel composition.) As purveyors of a defined entity, Christianity, Matthew and Luke are later, of course, than both Paul and Mark (and in viewpoint, if not time, John), but as messengers for the Nazarene they transmit what presumably precedes all these others. In sum, the relation of Christian myth to the teachings of Jesus remains to be defined.

Perhaps only in one's view of the relation of John to the writings of Mark and Paul does one feel any doubt as to the general conclusions of modern scholarship. When he seems to echo one in myth or the other in doctrine is he using them or their sources? Mark is par excellence the Pauline (not, as is often said, the Petrine) Gospel, simultaneously defining Christianity as opposed to Judaism while striving to create a new Judaic exclusive Christianity and, like Paul, using the most blasphemous (from the Hebraic standpoint) Greek myth in that effort. John, a subtler theologian than Paul, is also at war with Judaism, but he wishes to escape from it, not refound it. That much of his meditation is derivative, from Hellenistic philosophical commonplaces, among other sources, has long been noted, though in its new Christian setting creative in high degree. But neither Mark nor Paul creates the myth he is using either, or the essential lines of doctrine that must be derived from it. The personal intensity of Paul's writings, as well as his irreplaceable role in history, seem to have blinded critics to the degree to which his thought, too, is derivative; his prestige and passion have somehow obliterated the sense of his dependence on earlier creative thought or even its local transmission. Paul is a Lenin, not a Marx or Hegel.

Yet the critic of Hellenic myth will never hold that John is closer to the Greek than Mark or Paul — though that, too, is a common misconception. Quite the contrary. We shall see that well in the handling of the myth of incarnation. I go back to my own "dark period" for my own dark guess, which is not an ur-Mark, least of all an impossible ur-Paul, but a Greek-imbued mind quite unlike either Mark's or Paul's but earlier than either, which created the Christian myth, on which John, working sometimes independently (as in his handling of the resurrection theme), sometimes in oblique relation to earlier versions, could also call, beyond the writings of Mark and Paul. But as in the case of the late Matthew and Luke's reflection of the Nazarene, so in the different case of myth, Mark's rehandling of the postulated work of such an earlier unknown mind seems to me quite as clear as John's.

The original Hellenic form, as I conceive it, of the myth of incarnation is found in all four Gospels (Mat.3.16,17; Mark

1.10-12; Luke 3.21,22; John 1.32-34) and twice in three of them (Mat.17.5; Mark 9.7; Luke 9.34,35). The announcement at the Baptism and the announcement in the Transfiguration, or Metamorphosis, to use the Greek form, are doublets. The central fact in the so-called Baptism — we shall shortly see why the expression must be qualified — is the metamorphosis or transfiguration. I shall analyze only the Baptism version of the metamorphosis, but the criticism used there can be applied, pari passu, to the other version, where Elijah and Moses fill the part played by John the Baptist. In both cases Greek myth is presented as the "laying on of hands" by members of the Hebraic religious tradition — that is, in fact, the motive of the Gospel presentation — and both versions are the dramatized form of Paul's direct statement on his own authority, not the authority of projected drama, opening *Romans,* that the Son of God has been proclaimed by the Hebrew prophets in holy scripture.

I have said that the Baptism and Transfiguration are doublets, and I suspect the latter is the earlier version, not only because of the use of major, as opposed to a minor figure to figure the Hebraic transmission, but more importantly, because the opening of the ministry is clearly the appropriate place for the announcement of the Son of God, and the motive for the transference to that crux of the independent myth can be explained, whereas a rehearsal of the announcement is uncalled for and has, in fact, no clear dramatic *raison d'etre* in the dramatic sequence of any of the Gospels. The term, too, used in what I suggest is the earlier version is strategic: metamorphosis. It is the metamorphosis of Jesus of Nazareth as the Son of God, the prime factor in the creation of the Christian myth. And the creative mind of that myth, which I hold is none of the Gospel writers, made crystal clear in that term what he was doing, as none of them could have. It is the failure to understand that term and what it implies that led, in fact, in the later Gospel writers, Matthew and Luke, to the creation of the most popular of Christian stories of the parentage, conception, birth and early history of Jesus. But be it noted that these stories are *not* created to account for the historical Jesus — he would need them no more than Elijah or Isaiah — but to account for the

Hellenic *myth* of the Son of God, whose creation must therefore have as clearly preceded them as any historical life they might intend to magnify. Let us turn to the accounts of the Baptism.

> And it happened in those days that Jesus came from Nazareth of Galilee and was baptized in the Jordan by John. And straightway coming forth from the water he saw the heavens parting and the spirit like a dove descending upon him. And a voice arose from the heavens, "Thou art my Son, the beloved; in whom I am well pleased." And straightway the spirit sent him into the desert.[2]

In Mark the myth is the simplest 'as-if narrative' and therefore, clearly, the closest to the source. Luke piles up narrative infinitives, clearly restating a previous account, while keeping the direct discourse of the key declaration, whereas Matthew puts the declaration of the voice into the third person, "This is my son, etc." Yet Luke immediately juxtaposes the human genealogy, "as it was thought," of Jesus, a juxtaposition which echoes, for all the demurrer, the dual parentage of Christ in *Romans.* Matthew has, of course, placed the genealogy at the opening of his Gospel. Mark and John ignore it, but as Pindar should have taught us, it is an essential element of the myth, and in his poem the human genealogy of Castor stands side by side in direct discourse with the announcement of Polydeukes as the son of god. The noun *phone* of the Gospel version appears in its verbal form in Pindar (*Nemean* 10.76), as, of course, Zeus, the sky-god, a voice from heaven, addressing his son: *essi moi huios* has become *su ei ho huios mou.* And the dove? It is the heavenly equivalent of the mortal *sperma* found in both Pindar and Paul. It is, of course, the dove of the Annunciation, which is the ancient dove of Hera and Aphrodite, their male counterpart, the symbol of male generation, the same figure as the *strouthoi* of Sappho's hymn to Aphrodite, the "bird" of American slang. It is the symbol of divine parentage and therefore calls for the Lucan and Pauline juxtaposition of human parentage. This concrete symbol has disappeared in John, leaving only the abstract spirit or breath, *pneuma,* and

Matthew, as I have said, changes the declaration to the third person. Luke, then, is more faithful to Mark, or Mark's source, than the other Gospels.

Why do I make a point of the grammatical voice of the declaration of incarnation? Partly, of course, because the second person declaration in Mark, the earlier version, is a direct reflection of the Pindar line which, in a later form, I claim lies behind the Gospel myth. Matthew's unmotivated later variation – he is surely unconscious of changing the myth in any essential – is an easy instance of how myth loses its basic form in the hands of those who do not understand its mode.

For there is a more general point here than the dramatic Christian revival of Pindar's crucial version of the myth of incarnation. In myth, 'as-if narrative', speech revelatory of divine-human relation is projected dramatically, as of person to person, not only Zeus to Polydeukes but Aphrodite to Helen in the *Iliad,* or Aphrodite to Sappho, or Athena to Achilles, Dionysus to Pentheus. The poet's imagined symbolic figure reveals the dimensions or nature of its relation to the human being in dramatic converse. Only the imaged symbol is sanction for that relation, no poet, no thinker, no theologian. Both the mode and its revelation are purely imaginary, and no other authority intervenes to establish the nature of such relation. It is myth and nothing else. Matthew changes the voice and makes it not a *dramatic relation* but a *statement.* John goes even further and makes the whole *testimony.* In a few generations, the myth of the incarnation will be presented on the *authority* of Paul and the apostles, that it is myth entirely forgotten. Matthew in a small way begins the process that obfuscates the mode in which this revelation was created and earlier transmitted, unbroken and unobfuscated, be it noted, from Pindar to Mark.

John's version of the myth is shorthand here, for a reason I think will be clear in a moment. Elsewhere he has already expressed the doctrine of the incarnation in abstract terms, "And the Word became flesh and pitched its tent among us, and we beheld its glory, glory as of the only-begotten of the Father, full of grace and truth" (1.14). And his classic statement of the incarnation is the more famous, 3.16, "God so loved the world,

He gave his only begotten Son, that whoever believe in him should not perish but have everlasting life." Here, like Paul, he revives the inextricable relation of the two parts of the single myth, incarnation and resurrection. That juxtaposition, lost in the Gospel dramas of the incarnation, is to me another hint that John, like Paul, knew Mark's source first-hand and could use it in his own theological thinking and discourse. Like Paul, too, he is more interested in the theological *statement* of both elements of the myth than he is in its *dramatic* rehearsal as myth, less than Mark, or even Luke, following Mark, were. John's shorthand version in this location, however, is dictated by the necessity for some statement, at precisely the same location as in all the Gospels, of the incarnation, the beginning of Christ's ministry, the point in all where Jesus of Nazareth must become the Christ. In John and Mark, as in a different literary form, the salutation of *Romans,* this is the beginning of the entire Gospel, as, I would hold, it must be, granted the mythologization of Jesus. What precedes now in Matthew and even more extendedly in Luke is built precisely to accommodate a non-myth-appreciating audience to the declarations that open the accounts of Jesus in the earlier Gospels. Mary, Anne, Zebediah, Joseph, Bethlehem, Annunciation, Magi, and Manger, are the fuller "explanation" to a biography-hungry and not too theological humanity of this central announcement of Christ's nature and destiny. True, some of those, too, pick up earlier mythical elements, particularly as regards the role of Mary, but it is the earlier myth of the incarnation which has prompted their dramatic life, and only that myth, as theological abstraction, interpretation 'as-if narrative', which is our concern. And that myth is mythical deity become mythical man.

The 'as-if narrative' here is the man Jesus of Nazareth entering the waters of Jordan and issuing as the Son of God. The mind which created that myth, or rather, used an old myth in a new contemporary setting, which made that interpretation of the historical Nazarene, together with its interpretation of the death of Jesus as issuing in the resurrection of the Son of God, is the mind which forged Christianity. We are up against one of the most decisive creative or recreative moments of Western history, hypnotic in its implication of result spreading from image and its meaning held in a single mind to act on the lives of millions yet unborn.

That fascination both deepens and turns to scholarly humility, when we realize that we do not know and likely never will know whose mind that was. Without it Jesus would have ramained a clairvoyant teacher; there could be no evangel for the Gospels; no pole around which Paul's fiery energy could organize a neo-Judaic state as a church. To a Hellenist it has a further fascination: it is the moment when Judaic event is transformed as Hellenic myth making Christianity possible. No, not in the Church fathers but here, much earlier, the heritage of Greece becomes determinant of the Western religious tradition.

That mind was no more Mark's than it was Paul's. Mark, like Paul, is from the beginning engaged in making that neo-Hellenic, now Christian myth into something it could not have been as an original interpretation, and John is writing the first, and still one of the greatest meditations on myth already in being. The first line of Mark's Gospel has already summed up the doctrine of the incarnation, "The beginning of the evangel of Jesus Christ, the Son of God," where the human and the mythical are again sharply juxtaposed. This is precisely the point where Matthew places the *human* genealogy of Jesus. The two, as we have seen, are found side by side in Paul's salutation of *Romans*. It is at this point that John begins his abstract discourse on the Word which will shortly be made flesh. In their choices Matthew and John have both disclosed their guiding interest and temperament.

But it is what Mark does that most nearly concerns us. His handling of the myth, too, is a great creative moment, but it is creative just to the degree that it is misinterpretation. Mark does what Paul does in *Romans*: he transforms Hellenic myth back into Hebraic history, precisely the *opposite* dynamic of the mind which has created the myth he is using in the first place. "Jesus Christ, the Son of God, just as was written in Isaiah, the prophet, 'Behold I . . . .' "

Now to the Hebrews that is blasphemy, and the quotation which follows concerned, of course, with Israel's Messiah, not with the Son of God. That instinctive Hebraic reaction is, ironically, a far better guide to our understanding of what is happening here than the last century and a half of Biblical scholarship, since such reaction would make emphatic a distinction where such scholarship conceives a natural amalgamation. Again I indulge in unargued statement: to Christians, as opposed to Jews early concerned with Jesus and his teachings but not, I hold, to be designated "Christians," the concept of the Messiah has been of little moment, though the doctrine of the Son of God has been essential. The function of the Messiah in purely Christian discourse has been an ancillary one, deriving from the Mark-Pauline attempt to integrate Judaism in Christianity. But it has no more to do with the doctrine of the redemption than it has to do with the doctrine of the incarnation. Those are both cardinal to Christianity and, for all the variety of their Near Eastern expression, as found in Christianity derived from Hellenic sources. Focusing on a very narrow historical problem – the concern for the Messiah among those proto-Christians who did not forge or propagate Christianity, who proved, in fact, a barrier to its evolvement as a non-Judaic mission to the entire Mediterranean world – modern scholarship has of itself created a viewpoint that has entered into active theology, at least Protestant theology. It is an odd case where narrow scholarship, even at this late date, has had imaginative significance. It can also be considered a further 19th and 20th century attempt to Judaize Christianity, leading spectacularly to contemporary social Christianity. It has, however, cast a false light on the problem with which we are concerned, clearly reversing the relative importance at the very beginning for Christianity of the concept of the Messiah and the myth of the Son of God. Paul's epistles, historically, and the Agnus Dei or the Resurrexit, existentially, as sung in any Mass, should serve as constant reminders of how far modern scholarship has strayed in its accounts of the origins of Christianity.

We are here concerned, in fact, with Mark's attempt to place the Greek myth of the incarnation back into the setting of the Hebrew Messiah which both Jews and Hellenists, if not some Christians, realize is quite incongruous. And I am further concerned to point out that the mind which attempts that amalgamation is a mind which does not recognize the source of the myth it is using, that Mark, in sum, is not the creator of the vision of the Voice over Jordan declaring, "Thou art my Son." Had he or Paul been such a one, he would not, as both do, immediately turn and declare its source to be the teaching of the Hebrew prophets.

There is another deeply revealing indication of Mark's irrelation to his own source and the quality of its imagination. It is perfectly clear why, in the formal announcement of the incarnation, John the Baptist must enter the picture, as the living link between those earlier prophets and the new one, and in smaller compass the link between the figures used for the Hebrew tradition in the Transfiguration and the Baptism version of the Metamorphosis which, I have already said, I hold the later one. But if Mark were consistent, which means had he himself been the author of the decisive declaration, the proclamation would be in John's mouth. At his first designation of Jesus as the Christ, the Son of God, Mark juxtaposes Isaiah's prophecy. Its final counterpart is missing. Or rather, an inter-relation is suggested that reveals the deepest misunderstanding. The first designation of the Son of God is supported, if you will, by the "voice in the wilderness crying, Make ready the path of the Lord," and there is the clear suggestion that that "voice" is the early instance of the voice over Jordan declaring, "Thou art my Son." There is, of course, no more connection between those voices than between the Messiah and the Son of God. That Mark conceives such a connection is, however, revealing.

Yet it is only a suggestion. Mark does not act on it; he backs away from it in the end. The mythic statement stands in its own right, unbacked by any prophetic source. Mark does not, as he could have if that suggested interconnection were valid, put the proclamation in John's mouth. Or, as I would state it, he has at the last moment respected his source and revealed the incongruity of his dramatic setting and the myth he has placed in it. *The result is that the declaration has nothing to do with John the prophet whatsoever.* Mark has brought the character of John the Baptist into one of the crucial scenes of the Gospel and left him absolutely nothing to do. His function as the last link of the Hebraic prophecy of the Son of God is suddenly denied him, and *mythical voice speaks in its own right.* The sudden upsetting of the dramatic propriety derives clearly from the imposition of the myth into a new and false setting. And that in turn is to me a sign that the myth and its strategic application to Jesus of Nazareth existed prior to Mark's use of it in his Gospel. We shall come upon similar but even more marked dramatic discrepancies in John's account of the raising of Lazarus, pointing again to extant myth prior to John's attempt to integrate it in the sort of domestic scene which by his time was likely familiar to Gospel readers. I can only suppose that the key passage in this instance, the Voice from heaven declaring, Thou art my Son, existed and existed as applied to Christ in written form, and that its creation was the work of a mind which, if it did not know its clear Pindaric predecessor, did know some later Greek mythical version of it, knew and 'believed' in myth, that is, that unsupported mythic statement could be revelatory in itself, whereas Mark tries to turn the myth into history, tries in this case to make it pivotal of the prophet sequence from Isaiah to Jesus via John. It has, of course, no more historical connection with that prophet sequence than it displays dramatic accommodation in Mark's attempt to give it one.

And in that attempt to give the myth of incarnation a prophetic Hebraic home be betrays for the Hellenist his misunderstanding of a key term in the original myth: the desert. The more independent John omits the next part of the myth, though Matthew and Luke following Mark dramatize it. But I give John credit for his omission; not understanding it — since it can not become a part of his interpretative system — he forgoes it. Mark followed by the others has turned mythical abstraction of high order into local scenery, inspired, clearly enough, to his mishandling by the legends of the provenance of the Baptist. But the presence of his term, the desert, even as misunderstood, as local color rather than as theologically significant, is to me another sign that he was using locally known myth which had absorbed the basic structure and its basic terms in the original Greek. Its very misinterpretation points to its having been borrowed from a differently oriented source which maintained, as in the unsupported mythical voice from heaven, its original mythical or interpretative power.

Idas and Lynkeus, we may remember, were not other persons, historic individuals, but those aspects of human nature which prevent the realization figured in the sonship of Zeus and the resurrection of his son, representative of our sin as the failure to be aware of divinity disclosed in human form and action. Now, there is no reason why this contrasting aspect, this failure of realization should not be figured as a part of the *same* mythic figure which most fully realizes divinity in form and action, as his temporary or testing blindness. Christ, as both scion of David and Son of God, recapitulates both Polydeukes and Castor, the dual aspects of a single mythic entity, son of Zeus and son of Tyndareus. Similarly he could at the same time recapitulate Idas-Lynkeus, as tempting and rejected incarceration in individuality. Idas and Lynkeus as figuring that state as final are doomed to be deserted entirely of deity and, its realization. In the single figure for both poles it would be made image as temporary desertion and isolation. That is what the Son of God's desert doom figures. The word, *eremos,* is the same word as found in Pindar, and Greece, though arid and rocky, has no deserts. It is mythical image, of a state of soul, not a geographical type. The reiteration of *eremos* can be added to Thou art my son, the heaven speaking, and the word voice, *phone,* to deepen the ultimate connection between that poem and the myth re-expressed in the Gospels. That Mark should transform this term into the trans-Jordanian desert parallels Matthew and Luke's later familiarization of his and Paul's brief statements of the incarnation; it also shows that Mark has not understood the mythical or interpretative dimension of the term and hence once again can hardly have created the myth he is handling. But what has inspired his topicalization of a theological metaphor is the introduction of John the Baptist. Can we not glimpse, then, an earlier version of the myth with the correct valence for the "desert" without the Baptist? His 'reduction' of the spiritual wasteland as a literal desert seems to me, that is, not only to point to Mark's separation from the original form even of the Christian myth but to the presence of John in it as distinctly his contribution, accidentally and not happily accommodated to the earlier significance.

Now just as Mark attempts to interrelate the Hebrew prophetic voice crying in the wilderness and the Hellenic mythical voice out of heaven, so he attempts to coalesce the mythical status of the son of god and the prophetic baptism, and here, of course, Mark has been creative, that is, determinant of later appreciation, the Anointed One as the Son of God, the Son of God designated in the prophetic baptism. The result, for all intents and purposes, is what Mark implied but luckily, for our understanding, never quite brought himself to insist on, that the act of baptism invoked the voice of deity to proclaim the Sonship. Even in Mark, I repeat, that declaration is independent of the Baptist, their inter-connection in our text Hellenic myth incongruously projected into Hebrew rite. Current Biblical scholarship, long since divorced from the study of Hellenic mode or form, does not recognize this creative, if mistaken coalescence; popular theology, of course ignores it altogether, as it ignores myth as form, calling it the "revelation" of the Son of God.

But whether scholars are troubled or not, Gospel John was quite aware of the problem and clearly tries to integrate the dissonant parts. He renders the proclamation of the incarnation as *the testimony* of John, and even further, does place in John's own mouth the proclamation of the redeemer, "Behold the Lamb of God who takest away the sins of the world" (1.29).

This poses an intricate problem in form whose answer is a serious qualification of the general view of Gospel John's comparative relation, among the Gospel writers, to Greek mode. He is in some ways a more careful literary writer, aware of form, aware, it seems to me, of the incongruity of bringing the Baptist to the brink of the declaration and then abruptly denying him his function and leaving it a purely mythical voice from heaven. He smoothes that discrepancy, yet keeps the division, by making John the witness of what is not his own but another's declaration. Yet the total effect is to give John greater responsibility than in the rough carpentry of Mark's composition where John and the voice exist in mutual presence but in irrelation, and that effect is reinforced by making the Baptist, as Mark does not, the outright proclaimer of the Redeemer. That is an even greater historical incongruity, because concealed, than almost but not quite making the Baptist the proclaimer of the incarnation. We shall not be concerned with it, but the doctrine of redemption, despite scholarly effort to coalesce it with the Hebrew Messiah, is mythical, depends on relation to mythical figure for its effectuation, widespread in the Near East, absorbed by the Greeks and a major part of Greek religion, in the worship of Apollo, Zeus and Dionysus, among other cults. By the time of the Gospel writers it is as incontrovertibly Greek as the myth of the incarnation. But John's careful composition, this neat handling of the disparate voice of the incarnation in subordination to the voice of prophecy, and this compositional use of that prophetic voice to disclose yet another mythical role, that of redemption, this very sense for form in the end obfuscates myth — and its *never to be accounted for voice* — in a way Mark never does. Pindar never tells us his authority for Zeus' proclamation of Polydeukes' sonship, or Homer his for Athena's words to Achilles. The only authority is the imagined myth itself, and this "law" of myth is violated once the mythical announcement is subordinated to historic dramatic form, as in the prophet's testimony to the incarnation or his own proclamation of the redemption. Mark may not understand the mythic mode but he preserves it and jams its product right next to elements of a different provenance. It is he, not John, who gives us the clearer idea of what Greek myth "in action" is like.

Now Mark here may be more clumsily faithful to a common source, or John, as is the general view, simply rewriting Mark. The second alternative, in this particular instance, does not, of course, rule out Mark's own use of an earlier mythic version of the role and nature of Christ. Nor should it rule out the first by itself. John, that is, may have been cognizant of a brief original source and still base his composition on Mark. John, as we shall see, seems to have preserved, while again transforming stylistically, a Greek version of the resurrection lost in all the other Gospels. That should point to an anterior mythic version which, in the case of the incarnation, Mark has used more directly than John, but which John alone echoes in the resurrection. But though it is Mark, not John, who can here bring us closer to what is involved in seeing the Nazarene under the light of the Greek myth, since his clear motive, like Paul's, in presenting it is to read Greek myth as Hebrew tradition, I can not see how he is responsible for its creation.

In my imagination the hypothetical creator of the Christian myth, far more Hellenic in his mode of thought, is responsible for the creation of a Hellenic interpretation to which all the later writers, including Paul, are *reacting*. He, I would guess, would use the Nazarene or even the Hebraic formalization of him as the Christ as his new figure in Hellenic myth, much as a Classical poet could use any figure in his inherited vocabulary for its interpretative significance, Cheiron or Tantalus, Eteocles or Agamemnon. Since historic man or his Hebraic definition was simply his mythical pole, he would not be faced with any problems of historical or ritual incongruity; history or Jewish interpretation provided him with the "names" in his myth, and his whole energy could be focused on the realization of the mythic significance of the given figures. Such mythic projection is concerned with community only as appreciative audience, and it is concerned with illumination, not with social action. Those possibilities of illumination and interpretation were far too great and good ever to be ignored, but they could not of themselves serve the purpose of such as Mark and Paul. To bend that illumination to the creation of a community, to create "Christians" as an identity, subject to social form or organization, with the hope of later success and communal triumph: that was the mission of the missionaries, and in writing, too. Yet myth and myth simply as illumination were to live ever after within the community whose formation was their active motive.

But quite apart from such imaginative hypothesis, my main point is clear enough: in the last analysis the authority for Christ's revelation as the Son of God is the authority of myth, and only the study of myth in its own right will disclose what that authority is. Earlier chapters have been concerned with this subject, and it will not be rehearsed here, but it is in no wise the authority claimed for Hebrew prophecy. To see clearly that even in the Gospels the two can still be distinguished is my present purpose. That Christ or Jesus of Nazareth was also the

Son of God ultimately rests on the same basis as the Pindaric creation of the words of Zeus' statement to Polydeukes: "Thou art my son." Mark's clumsy juncture of John's prophecy and the voice from heaven, Gospel John's careful subordination of the separate voice from heaven to prophetic John's testimony of it mark that distinction between Hellenic myth and its new home. The incarnation is a myth, and valid, but valid as myth, and even Christian writers reveal that they are dealing with myth, for all that they bring it into history and tie it to a community's life and hope for future triumph.

It is in subordination to this point that I posit a mind which first saw historic figures as myth and made possible to men with different motives the building of a Christian, that is, a neo-Judaic community built around that myth. That creative act is fascinating quite beyond the interest of a Hellenist, for that creative act was the germ that made possible, through, it is true, the continuing community life posited by different motives, the illumination of Dante's verse, of Chartres' windows, of Michelangelo's frescoes, the glory of iconography, the glory of form, the glory of idea made flesh, of appreciation realized in material. And the glory of iconography is not the glory of Hebrew prophecy. To see how the Hellenic insistence on form resides from the very beginning beside its Hebraic denial is to see the irrelation between the voice over Jordan and the Hebrew prophet who stands by.

We shall not examine the variant Gospel accounts of Christ's resurrection, since they are not related to *Nemean 10* and hence lie outside the scope of this chapter. On the other hand, John's account of the raising of Lazarus is, I hold, ultimately if quite indirectly derived from Pindar's poem and calls for exegesis on the basis of that relation. I should like, however, simply as an aside, to suggest how my sort of criticism would approach the synoptic Gospel versions of Christ's resurrection.

Its theme would be the critic's need to maintain for every line the distinction between myth and history, a distinction which each Gospel writer in every line is seeking to break down. For example, as *history* the Johannine account of the resurrection is quite incompatible with the other three Gospel accounts, two of them, of course, based on the first, Mark. That incompatibility as history between Mark and John is a stumbling block to those trying to prove, as it is a weapon for those trying to disprove, the existence in the generations after Jesus of a generally accepted version of his miraculous escape from nature. In *Mark* a mysterious young man (16.6) announces to the mourning women, including the mother, "He is risen. He is not here." All apparitions of the risen Lord appear in later and separate contexts, whereas in *John,* where there is no such proclamation, Peter finds the tomb empty, and a little later Jesus in the guise of a supposed gardener reveals himself to Mary Magdalene (20.6-17). The historic personalities represented as present, as well as the way in which they discover the absence from the tomb and the mode of announcing its significance are quite different. Yet we are quite safe in assuming that John knew the other gospel versions, since he places (12) "two angels" or "messengers" at the empty bier, who are purely decorative — and hence derivative — since they do not fulfill the function of proclamation, using Luke's number, two, but Matthew's term, "messenger" for the instrument of the announcement, who appears as one "young man" in Mark. (Whatever his designation — the discrepancy should not trouble us — his presence in three of the Gospels is and should be naturally inexplicable. It is only important that he *not* be one of the human "characters" in the created historical drama. His only "life" is as vehicle in it of the announcement, put formally, the agent of myth. He is the equivalent of the voice from heaven in the Transfiguration or Metamorphosis and Incarnation.)

I consider, of course, any of the attempts to reconcile *John* with the other versions not only futile but clearly motivated, simply later men's efforts to *prove* the possibility of a miracle in history. But I find equally futile and motivated the attempts to *disprove* the resurrection by pointing to these glaring discrepancies. For both sides assume that they are arguing about a fact; the opponents on this issue are kin cousins, like the thinkers categorized in an early chapter as purporting to be on opposite sides of the issue of belief in deity. But as *differing historizations* of the *same myth* these contradictory accounts are compatible, their discrepancies as history immaterial, but their

301

differing ways of revealing the core of the myth illuminating and moving. John presents as dramatic image, Jesus as the gardener revealing himself to Mary, precisely what the young man or messenger or the two men announce — without the presence of Jesus — in the other gospels, "He is not here. He is risen." In both versions, that mythical core which has been preserved intact is at once presented as history.

The core of the myth we are dealing with is the apprehension of the son of god and his resurrection, god-given immortal form present in every identity but not defined by any identity. Jesus as the gardener is just such transposition of identity which reveals the living son of god. It were easier to comprehend, if we say that the gardener for an instant is revealed in his aspect relating him to the son of god, not as an identifiable gardener. But if we are using an already established historical identity as the figure for the myth, as the manifestation of the son of god, the gardener *as* Jesus expresses this dramatically. That gardener as Jesus can also serve to show us what doubting Thomas and the felt wounds amount to: the further attempt to demythologize the figure of Christ.

Now the creative, the Hellenized mind which took the decisive step of first proclaiming Jesus as the Son of God had a further problem in commenting for his Jewish followers upon his death. He faced a problem which we can pose in purely formal terms, how to express to these men the relation between the Son of God and the contents of that tomb? The decisive moment is the creative mind's transformation of fact into myth, not the other way round, though the next generation's effort is bent to just that, to turn the creator's myth back into history. His mythic comment to the mourning Jews is expressed dramatically within the Gospel accounts as the messenger's speech to the mourning women. "Jesus as the Son of God is not here. He is risen." But that mind knew, as the Gospel writers who are in the last analysis dependent on his creation did not, that the incarnation must be appreciated before the resurrection. Historization, failure of mythic appreciation, is already at work to change the myth in the Gospel versions. The *separation* of the Son of God proclaimed through the historical Jesus from any identity even, ultimately, that identity, and hence figured as his absence from the tomb, which is the dynamic of the myth maker's pronouncement, is turned at once into the historic absence of a historic Jesus from his tomb. Yet that appreciation of the absence of the Son of God from the tomb of Jesus in three Gospel versions is the same appreciation figured in the fourth as the apparition of Jesus as the gardener. The same creative dynamic is at work in all despite their obfuscation of it.

The announcement at the tomb is the parallel to the voice over Jordan designating that same singular human being as the Son of God at the beginning of his ministry, the end to match the beginning. The absence of the Son of God from the tomb of Jesus is the message of the creator of the Christian myth of resurrection. But just as in the earlier case the voice out of heaven, the same voice as appears in Pindar, is set by the Gospel writers in the context of the baptism in the waters of Jordan in the presence of a historical prophet, so the mythic answer to the Jews mourning Jesus is made history, with variant members of his entourage present in differing circumstances according to the varied Gospel writers.

As far as I am concerned, then, the announcement at the tomb is the only purely mythical part of the gospel accounts of resurrection and hence the product not of Mark but of the original myth-making mind, the rest historization related to the myth like the circumstances of the baptism to the announcement of the incarnation.

The following point bears not on theological interpretation of the resurrection narratives but on our critical thesis positing a now lost original mythologization of Jesus in life as in death. No one would claim that John created the myth of resurrection, yet his historization of it varies widely from the other Gospel writers. That I have used to illustrate mythical as opposed to historical compatibility, but it also points to the existence of the myth for John outside, beyond the historical accounts of it presented in Mark-Matthew-Luke. John did not create the myth of resurrection, but neither did he draw even his mythic appreciation, the transposition of Jesus as the gardener, from these others. Yet that transposition merely dramatizes the separation of the Son of God from given identity proclaimed as the meaning of the tomb in the other versions. If the same myth works differently in different imaginations which then attempt to illustrate it in varied putative historical circumstances, I think again we glimpse the existence of a basic myth of the ministry and life and death of Jesus apart from all the Gospel writing.

John's account of the raising of Lazarus is the late Christian version of the Hellenic myth of resurrection created by Pindar.

This tale is unique, of course, to John, but that does not mean, as some might assume, that anymore than Mark's dramatization of the incarnation as the Baptism, that its core myth, as opposed to its dramatic details, is of John's creation, or even its earliest Christian form. Once more we are up against the unknown source of the myth, but since this version of resurrection is found only in John, I feel that it shows that he, like Mark, but not the other Gospel writers, enjoyed direct contact with earlier Christianized Hellenic myth. Like the salutation of *Romans* and Mark's presentation of the incarnation he still preserves for our isolation elements of the original Hellenization of the meaning of Christ's ministry. Yet like those others his story is in its own right the Hebraization of that original Hellenization, not the original mythic interpretation itself. Its manner of turning myth into historical narrative obfuscates the nature of myth to a greater degree than Mark's version of incarnation and hence points to its lateness. Yet unlike the other Gospels, which limit themselves to the myth of resurrection clearly stated only as it applies to the person of Jesus, his sees the figure of Christ as instrumental rather than as the dramatic example of that myth. As such it must go back independently to such an earlier transformation of Jesus' ministry in terms of Hellenic myth. Such instrumentation (Polydeukes' decision brings Castor to life again) we saw in *Nemean 10* as one determinant form of the Hellenic myth in its own right.

Nor does this story reside in John as simply another miracle in the ministry of Jesus. In the exact center of his story, in as famous words as exist in any Gospel (11.25), it makes clear that it is the illustration par excellence of Christ the Son of God as the means to resurrection: "I am the resurrection and the life;

who believes in me shall live, even if he die." The following sentence, as I hope will be made clear later, is its contradiction. "And everyman who lives and believes in me will not die for eternity." That, like Mark's juxtaposition of the voice of the Baptist and the voice from heaven, discloses the Hebraic misunderstanding of the myth being used, while preserving its misinterpreted Hellenic core intact.

But the theological point I am making in contrasting these two sentences, which, as far as I know, have always been assumed to be corroborative, can perhaps be better understood in the context of my view of the account of Lazarus' resurrection. I can point to no better example of the Greek myth behind the putative natural history of Lazarus' resurrection than Polydeukes' restoration of his brother Castor to sight and speech, to the natural miracle of self-centered organic existence. That creative and determinant 5th century mythic version of resurrection is, I hold, the ultimate source of John's history-seeming account, though the figures in the myth may long since have been changed in later Hellenic versions, and Christian paradigms substituted for Hellenic mythic figures earlier even than John. In Christ's unmotivated tears (11.35), the never explained bond of love with Lazarus (36), and the now functionless apostrophe to heaven (41), it still trails, like the *phone, sperma, eremos* of the Gospel version of the incarnation, the intimate signs of its Greek source. Yet the tears, the bond of love, and the apostrophe to deity are not only integral parts of the Pindar version, they are also simply created by 'as-if narrative' of his myth as it unfolds. What is of necessity organic in Pindar resides as inorganic elements in John's story. That he keeps them in his story without either using them as they originally functioned or providing new ones is a clear sign that he is following another source. We have seen in the small a similar example in his presentation of functionless angels, a synthesized borrowing from Matthew and Luke, as pure decoration in his resurrection narrative. His borrowing from a later form of the Pindar myth is just as clear in the Lazarus story as his borrowing in that instance.

So also with the term *adelphos,* brother, which is properly the mythical brother, everyman, of the son of god, as John's

305

own paradigmatic statement (11.26) clearly shows, "everyman who lives and believes in me." This paradigmatic brother has, of course, in our account been humanized or particularized as the brother of Martha and Mary, which in no way supports John's own paradigmatic use of this figure. The core saying invites us, each and everyone, to identify with the resurrected one, but whereas we can define ourself as the brother of the son of god or as everyman's brother, as Paul reiterates in parallel passages, we can not identify with the brother of Martha and Mary. We can not, that is, annihilate our own identity in favor of another specified identity. Such osmosis is impossible. We can only identify, and hence be related as historical identities to one another, with a mythic figure for all identity. The "brother" of the son of god, with the significance earlier attributed to that term, is such a mythic figure. The failure to realize Lazarus as Christ's mythic brother, while abstractly basing the meaning of his own story on precisely such relationship, is the measure of John's failure to recognize the nature of the myth he is himself dramatizing.

The failure to define the Jesus-Lazarus relation not only leaves us without a dramatic base for the mythic or abstract meaning of the narrative; it also undercuts the possibility of psychologically convincing response within the narrative itself. By rights we should know, have posited for us, if only in the briefest compass, the bond of relation between Jesus and Lazarus to account for the former's love and its extraordinary result. Such a bond in family kin (even though that may be a misunderstanding of the mythic "brother") is posited between Lazarus and Mary/Martha, but that bond is essentially irrelevant to our story, and nowhere is the crucial axis of relation which issues in the resurrection itself defined. The result is that the meaning of the relation of Lazarus to Jesus, the deepest meaning of the story, has to be expressed through Martha — a point to which we shall return.

The explanation seems apparent. The characters of Mary and Martha are clearly borrowed from earlier Gospels to provide a familiar domestic setting for the myth which John, alone of the Gospel writers, attempts to transpose as historical narrative. But in order to incorporate the figure from myth in its new putative historical setting he uses as the relation between mythic figure and human characters the relation posited in the myth as between him who brings to life and him he resurrects. The relation between Castor and Polydeukes, or between other figures in a later form of the same myth, is here transposed into the purely familial and, as far as the meaning of the story is concerned, functionless relation between Lazarus and Mary/Martha.

We can see parallels to this hypothesis clearly enough in what happens to the tears and apostrophe to deity in Pindar's poem — elements which must have been preserved in the bridges between that poem and John — and John's use or rather misuse of them.

The tears (John 11.35), which should express pain, as in Pindar (75), at the death of one of one's "very own," imply a deep bond broken by that death, a bond, we reiterate, John never defines. Secondly, they should normally express, not only as in Pindar but in any convincing story, the human reaction of sorrow at the news of the death of the loved one. But it is not news and John has proscribed the possibility of sorrow. Lazarus' death has been foreseen and stated several times before Christ weeps. His tears even then have no psychological motivation, since John has made it clear that Christ has foreseen not only the death but the resurrection, has, in fact, rejoiced in the death as the means to display his God-given power for resurrection (11.4). In their present context Christ's tears are a contradiction of the previously posited peace in the face of the death. This is the sharpest possible contrast to Polydeukes' tears (75) as the expression of anguish in the loss brought by death and his sense, before the intervention of Zeus, of its finality. Polydeukes' tears are the expression of his overwhelming emotion; Christ by John's own account can feel no such emotion, and his·tears become meaningless.

And it is the anguish at death and the sense of its finality that lead to Polydeukes' cry to his father and the subsequent bestowal of the power of resurrection. But the apostrophe to deity is as functionless in John as the tears and makes them even more meaningless. For instead of being the cry that leads to the donation of the power that restores the dead loved one, it is in effect a boast before God to the audience for possessing such power, "Father, I thank Thee that Thou has heard me." Such boast contradicts the need for any tears. One should suppose that direct address to deity should be of crucial effect in narrative myth; here it serves only as John's underscoring of Jesus' foreknowledge of his own power. That very insistence destroys the usual function of apostrophe to God, the cry for help or relief. It might be noted that Jesus, as in other instances, of course, uses Father, *pater,* as the form of address here, the same word Polydeukes uses in his appeal, "Father, what loosing will there be from sorrows?" In his reply that Father brings forth the great sentence, "Thou art my son," which we have already seen is echoed word for word in the voice over Jordan.

But that there are tears and apostrophe to deity in John's narrative when they are either functionless or contradictory of the meaning he himself asserts in that narrative is itself significant. It should be evidence that he is following some source where tears and apostrophe did function. By the same token, what makes them functionless or contradictory in his own account is, one would normally assume, of his own making. The individual contribution in this case − what forefends natural sorrow or the need to appeal to God for release from it − is his view of Christ's foreknowledge of the death and of his power to cure it. What is of his own making does not organically fit the myth he is using. Yet this very irrelation is what discloses for us elements of an earlier form of the myth which are not absorbed in his own story, as well as his own intent which resists their absorption. Nor, of course, do I think it accidental that each of those unabsorbed elements, tears, apostrophe, and definition, brother, occurs in Pindar's version of the same myth.

For the myth is the myth of the son of god who brings man back to life again. John's narrative is built around that message: "I am the resurrection and the life; who believes in me shall not perish, even if he die." It is also the Johannine version of one Pauline statement − and there are others − without dramatic projection, which we have already considered in relation to Pindar, ending with the claim that the Supreme Power "rules over the dead and the living." (I do not think − and this pari passu might be applied to some other "Pauline" passages in John — that he need be indebted to the Epistles. In intent John clearly echoes Paul, but his use of a dramatic setting for his message seems to point to a common source for both, Christ the Son of God as the instrument of resurrection *as myth*. John's use may be later than Paul's, but that he makes his statement as dramatic history is to me a sign that he is inspired by an earlier myth, not a Pauline abstraction of it.)

That message — the son of god as the means to resurrection — is expressed only dramatically, never abstractly in Pindar's poem; it is that in which the myth, as-if narrative, resolves itself. Since that dramatic result is not cast either in contemporaneously social or abstract terms for our appreciation, we can not postulate resurrection outside the myth. We can not, that is, deny the medium of our appreciation in that very appreciation.

John reverses the process. That Christ as the Son of God can raise man from the dead is his starting point, and Lazarus is his illustration, and so belief must precede the historic drama to give it conviction, rather than, as with myth, issue as its imaginative result. Pindar through myth is trying to uncover what is required of the imagination to live with awareness of immortal power. John is trying to prove that Christ can raise the dead. But having borrowed the myth which provides in new form his case-illustration, having transformed the myth of Castor into the story of Lazarus, he then quite forgets to project *within the myth itself* his own historical use of it. The result is the deepest contradiction between that historical message and his case illustration derived from previous myth.

That message states that belief in Christ as the Son of God is what insures life even in death, yet nowhere is it revealed *that Lazarus so trusted or believed*. Our writer has overlooked *in his narrative* the most vital point of all: Lazarus' faith as paradigm for ours. Lazarus, too, should have been raised from the dead by the fullness of his own subscription to the reality of the Son of God.

It is not that John has for one moment forgotten the significance of that belief for resurrection. He dramatizes it as Martha's (11.27). But Martha is not raised from the dead, Lazarus is. Martha's faith lies outside the projected result of that faith as resurrection. The crucial absence within the narrative of a parallel faith on Lazarus' part is further evidence that John is working with two disparate elements and has failed again to coalesce them successfully, his own belief in Christ as the Son of God, and the myth of the son of god as the means to resurrection with no historical faith implicit in it. I am merely trying to mark the evidence within his overall account of the distinction, nay contradiction between that historical assertion and what he needs must use to illustrate it, an earlier myth of resurrection.

That John was rewriting earlier myth but rewriting it to make it appear as Christian history leads him into a final formal contradiction. As his tears and apostrophe to deity contradict his own interpretation of his story, so his putative historical account of Lazarus' raising denies the most urgent need in such case set up by historical writing, a need, however, never presented by myth. We end in Pindar with the moment of Castor's new sight and speech; we never go beyond. So in John we end with Christ's command to loose Lazarus' bonds and let him depart (11.44). As myth this is the final moment: the annunciation of the wonder of new life. But not at all as history. If this is natural history, then all the questions to the revived Lazarus and his answers are insisted upon by our equally natural curiosity. If he is natural man, what natural man has experienced, seen or felt, those four days in the monument, is demanded to close the account. The total silence as to Lazarus' reaction either to death or to his new life can not be reconciled to historical narrative. Yet once again it is easily understood if Lazarus is the borrowed mythical figure of the brother of the son of god mistakenly postulated in natural human event.

I point to this last unconscious revelation of the form John transposes not only to reiterate his dependence on earlier misunderstood form, but to juxtapose with that misunderstanding our consideration of his theological message which, I hold, is in the last analysis, dependent on a correct use of mythical form. The contradiction in this theological message, I earlier said, could better be seen in the light of his relation to myth, for that message reveals the same preservation of an earlier form and its understanding side by side with its contradiction.

Jesus' declaration (11.25,26), together with the passages from *Romans* and *I Corinthians* already noted, can stand as perhaps the greatest formative statements of the Christian doctrine of resurrection. This is the message of the Lazarus' story. John, it is clear, wants that message dramatized, which Paul felt no need for. Similarly, Paul's comment is always projected as his own, whereas John puts that comment itself in the mouth of Jesus. This, mind you, is not mythical projection at all, but "literary" dramatic form. In myth human characters can define their own relations to divine forms, can, in fact, react to or comment on those relations, as we have seen Helen, Pelops, and Achilles do. But what outside those specifically defined dramatic relationships we make of the divine-human relation for our individual understanding is strictly the mythic audience member's own affair. Myth like dream imagery is always dramatic presentation pure; analysis is a later and outside matter. John, so to speak, has placed his dream analysis in the center of his dream. Its central position, 25-27 within 46 verses, is clearly no accident.

As dramatic writing it is, indeed, very good. Martha, as we have already noted, is used, as her brother should have been used *within* the mythic narrative, as the representative of every true believer. To the question, "Do you believe this?," she replies, "Yes, Lord, I believe that you are the Christ, the Son of God who has come into the world." There is the central figure of Christian myth defined for all time by the character Martha. That definition, I would hold, is John's dramatic integration in his story of the earlier transposition of the historical Jesus as the mythical son of god. But before the question is posed, so that the dramatic representative of every true believer can reinforce His religious definition, Christ has himself proclaimed the privilege of that role in two contradictory sentences: "I am the resurrection and the life || Who believes in me, even if he die, shall live. *And* anyone living and believing in me will not die forever."

John's omission of Greek connectives is so consistent that his use of one when it is not absolutely necessary, just after he has omitted one that is, as Greek, altogether necessary, should make us stop and wonder. Where I have placed the bar there is no

311

connective, for the Classical ear an anacolouthon so rough — though frequent enough in this writer — that it sharply emphasizes the following connective which, given John's style, is quite unnecessary, far less needed than the one he omits. Where, with a change of subject, Greek style demands a connective particle, he omits it; where there is no change of subject and the meaning would be clear without a connective, he inserts one. I can prove nothing by this, but I am surely free to feel that John uses a connective in the second instance because he is juxtaposing two differently derived sentences. At least we need a reason that is not derived from grammar for it, since he is totally oblivious of such pressure. To me it is a hint, at least, that he has added his own comment on or enlargement of a borrowed and misunderstood sentence. (One can not overlook the possibility, of course, that the second sentence is not by John at all, that it was either originally a marginal gloss on his statement later added to the text, or that it was inserted in the text directly as expansion or corollary, as the writer understood it, of John's statement.)

For, like *Romans* 14.6-11 earlier considered, there is nothing in the first sentence placed in Jesus' mouth which contradicts the interpretation of the myth or resurrection I have given to the *10th Nemean*, whereas the second sentence, from that standpoint, is not its corollary but its contradiction. As I see Lazarus as originally the mythical brother of the son of god who wept his mortal brother's death and appealed to his father for release from such sorrow, transformed by John into the human brother of Mary and Martha, whose death and resurrection are both forseen by Jesus, making obsolete both tears and apostrophe to deity, so I see the first part of this message as the correct abstraction of the earlier myth of resurrection and the second as the direct denial of the imaginative act which leads to participation in resurrection. In both cases I feel the dynamic is identical, the turning of myth into human history. Since that seems to me John's motive in story and message alike, I find it as hard to conceive that he is himself the source of the first immortal sentence of the message which the second contradicts, as to conceive — which no one does — that he is the creator of the myth of Christ's resurrection or of his power to restore life.

His relation to the first part of the proclamation is precisely the same, I hold, as his relation to that myth — its purveyor — and his own contribution to the proclamation, the second sentence, of a piece with his humanization of Lazarus and his contradictory inclusion of Christ's prescience in the original myth of resurrection.

Though I should wish to avoid repeating at length the theological exposition of the *10th Nemean,* I have so many times stressed the contradiction between these two sentences of Jesus' self-proclamation, that the application is called for here. To say that no believer will die is not the same thing as to say that the believer will live, even if he die; the first assertion of itself prevents the imaginative process that alone makes it possible to understand how, if he die, the believer yet lives. To insist on the immortality of individual existence in defiance of organic process — the addition or gloss — is to block the appreciation of individual existence in its completely non-individual aspect. The insistence, in sum, is on what makes resurrection impossible: the definition of life by its individual organic unit. Resurrection springs from the relation of any individual organic existence to all other existence similarly organized and thus to its primal source or enactment imaginatively seized as a unity. (Source and enactment are synonymous here; there is no need to suggest conscious fiat or purpose "behind" the appreciated phenomenon of unified enactment.) Not only does the individual organic shape foretell all such shape in the future, as it rehearses all such shape of the past; it also exemplifies in its own right, as fully and clearly as any shape past or future, the nature of that immortal enactment as given to its actor.

The second point is, perhaps, even more important than the first for the understanding of the son of god as the instrument of resurrection. For by the figure of the son of god the entire process in all time is unified; the mythic figure subsumes all examples and by its name defines all those examples as imposed. To relate himself to that mythic form is for the individual to see himself no longer as a unique case but paradigmatically expressive, relating his dramatic enactment to its imposed form, revealing divinity in his own life and its action. As he sees himself only as he participates in that immortal form, its immortality is expressed through him. Death, with sleep, is the sharpest distinction between the individual's singular definition and the immortal pinions of his existence; it is his very death which truly celebrates the power expressed as his life. As he sees himself as expressing that power, as he identifies his aspect as reiterated form with that form seized as a unity, as he believes in the son of god, he can be said in one aspect, but in one aspect only − his relation to that son of god − not only to live on forever but to have lived from all time. "Before Abraham was I am." Resurrection through the son of god looks as much to the past as to the future; the present is simply individual celebration of that relation. But celebration as individual only in the sense that enactment as individual requires defined organic self-centered existence for its expression; it is celebration of the glory of form not celebration of identity.

The willful insistence on identity and *its* immortality is the denial of the relation to the son of god, who subsumes all individual cases, and thereby the occlusion of what relation to him brings, the individual seen not as identity but as expressive of divine form. Not only are past and future unified by the son of god, the present case is expressive only as expressive of him. Without the relation to the son of god the man must die: that is, he is simply defined as his identity. The second sentence attempts to state as the mode of resurrection what is, in point of natural fact, the eternal mode of death, life as defined by identity. Life as defined by relation to the son of god and life as defined by identity are antithetical.

Formally, the mythic figure is the imaginative means to resurrection. It bestowes an intellectual boon that turns into emotive privilege: self-realization in terms of the power of creation and dissolution. Natural self-assertion stands in its way, the delusion of the definitiveness of identity. Belief in the son of god is the individual yielding the construction of identity in favor of the figure for his, as anyone's, *given* existence.

In this sense Lazarus' resurrection is simply the appreciation of Christ as the Son of God, the appreciation Martha defines. Christ's resurrection is not, then, paradigm for the believer's; it *is* his, and he enjoys his own only as he "becomes one with

Christ," as he defines himself not as his identity but by his relation to that immortal form. The first sentence of the proclamation states this: "I *am* the resurrection and the life; who believes in me shall live, even if he die." Or, "My immortal existence is yours as you see yourself in me." In that sentence the mythic existence is equated to the believer's own immortality. Belief, then, is participation through symbol in unified existence and its given form. Self is not annihilated but grasped only as expressive rather than as definitive. When the self is made expressive, realized as the "brother" of the son of god, it can like Castor or Lazarus live forever, but only as dependent on, expressive of the immortal son, not as self but as Polydeukes' or Christ's brother.

To those professing Christians who might object that I have transformed or corrupted the miracle in nature of the only Son of God, Jesus of Nazareth, into a symbolic form, a mythical abstraction and, when so appreciated, an abstraction of form in nature, man's life not only as reiterative but totally given enactment, my reply is that the transformation and corruption are all the other way round, and the intent of this chapter has been to show just that, that in its original situ the myth of incarnation and resurrection was such symbolic appreciation of form in nature, and that it was historic misunderstanding of what they were using — but without which they would have had no new belief at all — that led 1st century Hebrews into such corruptions. My insistence is that Christian belief, at the most cardinal points of its dogma, be seen in relation to its Hellenic source. That source and its system is in every fibre and junction symbolic appreciation of natural form. These men of the 1st century did not invent what they are using. It is our task, as theologians quite as much as historians, to realize the nature of the myths on which the later religion is ineradicably founded. And it is at the very beginning, in the Epistles and Gospels, that we still get, I hold, the clearest glimpses, alongside their corruption, of the original Hellenic illumination.

John's relation to Greek myth in the Lazarus story and so ultimately to Pindar and the *10th Nemean* is but a single example of an intricate set of historical critical problems. My own effort as historical critic complicates a problem — which, I feel, has never been really faced – rather than posing any solution. I point to crucial lacunae; I can not fill them. I do not, of course, suppose that John knew Pindar; I am not even sure his Greek source did. The first gap lies between *Nemean 10* and the Hellenistic version or versions of the same myth, the next that version itself, thirdly, its first application to Jesus' life and ministry. That application is no more John's than Mark's or Paul's, the mythicization of Palestinian event or of Hebraic interpretation of it already in being. These writers, along with others, are bent on reversing the process, on turning myth back into history or supernatural event. These two processes are antithetical, and that, as far as New Testament criticism is concerned, is my major innovation. The mind which first saw Jesus as the Son of God turned him into a mythical figure, and it would not, normally, then turn and make him man again. I think the process of the Hebraic materialization of myth is fully apparent in all the Gospel writers as well as Paul; it accounts here for the transformation of the mythical brother into the brother of Mary and Martha. To the Hellenist this dynamic is insistent and consistent. And it is the dynamic pulling against the original mythicization. That original creative point has never been isolated; no one has located the moment or the motive for Jesus' definition as the Son of God, though John has made that the cause of his execution. I can not judge if this is historically sound or not; but if it is, the implication is clear that the mythical interpretation of Jesus' ministry was in process contemporary to it, earlier by a generation than any Epistle or Gospel fragment, as much lost to accurate history as that ministry itself.

Even if it can not now be precisely dated, it was in the longterm Western theological tradition a moment of the greatest creative impact. Nor can we appeal to Greek library, scholarship, or contemporaneous Hellenic intellectual history for the impetus to the new use of form or for that form itself. Anyone who has read Hellenistic scholia on Classical authors knows that their writers were as confused and confusing about the nature of Hellenic myth as any Gospel writer, and far less interested in its import for daily life and its understanding. These early Christian Hebrews are, in fact, far more creative, whatever their confusion in regard to Greek myth, far more responsible for its new life in the Western world than any precisely coeval Greeks. They established the forms of Christian myth in all essentials for later time. No Clement, Gregory, or Origen, after all, has had the influence of the Gospels and Paul's letters. It is historical irony that we owe to a few Hebrews not to Greeks themselves the most potent expression of Greek myth for later time: Christianity. I point to the creative moment for Christianity as the Hellenistic mythologization of a Hebraic religious biography and find it only natural that Judaism itself should reject it sharply. But what has been misleading in our view of this Hellenistic revolution is the critic's coalescence of two quite different stages in it, that before and that after the Gospels and Epistles. The earlier moment has been lost, and all the earliest Christian writers we now possess are engaged in the effort to minimize it, to reconcile the Hellenistic and the Hebraic, to construct through myth a new Israel in a church and to see myth as history or natural (or supernatural) event. But earlier than any writing we now have worked the mind or minds which first read Jesus as the Son of God, who turned a Hebrew teacher into a Greek mythical figure. The surge of appreciation thereby loosed was so great as to engulf Paul, Mark, and John in their various ways and with their various recalcitrances to its acceptance. Their writings are a continual revelation of these recalcitrances, but they must all be seen in relation to the very appreciation they struggle against. They are all, too, involved, again variously, in the forging and sustaining of the new Christian community, an evolvement from the Hebraic community, in the small as in the large of the inter-relation of local groups. But the hypothetical mind or minds I posit which first proclaimed Jesus as the Son of God and the means to immortality need not itself have been concerned with such community at all. To the mythmaker the only community is the audience which appreciates the myth. The creative moment is the free moment, untrammeled by the implications of its own act.

And if we bear in mind that there had been no creative evolvement in Greek myth and religion (which are synonymous) for four centuries, only slow denaturization, we can see that our sense of historical time is quite misleading as to the distance between Pindar and the first Christian. Not long complex development but slow obfuscation of the creative apogee of that myth is the separating veil, the length of years almost irrelevant. What Polydeukes had done for Castor, as Christ had done for Lazarus, another son of Zeus, in name, Dionysus could do in his own right, as in the other Gospel versions of the myth of resurrection. The son of Zeus interpreted as the son of Yahweh is the launching point of Christianity. Yahweh could not have any sons at all. That blasphemy is simply the transposition of Greek myth into Hebrew religious history. (The opposite dynamic, the transformation of Zeus, nature's unifying order, into willful Jehovah, in the syncretism of the Christian God, has concerned us in earlier chapters.) Only religious ethnocentrism, the insistence on uniqueness, a Christian inheritance from Judaism, would reject the creative moment of Christianity as the revival of Greek myth in new guise.

The nature of myth itself, from whose creative and appreciative apogee the earliest Christian writers were cut off, is, of course, obfuscated from the very beginning, and in the centuries immediately following the Gospels and Epistles the process of corruption went on apace. Perhaps no stranger document ever issued from the mind of man than the Nicene creed, its eschatology a Byzantine mélange of irreconcilable elements. Yet for all its weird syncretism it signally omits what Christians popularly suppose to be a part of their creed, the immortality of the soul. That doctrine is also Hellenic, for all its Christian history, and reached its expressive apogee, of course, in Plato. Like the Hellenic myth of resurrection its base is the appreciation of the individual's transient participation in imposed form, and the relation as psyche, appreciating center (soul), not as individual identity or destiny (body), to that form's imposition and continuing history. Such appreciation can not be reconciled to the image of the Last Judgment, when the world's immemorial corpses spring from their tombs or graves in fresh flesh. Such an image does not account for the soul's existence between death and resurrection nor does it permit of the all-important distinction between soul and body as the way to posit a relation of individual expression to continuing life. The belief in the immortal soul discounts any concern for the body's natural disappearance.

Later Christians have juxtaposed these incompatible images as somehow each other's counterpart. The Nicene declaration has transposed the earlier Hellenic appreciation of form separate from its individual enactment, the appreciation of man in the light of his expression of divine power, the myth of resurrection, as simply a term useful for the miraculous process of the Last Trump. Its "everlasting life" is material and individual, a denial of nature, as its "resurrection of the dead" is the body's renewal in the escape from the grave, not the appreciation of the individual's place in eternal divine natural process. Further, it has coalesced this material eschatology with yet another Hellenic myth, that of Heaven and Hell, the image of the punishment or reward, as if living, of the dead, a myth whose temporal or imaginative plausibility is not compatible either with the image of the Last Judgment or either Greek form of the myth of eternal form, resurrection or the soul's immortality. And it has, of course, insisted that the myth of the Son of God be construed as natural (that is, supernatural) history. Generations of Christians have quietly lisped this triumph of historical confusion as faith or belief. It is a far cry from such subscription, voluntary or enforced, to syncretic myth as fact, to belief or faith as a way of seeing life itself and rejoicing in it. But for the latter the Gospels, unlike that creed, do still recall the appreciation which in Pindar's time evolved for an audience listening to a myth, enunciated as myth, yet drawing a collective breath or breaking into quiet tears, as readers still may, as Polydeukes with his Father's power restores the sight and speech of his inseparable brother.

## APPENDIX

### An "Image"

Hera to Artemis:

"Since Zeus made you a lion to women and gave you
to slay whom you would."

*(Iliad* 21.483)

Prayer to the soma, while the soma sacrifice is being
made. sec.k.

Thou art a lioness, overcoming rivals, hail! Thou
art a lioness, bestowing fair offspring; hail! Thou art a
lioness, bestowing increase of wealth; hail! Thou art a
lioness, winning (the favour of) the Adityas; hail!
Thou art a lioness, bring the gods to the pious
sacrificer; hail!

Veda of Black Yajus School, trans. A.B. Keith
*(Harvard Oriental Series,* vol. 18.31)

In the first room to the left in the Acropolis Museum,
Athens, directly visible from the central vestibule as you enter,
a lioness is set to devour a bull calf she has killed. Her forepaws
clamp his haunches which her (now missing) jaws would chaw.
The bull, prone under her vast belly, comes up under her
loosely hung, her clearly nursing dugs (still crusted in red paint),
which brush against his neck. His neck is twisted, forehead
prone, jaws parted, gullet wide, the eyes blind in death. His
loins, shadowed by her heavy shoulders and left forepaw, yet
disclose his male ridge.

A 6th century sculpture (no. 4) from the pediment of one of
the temples burned by Xerxes' men, its theme is rehearsed in
even greater dimensions two rooms farther down. There (no.3)
a full-grown bull lies prone in death, but the mauling lioness or
lions are lost, and since the lioness is center of our "image," we
will remain with the smaller piece. Both are clearly from temple
pediments.

Here amid the remains of the religious center of ancient Athens within a short space two instances of bulls destroyed by the might of lions, in the case for our comment, a bull calf killed by a nursing lioness. This sculptural theme is clearly still a major religious ikon or "image" in 6th century Athens. In some way or other this sculpture depicts divine power in action. It poses a difficult task in understanding ancient imagery, in understanding how divinity is pictured in animal shape, and that animal shape depicted in the act of killing or dismemberment. We do not have any "primitive society" or "savage mind" to dispel or evade our perplexity or irrelation. Here in the full light of history, at a great apex of Hellenic sculptural mastery, we are presented with a grueling religious proposition: bestial mactation expressive of divine ordination. The lioness is in some way or other a form, one form, not an exclusive or definitive form, of divinity in action. Its absence in the next century in Athens will show how easily this disturbing yet compelling image is pushed aside, though what it 'points to' or 'declares' must be posited over and over again, in different fashion.

This is an example of divine power pictured in animal form, a major representation of divine power in Egypt, Sumer and Babylon, and in Greece, too, through the 6th century. Now amid the many interpretations, or misinterpretations of these animal shapes in human religion, there is one use, a freeing use, that has been generally overlooked. Theriomorphism, which begins, as far as we know, as early as anthropomorphism and maintains a position of equal status throughout the 'creative period' of mythology can collapse the whole theory of "projection," of "man projecting himself into the universe," of man replacing his disproved parent by a heavenly parent. The Lioness is a denial of the motive and continuing tenor of the Great Gods and Goddesses of antiquity as interpreted by the majority of modern critics. If animal shape alternates with human shape as the communication of compelling power, then it must spring from an analogous intellectual formulation and maintain a related, if not precisely parallel function for its audience, for those to whom it brought, presumably, their conviction, their view of divine power at work.

321

Now this lioness is killing and consuming a bull calf; she is doing that young bull no favor, showing it no kindness. Divinity as pictured here is not beneficent; it is dealing death. (Yet it is not to be defined as 'hostile' either; it is dealing death by instinct, and to feed its own energy which will nurse the young who use those dugs.) Divinity is not, then, concerned to confer kindness where it exerts power.

No lioness, either, can be read as the projection of a man or of a man's will; her power exerted in killing kine can not be understood as "wish-fulfillment", as "wish fantasy"; her consumption of the calf in no way exemplifies man's childlike "omnipotence of thought." The dimension of the externality of the lioness image, to man's person, hopes, or feelings, should be our means to remark, through this image as a realization of divine power in action, the externality of that power to man's hopes or feelings.

Yet this lioness does subtly, indirectly point to beneficent as well as destructive power; the figurative suggestion of her beneficence is those nursing dugs. And both the distended dugs and the bull calf's position under her, his haunches at her teeth and jaws, his head under her belly, "suppress," within this sculpture of killing, the age old "image" of continuous life or one carrier of life to the next, the cow and its calf, deer and fawn, or horse and colt, turned end to end. Perhaps this suppressed premise, in a representation of death dealing, may be made a little easier to accept by way of reference to a little noted but religiously illuminating pithos in the National Museum, Athens (no.355), given as Boeotian and dated by the museum to the 7th century. On its shoulders the anthropomorphic goddess, supported each side by a priestess or worshipper, is crowned by the vine-of-life which grows in wavy spaniels each side of her head. To her right and left a lioness — clearly an alternating shape. Beneath, in bands, first a row of does, and then the male stags. Those deer and stags can be thought of as the natural prey of the lioness pictured either side the goddess, but as much as the vine of life which proceeds from her head — her "power" — those same deer and stags may simultaneously be read as the offspring of the goddess. They can be understood at one and the same time as her donation and the natural prey of her destructive aspect. She is, in sum, both life-giving and life-taking.

For the Acropolis sculpture the only reminder of the life-sustaining power, realized as the vine-of-life on the pithos, are those nursing dugs. On the pithos, too, theriomorphic and anthropomorphic shapes are set side by side. To make the temple sculpture correspond the ellipsis must be filled by our knowledge that the temple itself is dedicated to a goddess and that its central pediment sculpture must be the image of divinity in action. The sculpture of the lioness by its position on the pediment of a temple "says" what the adjacent forms on the pithos "say": the power we are seeking to grasp may be pictured in either therio- or anthropomorphic guise, and it must be understood as both destructive and beneficent.

But how can a goddess be represented as a lioness, or better perhaps, how can the same divine power be realized as either a woman shape goddess or a lioness goddess? How are they interchangeable?

Never was Saussure's classic distinction between *signifiant* and *signifié* more crucial, more revolutionary, and more neglected than in the case of the shapes or figures of the great gods. Never, perhaps, can a series of errors — of which "identity" and "participation" are doubtless not the last — be more properly aligned along the edge, the failure to make that distinction, between the shape of the image and the intent or function or even referent of the image.

All the divine shapes, or serpent or bud or dove, or woman or bull, have slipped their natural moorings, have been separated in some fashion or other from the natural existences from which they, clearly, come. But it is that slipping which counts, the separation which alone makes possible their function as forms of divinity. What so many misleading interpreters, in many different ways, have done is to maintain a relation whose severance was essential to the shapes' new use, their ability to express not their natural counterparts but the divine power (whatever that is) which produced, dominated, and as a final sign of that domination, effaced those natural counterparts. Neither the human nor animal shape could be used to 'state' divine presence or will, if it were not being used in some new way.

We must try to define or understand that new way, the use of a natural creature's shape to reveal what is not seen in nature directly. How does the bud slip the bed of flowers, the serpent snakes, the dove a flock of pigeons? Above all, how is the Great Woman Shape to be distinguished from women, a Great God from such similar seeming men? What prompted this separation of the shape and its natural counterpart, the separation which alone makes it possible to play its new speaking role? How does the shape in its new role relate to the old natural shapes? For this set of intriguing questions, we can only hint at the outline of an answer.

Let me return to the 6th century Acropolis pediment sculpture and try to illustrate the disjunction between the "image" and the organic form from which it takes its shape, but which in its new use it deploys to reveal godhead in action.

The pediment sculpture shows a lioness, a lioness as in nature, killing a bull calf; both shapes and their formal relationship are rendered with the highest craft demanded by the new 6th century mastery of the carved rendition of natural shape in motion, the stone rendition of muscle in action, and arranged to meet the demands of design, to fit the architectural space. There is no way either the original spectator or today's interpreter can deny or evade the immediate conviction of natural beasts and 'realistic' bestial performance. Yet if we are to understand this sculpture's use in its religious setting, we may not rest in that impression. We have to 'read' it as an ideogram, and that reading, while using the intimate detail of the sculptural realization, the drama of the relation between the bull's life and the lion's power rendered in stone, will transform that image into an "image," whereby an act in nature reveals what is not physically seen in nature but *as if* act in nature, can hypostasize divine power as if the shape of a lioness killing and consuming a bull.

A few ordinary — but easily overlooked — suppositions of a 6th century Athenian audience may help us towards this necessary transformation, help us to read rather than simply react to our as if natural image, so that it may become an ikon or "image."

First we are concerned with a traditional image whose origins, in time or place, would have been unknown to 6th century Athenians. There were no lions in Attica in Classical times, or in Boeotia, either, to keep the pithos in mind. The citizens at a religious rite who use this sculpture for religious purpose had not likely seen a lion or a lioness. They had not likely seen a bull or bull calf slain by another beast. (It is interesting to speculate whence the sculptor himself drew his pattern, or, alternately, made his observations.) For those Athenian worshippers this is an image from another time and place, far off time and distant place. The comparable Delian use of such lion shape would, of course, be remembered, though by now the Mycenean had been buried. For the majority of the audience we can not, either, posit a firsthand knowledge of parallel Mesopotamian or Anatolian use of this ikon. Yet all of these, without specific reference, would have entered that original appreciation in the sense that the audience immediately recognized the lioness as an ancient image of god's power. The original audience, that is, is not using this sculpture to revive or judge firsthand observational experience; they are using a traditional image to grasp a traditional meaning, as we do with the Shepherd and His Flock, the Coronation of the Virgin, or, even more appropriately, the Crucifix. In none of those instances do the figures as natural representation yield their religious meaning; they point to it. So here the image carries with it its assigned meaning so that it can be transformed at once into an "image." We must not overlook, as they could not, that this is a temple sculpture, to be viewed on holy days. This context of itself excludes any purely secular or representational valence for the artifact. We are not intended to enjoy or deplore, or simply limit ourselves to concentrating on a lion killing a bull.

There is another rather ordinary observation which should qualify our interpretation of this religious sculpture for festival use. It pictures a death, but men and women are not usually religiously inspired or illuminated by the death of animals per se — least of all when one of the animals is of a species beyond their experience. Then as now, we might assume, men and women are concerned primarily with their own deaths, as with their

325

own living, and unless this animal act of killing illuminates the destiny of men, it is hard to understand its prominence in the religious architecture of the city. Instead, that is, of bringing parallel animal extinction to bear in their reaction to this sculpture, its social situation is such that it might the more readily serve as guide in their awareness of and reaction to the death of the city's warriors, or of young wives in childbirth, of easily stricken children, of aged parents. And if, in some way, that lioness is a goddess — though that way, admittedly, is our present problem — then it is god's power for or over human life which calls forth the concentration of an audience on a religious occasion.

Our last down to earth observation can serve to introduce our way of 'reading' this lioness as divine power.

The Athenian congregations which viewed this sculpture while, with a few possible exceptions, without experience of lions, would know directly the death of bulls or bull calves as a part of religious rite. To the city height where the temple of this sculpture stood, bulls of sacrifice were guided, driven — as witness the next century's Parthenon metopes — by filleted ephebes. The goddess' worshippers, then, were accustomed to the sight of the bull-in-death in religious service. Its presentation in this sculpture on this site would automatically recall precisely the same image of bull death in adjacent sacrifice. The stone bull or bull calf of the pediment sculptures points not to secular experience but to a parallel — and even more vivid — religious experience, the death of a living bull beneath the priest's sacrificial knife.

If the slain bull of the pediment sculpture must needs, for its original audience, recall the slain bull of sacrifice, then another parallel is at once set up, between the lioness and the priest, or, defined more strictly, between the act of the lioness and the act of the priest, between the animal's fulfillment in nature of its killer instinct and the priest's voluntary use of the killing knife in ritual. And though the two should not be "identified," each can point beyond itself to the same hypostasized death-dealing unity, god bringing death to natural life. Or, to use our terms, each is an "image," as different images, of the same power in act.

For the killing of sacrifice is conscious substantiation in rite of the everywhere enforcement of death in nature. Ritual, like any art form, is formal declaration, but, more ambitiously than secular art, attempts to present an imaginary divine program as ritual pageant, what is enacted in nature time and time again described in foreshortened terms as the structure of that enactment. Ritual's purpose is to disclose to an anxious audience the underpinning of that program, to confirm its major acts, to reveal the terrible power manifested in those acts.

The priest's use of the knife effects what, in nature, a lioness' teeth and claws might have done: so is ritual performance the formal, willed enactment of natural performance, and so the priest momentarily assumes or 'acts out' divine power. In Athens, as elsewhere in antiquity, the slaying or sacrificing priest is momentarily, or ritually, god-in-act. Divine power, in nature, kills continually, man who kills in sacrifice — appointed by the community for that function — puts on god's role, and the death of the active beast confirms his authenticity, makes clear or 'dramatic' his assumption of that terrible power. Rite is the conscious confirmation of the ordination of perpetual process. The priest, as actor, in words, gestures, and, climactically, in the killing act itself, becomes the visible agent of that process.

Here, more narrowly, the priest's act is echoed by one paradigmatic natural case, the lioness' rending of the bull, but that case, as presented in stone sculpture, like the priestly act, attempts to render or disclose the impelling power for all, so that the lioness becomes a goddess in act. Both lioness and priest have pre-empted one of the three great functions of divine power, to create creatures, to sustain their life and capacities, to submerge them in death. By its helplessness, for all its own fighting strength and evident fecundity, before the lioness' might, or the priest's knife, the bull proclaims the creature's subservience to divine ordination. Both slaying priest and killer lion concretize as images the divine command of life history, while the dead bull illustrates the condition of the creature's fulfillment of divine rule.

No 6th century priest in Hellas was in his own right held to incarnate god, and by the same token no specific lioness in nature (though any lioness, like any bull taken out of natural context, could be 'marked' for its divine function). A lioness of nature can as "image" take on the role of the lioness of myth, god in action, just as the priest of sacrifice takes on the role of god in his slaying act. But god and priest should not be called identical, nor lioness of nature and goddess. The figures of myth borrow their shapes from organic nature, because for their users there were no other unifying shapes, but the figures of myth are not the figures of the landscape, man or woman, bull or lion, tree or dove — though divine power can, for a moment, be realized in any one of these.

The lioness of myth who, in Greece, may be called, among other names, Artemis, has slain many women and children, as her 'brother' Apollo has slain many men, in battle, through disease, by 'old age'. *This* lioness is never directly seen, as lioness; she is only seen in her effects, the results of her power, the deaths of those she slays. Here we can understand why the lion image is so appropriate in lionless Hellas: might which, though never seen in and of itself, can be clearly, dramatically pictured. The animal, as illustration of the goddess, as "image," slays a bull, but the lioness as goddess slays many women, in childbirth, by disease, 'old age' — not as marauding animal.

The lioness of myth, then, is "image" of what can not, in fact, be seen in nature: the perpetual determination of life's term. The lioness "image" is the hypostatis of the *ordination* of natural effect, a declaration of a posited *command* of the cycle, birth, life, death.

In a very general sense the command of that cycle is the 'subject' of our sculpture: for it the image of the lioness had been conceived and used long before the 6th century, and far from Greece. The new Greek plastic verisimilitude in the presentation, in depth, of the muscled beasts may, like the humanity of the gods' sculptural presentation in the next century, confound in our minds the natural and the use of the natural as the form of an abstraction, perpetual power in recurrent circumstance. In this instance, if we concentrate on the bull's helplessness before the lion's strength, we do see in the flesh what can always be seen in the flesh, the *effect* of the divine power.

But divine power, its unified presence or its scope, is imaginary, made up, hypostasized *as if* one person, one will, one rule. It is realized through various images, but it is not defined by one. If we extrapolate a line through the priest's act of sacrifice and another through a lion's kill, we can arrive at a point beyond either where they cross which we might define, in contemporary not antique terms, as individual subjection to divine ordination, which is summed in death. Myth 'defines' as picture that divine ordination as a goddess or god, or a god's display of his sempiternal power. That divine power may be 'seen', realized as a lioness' devouring a bull calf, or a priest, with god's power, bringing a fecund bull's life to a close.

For the beneficent aspect of this power we may make similar converging extrapolations through the lioness of nature and through a nursing, nurturing woman of nature, to a point beyond each where we posit the divine goddess who may take, may reveal herself as either shape. The lioness in this usage does not 'stand for' a woman, or the woman for a lioness; either shape can be used as the "image" of a power exemplified in nature by either, and by many others. Viewed abstractly it is the system for all natural shapes.

Mankind's nurture by plants can be defined by woman shape (Demeter, Athena, Hera), as can human dependence, for sustenance, on animals (Artemis, Athena). Mankind's dependence on mothers in nature is a parallel system, so that, at the apex of the pyramid, the goddess as the institution of human mothers is in parallel case with the institution of plants or domesticated animals for human support. The same figure, or in Greece usually parallel figures, can be The Mother as Plant Life, the Mother as Animal Life, the Mother as Mother Life. In such a mode even the hypostatization as unity of mother-nurture is an abstraction of the *function* of the human mother, accurately realized as parallel to the function of plant or animal life for humankind.

Now this mother of mothers, of plants, and of animals, and of human mothers sustaining (and unraveling) mankind, at long last, in large settled communities, can be pictured as a woman, a woman with a citadel crown, a woman on the back of a lioness, or 'she' may be pictured as simply a lioness, or, as on the

Boeotian pithos, as woman and lioness side by side. Or, most elliptically, as the head of a lioness, as on the finial of a grave *stele*. If we grasp this (unnatural) nourishing aspect expressed by the lioness in religious iconography, we can free ourselves from an instinctive confusion between the lioness as the "image" of command or ordination of a life cycle and a lioness in nature. Similarly, when we see lion and woman shapes alternate, we should be able to free ourselves from the confusion between a goddess and a mortal woman, between the shape and its mythical function expressive of divine power. The hypostasized rule of the system of life and death uses an organic shape — a number of them — so that the system may be apprehended as a unity, a continuing unity, as a self-sustaining unity. The way-of-organic-life is summed, isolated, and announced by a single image, for our understanding, for our celebration, for our fearful worship and our praise.

In the larger hall, between the two rooms in the Acropolis Museum where the stone bulls lie with their heads upon the ground, there is a glass case full of terra cotta *ex votos* to Athena. One of them (13075) shows the goddess in a position to give suck to a lioness. That "image" should carry us beyond natural shapes into the extraordinary realm of purely posited power, ubiquitous, everliving power. The divine power may sustain lions in the same fashion as it sustains men or sheep or kine, and, though that power is pictured as a goddess, it clearly is not the enlargement or projection of a woman or woman's nature; that a lioness with folded ears should seem to reach for a goddess' dug should for us transform that woman shape into an "image" for the system which sustains the variety of organisms in this natural world. These terra cotta figurines like the sculptured stone forms of the Acropolis are meant to unfold for us what is *not seen* in the flesh *as if* it were visible in flesh, what is not seen directly in nature but realized in images taken from shapes which very much stir us in the flesh. So is natural form transformed as mythic "image" to release the recognition of the commanding powers under which as citizens we are born, flourish, die.

That lioness or woman shape as goddess does not directly 'stand for' process or system, anymore than it stands for a specific event or fact or creature in nature; it certainly can not be conceived as a picture of the *pattern* of a process. The relation to later analytic or scientific patterns is not as the first (erroneous) attempt at such pattern, but as the successful institution, intellectually, of process as entity, as determined and determining entity, as perpetual entity. The lioness does not 'stand for' but 'realizes' what is imaginatively postulated, and what it expresses must be seen, as much now as then, as 'existing' only as postulated. Process as commanded and commanding, not only determined but itself determining special effects is never a 'fact' but a transposition of many facts into an imaginative relationship for the observing and co-ordinating human mind. Such intellectual co-ordination is epiphenomenon, not a 'representation' of, or 'model' for a set of natural facts.

It might be said that the lioness shape 'sets in motion', in the mind not in nature, a variety of realizations themselves emerging from a set of relationships described or set up by the *as if* natural shape. For example, the lioness killing the bull calf dramatically reveals the subservience of bull life to lioness' power. But this singular dramatic killing — the dramatic relationship seen as a strong bull's impotence — is trigger to the realization of every man, woman, child's subservience to the ordination of death. The lion killing is not 'epitome', those men, women, children are not going to be slain and eaten by lions; they are going to 'succumb', in a variety of different fashions, to a variety of local destructions, but they are all going to 'succumb' to the 'law' of organic extinction. There is the point of unity. *The lioness, then, is the expression not of natural agent but of irresistible determination, not of natural pattern but of pattern as imposition.*

It is because the lioness does not, in killing, reflect in any way the modes of human death but their necessity that precisely the same image may be used in contrary case, as the everlasting sustenance of human or other organic form, the lioness of grave *steles*, or the lioness of Delos where no corpse should pollute the soil. In this other aspect, life-giving or life-sustaining, it is impossible for the lioness shape to express any specific act or fact or set of them, mode of birth or type of nourishment. The lioness is the postulated "image" of the system of such sustenance, not the image of any natural one of them. In this case the lioness, as we have seen, is an alternate of the commanding, nurturing human shape, the goddess. With the goddess as woman, of course, there is an unavoidable carry over of mother sustenance and mother love; the image sets up unavoidable human affect. (This may be why, in Greece, as opposed to Near Eastern and Indian iconography, the woman shape is no longer given the role 'command of extinction' — as with Anat, Kali, etc. There is a vestige of this goddess role in the Agave role in *The Bacchae,* life-giver as death-bringer. Yet so far removed is the 5th century audience from the basic myth that the playwright can use this role for its human horror without reference to its earlier significance. Note also the wolf shape in place of the lioness as image of sustenance in Roman myth-become-legend.)

Because the 'image' of *command* or *determination* of a process, while drawn from a natural shape dramatically related to other natural shapes, is no longer such a natural shape with its natural history in its use as the imposed unity of variegated process, its command of lives quite different from its own as a natural creature — lioness killing as death by disease, lioness as sustainer of the life of men and women — we must never yield to 'metaphorical' readings of myth. For example, Adolph Jensen's (*Myth and Cult among Primitive People,* Chicago, 1963) interpretation of the Dema-deity, Hainuwele, the god dismembered and parceled out as the food plant of the tribe, as the expression of 'life feeding on life'. This is seen too in Prof. Joseph Campbell's *Primitive Mythology*, New York, 1959, 176, 177: " ... the particular point is that death comes by way of murder. The second point is that plants on which men live derive from death. The world lives on death: that is the insight rendered dramatically in this image." Or Prof. René Girard's far fetched fancy that it is the act of violence, murder, which brings us into the world of sacredness, that life — *mirabile dictu* — is first sanctified by way of murder. *(La Violence et le Sacré,* Paris, 1972 *iterum et saepius).*

One life does feed on another, and a lioness on a bull calf shows that as vividly as any image in nature, but that image in its own right does not illustrate either the many modes of death or the realization of the necessity of death, its determination by supra-individual power. The same transformation is necessary with the image of the Dema-deity, divine death become a mode of sustenance and continuance, as in the Kore myth, or even later, Christianity.

We saw, too, that the priest's knife exerted the same power over the bull's life as the lion's teeth and claws, leading to the same result — in specific adjacent imagery, confirmable for innumerable occasions, on the Acropolis of Athens. This is not priestly "murder" but the ritual enactment of divine imposition. The ritual act, like the lioness' killing in stone nearby, is the "image" of a thousand thousand natural deaths, occurring, naturally, in many different ways, from disparate causes. It is death, not murder, but it is the phenomenon of death, and as phenomenon realized as the result of divine ordination, which is rehearsed in ritual death. All death, natural or violent, and the nature of all death is realized in the ritual act or "image." Death must be seen, too, as unconquerable, irresistible. We must, to be convinced, have a victim. In many places at many times that has been a human victim; in civilized antiquity it was usually, though not always, an animal victim. That status of the victim is an essential part of the priestly act as "image" condensing the subservience or subjection of myriad natural creatures to the necessity of organic extinction. And in ritual, too (unless, as with us, in the Mass, death is pantomimed) death must be enacted violently to take place, to be seen and realized.

Murder does not sustain or 'sanctify' human life; it destroys it, or pollutes the living; it is *miasma*. All ancient anthropology contradicts Girard's willful fancy. But the cycle of life and death is indissoluble, starting with copulation, leading to birth, growth, sustained capacities, and finally death. Though no one of the aspects of the cycle 'creates' or 'causes' the rest, any one may be singled out for ritual celebration, as the 'key', the momentary unifier of the cycle, as the critical expression of divine ordination. Such is the lioness killing the bull calf. At Eleusis all three, birth, copulation, death, were expressed imagistically, ritually, so that in celebration the human mind might hold them as unity, the imaginative unity of organic existence and non-existence expressed in a night of ritual. So individuals might grasp their relation to that dramatized unity, might momentarily grasp their relation to the divine program realized as ritual pageant.

# NOTES

## Chapter 1

1 Their full explication must await the analysis of the myth of *Olympian 1* in Chapter 4. As the quoted lines end, the poet states, "Witness to this — the interrelation of godhead and man's achievement — our present victor," which is the interrelation of Poseidon and Pelops in the later poem. These lines of *Nemean 6,* as one of the scholiasts earlier noted (A.B. Drachmann III 102), also echo the close of *Pythian 8,* which we read in juxtaposition with the *Olympian* ode. These lines of *Nemean 6,* written after Xenophanes' disclaimer of anthropomorphism, which we discuss in Chapter 5, are also, in a way, one of the subtlest "answers" to it since they disclose one strategic use or function of that anthropomorphic symbolism, at least, as neither arbitrary nor self-deluding but necessary.

## Chapter 2

1 This is also true of daydreams, or night dreams of social acclamation, where narcissism is the formulating instinct. The man as will must shake himself free of his passive relation to the daydream in order to assert himself and enact it. But it should be borne in mind that the successful man of action is still enmeshed in the residual contours of his daydreams or night dreams of social acclamation. Like the successful lover he has mastered the means of deploying the instinct, which propels the dream imagery, in accord with others' wills. Eventually, too, we must come to see the Freudian distinction between the conscious and subconscious not as a spatial or organic differentiation but as the distinction between the focusing mind and its given energies, capacities, and desires. They can not be divided in time or place in active history. The conscious activity is not only driven by but patterned by the (sometimes) unconscious instinct.

## Chapter 3

1 *Libro de la Vida* 29.13 where not only the sexual imagery — a little fire at the tip of the large gold dart which entered not only her heart but her entrails several times, leaving her burned by the love of God — but sexual sensation — pain that made her give out groans, the greatest pain which was also of such passing sweetness she did not want it to cease — is so explicit that the frequent criticism of Bernini for 'secularizing' or 'vulgarizing' her account is quite unfounded. The orgasmic affect is there in Teresa's writing before it appears on the marble face in Sta. Maria della Vittoria. No Greek, poet or otherwise, could possibly express his relation with deity in these terms. The *mythic* connection between mortal woman or boy and a loving god, or a mortal man and a goddess is the statement of an altogether different kind, as applied to earthly experience, as we shall see in the next chapter.

2 This writer has seen American soldiers in India sneer and spit at that; their personal practice later the same day was, of course, another matter.

3 This writer treated it at length in a series of lectures at Stanford on Plato and Eros, which is simply a way of saying that there are many many elements and much illustration omitted in this discussion.

## Chapter 4

1 Cf. also *Letters of Emily Dickinson,* ed. T.H. Johnson, II. 261, "I have a Brother and Sister — My mother does not care for thought — and Father too busy with his Briefs . . . . They are religious — except me — and address an Eclipse, every morning — whom they call their "Father".

2 For the statements in these paragraphs, see the author's (unpublished) doctoral dissertation, *The Chronology of Pindar's Persian War and Sicilian Odes* (Harvard, 1954).

Chapter 5

1 From the foreword to *A Choice of Kipling's Verse*, London, 1941.

2 *The Dial,* July 1929, quoted in *A Dial Miscellany,* ed. W. Wasserstrom (Syracuse, 1963), 356.

3 *Shores of Light* (New York, 1952) 436f. *T.S. Eliot and The Church of England.*

4 Some keep the Sabbath going to Church —
   I keep it, staying Home —
   With a Bobolink for a Chorister —
   and an Orchard, for a Dome — etc.,   (324)

5 *Ash Wednesday* should be read in the light of "As I ebb'd with the Ocean of Life"; "Bless me, Father"; "Kiss me my father"; apart from content the poetic form is in direct descent from the never fully acknowledged mastery of the earlier poet. The debt to Shelley in *Little Gidding* has been clearly acknowledged.

6 *The Nigger of the Narcissus*, Preface, last paragraph.

7 As printed in Morton White's *The Age of Analysis*, Boston, 1955, 27f.

8 *Reason in Religion*, the last paragraph of Chapter I. See The Modern Library, *Philosophy of Santayana*, ed. Irwin Edman, 152-3.

9 *Letters of Wallace Stevens*, ed. Holly Stevens, New York, 1966, 378. But there are similar statements at 348, 369, 70, at 402, 435, 438, and 729, as well as in *The Necessary Angel* (First Vintage Ed. 1965) 42, 51.


Chapter 6

1 Pericles uses precisely the adverb Homer uses — *pote* — 'sometime', vague but ominous.

2 It can not be overstressed, either, that the artifacts are presented as illustrations, by-the-way aids for understanding the intellectual nature of the social values. To make them primary has led to grievous misunderstanding of Plato's intuitions.

3 As paradigms of natural particulars the ideas play a minor role in Plato's own writing though it is the aspect Aristotle is most interested in, as it is center stage for English commentators. So complex is any natural particular the ideas simply do not work in this context, and Plato's references seem desultory, *pro forma*.

4 Quite clearly we have here assumed or created a parallel between our earlier (205-6) reference to the relation between word use or reference and codified word in a specific speech community, and the relation now limned between an instance of the deployment of given energy or capacity and the eternal god shape which donates that energy and the form of its deployment, both relations, we hold, echoed by the terms Plato uses for the relation between an eidos and its instantiation. Somehow or other all human intellectual structure derives from the matrix of speech; the formulation of divine shape, a controlling stabile unity for process, which made possible human intellectual 'control' of such process in diverse circumstances, is one of the greatest of those evolvements. Just how the relation between word use or reference and abiding word, and between example of energy deployment and god form are themselves inter-related would take us beyond the scope either of this chapter or of this work as a whole. It is an interrelation that should be further elucidated, elsewhere.

## Chapter 7

1 Cf. the author's *The Chronology of Pindar's Persian War and Sicilian Odes,* unpublished doctoral dissertation, Harvard, 1954.

2 For Hellenists let me note that I have translated *hama* (72) as temporal, not conjunctive. It is the blinding speed of their consumption, the completeness of divine ordination, which the poet is picturing. Lynkeus, in any case, has already been felled

337

by Polydeukes. The misinterpretation, as I conceive it, goes back to the scholiasts, revived by 19th century editors and followed without study by translators in this. The scholiasts, of course, are indispensable on language, but in interpreting are as open to error as any man. The destruction of Idas-Lynkeus is parallel in theological meaning and as mythical picture to the destruction of Cheiron and his patient in *Pythian 3,* where the parallel adverb is *okeos* (58), swiftly; Pindar has made the blast even swifter here.

## Chapter 8

1 Romans 14.7-12 — I render *eksomologesetai* as middle, not deponent, to make it parallel to *peri heautou logou.*

2 Mark 1.9-12. Nine is not a part of the Greek myth, hence the variation from the previous notation.

# INDEX